# THE GREATEST HOAX ON EARTH
## Catching Truth, While We Can

## ALAN C. LOGAN

with foreword by Paula Parks & Mark Zinder

ISBN 978-1-7361974-1-7
Library of Congress Control Number: 2020923114

Interior book design by Vince Font
www.glassspiderpublishing.com

Cover design by Judith S. Design & Creativity
www.judithsdesign.com

Visit the book website at www.GreatestHoax.com

*Dedicated to the memory of John "Bud" and Charlotte "Sparky" Parks*

*This book is based on an actual true story.*
*To respect the victims and the innocent, and to finally give them a voice,*
*the names, dates and events have NOT been altered.*

# FOREWORD

*The truth always emerges, in spite of*
*our best efforts to conceal it.*
Professor George Herbert Curteis, 1885

When truth has been submerged for too long, it will eventually rise to the surface. The time has come for the truth of this story to be told. It is a big story, about one of the most well-known figures in the world today, at least as he has become known through a best-selling book, a blockbuster movie, and a hit Broadway play. But few know the truth behind what has become one of the greatest hoaxes of our era.

The central character remains a mystery to most. Indeed, he has carefully concealed the real story of his life from the world—papering over reality with a colorful, fantastical creation that has been sold as "a true story." He has enthralled audiences the world over—for great fame and fortune. A man who, in telling the grand tale, proclaims to the world that he was one of the world's greatest con men—and indeed he may be, for his account has been believed. The story has been so magnified by others that it has become a legend. But it is really a myth. We may well ask if the title of his autobiographical enterprise is also an ongoing challenge—to "catch me *out*, if you can."

Our purpose here is not to catch him in lies, for that is too easy. It is to release the truth and those who have been bound by his lies.

# THE GREATEST HOAX ON EARTH

We have been part of the story of Frank W. Abagnale Jr., the real version, and it has been a privilege to work with Alan C. Logan to bring the truth into the light. This is a myth that has become so large that it is hurting those who live in knowledge of the truth—including the myth that "victimless" crimes have never hurt anyone. But it is bigger than that. This story is an example of the greater challenges facing a post-truth world where alternative facts can be created at will for profit and power, and the lines between fact and fiction have become so blurred that many can't tell the difference, or worse, don't care.

Our culture has shifted from a time when stories were told to inspire and to teach ethics and values for the greater good. Now, we live in a consumer society where our reality is bombarded with stories fabricated by those with largely ulterior motives—be they individuals, corporations or political factions. The world is waking up to this. And beginning to bring change by taking on the big stories, the ones that a minority have known to be truly false. But first, in order to restore our power to choose the truth, we need an awareness of how falsehoods fly.

At the beginning of this venture, we did not know each other. We each held different pieces of the puzzle. One of us, Paula, is a retired Delta Airlines flight attendant who met Frank Abagnale in the 1960s long *before* he started telling the fabricated version of his life. She has knowledge of Abagnale's very different actual life. His actions have had lasting effects on her family and community in Baton Rouge, bearing no resemblance to the stories he tells today. The other of us, Mark Zinder, was Frank Abagnale's booking agent and advance man during the early days of his reinvented career—*after* Abagnale had created a whole new life narrative in late 1970s Houston. Mark traveled with Abagnale on his speaking tours as he crisscrossed the country promoting his autobiography *Catch Me If You Can* into the early 1980s. He spent extensive time, night and day, with Abagnale and was able to share how the story unfolded during the early years of Abagnale's rise to meteoric fame following the release of his book.

It was through Alan that we discovered each other's truth. He had already conducted extensive research into the actual true story—through uncovering a vast volume of criminal and civil court proceedings, police department records, military service records, penitentiary files, census documents, university campus newsletters, and, critically, National Archives records in the United States, Sweden and France—not to mention thousands of newspaper articles.

Alan's research had already shown a very different story, one which nobody had ever fully pieced together before. Others had found fragments, to be sure, but not the level of detail that Alan had compiled to fully dispel the myth. Even we did not know all the details. In the course of his research, he shared his findings— and invited us to add our voices to the story.

Our partnership was formed, and from there we started reaching out to others who had been part of the true events, including those personally affected by the story. We knew that these accounts would bring the truth to life in a way that the documents alone could not. This has been an opportunity to release our own truths and finally begin to heal the pain of seeing the truth suppressed for so long.

*I teach ethics at the Federal Bureau of Investigation academy, which is ironic. But someone at the Bureau said, "Who better than you to do this?"*
Frank William Abagnale Jr., 2015[1]

At this time in history, we need heroes more than ever. Heroes who understand what the words ethics and integrity mean and how their definitions can be made real. Heroes who can help transform our society and provide meaning and purpose for the next generations. But those who deliberately deceive, sprinkling some grains of truth within a basket of lies, should have no place among our modern legends, save as a cautionary tale. Especially if they deceive in the name of ethics and truth while amassing a fortune.

For those of us who know the truth, the idea of Frank W. Abagnale teaching ethics at one of the world's most prestigious law enforcement training grounds is beyond the pale. The pages of this book will reveal why. If someone at the Bureau did indeed tell Frank Abagnale "who better than you?" to teach ethics, we might hope they knew only the myth, not the reality of decades-long deception.

For almost forty years, Abagnale has challenged media, law enforcement, academics, experts from trusted institutions, and the public at large, to *Catch Me If You Can*. And indeed, in the pages of *The Greatest Hoax,* that challenge has been met. History will be rewritten, correctly, in these pages. But our greater purpose is truth, awareness and the kind of justice that comes from shedding light on falsehood so that something better may grow. It is not retribution. It is not vengeance. It is for the love of truth, in a world that needs more love.

It is also important to note at the outset that this is not the story of Frank W. Abagnale. This is our story. A story of the actual lives he poured himself into. Shaken and stirred.

Alan has drawn from the historical record to give voice to the names and faces otherwise erased from all discourse. He has found heroes. And villains. The emotional aspects of our story are built on a firm foundation of facts and verified evidence. In many ways, if not most, it is more incredible, more humorous and far more sinister than the Hollywood fiction we've all been sold.

A story that has never told—until now.

Paula Parks Campbell
Mark Zinder

*Some of the most brilliant liars of antiquity are still very close to being best sellers . . .* [they] *made lies that had a face more beautiful than that of truth.*
Alan Chisholm, 1961[2]

# CHAPTER 1
# Uncomfortably Numb

*A lie can travel half-way around the world*
*while the truth is putting on its shoes.*
Mark Twain

"Hey, Z!" The voice was unmistakable. There was only one person who ever called Mark Zinder "Z." Usually confident and self-assured, Mark was frozen in shock. He had been lost in thought, looking up at the airport departures board, trying to locate his gate when that voice stopped him in his tracks.

Mark Zinder is a frequent traveler, often on the road hop-scotching between regional airports. As a seasoned keynote speaker in the field of finance and economics, the former national spokesperson for Sir John Templeton and the Templeton Group still makes regular appearances on cable news channels. Given his schedule, and being well known in the world of business, it is not uncommon for Mark to bump into people who know or recognize him. But this day was very different and shook him to his core.

It was inevitable that they would meet again, in some ways surprising it had taken so long. More than twenty years had passed since they parted so dramatically under such dire circumstances. And it was oddly fitting that they should meet in an airport—the scene of Frank Abagnale's most audacious con posing as an airline pilot.

Many decades after Abagnale began spinning his saga as a great imposter, the legend of his feats has not faded, but the glamor of air travel certainly has. Now, highly stressed, weary and impatient crowds jostle through security before spilling into the appendages of the terminal. Thousands of parallel lives passing, rarely interacting, as they scuttle to find their departure gates, carry-on luggage in tow.

Mark was momentarily frozen in what now seemed like an icy stream of faceless travelers. His mind was racing as he turned to face the man who had left such a scar on his life. The hands of time hadn't been kind to him, but there was no mistaking who it was. Mark could never forget that face. In his mind, that man still lived as he had appeared in the 1980 glamor headshot—the polished photograph he knew so well. He tried to reconcile that memory with the old man who stood before him in the bustling airport—a man he had not seen for decades—since that fateful day in 1982 to be exact.

Perhaps he paused a millisecond too long, so the man tried to help him out.

"It's me. Frank!" he exclaimed, walking toward Mark, hand outstretched, as though nothing had happened.

Mark had often wondered what he would do if he did eventually see Frank W. Abagnale Jr. again. Would he challenge him? Call him out? They both traveled a lot, both on the same speakers' bureau, so in a way it was remarkable that it took twenty years for their paths to cross again. Caught in the unexpected surprise, Mark stepped forward and shook Abagnale's hand, feeling surprisingly little emotion, at least initially.

They made small talk for a few minutes, both affable, like old friends.

"He was a master of conversation and instinctively made the chance meeting about me, not him," Mark later recalled. But then Abagnale shifted the conversation.

"How's Fran?" he asked. It seemed polite. But also loaded.

"Oh, that didn't work out—we ended up divorcing," Mark explained, still without time to process the whole encounter.

"That's too bad," Abagnale replied, mysteriously adding, "I've always wanted to call you and apologize for that."

For *that*? For what?

But Mark was left wondering, because Frank William Abagnale's next words were some form of farewell. With luggage in tow, he disappeared into the steady stream of business travelers, just as quickly as he had appeared. They had politely shaken hands and parted ways before Mark even had time to think about what happened. If captured on a stopwatch, the exchange could barely be counted in minutes. It was jolting but fleeting, like the grand finale in a fireworks display—leaving a strange smoky shadow hanging where it had just exploded. Mark's head was already bursting with vivid memories, all the while wondering what Abagnale meant by the apology concerning his ex-wife, Fran.

He stood alone, oblivious to his gate and departure time.

"I thought I had shut that door," Mark recalls today, still surprised by how much he had done to suppress the past, "but it opened old deep wounds I thought had healed. I had done everything I could to ignore that episode of my life. I had avoided the Spielberg film. Made every excuse when the Broadway musical arrived in Nashville and my family wanted to go. The very notion of a musical to celebrate his life was farcical. A bridge too far. Did they really not know he had fabricated most of it?"

Strangely, amid his resurfacing emotions, Mark Zinder's

thoughts went straight to the swimming pool in Frank Abagnale's Houston home, back when he worked as Abagnale's booking agent and event manager. Abagnale loved horsing around with him in the pool. He would insist on playing a wrestling game, each trying to dunk the other to the point of surrender. The outcome was predictable.

"Frank was the winner. Except for just one time," said Mark recalling Abagnale's silent fury when his younger subordinate got the better of him. "I never saw him lose his cool, he was always smooth as silk, but I certainly knew when he was angry or displeased. He always liked to have the upper hand and be in control. The day I dunked him to submission I actually thought he was going to fire me as his agent . . . for the second time."

In those moments at the airport, as Mark felt the specter of the strange alternative reality of Frank Abagnale looming again, he realized how powerless he had felt to stop it, and the guilt he still felt to have been part of it.

In the autumn of 1982, with many of Frank Abagnale's tales proven to be false, Mark Zinder had been convinced that his client's career was over—at least as far as peddling the hoax that had seemed to convince so many for so long. The self-proclaimed con man had just been publicly called out on his lies, his college campus speaking tour all but canceled. That was the moment Mark realized he had been an unwitting pawn in a grand hoax. He recalled his disillusionment. His fear. And the enormous relief when he walked away. In all the years that followed he had watched in disbelief as Abagnale resurrected his story for millions of still willing believers.

Seeing him again had been disturbing. It ignited the old desire of wanting to tell the world the truth. But he had tried that before and knew how it ended—in radio silence.

"Somehow, someway, I found my way to my gate and onto

the airplane. But I do have one very distinct memory from that flight," said Mark. "I will never forget looking out the window of the airplane as it lifted off, thinking surely someone else out there, someone, must know the real story."

\*     \*     \*

*'Tis strange, but true; for truth is always strange; stranger than fiction; if it could be told.*
George Gordon Byron, 1823

Many epic tales must be viewed across the expanse of time, as the lens of history gently refocuses the past, drawing its characters into new light, to offer redemption in a greater truth. And this story is no different. But its truth is not yet set into stone, and the final chapters are still to unfold.

More than fifty years in the making, the story began with a small seed of deception planted from the imagination of a man who may have never expected it to proliferate into one of the best-known stories of modern history. Spreading with runaway momentum, it has enthralled the world for decades, capturing the possibility of imagination, audacity, and daring exploits intertwined with youthful tenacity. There are now very few who have not heard of it—through the initial autobiography, the movie, the Broadway play, or the countless interviews celebrating the brazen antics dramatized in various forms under the contagious branding of *Catch Me If You Can*. The story of a man who told the world he was the greatest con man in modern history has been made all the more appealing by his tale of reform, redemption and professed reparations to all his corporate victims. For many, he has become an archetypal modern hero in true Robin Hood style.

But the truth is very different. In so many ways, the real story is even more strange and remarkable than the still revered legend of Frank William Abagnale Jr. Yet that story has not been told. Nor have the real stories of those embroiled in the theatrics he created, their truth discarded on the cutting room floor of history. All the while, his *greatest* hoax concealed.

The central figure remains the man who miraculously turned his life around and, in the process, dramatically changed his fortunes. But, in a world of mirrors, the facts show his still considerable achievements in a very different light. Incredibly, his greatest triumph as a self-proclaimed con man is not even known—and once exposed may indeed justify any claim that he *is* America's greatest hoaxer. As the true story comes into focus, so does one of the largest, longest hoaxes in history—crossing generations and spanning continents—in an illusion that still touches people today. In one form or another, the tale known as *Catch* has generated a billion-dollar industry on film, in books and on stage. For more than forty years it has reached the awareness of countless people across the globe.

As we enter this story, we may surely face the dangers of being bedazzled and enchanted by the con man—like the millions of willing believers. Most still believe the tale is true. Or want to. Even as the truth is revealed, we may be tempted to believe that it does not matter. That it was all a harmless lark.

But Abagnale's tale is a dangerous hoax. It erodes trust and muzzles victims. At a perilous time in human history, it insinuates fiction into institutions that are thirsty for facts and evidence. A menace must be understood and remembered. No matter how entertaining. No matter how likable the romanticized perpetrator. No matter how much we want to believe rollicking chicanery is true, awareness of the harms induced by grand falsehoods is vital—especially in the context of global erosion of truth.

[Hoaxes] *endure even though the most positive proof is shown of their untruthfulness. They express something which a portion of the people want to believe, in spite of the truth . . . we may battle with it, as of course we should, but it is folly to expect that the struggle will prove an easy victory for truth and fact.*
W.J. Ghent. The Independent, 1913[3]

\*   \*   \*

The strange airport encounter with Frank Abagnale happened over ten years ago. By the time Mark Zinder's plane landed at his destination he had recomposed his reality, ready to rebury his memories and move on again. All his life, he had searched for truth and meaning, but he was also a realist. As a highly successful futurist and leading trend forecaster specializing in the areas of finance and economics, he had no desire to be drawn back into the shady world of the great con man.

Life returned to an even keel. It was only when this author contacted Mark in 2019 to ask him to share his experiences that Mark realized how much Abagnale still haunted him. How he had been uncomfortably numb for so long, kidding himself that he had never looked back. In those moments he agreed to reopen the door to his past—one he had kept closed for decades, waiting for the right time to open it again.

"I have been waiting for this call for over thirty years," was the first thing Mark said when he learned this author was interested in the facts of what really happened. Invited to tell his story, Mark began to realize just how much he wanted the truth to be told.

Perhaps this time, someone will listen to the truth, he thought. And that was before Mark even knew the bigger story—the story Abagnale had been hiding all along.

# CHAPTER 2
# To Tell the Truth

*It is easier to fool people than to convince them
that they have been fooled.*
Anonymous

"Have fun and lie well," were the famous backstage instructions given by public relations man Dick Craven.[4] Inside NBC studios he was busy prepping his cast of two imposters for the once-popular TV show *To Tell the Truth*. They had each received their customary fifty-dollar stipend, scored some show swag, and been treated to a room at the Berkshire the night before.

The premise of the show was simple. Showbiz panelists would be presented with three contestants, one remarkable true story, and a limited time to question the contestants in order to guess who might be the sole legitimate owner of the factual narrative. Two imposters were permitted to lie. But not the third. That person, known as the central character, the holder of the authentic lived experiences, was instructed to *only* tell the truth.[5]

Not yet thirty years old, Mr. Frank Abagnale Jr. was to be the central character, promising to tell the truth. When he showed up dutifully at the midtown-Manhattan studios, in the spring of 1977, *Truth* ratings were sliding. Entertainment was the name of the game. They needed better material. This central character,

Abagnale, had a triple-shot-of-caffeine type resumé. In the entire twenty-two-year history of the show, the *Truth* producers had surely never encountered such an audacious tale!

Although Craven has been credited as the official researcher for *Truth*, it is not clear how much fact-checking was performed to verify the story of their central character that day. All indications suggest very little—if any. But there is almost no doubt that the producers knew the biography provided by Mr. Abagnale would be a huge hit with the audience.

The legend of Frank Abagnale, at least as we know it today, had its prefab origins in Houston, Texas, circa 1976. He began telling his stories at small local venues in the Lone Star State, but it was his first major television appearance on *Truth* that catapulted the emerging hero toward national fame.

This appearance is now better known in its dramatized form—in the opening scenes of Steven Spielberg's famous film *Catch Me If You Can*, the celluloid adaptation of Abagnale's autobiography. Re-enacted scenes with actor Leonardo DiCaprio were spliced into original *To Tell the Truth* footage. The dialogue in Spielberg's movie version of the *Truth* appearance was altered from the original 1977 broadcast—the biography used to introduce DiCaprio playing Abagnale was amended to better fit the film's storyline.

But the version below is the actual biography proffered by the real Frank William Abagnale on the stage of Studio 8G at Rockefeller Center in New York City in early 1977—the one actually read aloud to the studio audience and ultimately broadcast nationwide.

\* \* \*

The brightly lit stage is set as the expectant audience awaits the appearance of the three contestants from behind golden sliding doors, each door emblazoned with a blue tuxedo-clad figure, right hand raised as if to swear to tell the truth. Moments before the doors open to reveal the contestants, Dick Craven works the studio audience, jazzing them up in anticipation of the unbelievable true story they are about to hear from *one* of the program's contestants.

But who will it be? Which contestant will be telling the truth?

The audience is hushed as the host of the show, affable ex-baseball player host Joe Garagiola, welcomes his audience and warns that they are all about to meet an outrageous real imposter!

It's showtime!

The golden doors slide open.

"Applause" lamps flash on, and the studio audience obliges. Frank Abagnale strides forward dressed in a pilot's uniform, the cap tucked under his arm. He is flanked by two fake imposters, one dressed as a doctor, the other in a cartoonish jailbird outfit.

Garagiola then reads out the signed truth affidavit—the sworn biography belonging to the as yet unidentified Frank Abagnale, one of the three men standing under the bright lights:

*"I, Frank William Abagnale, am known as the world's greatest imposter. And no wonder. In the course of my nefarious career I've palmed myself off as a doctor, lawyer, college instructor, stockbroker, and airline pilot,"* reads Garagiola as the camera pans across the poker-faced candidate imposters. *"To become an airline pilot, I merely bought a plastic ID card for five dollars, affixed an airline logo from a model plane hobby kit, and in no time at all was co-pilot for a major airline,"* he continues as the audience can be heard gasping and muttering with surprise.

*"As a bogus lawyer, I actually worked on a state attorney general's staff, for six years I also cashed over two million, five hundred thousand dollars in*

*bad checks in twenty-six countries. Ultimately, I was sentenced to seventy-two years in prison,"* Garagiola is now chuckling himself as he reads the final words of Abagnale's incredible statement, *"I served one year in France, one year in Sweden; I then served four years in a federal prison in this country. Paroled, I now devote my life to the prevention and detection of crime. Signed, Frank William Abagnale."*

The audience erupts in applause as the three imposters take their seats and prepare to be challenged by the panel. Garagiola reminds the audience and his panel of the rules.

"For the first time he's gonna have to tell the truth," pledges Garagiola, almost certainly not realizing this was a promise about to be broken.

Then, the questioning from panelists begins. In order to sound convincing, the two "imposters" are already primed with elements of Abagnale's story, including his claim to a falsified law degree and his work at the Louisiana State Attorney General's office in Baton Rouge, Louisiana. In Abagnale's own responses he provides additional specifics, claiming that he worked as an assistant state attorney general for "approximately one year."

When quizzed if he had ever given medical advice, he responds, "Ah, yes, I worked for a year as the chief resident of a hospital. It was the Cobb County General Hospital in Marietta, Georgia. I had no problems," going on to state, "I am the only man to ever successfully escape from the Atlanta Federal Penitentiary in Atlanta, Georgia . . . I impersonated a federal prison inspector and walked out of the prison."

When celebrity Kitty Carlisle asks Abagnale, "What is the first thing you stole from?" presumably meaning what kind of business outlet, he responds that he "ah, never actually stole anything."

In what seems like the blink of an eye, the time for questions is over. Time for a decision. Remarkably, in true dramatic style, all four celebrity panelists are fooled. None identify Abagnale as the supposed authentic imposter.

"What chance did we have?" joked one of the celebrities. After, all he was a masterful con man! The prize for fooling all the panelists was $500. A small reward compared with the vast, biography-based riches soon to follow.

Garagiola closed Abagnale's segment by simply saying, "How about that one!" How, indeed. Nobody appeared to have investigated his story. A year working as a doctor and another as a barrister with the attorney general? For the media swooning that would follow, his appearance on *To Tell the Truth* seemed validation enough.

Not long after, Abagnale started passing out his press kit with an impressive sixteen-page booklet of achievements. Inside its sleek pages, filled with his many outlandish capers, he added in large-type bolded letters that "Frank fooled the entire panel on *To Tell the Truth.*"

Yes, he did. But in layers of deep irony, which would not be appreciated for decades, his deception was far greater than fooling the washed-up celebrity panel with "the truth." On that day, the rules of the show, and much more, were broken. *Truth* had taken the form of "Fool's Gold." None of the contestants spoke the truth, especially not Frank William Abagnale.

In a strangely symbolic twist, *Truth* was canceled not long after Abagnale's appearance. Looking back, this moment could very much be seen as the dawn of the post-truth era, where entertainment trumped truth, and no one seemed to care.

"Truth" was indeed canceled, in more ways than one.

*All pathological liars have a purpose, that is, to decorate their own person, to tell something interesting, and an ego motive is always present. They all wish to lie about something they wish or possess to be.*
Psychiatrist Max Köppen, MD, 1898

\* \* \*

Abagnale hauntingly disappeared off the set of *Truth*—exiting stage left through the side door with what appeared to be a victorious bounce in his step. After breaking the rules of the show, to the victor went the spoils. Freeze-framing his exit from the *Truth* set is a worthwhile exercise—it was a remarkable moment in time, far bigger than anyone appreciated then, or now. Showbiz media wanted Abagnale, and history would show he wanted them.

It set in motion a cascading series of events, his story expanded and took him so quickly to unexpected heights. Perhaps not unlike the tragically true story of the Scottish tourist desperately clinging to the bottom basket of a rapidly rising hot air balloon. Instinctively gripping—unable to let go immediately for fear of short-term injury. But the longer he holds on, the harder the fall.[6]

And this is where this our story takes a very different turn from the well-known fable told in the 2002 movie *Catch Me If You Can,* which also launched its narrative from the set of *To Tell the Truth.* The movie captured the highly entertaining autobiographical claims of Abagnale himself. The important word in that celluloid effort being *claims.* But this story will focus on what *really* happened. The truth—which is in many ways more astounding. For that, we first need to understand the mid-1970s cultural Petri dish, the ideal conditions for the germination of Abagnale's hoax.

> *When I was sixteen years old I successfully impersonated an airline pilot for Pan American Airlines for two years until I was eighteen. At the age of eighteen I became the chief resident pediatrician of a Georgia hospital where I practiced medicine there for about a year. At the age of nineteen, having never been to law school in my life, I took the state bar exams in the State of Louisiana, I passed the bar and became a licensed attorney. Before my nineteenth birthday was over, I was appointed the Assistant Attorney General of the State, where I practiced law in that position for about a year. At the age of twenty I was a college professor at Brigham Young University in Provo, Utah. I taught two full semesters there as a PhD. Of course, before I was old enough to drink I was a millionaire twice over."*
>
> Frank W. Abagnale, 1994[7]
> In his own words from a recorded speech
> summarizing his life experiences.

# CHAPTER 3
# In Search of a
# New American Hero

*The culture of illusion thrives by robbing us*
*of the intellectual and linguistic tools*
*to separate illusion from truth.*
Chris Hedges, 2009[8]

As newlywed Frank William Abagnale Jr. made his way to
McAdams Junior High School on Saturday, January 29, 1977, he
couldn't possibly have known he was moving toward a sliding
doors moment in American cultural history. Few could. Events
about to unfold would set one man on a Houston moonshot
toward fame, as another, miles away in Chicago, fell from favor.
One American hero's countdown to liftoff was about to
commence, just as the other came crashing down.

The 28-year-old Abagnale was about to give a lecture in a
school cafeteria in Dickinson, Texas. Still an unknown, he was
booked by the local chamber of commerce for their annual
banquet—set to kick off at 7:30 p.m. Just seven bucks for a
ticket, including a nondescript meal, promise of cake, and
entertainment by a man few had ever heard of before.

In a bizarre coincidence, that was the very weekend Evel

Knievel's hucksters were hyping the shark jump that would mark the end of the world-famous daredevil's career. The nation had already shown its great appetite for flamboyant hoaxers and flashy showmen who would stop at nothing for fame and fortune. Western culture was already in the grip of a deep love-hate relationship with Evel Knievel, one of the decade's most outrageous flim-flam men. But by 1977, that relationship was shifting more toward hate and disillusion. There seemed no end to his grandiose promises. Failure became inevitable as each promised feat became more outlandish. But not before he convinced the public and sponsors to part with tens of millions of dollars.

American mid-1970s culture was in the doldrums. After the legacy of Vietnam, Charles Manson and Watergate, cultural leaders like Andy Warhol described the era as "empty." In his book, *From A to B and Back Again,* the artist reflected on the loss of trust, ideals, patriotism, and love.[9] In her own reflections on Warhol's book, *New York Times* critic Barbara Goldsmith captured the melancholy, and perhaps a glimpse of the post-truth era on tap. "Warhol poses the quintessential philosophical question: What is image and what is real? Can we answer? I remember reading somewhere that almost half of the people polled after a 1972 moonwalk did not believe in the man on the moon. They thought they were watching a television simulation," she wrote. "We have seen too many simulations, and the emotional signposts that once marked the road to truth have been obliterated."[10]

On January 31, 1977, Evel Knievel looked at the ramp that would help propel him over a pool filled with thirteen lemon sharks. It was just two hours before the much-ballyhooed jump. A live telecast was due to be beamed into homes nationwide, filmed in front of thousands in the sold-out International

28

Amphitheatre in Chicago. Against the wishes of advisors, just before the arena doors opened, he decided to do a pre-event rehearsal jump. Big mistake. He didn't know it yet, but it would be his last jump.

It ended badly, sending him to an area hospital. Soon after, thousands already inside the arena booed when co-hosts Jill St. John and Telly Savalas announced that Evel was out of commission, there would be no shark jump, and fans would have to settle for low-level stunts by other risk-takers.[11] The phrase "jumping the shark," emerged as a social meme around that time—derived from a sitcom episode based on Evel's shark jump, it symbolizes that the envelope has been pushed so far that suspension of disbelief can no longer be held, and the halcyon days of an individual or cultural entity are over. Crossing the line into ridiculousness.

The shark hype was disproportionate to the live reality. It seemed to be a repeat of his aborted 1974 canyon jump, which prompted speculation that Evel had intentionally deceived the world, after raising over twenty-two million dollars in the pre-event hype.

"Was the fix in?" wrote journalist Michael Duffy reflecting on the canyon event. "It's hard to say . . . but that would be attributing the worst of motives to an endangered species—the genuine American crazy—of which Evel Knievel is one of the last living examples . . . so Evel's secret is safe. He lives to con another day. But I'm just as happy. I like Evel Knievel. And American heroes, fallible or not, are at a premium these days."[12]

The mid-1970s desperation for American heroes allowed ne'er-do-well candidates to look shiny and virtuous. But by January 1977, the sharks had gnawed through the gloss. At least for Evel, anyway.

Several months later, Evel Knievel was arrested for assaulting

29

his agent Shelly Saltman, shattering his arm with a baseball bat. He didn't care for the tone of Saltman's new tell-all book or being referred to as a sex-driven con man.[13]

Saltman, now with metal screws and plates holding his fractured arm back in place, did his best to explain the growing media hunger for sensation and entertainment, the building of heroes at almost any cost. "All of us are victims of the kind of media buildup with which I was engaged," said Saltman. "Success depended on the symbiotic relationship that exists between promoters, such as myself, and the news media. We needed them to get the public interested, they needed us . . . on both sides it's a con game, and the world is a sucker."[14]

Evel action figures were, seemingly overnight, placed on discount racks and inside discarded boxes at lawn sales.

America was already searching for a new hero.

And so, the scene was set for the arrival of another daring figure to feed the growing appetite of the media and the audience they yearned to attract. Opening this cultural time capsule shows a world that was sitting on edge, fracking for the next outrageous hero—ready to drill down, hit rock bottom, and keep on digging, far down to the soulless inferno to find one, if necessary. Perhaps the next audacious candidate might be more reliable than the last? Even if that hero were to be a con man.

*During a time which has seen America put its tail between its legs and retreat from a no-win war, then watched in awe as first its vice president and then president resigned in humiliation, the nation has been ripe for the emergence of a high-class national hero . . . yet the man called 'Evel'* [Knievel] *seems to possess questionable traits . . . and one other thing along with them—flim-flam.*
Randy Wheeler, journalist, 1974[15]

\*    \*    \*

Evel had jumped the shark that weekend in January 1977. He was done. But back in Texas, at an obscure venue in Galveston County, just hours earlier, a fuse was lit underneath the Houston rocket that was to be Frank Abagnale's meteoric rise to national fame.

It was a chilly Saturday night in Dickinson. The cafeteria inside the McAdams Junior High School had been rearranged to accommodate the chamber of commerce's soiree. The billing in local Galveston newspapers promised that the chamber had landed a big fish for its small crowd that evening. According to chamber officials, Abagnale's stories as "an airline pilot, physician, lawyer, stockbroker, and college professor will keep banquet participants waiting for more." Abagnale had informed the organizers he was "the subject of a planned motion picture." The local paper headlined the event on the front page and simply repeated his claims.[16]

Nonetheless, the *Galveston Daily News* was more cautious than most major media outlets would be in the future, noting that Abagnale had self-styled *himself* as "the most preposterous hoaxer who ever hoodwinked the world" with his claims that he "has assumed five different personalities and professions." They took a chance. A year earlier, the chamber's annual banquet was a yawn fest. No speaker at all. The featured attraction was a slide show with touristy photos of the Dickinson area. What a difference a year makes!

It was Frank W. Abagnale's first semi-publicized public gig. And he delivered! He was a huge hit and soon celebrated as a new hero.[17]

The small crowd adored his wild escapades, his gumption, and his good-guy story of redemption, all repurposed for an anti-crime crusade! If this was his screen test, he proved himself the leading man in his own self-styled role. On the edge of their seats, chamber officials loved it so much that they wanted the wider community to hear the tale. And Abagnale was immediately rebooked by the chamber, announcing a larger public lecture—he would reappear within the month for an Everyone Welcome anti-crime lecture!

But no one seemed to ask the obvious question. With a resumé to rival James Bond, why hadn't he been featured in any southwest Texas area newspapers in 1975 or 1976? No one seemed to know where this guy came from. It was as though he was shot out of a circus cannon, somehow landing into the soft net of a relatively obscure commerce group. Whatever speaking their speaker had done previously, it hadn't been publicized. But thanks to the public outreach put into motion by the chamber and the soft-serve local reporting that followed, Abagnale would be obscure no more. He would henceforth receive a hero's welcome!

As Abagnale took the podium at McAdams Junior High School that January, *Time* magazine's cover story featured "America's Mood." Senior journalist Hugh Sidey concluded that America was "trying to get a grip on its soul," and that growing numbers were searching for "guidance" through religious revival and membership in cults.[18] The desperation for leadership was so strong, it created an opening for cult leaders and self-styled, narcissistic mega-church, incorporated ministers.

For many, America seemed out of control, and a desire for "law and order" was part of that religious surge. Lawlessness was all around, and vigilantism was in vogue—it was not by chance that rogue cop "Dirty Harry" was challenging punks if they were "feeling lucky." Check fraud was a billion-dollar problem in

America. Moneymen were mad-as-hell, and public confidence in the business community was cratering.[19] There was a market void to be filled—a promising landscape for a reformed con man on an anti-crime campaign. In Galveston County, the business community had just found a savior, a fervent crusader and a comic-book-style hero—all in one.

Indeed, in the years to come, Frank's fans did want to know if he had found redemption through religion.

"People from the crowd would often ask me that, knowing I worked closely with him," recalled his agent Mark Zinder. "So, I did ask him if he had. But he just scoffed at the question and waved me off."

Mark took that as an emphatic no. But not long afterwards, Abagnale appeared to rethink the Bible Belt optics.

"After that, I was instructed to tell people that yes, he had found God," said Mark.

While Abagnale had already given a few talks to retail outfits and some high schools around Houston,[20] it was the wider networks of chambers of commerce that sparked his trajectory to nationwide publicity. Dickinson was really the point of origin, at least as far as a public test of his biographical claims. And so it was that Frank W. Abagnale Jr. began his forward motion, actually by looking backwards, rewriting a decade of history between 1965 and 1975, and freefalling into fame and fortune.

In the lead-up to the gig at McAdams Junior High School, Soll Sussman, a local reporter with the *Galveston Daily News,* had written a profile piece on the "real con artist."[21] At this point Abagnale wasn't shying away from press attention. It was the first big story covering the self-styled imposter, and one of the rare occasions that Abagnale would take a direct interview with a reporter. In fact, it was he who walked into the newsroom to meet Sussman.

Anyone meeting a known con man might be wary. But this one was reformed. And he was easy to believe, according to Sussman. Perhaps it was in his nonthreatening "everyman" appearance. He was tall and thickset, with a forgettable face, sporting the bold sideburns of the day. His voice was strangely mesmerizing. Everything made his farfetched claims somehow easier to believe.

The life story narrative that Abagnale offered Sussman certainly defied belief. So strange that perhaps it was true. Who would dare make it up?

Much as he claimed on *To Tell the Truth* a couple of months later, he told Sussman that he made 2.5 million USD off forged checks, often adding a Pan American Airlines decal to them for authenticity.

"I supported Revell Model Co., I probably bought two thousand model airplanes," said Abagnale, inferring that he wrote that many Pan Am checks during his writing spree.[21] He also recounted his exploits as a physician, an attorney, and a university professor, and his imprisonment in France and Sweden. He told Sussman of his deportation to the U.S. from Sweden, the awaiting authorities at JFK airport, and how he brazenly escaped through a toilet hatch when the airplane landed. With deadpan humor, he even scoffed at the experts he impersonated.

"I think being a lawyer is just being a good con artist," he said.[21]

Finally, Abagnale mentioned Fred Demara, the once legendary imposter who was the legitimate subject of a best-selling book and major motion picture starring Tony Curtis, almost twenty years earlier. "Nobody remembers Ferdinand Demara, The Great Imposter," he told Sussman. It is unclear why Abagnale was preoccupied with Demara, or if he had taken Demara as a role model of sorts.

"Abagnale said he realizes that he still has the power to manipulate people," wrote Sussman, "but he's trying to use it in positive ways."

The *Galveston Daily News* story went out on January 27, 1977, two days before his event in the junior high cafeteria, and no doubt drummed up more attention. Along with a photograph of Abagnale dressed in a pilot costume, Sussman included a separate front-page photo of the imposter with his arm around his new bride, Kelly Welbes. They posed together outside the old news building on Mechanic Street. For the casual reader, her presence seemed to add legitimacy to the whole affair. Sussman said so.

Still, the journalist appeared to have doubts and hedged his bets.

"I'm just waiting for someone to call me with the news that Abagnale is really just a little old pizza twirler, and this is all a con," said Sussman in his closing. The con man did have some documents. Those were helpful in convincing the journalist, but Sussman wrote that he was reassured because Abagnale had a "sincere look in his eye," and after all, "his wife was with him."

The final words of Sussman's two-page article provide the cautionary tale for those interested in facts and truth: "I couldn't help it. I believed him."[21]

Remarkably, Sussman's *Galveston Daily News* story was picked up by United Press International, and abridged versions appeared in affiliated newspapers throughout Texas, with many takers.[22,23,24] But all the syndicated versions removed Sussman's expressions of doubt that the whole thing might be a con job.

\* \* \*

Frank Abagnale and Kelly Welbes, Galveston Daily News
building, Texas, 1977. (Copyright 1977. *The Daily News.*
Used with permission.)

On Tuesday, May 17, 1977, in the small Gulf Coast city of
Nederland, Texas, Abagnale sauntered into a local restaurant.
Waiting for him inside was a small group of high school students
who had signed up for a vocational learning credit in marketing
and sales. And it would be memorable!

Local journalist Jeff Meyer was in the eatery ready to take
notes. It was still the early days of Abagnale's storytelling, but he
already had *Truth,* the show, on his resumé, and his young
audience was already impressed even before he boasted that
MGM was about to begin filming his life story. Actually, in about
six weeks, Abagnale said, but he still had to sign off on the final

36

script. He told them he was delighted with the choice of Dustin Hoffman to play his younger self.

"[Hoffman] spent a month with me while he was filming *Marathon Man*, watching everything I did. His intensity is amazing," crowed Abagnale to the captivated students. "He wanted to spend that month studying my mannerisms, everything about me. In real life, he's very clumsy. I was surprised," he added to the stunned group.[17]

Perhaps Abagnale didn't know that *Marathon Man* had actually been filmed in autumn 1975 on a tight four-month production schedule in New York, Paris and Hollywood[25]—another journalist Linda Stowell would later contact Hoffman's office, confirming that the Hoffman team had never heard of Abagnale or his movie.[26] But on that night in Nederland, Texas, no one questioned it. Not even journalist Meyer.

Abagnale told the students of his days as a doctor, lawyer, co-pilot and professor. He told them how he fled authorities through the jetliner toilet and his brazen escape from the ultra-secure Atlanta Federal Penitentiary. Without a whiff of irony, Abagnale turned to Meyer and told him that "the education I'm giving them is something they won't get on the job."[17]

\*   \*   \*

There appeared to be no fact-checking, and the veracity of Abagnale's claims went unchallenged. Instead, the United Press International provided a stenography service to a man with wild claims. Of course, each article became a circular means of verifying the Abagnale press kit—a self-styled life story dossier. Very good for a growing business.

In the spring of 1977, Abagnale started distributing a photo of himself to multiple media outlets—the same one Sussman used in his article. The *San Antonio Express* published it with the companion headline "Con Man Tells His Wild Story."[27] In the photo, the chunky, side-burned con man is wearing a Pan Am pilot's uniform. It was originally taken at Ferrel Massey's portrait studio in Provo, Utah—likely when he was twenty-two years old. Abagnale was careful to conceal what he was *really* doing in the college town during the autumn of 1970—those details would have proved incompatible with his new alt-reality.

But these small news articles in various Texas towns were merely setting the table for the big one! On the humid morning of June 19, 1977, Houston awoke to a full-color photograph of Mr. Abagnale filling the entire cover of the Sunday *Houston Chronicle* magazine—with "IMPOSTER" stamped diagonally in red across the Massey studio portrait. Abagnale had landed a five-page feature story in his hometown paper! At the time, the Sunday edition of the *Houston Chronicle* had one of the largest circulations in the nation.

Like the McAdams Junior High cafeteria appearance and *To Tell the Truth* several months earlier, this was an inflection point in the construction of the greatest hoax. And the man at the helm of the *Chronicle* story was none other than veteran reporter Stan Redding, the same man who later co-authored Abagnale's now best-selling autobiography—the basis for the Spielberg movie *Catch Me If You Can*.

Redding used the Sunday *Chronicle* to simply reinforce Abagnale's claimed capers posing as a pilot, supervising pediatrician, assistant district attorney, and college professor. No corroboration. No journalistic skepticism. The newsman with greased-back hair and the look of a used car dealer simply served as Abagnale's scribe—providing the equivalent of a free high-impact advertising flyer for the con man, direct to doorsteps across that corner of Texas.

"That was me, all of them," confirmed Abagnale to Redding, who happily printed his words without question. "I didn't keep any books, but the FBI says I cashed $2.5 million worth of fraudulent checks. The figure sounds reasonable," he claimed. Like many other articles and orations that would follow, Abagnale characteristically dropped influential names to add credence to his story. This created the illusion that he was merely repeating what purportedly "Pan Am says," "the FBI says," "*The New York Times* says," "*The Wall Street Journal* says," etc.[28] In Abagnale's world, a lot of people "are saying."

"Money was just a part of it. I did have fun fooling people," he told Redding. "It was exciting, and at times glamorous, and I became so good at what I was doing that it just became natural for me to assume an identity other than my own."[29]

Abagnale also started to flesh out his story with more details, including his European tour for four months with the student flight attendants he said he recruited. There was still no apparent investigation to confirm the truth of any of these claims.

It did not seem to matter. Despite being one of the worst pieces of journalism in the history of the newspaper, Redding's feature article was a smash-hit!

Abagnale soon had speaking engagements at exclusive country clubs across Texas, as his story spread like wildfire. By the end of 1977, Abagnale was traveling throughout the United States, retelling his story with even more additions and bravado.

Redding's advertorial, in tandem with his appearance on *Truth,* propelled Abagnale onto the major high-impact television programs of the day. He set himself up as the mechanical rabbit, and the greyhounds of infotainment gave chase. Very few seemed to care about who this guy was, really.

One appearance fed quickly into another. From *Truth* he was picked up by the *Today* show, interviewed by famed journalist

Tom Brokaw. Audiences loved it. No tough questions. It was all about the entertainment. Incredible stepping stones for Abagnale, as he made a lightning hop, skip and jump toward the coveted showbiz media pot of gold—*The Tonight Show* with Johnny Carson.

*Truth*, *Today* and *Tonight*—it was clear NBC studios loved the con man.

On April 6, 1978, Abagnale scored his first golden booking on *Tonight*. An appearance with Johnny Carson was the ultimate endorsement—instant transformation from fame seeker to fame hero. With Carson's *The Tonight Show* added to his resumé, multiple doors were flung open.

Curiously, in this appearance he was officially listed as a "writer"—although his only publication appeared to be the sixteen-page tract taken directly from Stan Redding's *Houston Chronicle* article, which boldly announced "He was a millionaire twice over before he was twenty-one. He stole every nickel of it." That small dossier—still only sixteen pages—would soon prominently feature his appearance on Carson's *Tonight*, and be marketed as though it was an international best-seller, emblazoned with "Now in its Seventh Printing."[30]

The media seemed mesmerized. Captivated by Abagnale and his story—providing enormous publicity for what was still almost completely unverified. Indeed, this was strangely reminiscent of how Evel Knievel himself once captured the media—with the exception that Knievel actually *did* jump buses, fountains, canyons and sharks, sometimes successfully.

"A lot of reporters who have never met me before are starstruck. No, not starstruck—they're astounded," Knievel had said.[14] His agent Shelly Saltman also explained how it was that those astounded reporters reacted to Evel's talent for promotion and his audacious courage by giving the canyon jump probably the most widespread publicity that any special event ever received.[14] And the media machine was most certainly doing the same for Abagnale.

Unlike Abagnale, Knievel's ever-growing claims had been about his *future* stunts, risking inevitable failure, and his life. But Abagnale's claims were safely in the *past* where they could be happily exaggerated with little risk. By many accounts, even as Abagnale beclowned the media that mollycoddled him, the man was hypnotically convincing.

"He looks you in the eye constantly. It constantly feels like he is drawing you into the world that he's talking about," said actor Leonardo DiCaprio, who later studied Abagnale for his role as the con man in the 2002 film.[31]

All the more reason not to waive journalistic inquiry, especially when dealing with a known con man. More likely, the runaway story was propagated through compounding assumptions—each journalist content to repeat the stories of the last, assuming that the hard work of verification had already been done.

Even today, giants of journalism are still lured in. In October 2019, Australia's *60 Minutes* aired its interview with Abagnale. There to peddle his latest book, he sits eye-to-eye with award-winning Australian journalist Liam Bartlett—telling the same story, unchallenged, on Australia's Nine Network.[32]

The lulling narrative may be more sophisticated now, peppered with philosophical reflections, but the core story is the same. With a steady gaze on Bartlett, Abagnale reminds his audience that he was "just a kid"—a teenage boy trying to survive, adding that he truly believes that he "would probably not have done it" if he had been older. It is a sympathetic narrative, and Bartlett nods, offering the "naivety of youth" as "a good excuse."

Abagnale also reminds Bartlett that he is now a man of

integrity.

"My conscience started to bother me," he says, then agrees with Bartlett that "you can't have a conscience and be a con man."

"I paid back two million dollars of that money because I hadn't spent it. And I eventually paid the other half a million dollars back because I felt it was right to pay all the money back," added Abagnale, inferring that he had stashed the unspent loot somewhere during his youthful escapades, and eventually dug it out, Shawshank-style, to make amends.

For years he has maintained that he never targeted individuals or small businesses. And he was quick to point out to Bartlett and *60 Minutes* that "the people most upset with me" were the people he was most generous to! "All the people I met that I really never did anything to, in fact, I took them places, I spent money on them, I bought them lots of things," he explained, "those people felt deceived."[32]

Of course, he never mentions his actual victims, the individuals and the families he really stole from. Those people belong to a different story. The real story that he never tells, and by extension, the story Spielberg never told.

*       *       *

Forty years may have passed, but there is a direct line between the cafeteria in McAdams Junior High, Abagnale's breakthrough appearance on *Tonight* with Johnny Carson, and his continuing narrative today—the core claims remain essentially unchanged. The impact and the reach of those early appearances cannot be overestimated, beamed into the homes of millions who stayed up to watch the enormously popular *The Tonight Show* in 1978.

Abagnale must have known that some of those who knew who he *really* was could be watching Carson that night—people who knew the real story.

\*    \*    \*

In Louisiana, John "Bud" Parks and his wife Charlotte Parks were both momentarily confused when Abagnale's face appeared on their television that night. Then disbelief set in. There must be some mistake. This could not be the same person who had broken into their lives. But it was.

As that reality became clear, Charlotte Parks became physically ill. All her anxieties returned. She had never really recovered from the day that he crossed the threshold of their home and hearts and stole their trust.

Bud was just angry. He could not believe what Abagnale had gotten away with. And now he was making up more lies on national television. Worse still, these people seemed to believe it!

Even the most elaborate lies are often formed around small grains of truth. And some of those tiny grains were known to Bud and Charlotte. But Abagnale's version of events was *so far* removed from the facts, especially concerning his time in Baton Rouge. It seemed impossible to believe that no one had realized.

They wanted to call their daughter Paula immediately but waited a sleepless night to call her first thing in the morning. When they did get through to her, Paula Parks was just as shocked. Abagnale's shady trail of destruction had left a mark on all their lives. It was outrageous. Most of all, it was painful to see the effect the memories still had on her mother, Charlotte.

But the Parks family were not the only ones sitting watching in disbelief.

# THE GREATEST HOAX ON EARTH

*The mythomaniac, like the fiction writer, after he has
lovingly wrought his lie, is rather apt to take it to market
to see what he can get for it.*
Anonymous, a substitute for
the plain word "liar," 1908[33]

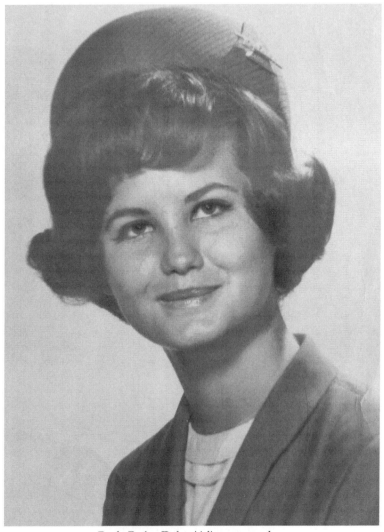

Paula Parks, Delta Airlines stewardess
(flight attendant), circa 1969.

# CHAPTER 4
# The Smell of Fear

*He was, by his account, a magnet*
*for attractive stewardesses.*
Journalist Bob Baker on Abagnale, 2002.[34]

Paula Parks first encountered Abagnale on a fateful flight to Miami around New Year's Day, 1969. It was the dawn of what would be one of the most tumultuous years in American history. A year of change that would leave an indelible mark on the social fabric—a moon landing, Woodstock, the Vietnam quagmire, civil uprising and restless energy. A year of unprecedented feats. It was also a year that would forever change the Parks family of Baton Rouge, Louisiana.

Paula was a flight attendant for Delta Airlines, and a member of the crew that day. Confident, beautiful and poised, it was obvious why Abagnale might be drawn to her. Even now, fifty years later, she has an ever-attractive air of dignity and great resilience. She is not bitter but has always felt that the truth should be told—because Frank Abagnale was *still* deceiving the world, and despite what he told Liam Bartlett on *60 Minutes,* he has not made restitution to those he has hurt.

\*   \*   \*

It was a cold New York night, and the crew couldn't wait to head back to Florida. Delta Airlines' marketing tagline in January 1969 was "Delta's ready when you are!" But the flight was already late departing, and it was a chance for a "deadhead" co-pilot from Trans World Airlines (TWA) to come aboard with a jump seat authorization slip.

"All the paperwork was in place, we were already past time," Paula recalls. Passengers waited as the Delta Airlines DC-8 got the signal they could push back from the gate. "The TWA man only just made it as we were about to close up the cabin door," she added.

The spare seat in the cockpit was often used to transport flight inspectors, as well as crew making their way to the destinations that demanded their services. This included pilots, co-pilots and flight engineers from competing airlines. Sanctioned hitchhiking in the friendly skies. At the time, if a jump seat was open, it really wasn't that difficult to secure a deadhead authorization. Beyond airline crew, the jump seat was a perk once shared by over 16,000 flight controllers working in the towers. An ID card would suffice.

And on this night, a reasonable looking ID card and TWA costume brought Frank William Abagnale onto Paula's Delta night flight from New York to Miami.

Paula welcomed him aboard with a smile. "I'm glad you made it!" she said warmly.

And the man in the TWA uniform responded with a sly grin. Average looking with some premature gray hair, he looked to be in his mid-twenties. But strangely, the *very* first thing that Paula recalled after fifty years was the overpowering smell. Since the sense of smell is so closely linked to memory and emotion, just asking her to think of these events triggered subconscious associations she had long forgotten.

"We all noticed—it was something more than normal body odor. My colleague thought so too—like a wild animal," Paula says with a mixture of surprise at the memory, and embarrassment in saying it. "Whatever it was, it couldn't be masked with English Leather cologne."

Oddly, their deadhead passenger did not head for the jump seat.

"He chose not to sit in the cockpit with his fellow pilots, and instead made his way to an empty seat toward the back, near to the galley," Paula recalls. "I now realize he was most likely avoiding anyone who might ask him some tough questions about instrumentation."

Once airborne, the attendants got to work and paid little attention to the TWA man with three golden stripes above the cuff of each sleeve.

"There were six flight attendants on our crew that night, although we were called 'stewardesses' in those days." It was truly the golden age of North American aviation. Like other airlines, Delta advertisements of the era glamorized the attendants. In print marketing they positioned the stewardesses as "The Star of Our Show" and "Our Leading Lady." One Delta ad campaign captured the Broadway lights zeitgeist: *"She's on stage for every performance. And gets rave reviews! She's a solid hit. Catch her act between fifty-eight cities nationwide."*

But on this particular night, after the passengers were wined and dined, the attendants were the ones who were entertained— by the man in the TWA suit.

"He joined us in the galley on our mid-flight break and really turned on the charm," says Paula. He told them his name was Frank Abagnale, and that he was from Bronxville, New York— one of the most affluent towns in the United States. Not to be confused with the Bronx, where he was really born, but he never mentioned that.

"This guy could talk. And he was funny. A real smooth character. I can't remember the specifics of his madcap tales, but I clearly recall that the whole group was very entertained."

In reality he was almost twenty-one years old. Certainly not a teenager as he would later like to claim. But he seemed quite unfamiliar with the airplane and airlines—as though he was completely new to the game.

When the flight landed, Frank invited all the flight attendants to join him for a meal. It was after midnight, and everyone was tired. Each respectfully declined.

"But he was quite persistent with me," recalls Paula with some discomfort. "I didn't want to hurt his feelings, so I caved. But there was no way I was going alone. So I convinced my Delta roommate to tag along. If she hadn't agreed, that would have been the end of it!"

It ended up being a hard task to find an open restaurant, so they settled in on hot dogs in the warm Miami night. Frank entertained them with more stories for an hour or so, and then Paula and her flight attendant colleague went back to their hotel room for some much-needed rest.

"We thought that was that. But the next morning my roommate noticed that the red message light on our room phone was flashing. There was a message simply to call the front desk. Which I did. The receptionist said I should make my way down to the lobby desk right away. They wouldn't say why, but she insisted everything was alright. 'Are you sure?' I was concerned. 'It's a good thing. Honestly. But you really should make your way down,' the receptionist insisted. I thought it was a prank."

Down in the lobby, the youthful receptionist was grinning from ear to ear. Romance was in the air, or so she thought.

"Aren't you the object of someone's attention?" the breathless receptionist said before she handed Paula two dozen red roses and a five-pound box of chocolates. There was a card attached.

It was from Frank, the TWA man. "Let's have lunch," it said.

Back in the room, flowers and candy in tow, Paula hemmed and hawed. She wasn't interested in him romantically. On the other hand, it might be fun. He was a character. Again, there was no way she was going alone.

Paula's colleague smiled and said, "What the heck," agreeing to chaperone. So lunch was arranged. Soon after, Frank Abagnale pulled up in front of the hotel in a massive, late-model convertible.

"Even now, I'll admit it was pretty cool. Off to lunch we went, the three of us, and once again, we actually had some good laughs," admits Paula.

After lunch Frank drove Paula and her colleague to Miami International Airport where they were going back on duty for their next scheduled Delta run.

"As we were leaving, he asked for my phone number and my heart sank. I really did not want to give out my number. He may have been charming, but there was no spark for me. Not at all. But more than that, my intuition was rumbling. There was something off about this guy. Cliché to say, I know, my sixth sense was tugging hard on my gut, saying 'good from far, far from good,'" she recalls. But Paula's instincts gave way to her ingrained Southern manners, which dictated politeness. She reluctantly gave out her number.

"I wish to this day that I hadn't."

In their previous conversation at lunch Paula mentioned that she lived in New Orleans, and her flippant departing line, "call me if you are ever in town," was also mere politeness. She had already declined his offer to make specific plans to meet at some point soon, hoping that the signal had been obvious. Paula was relieved to be leaving on a jet plane, unlikely to ever see the guy again.

She flew out of Miami on her routine sectors and was soon heading back to her home base in New Orleans, looking forward to a brief rest. But there was the TWA pilot again. Waiting when she landed. The odds that this was mere coincidence were near nil.

"When I returned home to New Orleans airport, he was right there, waiting for me. He knew where I was going to exit and was there with the gleaming convertible," said Paula. "This time he had a bunch of plastic flowers in hand. It was so weird. Who gives someone a handful of plastic flowers? Immediately, I wondered if they had been retrieved from a local cemetery!"

He made up a story about his flight being canceled, claiming to have a few days off. Paula had pangs of doubt. This was getting a bit much.

"'Well, I don't have a few days off,' I told him pretty firmly, hoping he would get the message this time. I said I needed to get some sleep, and that I had a flight to Washington, DC the next day. We quickly parted ways at New Orleans International, without one ounce of remorse on my part," recalled Paula.

But it did not stop there. When Paula's next round of scheduled flights ended in Washington, DC, Frank was waiting once again. Mysteriously, with more time off.

"This time he offered to take me sightseeing around the National Mall in DC," said Paula. It was daylight, and she thought there would be no harm in a short outing, so she agreed. "He was still wearing his TWA uniform as we headed downtown."

First, he took Paula into a shop.

"He bought me a gift," she said. "A Polaroid 800 Land

Camera."

Paula thought it was rather a strange and expensive thing to give someone who he hardly knew. Abagnale bought it with a charge card.

"It made me very uncomfortable, and I respectfully declined," said Paula. "But he insisted it was so I could take pictures of the Washington Monument and the other sights. I said I would be happy to take photographs, but the camera was his. He would not take no for an answer, so in the end I reluctantly accepted it. I still have that camera today."

After taking in the sights, they decided to find something to eat a few blocks away from the mall. Just a light meal, nothing fancy. But the shop only took cash.

"When we went to pay, he told me that he didn't have any cash," said Paula. "It was not an expensive meal, and I gladly paid, especially after he had spent so much money on the camera."

After this, Frank wanted to go shopping again. Although he wasn't flush with cash, he had the charge card and gave the appearance of a man with means. They were around H Street and 11th Street. It appeared to be a mini garment district, and there were three or four different uniform shops.

"I'm not sure why Frank wanted to buy a new uniform on a sightseeing jaunt," said Paula, "but he emphasized he was a veteran TWA man who needed to upgrade his uniform."

They went into a run-of-the-mill uniform shop with physicians' scrubs, nurses' whites, military uniforms, doorman outfits and many more besides. Other than the stitching on the gold bands, a pilot's airline uniform wasn't unique or hard to get.

"I watched as he walked into one of the shops, wearing his uniform, showing what I now know was a phony TWA ID card," said Paula. "He purchased another full uniform and several white shirts. And he charged it to the same card he used to buy the Polaroid."

After the outing, Paula again made excuses and made her way back to her room. She was thankfully not disturbed again, and glad to leave Washington without another awkward goodbye.

But, not long after, she was surprised and spooked to learn that Frank appeared to have used some form of deception with the Delta Airlines supervisors to discover her work schedule.

"It was just creepy," she remembers. "I really felt he was stalking me,"

Over the following days, this routine continued, not just when she returned to New Orleans, but in at least two other layover cities. Paula knew these were no coincidences, as she made every excuse to get away from him.

"I knew he was following me. No doubt. Wherever I landed, there was Frank waiting, as I clocked off duty for the night. I was cordial in rebuffing him. But he still did not get the message."

When Paula finally arrived back home in New Orleans for a solid few days off, Frank was there yet again—this time with a gleaming Chevrolet Impala convertible.

"I honestly didn't know what to do with this guy. On the spot, stressed, and trying to get rid of him again, I told him I was going to Baton Rouge to see my parents," Paula said. "I was hoping he would let me go." It didn't work.

"Great, I'll drive you," he responded.

Betwixt and between and under pressure, Paula said yes.

"But I was committed to using that driving time, while his hands were on the wheel, to make it very clear to Frank that there would never be anything romantic between us. Ever."

So, with the weather cooperating, they drove down to Baton Rouge with the top down. Paula found it very strange that Frank was driving so slowly.

"I asked him why he was going so slow the entire way—fifty-five miles per hour in a seventy zone."

"I like to stay on the far-right side of the law," he said. Paula found that even more odd, but she did not know that the big shiny convertible was not owned by Frank W. Abagnale. Or that it was originally rented by a guy named George Collins almost one thousand miles to the east, in Miami, Florida. According to Collins' contract, it was not to be driven outside Florida.

Paula still felt cornered into the trip and continued to disabuse him of any notion there could ever be anything between them. She was relieved that he seemed to be getting the hint at last. When they arrived at Paula's family home in Baton Rouge, she planned to extricate herself from the situation and send him on his way. But that's not what happened.

"I wasn't anticipating that my parents and my brother would fall backwards into the Venus flytrap of Frank Abagnale's charms," Paula laments. "They weren't seeing what I saw. Weren't sensing what I sensed. They adored him—until they didn't."

*The trust of the innocent is the liar's most useful tool.*
Stephen King

Top: Frank Abagnale and John "Bud" Parks, Baton
Rouge, Louisiana, 1969. Bottom: Frank Abagnale
and Charlotte Parks, Baton Rouge, Louisiana, 1969.
(Both courtesy of Parks family collection.)

# CHAPTER 5
# At Home with the Parks Family

*Everyone is just wonderful, and what hospitality!*
*I've often heard mention of Southern hospitality,*
*and believe me, it's real!*
Pioneer New York sportswriter Elinor Kaine
visiting Southern Louisiana, 1965.

John and Charlotte Parks had everything Abagnale craved. Love. A wonderful family. A happy home. They had it in spades. They worked hard for everything they had. With their generous hearts, they were beloved in the community. "Bud" to his friends and family, John was a music educator, known locally and throughout Louisiana. Charlotte was a nurse. Both were veterans of World War II, Bud in the United States Navy, and Charlotte commissioned as a second lieutenant in the U.S. Army Nurse Corps.

"We were not rich," Paula said. "Not at all. We didn't live in Bronxville. But generosity ruled."

It should have been no surprise that they opened their door to Frank Abagnale when he arrived at their house that fateful day. As soon as he saw them, he went to work on a charm offensive. They welcomed him in before Paula could wave him off for good. He was talented, charming and accomplished—what was not to like?

"In fact, he went so far overboard with stories to impress them, I am sure they were confused," recalls Paula. "I am still not sure who he was really trying to impress. He hardly paused for breath. It was bizarre and chaotic."

After being introduced as a TWA pilot, he told them how much he loved kids. Then he told them how he held an advanced degree in social work from New York's prestigious Cornell University. Actually, he said, he was looking for a job working with kids in this area. A highly trained pilot *and* an Ivy-League educated professional? What a man.

Naturally, Bud was confused and asked why Frank was not planning advancement in his career as a pilot. Perhaps a promotion to captain, Charlotte wondered? No. Flying was just a short game, Frank said. Over the long term he really wanted to work with kids. He made it clear he was a generous soul and wanted to help those in need.

"He discovered that mamma liked fishing and he asked if she would teach him. It was crazy. In what seemed like only minutes, they were wondering why I wasn't swooning for this man. He was a catch, they said later." Paula cringed at the thought. "They were certainly more enthralled with Frank than I was."

Soon enough it was time to leave, and by then, Paula was resigned to just make the return journey with Frank in the convertible, back to New Orleans.

In true Louisianan style, her parents were polite.

"Come back and visit us some time if you are ever passing by," they called as Frank and Paula drove off. Baton Rouge pleasantry. Sincere, of course, but never expecting he would be back.

Frank took Paula on another slower-than-speed-limit drive. On the way, Paula started wondering more about how long he had been a co-pilot. There were obvious inconsistencies, and he seemed unaware of pretty routine airline employee dialogue.

"Back in New Orleans I said goodbye to Frank. I think he finally got the message as far as romance was concerned. Even friendship, for that matter. We had little in common."

Parting ways was a relief, but the distress was still there. At each layover location, Paula had a more rapid heartbeat, expecting to see the shadowy figure with plastic perennials.

"I truly felt stalked by Frank Abagnale and make no apologies for saying so. I felt harassed by the unwanted attention. It was creepy that he was following my work schedule and dressing in a costume to track me. It was repeated behavior, and he knew he was making me uncomfortable. That's stalking by definition," Paula said.

After a week went by, she thought she had finally seen the last of him. She could take a breath. It was done.

Nothing could have prepared her for what he did next.

\*     \*     \*

Just days later, Paula received another call. She had just returned to her New Orleans apartment from Atlanta. It was her mother, which was not unusual. But what she had to say certainly was. Paula had to sit down in shock.

Charlotte explained that Frank Abagnale had moved into their house.

*What!? Why?!* Paula did not know what to say. It was so weird. Why on earth would he do such a thing? But her first thoughts were for her parents and brother. Was everyone okay? They really did not know anything about this man.

"I was really worried that there was something off about him. And it was not just that smell. He had been stalking me. And now my parents. It was just not normal behavior." It was natural for her to worry about their safety. After assurances that the family was fine, Paula wanted to know what had happened.

Charlotte Parks explained that a few days after Paula left, Mr. Abagnale had turned up on their doorstep in Baton Rouge, unannounced.

"Remember me, Paula's friend?" he asked Paula's surprised parents. "I'm here for those fishing lessons."

They didn't know what to do. Because he had visited about a week before, and appeared to be an airline colleague and at least an acquaintance of their daughter, they thought it was only decent to invite him in for refreshments. Drinks turned into dinner. And dinner turned into a room for the night. Anyone who lived in Baton Rouge in those days could understand how that might work. But then he just didn't leave!

Paula could barely believe it. Then again, knowing her parents' kindness, generosity, and Louisianan benevolence, she could well imagine how he had steamrollered them.

As she digested the news, she had an alarming thought.

"He's not staying in my room, is he?!" she asked her mother.

But she already knew the answer. Frank Abagnale was sleeping in her bed, surrounded by all of her very personal childhood keepsakes. She was chilled at the thought of him going through her things, and he almost certainly was. He was there for fishing.

"I felt sick," she said recently, recalling just how disturbing this had been. "It amped up the creep factor so much that I never wanted to stay there again."

Of course, Paula never blamed her parents for simply being generous.

"My parents did what any good-hearted Southern Christian family would do. They opened the door and gave him a room in the house. By the time I heard about this, mamma was cooking his meals and cleaning up after him!" recalls Paula, still incredulous. "They had even cut him a set of keys to the house!"

Even now, Paula remembers it like a creepy Hollywood thriller. A strange man she hardly knew—who had already been stalking her with graveside plastic flowers—had now moved into her parents' house! Made all the more sinister because he was mesmerizing them with his charm. And it seemed to be working. He was, in their words, "harmless." But Paula just didn't trust him.

Paula told her parents that she loved them dearly, but so long as Mr. Abagnale was in the house, she wouldn't be returning to Baton Rouge. She couldn't even bear the idea of a visit.

Over the next month, Frank helped himself to what was in the fridge, enjoyed home cooking and scooped up their hospitality. On occasion, he left for a few days. They were not sure where he went, but before long, that big Chevy convertible—with Florida license plate 1E36687 on the back—would roll back into the driveway. Paula's parents wondered about the Florida car, and the pilot explained he had been living in comfort in Miami. He had family connections there—his uncle Roy was a big shot banker in Miami, he said.

But it wasn't all a one-way street. To show his appreciation, Frank would take Paula's parents out to dinner. They were touched by his generosity. Especially her mother.

"Frank bought mamma a big, beautiful bouquet of flowers. Real ones. She loved it. She really thought he was wonderful," Paula recalls, still touched by her parents' trust. Hearing of his kindness, she had wondered if her uneasy feeling was ungracious.

With startling speed, Abagnale began insinuating himself into the local community. He said he wanted to be involved with a church and do something good with his Cornell social work degree. Naturally, he accompanied Bud and Charlotte to their church and asked them to introduce him to influential people in their community—and to Paula's attractive cousin, who appeared to be the new focus of his amorous affections.

"Before long, Frank started dating my cousin. I could hardly believe it. Mamma said it was my loss," says Paula, adding that she was secretly very relieved that he had turned his attentions elsewhere. But on the other hand, she was concerned for her cousin.

Although Abagnale still claimed to be a pilot, and occasionally put on his costume, he told them he was now "on furlough" and showed no sign that he was working. Instead, he seemed intent on his plan to get a job working with local kids. Vulnerable children. He had even got involved in a youth group at the local church. This seemed an odd career change, but Paula's parents thought this was admirable, and decided to do everything they could to support this, by enlisting the help of Reverend Earl Underwood from their church.

"Reverend Earl was a truly wonderful person, well known and highly respected in our community," Paula says of the man who performed her own wedding ceremony years later. The reverend was very well connected, with many friends and colleagues in academia, including at Louisiana State University (LSU). He welcomed Abagnale to their congregation and was happy to help the TWA co-pilot with his new career plans. The Cornell man, Reverend Underwood thought, should be able to find his feet quickly and make a contribution to their community.

But there was also something else about the young man that drew the reverend's sympathy. For all Frank's superficial confidence, the reverend sensed there was also something lost and broken. Reverend Earl had spent a long time working with people in pain, and he could tell that Frank was a man in need of kindness. And as a man who dealt in kindness, the reverend took the time to help Frank—not just with finding work, but to provide any spiritual support he might be willing to take.

And so, the reverend introduced Frank Abagnale to several others in the community, including people from LSU, with the intent of helping him find a suitable position.

"Frank had already played several rounds of golf with these folks before I heard about any of this," recalls Paula. "He certainly seemed to get around."

While the LSU academics were looking into a position for Frank, he was befriending Paula's 18-year-old brother, John, affectionately known as "Bubba."

"Frank seemed to have a Rasputin-like hold on him," Paula says, remembering the same hypnotic stare that Leonardo DiCaprio later described.[31] He loved an audience and looked for opportunities to impress local teens with his stories as a pilot.

"He even arranged to speak at Bubba's high school about a pilot's life," said Paula. "Mamma told me he dressed in his uniform for the event. Everyone was very impressed. They took a photograph of him to mark the occasion."

Frank Abagnale (aged 20) behind the wheel of a Chevy Impala that did not belong to him. Here he takes a local woman (not identified) on a picnic date, Baton Rouge, winter 1969. (Photographs courtesy of the Parks family.)

Paula's brother also described how Frank was quite keen on their cousin, and how Bubba and his own girlfriend would go on double dates with Frank and their cousin. Picnics, horseback riding, and so on. Frank was such a charmer. They all liked hanging out with the worldly man, who was pretending to be ten years older than them. Bubba recalled that Frank would still come and go, and he was not entirely sure where his new friend would disappear to.

All the while, Paula stayed away from the house. She wanted to keep her distance from the strange goings-on—but checked in regularly by phone, to make sure that everything was still all right.

"The uneasy feeling would not leave me." Paula would call from each layover and from her apartment in New Orleans. Her parents kept insisting that all was well. They appreciated Frank's gratitude for their hospitality. The dinners. The flowers. They did not have much money and were not used to such treats or attention.

"It was actually quite exciting for them. Entertaining stories. He had them in the palm of his hand. And they loved it." Paula adored her parents and was glad to hear they were happy. They were providing a home for him, spending extra money to have him there. At least he was reciprocating their kindness by spending money on them in return.

"Still, on each phone call home I repeated my doubts. They were in the middle of the situation and could not see it. With the benefit of distance and my previous experience with him, I felt something just didn't add up with this guy." And she kept telling them so. But they would not have it.

"We love Frank," said mamma. "He'd make a fine son-in-law." They seemed thoroughly disappointed that Paula was not interested in him.

But perhaps it was not all roses.

"Literally. The smell was starting to get to them too," said Paula.

For all their politeness, Paula's parents had to mention it eventually.

"It was Daddy who said it first. He had been trying to usher Frank toward the shower as soon as he got there. But it was something else he said that struck a chord. Daddy said Frank had 'the smell of fear about him.' I knew what he meant. It wasn't normal body odor. Just like my Delta colleague noticed it. It was like an entity. A living beast. This seemed to be a strange concoction of stress hormones and who knows what." Paula knew her father was not being unkind. If anything, her parents were just showing their concern for Frank. And trying to help.

Bud also remarked that there were other things that were starting to bother them.

"He would pace the floor here at night," Bud Parks said later to a local reporter.[35] Frank seemed to hardly sleep and appeared to have a nervous fear.

"My daddy was right. I believe Frank was living in fear—the constant fear of discovery." Paula knew Abagnale was certainly hiding something.

It would not be long before Paula's concerns were justified.

"I got the call on the first day of Mardi Gras, 1969. It was mamma again. I was in Washington, DC. The moment I heard her voice shaking over the line, I knew it was about our house guest."

Frank Abagnale, shortly before his 21st birthday, at home at the Parks residence, Baton Rouge, 1969. (Courtesy of the Parks family archives.)

# CHAPTER 6
# The Convict Who
# Makes Up Crimes

*The mythomaniac has told things about himself that might be highly incriminating, and when questioned, made quick use of his presence of mind to strengthen the circumstantial evidence against himself.*

Popular Science, "Mythomania,
When lying hurts the liar," 1921[36]

In the 1970s, Johnny Carson's top-rated *The Tonight Show* was the pinnacle of cultural success. An appearance with Carson was worth more than money and prestige. It was a mystical transformation. *The Tonight Show* supplied "a public rite of passage from obscurity to official term for the fame hero," and Johnny Carson was considered the high priest of fame.[37] An invitation was tantamount to a blessing.

"Johnny Carson is royalty," explained one promoter, "the king of show business. If Carson puts his hand on your shoulder and says you're acceptable, you're welcome to the court."[37]

Carson created celebrity and success like no one else. He made the careers of a legion of comedians, authors and musicians. Too many to mention. A moment on Carson's *Tonight* stage was life-changing.

"It was like going through the looking glass in *Alice in Wonderland*," said comedian Steven Wright, who made an appearance in the early 1980s.

Abagnale entered that wonderland on an overcast day in Los Angeles, April 6, 1978, inside 3000 W. Alameda Avenue, on the Stage One set of *Tonight*. His myth was growing—thanks to an increasingly robust press kit and the sixteen-page dossier, now "verified" by the added credibility of his appearance on *Truth*, Redding's *Houston Chronicle* cover story, and multiple puff pieces in Texas newspapers.

Johnny Carson was famous for not pre-interviewing his guests. He was cloistered away from his cast before and after their on-camera appearances. It was said that he preferred the spontaneity of a first-time meeting and the resultant conversation at his desk, in front of the live audience—it was far more natural. But Carson's aloof approach also added more to his mystery and his power, like an oracle in a religious sanctuary.

This meant Carson required a team of talent coordinators. This advance team went to extraordinary lengths to ensure that by the day of taping, each new guest would be primed for rapport with Carson. They screened candidates with multiple phone and in-person interviews in luxury hotel suites around Los Angeles. They had the power to determine who made it to Carson's couch in the first place.

And none was more influential than socialite and former model Shirley Wood—Carson's senior talent coordinator.

"Johnny Carson does the talking, but coordinator Shirley Wood puts the cast on the couch," wrote *People* magazine in 1982. Carson may have been the high priest, but all new talent had to first be filtered through Shirley Wood and her team of talent managers before they would even get near the kingmaker.

"There isn't a recognizable person on the face of the earth she [Shirley Wood] hasn't dated, interviewed, coddled or coerced. The most cynical lady I have ever met and, at the same time, a certified marshmallow," wrote one former colleague, a producer for *Tonight*.[38]

The hard-nosed socialite had already married and divorced three tycoons before joining Carson full time in the late 1960s. That included the Los Angeles drugstore magnate Samuel Sontag, publishing mogul Arthur Dettner Jr. and wealthy New York advertising executive Robert Milton Sherritt.[39,40] After all that, she acquired a new boyfriend who happened to be a producer at *Tonight*. Presumably on her own merit, the one-time perfume pitchwoman Shirley Sherritt was hired at *Tonight* and took on the new name of Shirley Wood.[41,42]

Wood's influence behind the scenes was legendary. She was the one to please. But she was not easily impressed. In a behind-the-scenes book about *Tonight*, another colleague described her as a colorful character with a "hard-bitten outlook."[43] Carson liked her, and that's all that mattered.

New talent like Frank Abagnale had to run the gauntlet through Shirley Wood's rigorous process of pre-interviewing, and for those that made the grade, she also handled preparation for their brief onstage encounter with Carson. Once in the fold, they might hope to make return visits—if Shirley Wood was impressed enough. She is credited with discovering former unknowns, like the now-infamous Bill Cosby and Robert Blake.[44]

Those who worked behind the scenes with Carson conceded that *Tonight* was all about illusion and "glorifying the power of suggestion over truth."[43] With that description, surely Wood had found the Rosetta Stone in Abagnale. He clearly impressed Wood and those at Carson's house of fantasia. Their work was likely made easy. They could lift questions for Carson directly from

Abagnale's self-styled dossier. And Abagnale knew his lines well.

\*     \*     \*

With a cheeky grin, Frank Abagnale emerged from behind the curtain, complete with his tall stories—from the same script that he used on *To Tell the Truth*, only now with new embellishments and extra thrills. The crowd was pleased. And so was Johnny.

"I find this absolutely mind-boggling," Carson said in amazement, further roiling up his studio audience.

Though it was a short segment within a ninety-minute show, it captured enormous attention. But not everyone was happy. Afterwards, the show received mail from concerned viewers—not about its veracity but with the way in which *Tonight* was aggrandizing unlawful behavior. This prompted a brief return appearance the following month to set the record straight—only adding to Abagnale's publicity. And a chance for him to expand his redemption narrative.

Carson introduced Abagnale once again and recapped his biographical feats.

"Everybody kind of went, 'You've got to be kidding,'" said Carson about Abagnale's appearance the previous month. "Maybe we should set something straight. We received quite a bit of mail and the general tenure of it, as I'm sure you know, was that we seemed to be glorifying crime," added Carson.

This time Abagnale gave tedious crime prevention tips on how to avoid getting shortchanged when breaking large bills and briefly mentioned the horrors of his French prison stay. Not the kind of stuff that lights up the house band and laugh lamps. But the message was clear. Crime doesn't pay. It ends horribly for the perpetrator, and Abagnale was here to protect and serve.

Mission accomplished. Abagnale left the set with an ever-expanding resumé and a list of speaking engagements. By the time he reached Hawaii in the summer of '78, he was flying high. There he was reported as "a man who eluded the FBI for six years, who successfully impersonated an airline pilot, a doctor, a lawyer, a college teacher, a stockbroker . . . who played cat and mouse so slyly with INTERPOL."[45]

"People love to think of someone who got away with all this. Everyone would love to do something like that. They dream about it, but they'd never do it. It's all fantasy," he bragged to Hawaiian journalist Beverly Creamer.[45] Three seemingly innocent but significant words spoken to the journalist. It's. All. Fantasy. Was he actually hiding the truth in plain sight for his own amusement?

Within six months Abagnale was invited back to Carson for his third appearance on *Tonight*—on October 4, 1978—along with sibling entertainers Donny and Marie Osmond, ventriloquist Señor Wences and comedian Kelly Monteith.

Carson introduced Abagnale and his now well-worn story, with a few extra details, such as how Abagnale had cashed *seventeen thousand* bad checks in his short but illustrious career as a con man. But he had some new material to share, including how he cashed a check written on a paper napkin.

"I've gone into a bank, even under a hidden camera, just to prove a point, and pulled up to the bank in a Rolls Royce with a chauffeur, three-hundred-dollar suit with a cane and gloves, and walked in and wrote a check on a paper napkin. And the teller has cashed it," said Abagnale to an enthralled audience. "And later on [I] asked why she cashed a paper napkin for a check. She said that when she saw me come into the bank, getting out of the Rolls Royce, dressed the way I was, she would have cashed a roll of toilet paper if I gave it to her."

The audience laughed loudly, as the fantasy of a swooning,

timid female bank teller hung in the air. The power of confidence and a man with a cane. Perhaps some recalled that Evel Knievel also famously carried a cane.

Running with the theme of Abagnale's magnetic charm with women, Carson posed another question. "You managed to take eight girls all over Europe as phony stewardesses, right?"

"It's true," Abagnale responded, before painting a picture of his extensive hiring process. "I interviewed about ninety girls, selected the eight girls I wanted," he said, adding that he told them that "we [Pan Am] would like to take you on an advertising campaign, [and] that we would like to use you this summer to shoot some stills over in Europe.

"So, of course I convinced the eight girls, dressed them up in the uniforms, [and] over to Europe we went," he told Carson's stunned audience. More male fantasy. *He dressed them up in uniforms?*

"And, they traveled with me for three months. Never knew what was going on," Abagnale continued, like a puppet master, referring to co-eds he claimed to have recruited from an unidentified university out west. "The photographers who were doing all the commercial photography work—I'd hire freelance, each one in a different city—he'd say, 'What do you want me to do with these proofs?' I'd say, 'well send those proofs to the advertising departments of Pan American Airlines.' In New York, the advertising department was getting hundreds of these photographs. Who the hell are these girls? And nobody knew. And they'd send them out to the [airline] bases and the chief stewardesses write back, 'These aren't my girls.' And the chief of security there of course was looking for me for years and said, 'I know this Abagnale is behind this somewhere,'" Abagnale told Johnny.

"How long did you do this?" Carson asked.

"We did it for three months and finally I took the girls back to the airport," Abagnale said. "I told them return to school, keep your uniforms, your ID cards, your [pay] stubs. I did that in case they were questioned, they could prove what had gone on. I said go back to school, and I said you'll be hearing from the airline shortly."

Abagnale told Carson about another caper that appeared to be a recent addition to his claims. It seems he needed new material because this whopper was strangely absent from his dossier—he started road-testing it in the days leading up to the *Tonight* taping. According to this story, Abagnale had made up a professionally printed sign indicating that the First National City Bank night deposit box at Boston's Logan International Airport was out of order. Unsuspecting businesses handed over their daily takings to the security guard standing at the alternate deposit receptacle. Abagnale claimed he was that security guard.

"The bad part about it was I couldn't get it [the cart with alternate deposit box] moving because it was so heavy," he told Carson. "All of a sudden, I hear two people coming. I turn around, it's two Massachusetts State Troopers. I said, 'I can't get this thing out the door.' They helped me get it out, load it into the car."

The audience laughs it up over the notion of buffoonish policemen. He had the audience in the palm of his hand. And he seemed to know that the more implausible his stories, the more they would be believed. Bizarrely so. When he walked off the set of *Tonight*, the mask had become the man. He was America's favorite con man.

Abagnale grinned, and the studio audience chortled, but having a go at the Massachusetts State Police, making them out to be as dumb as bricks, was a sure-fire way to invite deeper questions. And it did. One young man in San Francisco, a rookie reporter, decided it was time to investigate.

In the meantime, Abagnale's dossier grew ever more impressive. The power of *Tonight* in 1978 can be measured by mentions of Abagnale in American newspapers, which increased ten-fold between 1977 and 1978. These were almost exclusively puff pieces—hundreds of original and syndicated articles that simply repeated the press kit narrative.

Local journalists would sit in and transcribe Abagnale's words as he delivered them at lectures in community centers, colleges, high schools, chambers of commerce, country clubs, banquet houses and Interstate-exit motel conference rooms. Very few journalists included any qualifying statements or terms such as "allegedly," "he claims," or even acknowledged that the stories were based on what "he says." Put simply, the claims in his talks were largely written up as facts. Of course, there was an upside. Local journalists did record Abagnale *in his own words*, and those transcripts are invaluable for anyone trying to peel back the history, or rather the "his-story," of the hoax. Today, they are akin to holding a mirror up to Abagnale's face.

> *Public credulity seems to be the mark of our age. We're ready to swallow anything shown on television, whether it has any basis in fact or not . . . when people are searching for a name for the age we live in, they sometimes call it the Age of Anxiety. How about . . . the Age of Fraudulence?*
> Barbara W. Tuchman, 1988[46]

\* \* \*

Stephen S. Hall, beat reporter for the *San Francisco Chronicle*, was the young man unwilling to suspend his disbelief about two Massachusetts State Troopers helping Abagnale load a cart full of loot into his station wagon. He set out to examine Abagnale's claims. Although it is often said that journalism is dead in America, there are good journalists, those who stick to the professional code of ethics—and Stephen Hall was one of them. He still is.

As a committed myth-buster of the day, Hall's quest for truth took him in many directions. Just one week earlier he had published a serious but highly entertaining full-page exposé on the deceptive ads in the back of comic books—X-Ray Specs, instant muscle-building plans, secrets of attracting girls, switchblade combs, UFO photos, and magic brine shrimp.[47] One of the ads captured in Hall's piece was for a product, by huckster Scott Reed, a self-styled Metaphysician, promising to "put you on the road to a new life filled to the brim with riches, love, pleasure, and all the wonderful luxuries of the world!"—with a caption that screamed, "How to make others secretly DO YOUR BIDDING with the astonishing power of automatic mind control."

It was just the sort of control Abagnale seemed to have over most of the media, and the folks at *Tonight*, all doing his bidding and providing free publicity for his stories without question. The road to wonderful luxuries and filled-to-the-brim riches.

But Hall was not buying what Abagnale was selling.

He began his own fact-checking and within two days had published his findings. The headline from Hall's front-page *Chronicle* article reflects his conclusion about Abagnale's claims on the Carson show: "Johnny is conned. A convict who makes up crimes."[48]

Hall's piece provided the first point-by-point investigation of Abagnale's claims, including the gem in which he said he hoodwinked the Massachusetts State Troopers at the First National City Bank of Boston. There was no such bank. No banks anywhere near Logan Airport reported such a theft. Hall contacted the legitimate, similar-sounding First National Bank of Boston. They had already investigated the claims, not only at their own bank but in the wider area. The bank spokesperson concluded, "It never happened at our bank, never happened in Boston, never happened at Logan, and never happened at the only bank that has a night deposit box out there [at Logan, that is, Shawmut Bank of Boston], and there you have it."[48]

Abagnale claimed then, and throughout the decades, that people involved in his ruses often didn't report it to avoid "embarrassment." But Hall and the Boston-area bankers knew it would have been reported because theft of large amounts of currency from a banking institution requires mandatory reporting.

Next, Hall debunked Abagnale's claim that he was chief of pediatric residents at Cobb General Hospital (CGH) in Marietta, Georgia, for nearly a year. This was impossible. CGH didn't even have residents at the time. Hall's source was executive administrator Betty E. Whisenant, who was there when CGH first opened its doors June 3, 1968. She knew its history and its personnel very well. It was a small community hospital back then with only fifty-eight medical staff and 150 employees in total.[49,50] They were a close-knit bunch, and everyone knew each other.

Hall then examined Abagnale's claim of being an assistant district attorney under Attorney General P.F. "Jack" Gremillion in Baton Rouge, a job he said he secured after passing the bar exam. For that, Hall's source was another assistant district attorney, Kenneth C. DeJean. If Abagnale had really worked in the Baton Rouge Civil Division, Kenneth C. DeJean would know him well. DeJean had worked in the attorney general's office since the mid-1960s. He had risen through the ranks and was now head of the Civil Division. He knew all of the people who had worked in his office over that period, and there was no question—he had *never* seen the man who had appeared on

NBC's *Tonight*, under *any* name. Abagnale never worked there.

DeJean, it turned out, had already been proactive in trying to debunk the bunko. Immediately after the Carson show had gone to air, he contacted NBC to correct the record. He underscored that Frank W. Abagnale Jr. was never an employee in his Baton Rouge government office. But NBC was unresponsive.

Still, DeJean had a clever request, hoping to catch Abagnale out. He suggested that Stephen Hall ask Abagnale what floor of their Baton Rouge building that the Attorney General offices were located on. If Abagnale worked there for almost a year, he should know. The question was posed, and Abagnale guessed the second floor. In reality the offices were twenty stories higher and spread over two floors. Abagnale didn't have a clue. He did not even pronounce AG Gremillion's name correctly.

Abagnale's claims of a two-semester professorship at Brigham Young University were just as easily debunked. Sociology professor Spencer Condie told Hall that BYU was a religion-affiliated institution, and as such, detailed references from ecclesiastical advisors were an added part of the extensive hiring process. They even listed newly hired faculty in the local papers, as a public service. Condie was clear. "Professor" Abagnale was pure fantasy.

Hall then moved on to examine the claim that Abagnale was the only person to have ever escaped from the ultra-secure Atlanta Federal Penitentiary. In this preposterous claim, the one he recycled from *Truth*, the game show, Abagnale said he posed as a prison inspector and walked right out the door. "Only two guys have escaped by what we call unexplained means in the last forty years, and neither one of them was named Abagnale," said U.S. Bureau of Prisons spokesperson William Noonan, in reference to the Atlanta Federal Penitentiary. Another falsehood.

# THE GREATEST HOAX ON EARTH

*Mythomaniacs are subject to memory fabrication and seek
page one publicity for imagined crimes.*
Max Bahr, MD, Psychiatrist, 1935[51]

\*　　\*　　\*

Hall's article "A Convict Who makes Up Crimes" ran in the *San Francisco Chronicle* on October 6, 1978. His introduction explained how Abagnale "is finding willing believers as he promotes and invents a more varied criminal past." Kind of like the comic book ads. Willing believers, except this time it wasn't insecure adolescents seeking a body-building blueprint to avoid getting beach sand kicked in their face, but bankers, business and media execs desperate for a hero, something out of the ordinary. Their personal Sea Monkey. And how they had watched him grow!

The rival *San Francisco Examiner* ran a smaller story, but the conclusions were the same. Abagnale "made up the series of epic con man stunts that he described to national and San Francisco audiences," they wrote.

Ron Ziskin, the producer of KGO-TV's "A.M. San Francisco," put it in plain language when he just said, "We were had."[52]

\*　　\*　　\*

Abagnale's reaction to the negative publicity was to cancel his next California gig and get out of town. This would become a recurring pattern whenever anyone challenged his stories in the years to come. Several days after Hall's story broke, social columnist Herb Caen reported Abagnale's departure.

"Frank Abagnale, the 30-year-old con man who conned

Johnny Carson about a bank robbery that never happened, stood up the California Apartment House Owners Association, ducking a scheduled speech at Civic Auditorium 'because of negative publicity generated by the Carson show.' Grandly, he waived his lecture fee but stuck the landlords for $500 travel expenses," wrote Caen in the *Chronicle*.[53]

Abagnale bailed on a convention that would likely have been his largest live audience yet, at least at that point in his career. It was a colossal "How to Succeed in Real Estate" gathering attended by around ten thousand people.[54] An enormous lost opportunity.

In Burbank it would seem Johnny was personally embarrassed by the media fallout four hundred miles to the north. Although Abagnale did get back on *Tonight*, once in 1979 and once again in 1980, it was not with Johnny—only while guest hosts George Carlin (1979) and Joan Rivers (1980) were at the helm. Johnny would never interview the con man at the *Tonight* desk again.

When challenged with Hall's long list of denials, including contacts from almost all of the institutions involved in his scams, Abagnale had a ready disclaimer.

"I've run into this before when people confronted me and asked me to prove it . . . but due to the embarrassment involved, I doubt if anyone would confirm the information," retorted Abagnale, already off to greener pastures.

The negative publicity was contained to the Bay Area, and he was still enjoying very favorable press elsewhere. It was quickly offset by a puff piece that regurgitated his press kit story and, thanks to Field News Service, ended up in dozens of newspapers from coast to coast. The headline "Shyster Capitalizes on Years as MD, Lawyer, Pilot"[55] is a clear indication that Hall's exposé had not penetrated general awareness—or that it was more convenient to ignore reality.

Before the digital age and the internet, unless a story was picked up by the Associated Press or United Press International, or sent out through syndication, a story like Stephen Hall's in San Francisco or any other big city, was largely confined to its home audience. Hall fired a tranquilizer dart at the gargantuan myth charging around America. But it barely sedated the beast. By the time Hall fired his shot, the Abagnale craze had already been running wildly through the Zenith wooden-console-encased television sets as *Tonight* beamed nationwide into fifteen million American homes. Not once, not twice, but three times with Johnny. Hall's isolated report was no match.

For the rest of October, through November and into early December, Abagnale's lecture schedule was full, with packed houses across the Midwest. He was a guest on other major talk shows, including *The Phil Donahue Show*, and *Catch 21* on PBS. The mainstream media was gleefully feeding the beast.

By the end of 1978, Abagnale was also being paid handsomely for seminars offering to save business executives millions by cutting white-collar crime.[56]

"The man with a pen steals more than the man with a gun," became one of Abagnale's hackneyed lines, with various embellishments.[57] And they were buying it—oratory opium for the masses in banking, financial barons and C-suite boys—he was booked solid. "White-collar crime costs businessmen and consumers in America $40.5 billion annually. I think I am in a unique position to cut those losses. There is more than a little truth in the old maxim 'set a thief to catch a thief,'" Abagnale told his audiences. "I am no longer a thief myself, but I know the ways and means used by thieves. At any rate—I enjoy it."

Abagnale told audiences that banks, major department store chains and at least seven police academies had hired him for his services.

It seemed that Stephen Hall's exposé in the *San Francisco Chronicle* had failed to get any traction. His heroic lone efforts to rescue truth seemed in vain, as Abagnale headed back to Oklahoma—the home of outlaws, con men and gunslingers—where surely he knew he would be welcome. But things did not go quite to plan.

> *We see from what has taken place in our own days that princes who have set little store by their word, but have known how to overreach men by their cunning, have accomplished great things, and in the end got the better of those who trusted in honest dealing.*
> Niccolò Machiavelli, *The Prince*, early 16th century.[58]

Ira D. Perry, young journalist for the
*Daily Oklahoman*, in 1978.

# CHAPTER 7
# Truth and Daring

*In a time of deceit, telling the truth is a revolutionary act.*
Quote attributed to George Orwell

Ira D. Perry was a 22-year-old journalist, new to the game. He had just landed a job as the assistant to the city editor of *The Daily Oklahoman*. Fresh from Texas Tech University in Lubbock, he was hungry for a good story to launch his career. Only months earlier, as a student, he had won a prestigious award in a nationwide journalism contest sponsored by the William Randolph Hearst Foundation.[59] It was the first of many awards in what would become a celebrated career.

By December 1978, Abagnale had familiarized himself with folk from the Sooner State. With his one-man Barnum act, the Bronx man had already given twenty-seven seminars in nine Oklahoman towns and cities on behalf of the Oklahoma Banking Association, getting paid more than $600 for each appearance—plus expenses.[56] Billing himself as "The Skyway Man" and "one of the world's most sought-after con men," Abagnale was a favorite with bankers in rural Oklahoma. He had penetrated their insider's club, the inner sanctum of those who orchestrated life from behind mahogany desks.

Now he would try his hand in the big smoke, Oklahoma City.

When Abagnale's press kit came across Perry's desk, it immediately triggered his suspicions and sparked his youthful enthusiasm for a good fact-checking challenge. The perfect opportunity to put his journalistic training to the test.

Oklahoma was proud of its history of renegades, outlaws and heroes of individualism. There had been plenty of material for books like *Oklahoma Scoundrels: History's Most Notorious Outlaws, Bandits & Gangsters*, and *100 Oklahoma Outlaws, Gangsters & Lawmen*—including Robert Vernon Spears, one of the truly notable con men of the twentieth century.[60] These legendary outlaws and confidence men were authentic—with gritty, oft-ugly life experiences. But their stories were real.

For Perry, Abagnale's sixteen-page press dossier was dubious. It smacked of Madison Avenue marketing speak, even after a superficial read. Abagnale did not look fit to carry the saddle of a real Oklahoman hustler.

The dossier stated that during the course of five years Abagnale amassed over 2.5 million dollars, but he "blew it all on world travel, beautiful clothes, gourmet food, choice wines, fine lodgings, lovely ladies and other goodies," and that he "partied in every capital in Europe, and lived it up in South America and the Orient." He would rent Rolls Royces in various cities, cash some bogus checks and "catch a plane to Rome or Hong Kong." It proudly stated that he was "slippier than a Vaselined shoate [goat]," always several steps ahead of his pursuers.

None of this seemed to fit with his narrative that he had returned all the money he stole and that no one was "out one dime."[61,62]

Perry knew the slippery showman was scheduled to take his act to the Holiday Inn South, at the intersection of I-35 and SE 29th Street in the city nicknamed "The Big Friendly." As an editor's assistant, the young journalist could have done as expected and just written another promotional puff piece to announce the event, like countless journalists before him. But his fresh-eyed journalistic integrity called him to investigate each of Abagnale's statements first. Because of the sheer number of claims the con man was making, it was a tall order.

With only days before Abagnale's December 14 lecture, Perry had to act swiftly. First, he had to convince his editors to give him the story—and the column space he would need to deconstruct the myth line by line. They did. But only if he could come up with the goods.

Hoping this would be his big break, Perry set to work—like David taking on an ever-growing Goliath on a deadline. Working around the clock, he went right back to the very beginning of Abagnale's story—his birthplace—and discovered that even that proved to be untrue.

Abagnale claimed he was born in affluent Bronxville, New York. But when Perry checked birth records with officials in Bronxville and surrounding Westchester County hospitals, they had no birth records for Frank Abagnale, or anyone resembling that name, between 1946 and 1950.

In reality, Frank William Abagnale Jr. was born on April 27, 1948, in the Bronx, New York—a far cry from elite Bronxville, a place where U.S. presidents retire. Perry did not discover this at the time, but research for this book confirms this and shows the Abagnale family was living at 1551 Unionport Road in the Parkchester section of the Bronx. Court records show his mother Paulette filed for naturalization on June 7, 1948, not long after Abagnale's birth. Frank was her second child to Frank Abagnale Sr. after they met during World War II. Perhaps Frank Jr. thought the social cachet of origins in exclusive Bronxville would play much better with bankers and businesses hiring him as an anti-crime expert.

Next, Perry started examining Abagnale's core claims, beginning with Pan Am. In billing himself as the Skyway Man, Abagnale was framing the success of his five-year on-the-run criminal career around his airline scheme. And so, Perry contacted Pan Am spokesperson Bruce Haxthausen about the massive 2.5 million dollar loss (the equivalent of somewhere between 16 and 20 million dollars today) that would have been incurred from Abagnale's forged Pan Am checks. Notably, even bogus checks would ultimately make their way through channels back to both Pan Am and banking authorities. The loss would have to be recorded somewhere.

"It never happened," Bruce Haxthausen told Perry. "I've checked with the security people and everyone here, and it never happened," he said, adding, "You don't forget $2.5 million in bad checks. I'd say this guy is as phony as a $3 bill."

Pan Am chief of security, Joseph Sullivan, concurred, adding "I've never heard of any losses in these dimensions at all. And the stewardess [recruitment] thing is ridiculous."

Sullivan was referring to Abagnale's oft-repeated story that he recruited young women at the University of Arizona and toured them all over Europe on Pan American's dime. "They loved it." Abagnale was still saying. "We went all over Europe together. I forged nine checks at a time and paid them."[63]

This fantastical scene still made it into Spielberg's film over twenty years later. In 2002 Barbara Walters and Leonardo DiCaprio discussed it on *20/20 Investigates* as though it really happened—including how Abagnale, with eight stewardesses in tow, slipped right past federal authorities.

"He goes right by them [federal agents] and leaves the country. It was one of his biggest cons, and it's amazing," DiCaprio would tell Walters, with the same confidence of the grifter he portrayed in the film.

In the late 1960s, Pan Am *did* actually have a well-publicized and highly coveted flight-attendant-for-a-summer program, recruiting young women from North American universities for the dream summer job. From a high volume of applicants, only forty winning candidates were chosen. After four weeks of training in Miami, the co-ed Jet Clippers were qualified for a month of international travel and glamorous work with Pan Am.[64] The program was discontinued in 1969.[65]

Abagnale claimed he had recruited women for his European Pan Am caper from Arizona. So Perry went straight to the long-time director of career services at the University of Arizona, Ronald Hummel, for comment. He learned that Abagnale had indeed been there and tried a scam on just a few co-eds—but did not get away with it. First of all, he tried this in 1970 *after* Pan Am stopped their program. Second, the authorities were fully aware of him and put a stop to it immediately. He would have been twenty-two years old at the time, *not* a teenager as he had claimed.

"He just walked in the office one summer [the summer of 1970] wearing his uniform and said he needed to recruit some girls," Hummel told Perry. "We got together six or seven one day, and two or three the next day, but before anything happened, the FBI was here calling the girls. He told *The Tonight Show* he interviewed seventy girls or so, and at most he talked to twelve, and none of them went anywhere. The FBI told them [later] this guy was a fake . . . and it was pretty obvious anyway."[56]

Abagnale's press kit dossier featured a photograph of a half-dozen uniformed Pan Am flight attendants he claimed to have taken on tour. As if Perry needed any more reason for suspicion, the women were in the early 1970s variant of the uniform, with oversized Pan Am badge pinned to the bowler hat—not the uniform they would have been wearing at the time Abagnale claimed he was escorting them on his European jaunts. They also each had a lapel corsage, a standard addition for Pan Am graduation photographs, complete with the typical champagne to toast their special day. Even more notable, the photograph featured a black woman, one of the first to break the color barrier. It was not until 1971, when Abagnale was in already in prison, that Pan Am began hiring black women in earnest and released press photos to celebrate their efforts in promoting diversity.[66] Before 1970, it is estimated that African-American women accounted for less than 1% of Pan Am's flight attendants.[67] Abagnale appeared to have secured a press photograph celebrating diversity of women toasting their own success—and replaced it with a caption reading "Stews on a four month tour of Europe toast Frank."

He continued to extend this audacious fabrication on his speaking tours.

"On my eighth visit on [*The Tonight Show*], it was my birthday, and as a surprise for my birthday Johnny brought the eight girls on the show," Abagnale later told a crowd of bedazzled finance professionals. "All of them are married and what shocked me was, of course, there were no hard feelings or anything, but three of them have been, and are today, career flight attendants for Pan Am. So kind of on-the-job training," claimed Abagnale.[68]

Even his claim to have been on *The Tonight Show* eight times [68] is at odds with the facts. But Abagnale knew the power of his association with Carson's *The Tonight Show*, and inserted Carson into an event that never happened—the fantasy that Carson "re-recruited" Abagnale's college co-ed Pam Am recruits just to please his guest! It is no wonder that the relationship Abagnale so prized with Carson became tainted by his own compulsive exaggerations.

*Like any good confidence man, he practiced alchemy. He
melded truth with fiction and avoided detail.*
On Robert Vernon Spears, con man, *Self-Styled*[60]

Next up, Perry contacted the offices of the Baton Rouge
Attorney General to investigate claims that Abagnale had worked
there as an attorney for many months under the alias of Robert
"Bob" Conrad. By Abagnale's telling, he didn't just work there;
he was a crackerjack barrister who won thirty-three cases for his
boss, Jack Gremillion. Abagnale claimed he passed the bar on his
third try. Perry spoke with Thomas Patale from the Louisiana
State Bar Association's committee on professional responsibility.

"We had so many complaints from lawyers and alumni and
judges after this guy got on the Carson show that we couldn't
believe it," Patale told Perry. He explained that the attorney
general's office in Baton Rouge and the Louisiana State Bar
Association had launched a series of investigations. The Bar
Association had already reconciled each candidate who took the
bar exam with their current whereabouts.

"We checked each name against each person. We checked the
tests [bar exams] and have no one unaccounted for. We know
who everyone who took the test is," said Thomas Patale. At that
time, the bar exam was only offered every six months in
Louisiana. For Abagnale to make three attempts before passing
would have taken at least a year if not much longer, not thirteen
weeks as he later claimed in his autobiography.

When Perry asked Patale if any portion of Abagnale's tales of
closing thirty-three "trespass to try title" cases could be true, he
responded with just one word, "Never."

Kenneth C. DeJean, head of the attorney general's Civil
Division, was as adamant that this had never occurred in his
office, as he had been when he spoke to Stephen Hall. He went

further, pointing out that "trespass to try title" actions were not even part of their legal activities in Louisiana. "I've never heard of trespass to try title action," he later said about the term.[69] Notably, however, this term *was* instead part of the Texas Property Code[70]—which was Abagnale's home state when he was constructing his hoax and writing his dossier.

It also appeared that Abagnale had not accounted for strict civil service processes and decades of verifiable government records. Perhaps he overlooked the fact that working for the Baton Rouge Attorney General's office was a government post, and that state officials must keep detailed records on all staff, including all payments to employees. There was no Robert "Bob" Conrad on the Louisiana payroll.[56,71] Not to mention that no one recognized him from his television appearances.

"We have no listing of ever paying anyone by any of the names this man has used," said Jim Mitchell, personnel administrator for the Louisiana Office of the Attorney General. "We checked with all the former Attorneys General, and he wasn't there. We don't even have a record of paying *anyone* for only six months," Mitchell added. Abagnale's retort that his stories were too embarrassing to confirm was equally ridiculous—as many of the institutional documents are a matter of public record. Just like the banks around Logan Airport, they couldn't cover it up if they wanted to.

*With my photographic memory, I could easily memorize anything. They arranged an interview for me before a panel of six doctors. I passed. The rest was easy. I just took on an Alan Alda-type attitude.*
Frank Abagnale on being interviewed and hired as a supervising physician[72]

Like Hall before him, Perry contacted Betty Whisenant at Cobb General Hospital for more information on Abagnale's physician claims. By then, Whisenant was vacillating between annoyed and amused, but she confirmed what she had already told Stephen Hall.

"We don't have any interns [residents], never have had . . . this always makes me laugh. This guy's story gets better every time he tells it . . . he was never here as anything," Whisenant told young Perry.[56]

No one knew the hospital and its people better than Whisenant. She was already working for CGH before it even opened its doors for business and helped with the hiring. By the time Perry contacted Whisenant, ten years after CGH opened, she had worked up through the ranks and was the assistant chief administrator.

Abagnale claimed to have supervised the nightshift. An impossibility. While several of the nurses did work overnight, there was no steady midnight-to-eight shift for physicians when the hospital first opened.[73] No one at CGH emerged to confirm that Abagnale—as "Dr. Frank Williams" or any other name—had worked among them. Not a single document from the Georgia Medical Board (or any other regional board) corroborated his claim of a successful interview with the Board and his claim of being granted a temporary license. The chair of the Cobb County Hospital Authority, Dr. W. Harold Dellinger, CGH's chief of medicine, Dr. Richard Hammonds, and the CGH chief administrator, William H. Shepherd, would have known if Abagnale had been among them.

Bizarrely, Abagnale would later double down on the story, telling audiences that he watched other doctors scribbling unintelligibly in the medical charts and that he did the same. At one recorded speaking engagement, Abagnale even claimed that

*The New York Times* published his patients' charts, which showed "they say absolutely nothing" because of his illegible scribbles.[74] Of course, the *Times* did not publish anything of the sort. Not only did Abagnale know nothing about medicine, as he admitted, he also clearly knew nothing about ethics and laws surrounding patient confidentiality.

Perry's fast-paced investigation moved on to Abagnale's teaching claims at Brigham Young University; he reached out to Hall's source for anything else to help debunk the claims.

> *It was the easiest con I ever pulled, I just read ahead a*
> *chapter ahead of all my students.*
> Frank Abagnale on being a two-semester PhD-
> level university professor.[75]

Dr. Spencer Condie, the Chair of Sociology, emphasized that the professors all knew each other. In the late 1960s, the campus was relatively small, the sociology department especially so.

"We can tell you who taught here since 1935. We know who everyone was and where they are now, and this guy was not one of them under any name. There isn't even the most remote possibility," confirmed Condie.[56] Like many contacted for comment, his department was frustrated with Abagnale's blanket comment that university officials and others would not confirm the information "due to the embarrassment" of being conned. Ridiculous.

Condie also reiterated that BYU required multiple checks of basic references, and as a private, religion-affiliated school, "we also require an ecclesiastical reference from a recognized church leader."

And why had no one noticed that the dossier photograph supposedly taken as a "college professor in Utah" was clearly faked? There's a "Mr. PiBB" soda can sitting on his classroom desk—a product that did not even debut until June 1972!

> *I'm the youngest man ever confined behind the walls of the*
> *Atlanta Federal Pen . . . it had never had an escape there*
> *since 1902. I was there thirteen days when I became the*
> *first man ever to escape the Atlanta Federal Penitentiary.*
> Frank Abagnale, recorded speech, 1984[76]

Perry's source from the United States Penitentiary, Atlanta, was the warden himself, Dwight Amstutz. Not only did Abagnale not escape, as he claimed, he had never even been housed there. Miraculously, with his *Daily Oklahoman* deadline looming, Perry did discover the likely grain of truth at the core of Abagnale's wild escape exaggerations.

The escape story was based on a real incident in Marietta, Cobb County, Georgia. It showed that he certainly was there—but not working as a pediatrician. Instead, he was being held in the Cobb County jail awaiting a federal trial in Atlanta in February of 1971. Abagnale walked out of the booking room while the deputies were processing some paperwork. Perry spoke to Sherriff Bill Hutson at Cobb County jail, who was more than willing to admit this, without any embarrassment. Abagnale was recaptured within two days and pleaded guilty to the escape charge in March of 1971. He was transferred back to Georgia for federal forgery charges, but we will get to that later. There is a very big difference between escaping from a local county jail and one of the most secure penitentiaries in the United States.

Abagnale not only exaggerated his crimes, but also the charges. His dossier claimed he had so many counts against him, and was wanted by so many states, that federal and state authorities finally agreed on a "package deal." It added that he was tried under Rule 20 of the U.S. Penal Code, an act that covers "all crimes, known and unknown."

This also had no basis in fact or logic. It was preposterous to propose that any criminal could get a deal on all their unknown "yet-to-be-discovered" crimes! Rule 20 simply allows United States attorneys to transfer an indictment to another district where the defendant will make a plea or be sentenced. For example, if a defendant in Georgia is wanted for a crime in Arizona, Rule 20 allows the defendant to plead to the crime while physically present in Georgia, without having to be transferred to Arizona. For completeness, Perry sourced a local U.S. assistant district attorney who confirmed the impossibility and absurdity of Abagnale's claimed deal on "all crimes."

Abagnale's parole officer, Jim Blackmon of Houston, refused to be quoted for Perry's article, but he indirectly confirmed that many of Abagnale's escapades were phony. Perry noted that in his glossy brochure, Abagnale claimed he was paroled from Petersburg, Virginia, on February 8, 1974. As we will see, Abagnale was already back out, floating around Houston in 1973.

Perry also spoke to former FBI agent Eugene Stewart,[77] who was the current Delta Airlines' vice president of corporate security. Stewart said that most of the airlines were well aware of this small-time crook dressing in an airline costume to cash personal checks.

"It's more of a harassment than anything else," Stewart said.[56]

And Stewart was in a position to know just how ridiculous Abagnale's story was. During his esteemed thirty-one-year career with the FBI, he had been a long-time boss—assistant special agent in charge, no less—at the Atlanta division of the FBI.[78] The very place where Abagnale claimed to be the focus of a whole task force of agents—a supposed war room dedicated to the capture of a "master thief" who had been eluding them for five years. The very place where he was supposedly practicing as a suburban chief of pediatric residents for a year.

Before filing his article, Perry tried to contact Abagnale for comment. But Abagnale refused to return his calls.

Perry's in-depth article was so well received by his editors at *The Daily Oklahoman*, they decided to give him the front page.[56] It went to press on Thursday, December 14—the day of Abagnale's scheduled appearance in Oklahoma City. The detailed twenty-eight-column, four-page exposé was headlined on each page with a large caption that clearly called out Abagnale's hoax, including "The Great Imposter Is at It Again" and "Inquiry Shows 'Reformed' Con Man Hasn't Quit Yet" and "People, Places in Abagnale's 'Past' Vanish Into Thin Air . . ." and "Sometimes He Managed to Be in Two Places at Once." The meticulously researched piece left little doubt that the con man was still working a gullible public. Lies built upon lies.

In the closing of his original *Daily Oklahoman* article, Perry had thoughtfully referred back to Eugene Stewart at Delta Airlines. As a former FBI guy and an airline executive, he was well placed to see this from many angles. Stewart made it clear he would not hire Abagnale as anti-crime consultant.

"If you were to ask if we [Delta] would hire him, the answer would be no . . . we would not use him. We could easily find someone more appreciative of the total problem. It's one of those things where the public must decide where they want their information to come from," Stewart said, pointedly.

He wasn't being cynical. He was simply inserting a greater perspective that included the shifting public appetite for sensation and infotainment over substance. The media was feeding that ever-increasing hunger, and no doubt manipulating the nature of that craving. But how powerless are we really in deciding our fate, and the kind of world we want to live in?

\*　　\*　　\*

In 1984, Ira Perry was recognized by the Texas Bar Association for his outstanding journalism, including work that "helped foster better public understanding of the values of the legal and judicial system."[79] Unfortunately, his incredible work upholding truth in the face of Abagnale's alternative facts was not afforded the same level of recognition.

Perry's work was so compelling it *should* have been the last word on the subject. But of course, it wasn't.

> *To abandon facts is to abandon freedom. If nothing is true, then no one can criticize power, because there is no basis on which to do so. If nothing is true, then all is spectacle. The biggest wallet pays for the most blinding lights.*
> Professor Timothy Snyder, *On Tyranny* (2017)

# CHAPTER 8
# Collusion by Convenience and Complacency

*This kind of thing is frightening to me because it gives me
the feeling that the very concept of objective truth is fading
out of the world. Lies will pass into history.*
George Orwell on media-fueled misinformation,
1942[80]

Abagnale had an agent, a vicious defender who was there to help
ward off overly inquisitive media or anyone else who tried to
challenge her golden goose. Marjel Jean DeLauer. She was
ferocious. And not too happy with Perry's story in *The Daily
Oklahoman*.

DeLauer was a controversial figure with a colorful past of her
own. She once claimed to have found secret documents
belonging to billionaire Howard Hughes. In 1968, while briefly
working a low-level job for KLAS-TV in Las Vegas—at the time
the station was purchased by a larger corporation controlled by
Hughes—she claimed to have happened upon a treasure trove of
Hughes' confidential personal documents. DeLauer declared that
she used the documents as key research for her book *The Mystery*

*of the Phantom Billionaire.* Although fictional, the book was loosely based on Howard Hughes' life.

Around the time of the book's release in 1972, DeLauer reported that her home was ransacked.[81] This prompted a series of news stories, initially citing her as a key witness in a grand jury hearing probing the real-life drama of Hughes, the eccentric hermit mogul. DeLauer insisted that nothing was taken in the break-in, but that she believed the intruders were searching for the secret documents of her former employer, Hughes.[82] Later she even asserted the CIA was behind the break-in.[83] KLAS-TV executives laughed off her wild claims, pointing out that she had only worked in a low-level public relations spot for two months and did not have access to any such material.[81] The press soon suspected that it was all just a publicity stunt for her book.[84] They quickly ignored her dubious claims.

Once a C-level chorus girl and secretary to mobster Louis "Russian Louie" Strauss, DeLauer (then Marjel Atkins) was with him in his car as he fled murder charges in 1947. In a high-speed chase, their vehicle was run off the road by police. She flipped on her boss, becoming a material witness in the case.

With her background in grandiosity, DeLauer appeared to be a heavenly match for Abagnale's claim-heavy campaign—a job she took before eventually making an unsuccessful foray into politics.

When Perry initially contacted DeLauer to verify Abagnale's story, she immediately directed him to a retired FBI contact. When Perry asked if she had confirmed Abagnale's story herself, she brought out her inner honey badger.

"You're damn right I checked, and if you're going to do something bad on him, I'm not going to give you a damn thing. He's like a son to me," she said, going after Perry. She referred him to the FBI again.

It appeared that DeLauer's standard response to the press and other callers with questions about Abagnale's credentials was "check with the FBI." She threw out several names, including FBI agent Robert Russ Franck. This is what she had told Houston University law professor Matthew H. Talty III when he arranged for Abagnale to speak to students on white-collar crime. Talty told Perry that "he [Abagnale] can put on a hell of a show" and confirmed that DeLauer told them to get in touch with "former Atlanta FBI agent" Robert Franck if they needed verification.

So Perry also tracked down FBI agent Franck for comment.

The journalist learned that Robert Franck was indeed a career FBI man. He had just retired, months earlier, as the boss of the Houston Division. But he'd never met Abagnale, nor had he ever worked in Atlanta.

"That damn Abagnale uses my name all over the place," was Franck's immediate reaction. "But I've never even met the guy," he added, wondering how people had got his number. Yes, he had heard legendary stories of Abagnale—mostly from the people who kept calling him![56]

In the same way active agents are trained to reserve comment about information in the public domain, Franck could neither confirm nor deny Abagnale's claims, nor the very reasonable suspicions of those who were cynical.

"I know about what I've heard," Franck said, "but I never checked the guy out. I can't prove it, and that's all I can tell these people that call. I've heard of it, but I can't prove it."

Perry also contacted NBC to find out how Abagnale was getting past their fact-checkers. He went straight to renowned talent coordinator Shirley Wood—"researcher" for Johnny Carson's *Tonight*. Had they made any effort to verify the claims and content of Abagnale's sixteen-page dossier? Shirley Wood wouldn't comment. As an assistant to a city desk editor at an Oklahoma newspaper, Perry was likely deemed unimportant.

Perry was pawned off to Wood's assistant, who made a statement downplaying any future appearances by the con man. The assistant emphasized that Abagnale's resumé had been verified during the booking process. Who did the show contact for verification? Perry asked. Ken DeJean in Baton Rouge? Betty Whisenant at Cobb County General? Wood's assistant conceded that their verification source was a woman by the name of Marjel DeLauer! With the exception of Abagnale himself, literary agent DeLauer was probably the least reliable person to verify the facts.

*　　*　　*

Perry had unmasked the entire operation. Not just the original lies but the layers of deception that held them in place. He also had revealed how the Abagnale machine was still building the Barnum-like big-top tent, capitalizing on the names of reputable companies every time he spoke, falsely claiming employment to trump up his credentials—as he did with the prestigious Neiman-Marcus department store chain.

The Neiman-Marcus store in Dallas had hired Abagnale to give a brief session on crime prevention, Perry discovered after talking to Frank Ball, vice president of operations at the Texas-based store.

"We could have gotten the same information someplace else. He just came to our door," said Ball.[56] "The thing that concerns us now is that he is saying that he was employed here," he added with exasperation, "and he was *not*—under *any* circumstances."

In a gross exaggeration, Abagnale publicly announced he had saved Neiman-Marcus three million dollars in internal losses in the last year.[56] It was a complete fabrication. Frank Ball explained that Abagnale had only spoken about bad checks to a small group of twelve employees and never even talked about internal theft as he claimed. Ball also added that they did suspect that "his credentials are not as solid as he claims."

This was a recurring theme. Leveraging the name of prestigious companies and institutions was perhaps the most audacious way of selling a false veneer of credibility—so people would simply accept his exaggerations and not look too deeply into the details.

"The Great Imposter is apparently at it again," said one of Perry's confidential sources. "Frank Abagnale probably knows less about white-collar crimes than most well-read 15-year-olds."

Perry had won the day. Abagnale and DeLauer were found out. Leveraging the name of a senior FBI official who had never even met the con man, they were knowingly perpetuating and amplifying the deception to a largely unsuspecting public, including the individuals and businesses who were paying to see Abagnale "tell the truth" of his larger-than-life exploits and reform from a criminal past.

Abagnale canceled his scheduled appearance as soon as Perry's first article appeared on December 14, 1978. Just as he had in San Francisco two months earlier when things got sticky after Hall's article appeared.

Like a gunslinger at a high-noon standoff, Perry had run the fake Bronx outlaw and his chorus-girl sidekick out of the Oklahoman town. Fans making their way to the Holiday Inn were disappointed. The Oklahoma City Personnel Association that had arranged the event was embarrassed.

Association president, B. Chris Henninger, confirmed that Abagnale canceled without challenging the accuracy of Perry's reporting.[85] And Perry knew he couldn't challenge it. With some irony, the Association replaced Abagnale at the dinner event with a local magician, John Panze—another illusionist, but a man who didn't try to conceal that he was one!

For a follow-up story, Perry called down to Abagnale's Houston office again. He secured a comment from an unnamed secretary who said the showman wasn't in town.

"There was some problem with the newspaper article," she said. "They decided that because of the way the article was written, he should not make that appearance."

Who was she referring to when "they decided" to pull the plug? Were others party to the hoax? DeLauer? Even today, Abagnale says DeLauer did so much for him. Certainly, she was tight with Wood and the folks at *Tonight*. And what was Stan Redding's role? It was not clear who else was actively involved in engineering the Abagnale hoax—at least not yet.

In his follow-up *Daily Oklahoman* article "'Con Artist' Cancels," Perry got another statement from Thomas Patale on behalf of the Louisiana State Bar Association. Their frustrations were still running high, and they were considering a civil lawsuit against the con man.[85] Other organizations in Oklahoma were also considering canceling planned engagements with Abagnale, who had already garnished over $5,000 (about $20,000 today) in speaking fees in the area.[85]

Perry likely thought that his epic efforts would put an end to the spread of Abagnale's lies in Oklahoma and beyond. If so, that would have been the naivety of youth. His story was tightly contained in Oklahoma City. Just before Christmas, in the midst of the shopping season, attention was elsewhere and Perry's work was overlooked and forgotten as 1979 loomed on the horizon. His courageous efforts merely glanced off Abagnale's Teflon armor.

Perry had confronted the wrath of Marjel DeLauer, but she had the last laugh. In less than twenty-four months, she would go on to become the literary agent for a book that would sell by the millions—*Catch Me If You Can.*

As the Abagnale juggernaut continued on into an even more prolific phase, she was ready to viciously guard Abagnale's interests as if he were her own son.

\* \* \*

Ahead of the book launch, Marjel DeLauer was poised to defend Abagnale's reputation—any more articles stating that the con man *wasn't* such a notable imposter might damage his reputation and be bad for business. Fortunately for her campaign, there seemed to be no further assaults on Abagnale's integrity as a con artist.

Mark Zinder had not yet started working as Abagnale's booking agent. By the time he did, almost two years after the bad press from Stephen Hall and Ira Perry, their journalistic efforts had been long forgotten. Mark was not even aware of them. And Abagnale certainly never mentioned it.

Marjel looked after the early aspects of the book process, whereas Mark managed the speaking tour post-publication, and they did not have much to do with each other.

"Marjel may have had an intimidating reputation," said Mark Zinder, "but she was always nice to me. Probably because I was helping her with good exposure for the book."

It was not long before she moved on to other clients and her brief political career.

"I did get a call from her later," said Mark. "She told me that she had another ex-criminal client and she wanted me to do the bookings—but I declined. I got the feeling that she really believed in Abagnale. I certainly did."

Mark remained unaware that there had been any challenges to Abagnale's veracity.

"I never really saw any evidence that he was fabricating these stories. There were inconsistencies, yes, but I considered that was just part of the game—comedic flair, or artistic license to engage the audience. There were so many other reputable publications and TV shows endorsing him, who was I to think that I knew something they didn't," Mark said.

"He had everyone around him so convinced," he added. "Looking back, it was like being in a cult—one that his audiences, and the media for that matter, didn't even know that they had joined. Brainwashed and wanting to believe in it. When the guy is associating himself with the FBI, you can't help thinking about their famous guiding words—Fidelity, Bravery and Integrity—surely it must be true."

With the benefit of forty years' hindsight, Mark admits, with much discomfort, that he had been oblivious, caught in the excitement of working with such a dynamic man with such a powerful story of reform.

"I really had no idea," he said, still struggling with the guilt.

But neither did the mainstream media. Ignorance seemed to prevail—even when the facts were presented to them. NBC had received a number of calls from people who were concerned that the truth was not being told, an assistant attorney general and a victimized family in Baton Rouge among them. Other local officials also knew better. So did the small businesses and families who had been defrauded by Abagnale under very different circumstances than he was describing. It could have been an even bigger scoop.

"The media was certainly his biggest asset," Mark agreed. "In the beginning it was a mutually beneficial relationship. He loved the publicity and they loved a good story. Convenient for everyone. After a while everyone just assumed it was true, and no one cared to look any deeper. All rational thought seemed to go out the window."

Collusion by convenience and complacency. No one in the media seemed to be questioning their assumptions.

"The attention was like a drug to him. He craved it and could not get enough. And we kept supplying it," said Mark.

\*   \*   \*

In early 1979, Abagnale was riding high as though nothing had happened. His appearance on *The Phil Donahue Show* was re-aired through January. He was also featured on the popular nationally broadcast *Mike Douglas Show,* adding to his still-growing fame. The voices of Hall and Perry were easily drowned out by the enthusiastic national media tsunami. Their articles could not compete with television coverage reaching 80 million American homes.

By August, Abagnale was back on *Tonight*, this time with George Carlin as the guest host, reinforcing his sixteen-page con man dossier—now in its seventeenth printing! And once again, the various local institutions, the places where Abagnale supposedly worked, suffered the consequences of having "allowed" Abagnale to take on roles of responsibility even though he never had. Not only did these places—Cobb General, Brigham Young University and the Louisiana Attorney General's office—have to engage in yet more debunking, they had to contend with a deluge of inquiries from clients, staff or students asking how they could have let this happen.

Like many, the sociology department at BYU was exasperated. "He has never, never been employed by BYU. We checked this out fully a year ago. He's a double con. He gets on the Johnny

Carson show and says he's done these things and he never has," said Barbara Jenkins in a statement on behalf of BYU.[86]

But these fact-based responses evaporated into the ether. The voices of experts appeared to have less weight than the self-proclaimed con man and convicted criminal. Abagnale put the burden of proof on the disbelievers. And continued to discredit them by suggesting they were in a conspiracy of denial, huddling together because they were embarrassed by Abagnale's truth. The media only perpetuated this by reporting factual expert statements as though there was room for doubt, exploiting public distrust in authority. It was becoming increasingly difficult for experts to debunk falsehoods with facts.

The Abagnale phenomenon was cultivating a new jelly-like culture that would become known as post-truth—a new world where undisputed facts would be viewed only as an alternative perspective, a place where it would be equally valid to accept a more convenient alternate version of events. A truly golden age for the media. An era that heralded a new kind of celebrity.

And it was very lucrative.

Already in late 1979 Abagnale was openly telling crowds he was hauling in over three million a year in consulting and speaking fees. Even if this was another exaggeration, there is no doubt that he was earning big-time. His speaking engagements continued to increase, and so did his speaking fee.

But all of this was merely setting the table for the release of his soon-to-be best-selling book in 1980, *Catch Me If You Can*.[87] From a respectable publishing house, this was his new calling card. No more dossier.

The cover of the first edition states: "This is the true story of Frank W. Abagnale, alias Frank Williams, alias Robert Conrad, alias Frank Adams, and Robert Monjo—for five years the world's most hunted forger, fraudulent check writer, imposter and con man extraordinaire."

In effect it was an expanded dossier, a fantasy-filled autobiography in which Abagnale brought even more color to his many already well-known claims—by adding a new layer of numerous sexual exploits. He described many encounters with besotted women across the United States and beyond. This included bizarre scenarios, such as how he was entertained by women while being leashed like a dog during his extradition from France to Sweden on a commercial train. The gendarmes, he says, invited "three vivacious, pretty American girls dressed in a minimum of silks and nylons" to sit in his train compartment where they discussed their graphic sexual exploits, uninhibited by their male company.

Curiously, it was during his chapters about his time as a lawyer—which he had previously said was in Baton Rouge, Louisiana—that he wrote about how he developed a friendship with a "lively, personable, vibrant girl" from a staunch Methodist family, a young woman who would not give in to his charms.

"I was learning that a woman can also be delightful with her clothes on," wrote Frank. Interestingly, he also describes forming a close relationship with the church pastor who persuaded him to become involved with the church's youth programs. It is hard not to see the parallels with Paula Parks and Reverend Underwood. Always a grain of truth—although what really happened was vastly different.

Many newspaper reviewers loved the book and fueled Abagnale's narrative. When it was released, many US newspapers printed large excerpts, some even did so in serial form. This helped to harden the foundations of credibility.

"The reader will wind up chortling with and cheering along the criminal," wrote one enamored reviewer.[88] "Reads like a fast-moving novel; it's exciting, well-written and fun—almost unlawfully so, even as are Abagnale's frolics," wrote another.[89]

Elizabeth Wheeler of the *Los Angeles Times* was one of the few exceptions. "According to his breezy and self-serving book, Abagnale impersonated an airline pilot, a doctor, a lawyer, and a professor, picking up oodles of money and enough women to qualify for a Guinness Record. He presents himself as a thief so charming that even the bilked love him," wrote Wheeler. "Sounds like another con to me," she concluded.[90]

In Berkeley, California, critic Robert Manor excoriated the book under the headline "Bad Check Artist No Better at Books." Manor was skeptical of the claims. But more importantly, he was deeply troubled by the ways in which the book denigrated women.

"The anecdotes betray a pathetically twisted way of looking at women," wrote Manor.[91]

\* \* \*

Although a handful of journalists would superficially question the truth of Abagnale's stories at various times, to this day Stephen Hall and Ira Perry are still the only journalists to systematically debunk Abagnale's claims. Fayette Tompkins of the *State-Times* in Baton Rouge also played an important part in shredding Abagnale's story—but more on that later. They all did exceptional work trying to prove Abagnale was *not* where he claimed to have been and did *not* do what he had claimed to have done.

But Abagnale found it too easy to slip through this net—and in his book he made this even easier by adding a disclaimer that "all the characters and some of the events have been altered, and all names, dates, and places have been changed to protect the rights of those whose paths have crossed the author's." To paraphrase, for anyone expecting to find verifiable facts, don't bother.

Abagnale had learned his lesson from Hall and Perry's critical appraisal. He was changing his narrative to slowly walk back the detailed specificity that he had so clearly laid out previously on *To Tell the Truth* and in print media outlets during 1977 and the first half of 1978. Had Hall and Perry been able to show where he *actually* was and what he was *actually* doing from 1965 to 1970—at the time of the alleged capers—there would have been no doubt it was a hoax.

After Abagnale's book was released, Linda Stowell of the *Arizona Republic* appeared to be among the skeptics. When Abagnale passed through Phoenix in 1981, telling his tales to the Institute of Internal Auditors, she raised questions about his content, but also his "big sell" approach. She noted he was peddling audio-visual training programs for $175, and charging bankers $1,000 per lecture for information law enforcement experts offered for free. Especially when what he said concerning his life was so dubious.

"Some of his claims indicate there is still a little conning going on," Stowell wrote. She called out a number of his false claims, including that he had worked with Dustin Hoffman and escaped from the Atlanta Federal Penitentiary.[92]

"He dresses in $800 three-piece suits. He is articulate and brash when he talks about his earlier years of hiding from law enforcement officials and his love for a playboy's life," she wrote. Stowell was not buying the flim-flam and wondering why the bankers were.

But her comments barely registered.

Still, nobody had discovered Abagnale's true whereabouts, which would have made it clear why the story, as he had told it, was completely impossible. Instead, it was the beginning of a new chapter of roaring success.

> *Nothing is so firmly believed, as what we least know; nor any people so confident, as those who entertain us with fictitious tales.*
> Michel de Montaigne, 1580

Reverend Earl Underwood, Baton Rouge, late 1960s.

# CHAPTER 9
# Mardi Gras 1969

*You people have showed* [sic] *me more love in 6 weeks*
*then* [sic] *I have ever saw* [sic] *in my life time* [sic].
Frank W. Abagnale Jr. in a letter to Mr. and Mrs.
John and Charlotte Parks dated March 3, 1969.

Reverend Underwood had been trying in earnest to secure Frank
Abagnale a job befitting his Cornell University graduate degree.
He had made introductions and facilitated several meetings for
the furloughed pilot so desperate to work with kids. So, it was
unsettling for the reverend to get a call from one of his contacts
at Louisiana State University, shortly after they met Frank.

It has been pretty obvious, the academic told Reverend
Underwood, that Mr. Abagnale hadn't the foggiest notion about
academic psychology, social work or formalized work with
children. He was quite a talker and very entertaining. He seemed
to know a little bit about everything, but a whole lot about
nothing. Nevertheless, he did not appear to have any appropriate
knowledge or training related to the field in which he sought
employment. His story did not add up, and neither did his
credentials. It had only taken a few phone calls for the LSU
academics to determine that Frank Abagnale had never attended

Cornell, nor graduated from one of its advanced degree programs.

For the man who would later call himself The Great Imposter, the jig was up, before it even began.

They had asked if the reverend knew much more about him, and he was rather embarrassed to admit that he did not. He was very apologetic for having troubled them and for making the referral in the first place.

This was unwelcome news indeed. But Reverend Underwood was not yet sure what to make of it. Frank was living with the Parks family, so he assumed that they must know more about Frank Abagnale than he did. But he did not want to worry them until he made further investigations of his own.

The reverend's concerns about Frank were more about his psychological well-being than his academic credentials. He seemed a very troubled young man. The lie about Cornell appeared to confirm that Frank seemed desperate to belong, and had been trying hard to befriend people in their community. Possibly too hard? Something was not right, so the reverend wanted to find out more about this recent arrival to their community.

Since Frank had been passing himself off as a TWA pilot on furlough, that seemed to be the obvious place to start. Reverend Underwood began by calling the TWA hub in nearby New Orleans. He was a little surprised by their response.

The TWA office knew him very well.

"They knew him right quick!" was how Bud Parks, Paula's father, later relayed the bizarre exchange about their house guest.

The airline had already been watching the man who had been hanging around airports in a TWA costume and attempting to pass bad checks. He was more of a nuisance to them than a serious security threat. Unlike the elusive, debonair character portrayed in the film *Catch Me If You Can*, the airlines viewed him as an unsavory character who stuck out like a sore thumb. They knew exactly who he was.

"He was a grown man, almost twenty-one years old—not some innocent kid dressing up in a uniform. He knew exactly what he was doing," said Paula, in response to Abagnale's ongoing false claims that he was just a wayward teen, a 16-year-old who didn't know any better.

"TWA knew he was a phony, and told Reverend Underwood so," she added.

Although this was shocking news to the reverend, it was also starting to make sense. There had been a number of incidents in Baton Rouge, and he began to suspect that Frank might be involved.

Bad checks had been floating around Baton Rouge. Money had been stolen from small businesses, including Dooley and Son, a local small business selling fire safety equipment. Although that may not have been unusual in itself, there was a possible connection to Frank. He had been hanging around the premises with the manager's son. It was consistent with what the reverend had just learned from TWA.

"My parents still had no idea about any of this," Paula recalls, "and neither did I. It was not a great feeling to have my suspicions confirmed when we finally did find out what he had been up to. There was no relishing 'I told you so.'"

At the time Reverend Underwood was making his discoveries, Frank announced that he was moving out of the Parkses' house. He had found an apartment and paid the deposit to secure his new rental—the Broadmoor VIP Apartments at 9262 Florida Boulevard. His new digs were advertised as large, quiet and comfortable luxury apartments in the city's finest residential section. Frank was moving up in the world.

"I think my parents were actually sorry to see him move out," says Paula, "but he had every intention of staying in touch. There must have been some incentive to leave the home comforts and mamma's cooking. He was dating my cousin, so I guess he was trying to impress her with a new bachelor pad and give himself some independence."

Paula is still grateful that Frank had already moved out by the time that Reverend Underwood made his call to the police. Much as he liked Frank, he could not ignore the concerning information that he felt needed to be reported.

The Baton Rouge PD quickly interviewed a number of witnesses, and the description of the man trying to pass the hot checks fit Frank.

The more difficult phone call Reverend Underwood had to make was to Paula's parents. They were about to discover Frank had been stealing from them the whole time he was sleeping under their roof and eating at their kitchen table—helping himself to their checkbook as he stole their trust.

*I was proud of the fact that I never swindled an individual,*
*just companies that could afford it.*[93]
Frank W. Abagnale, 1985


\*    \*    \*

Frank Abagnale (aged 20) in TWA costume shortly before
his arrest in Baton Rouge, 1969. (Parks family collection.
Used with permission.)

By Valentine's Day, 1969, Abagnale had already settled into
the VIP Broadmoor Apartments. The cult classic film *The Other
Side of Bonnie and Clyde* was playing at the nearby Tiger Drive-In. If
the grifter had any romantic plans that evening, they were about
to be ruined by the Baton Rouge Police Department. And, if he
had seen his daily *Horoscope by Stella* in Baton Rouge's hometown
*State-Times* paper, he would have been warned that he had "A
better-than-average chance of gaining recognition today among
co-workers."[94] In Frank's case that might have meant his
fictitious TWA co-workers, or perhaps his fictitious legal
colleagues. Indeed, he was just about to gain recognition with law

117

and order in Baton Rouge—the very place he later claimed to work, with the State's Attorneys' office.

At around 9:30 a.m. on Friday, February 14, the police rolled up on busy Florida Boulevard to question Frank W. Abagnale Jr. He had just come out into the parking lot to get behind the wheel of his frost-lime Chevrolet Impala convertible with the Dover-white colored top. If he was en route to pick up roses and few pounds of chocolate, the plan was foiled.

Frank was invited to move away from the vehicle—but he already knew the routine well.

True to form, Frank Abagnale had plenty to say. As detectives questioned him, his story kept bending, weaving and shifting direction. First, he was quick to point out that he was a TWA co-pilot. Then, he conceded, no, he was a student pilot, a trainee. The detectives were already aware of his small-time TWA scam. The arrest report[95] shows that investigating officer, Lieutenant E.R. Thompson, had already spoken with TWA's crew manager in New Orleans, E.A. Rossi, about the easily identifiable amateur imposter. Rossi had confirmed that no one by the name of Frank Abagnale had ever worked for the airline. Finally, Abagnale conceded he was neither a co-pilot, nor a student pilot, nor any kind of pilot. He just wore the uniform.

Abagnale had shown Lieutenant E.R. Thompson and Sergeant Sanders the fake airline ID tag as his identification—claiming to be 30 years old.[95]

TWA's director of security, William M. West, also told the Baton Rouge detectives that TWA already had a file on this subject. Over the previous six weeks, they had received numerous complaints about him posing as a pilot or a flight officer. In contrast to Spielberg's film, many airline workers who interacted with Abagnale were not fooled. Still, West conceded that the imposter had taken at least one flight on TWA posing as a flight officer. They had been tracking his movements, which corresponded to the locations where Paula had seen him—when he "just happened to be there" at her flight destinations.

West had also determined that during the previous month, Abagnale had stayed at hotels in the vicinity of airport hubs: the Sheraton-Delta and the Sheraton-Charles in New Orleans, as well as other hotels in Indianapolis, Atlanta, and Louisville. Dressed as a TWA pilot at checkout, the petty thief would use a personal check in his own name—checks which bounced from accounts with insufficient funds after his departure.

Armed with this information and Abagnale's own admission, the detectives took him into custody. They also tagged and held his pilot's uniform, complete with cap.

He was initially charged with vagrancy. This Louisiana crime targeted "undesirable characters" loitering in public without lawful purposes or lawful means of support—a fairly broad crime prevention justification. With false identification and unable to produce evidence of lawful means of employment, Abagnale fit the bill.

Abagnale insisted that he now lived in Baton Rouge. He had moved there six weeks earlier, he said. In effect, he was time-stamping this move to around New Year's Day, when he met Paula Parks on that fateful flight out of New York. It would soon become apparent that the flight with Paula was one of the first occasions on which he tried the jump seat scam—and why he had *not* been doing it regularly since he was sixteen as he has claimed since.

Based on his conflicting stories, they also impounded his car while they investigated whether it was stolen.

Detectives quickly learned that the Chevrolet Impala belonged to National (then called Morse-National) Car Rental in Miami. They spoke to Herman Davis of National's office there and learned that the vehicle was originally rented by a man named George Collins and was by now weeks overdue.[95] The mysterious Collins had placed Abagnale's name on the rental agreement as a second driver. National had been looking for it and were about to press charges. Given the car had turned up in Louisiana, those charges would also potentially include driving the car illegally over Florida state lines.

Abagnale knew he was in hot water. And it would only be a matter of time before Lieutenant Thompson discovered he had been stealing from the Parks family and at least one local business.

*I always avoided small merchants.[96] I would never cash a check in 'mom and pop stores' but rather against banks and airlines where I thought it really wasn't hurting them.[97,98]*

Frank W. Abagnale

\*     \*     \*

"It is strange how life can change in an instant. How a single moment can change how you see the world, and take away your trust," said Paula Parks. "That is how it was for my parents. Especially my mamma."

Reverend Underwood called Bud and Charlotte Parks soon after he spoke to the police. With Frank Abagnale's almost certain arrest, he wanted to be the one to break the horrible news and to warn them that they could expect a visit from detectives.

"The bottom just fell out of their world," said Paula.

The reverend told the Parks family about his investigations, including what he had learned from TWA about Abagnale's sinister behavior and that Abagnale's solicitations to LSU were also based on fraud. Finally, he said police were suspicious that Abagnale was stealing from locals and warned Bud to check his personal accounts and checkbook immediately.

"They couldn't believe it to start with," Paula said. "It did not fit with the picture of the person who had been living in their home. But when Daddy saw his checkbook, there was no question. That was the moment that made it horribly real."

Like a *Lifetime* made-for-TV drama, Abagnale had been rifling through the family's possessions when their backs were turned. He found the desk containing their most personal papers and vital documents. There he discovered what he was really looking for—checkbooks. He peeled off some checks from the back of the checkbook in order to minimize the risk that it would be noticed. Signing John Parks' name, he had been siphoning their account. One of the checks was for $150, which is the equivalent of over $1,000 today.

"They were not wealthy people, and he knew it. But that wasn't the point," said Paula, "They had shown him so much love and generosity, and you can't put a price on the trust that he took."

"I fed him. I cooked. I think the thing that hurt me was that someone would come into our home and do this," said Charlotte Parks years later. "I don't trust people as much anymore."[35]

The generosity Frank had been showing them in return for their Louisianan hospitality wasn't just insincere, he had been spending what he had stolen from their own savings—including the dinners and the flowers he had so flamboyantly given Charlotte!

"The deceit was so hideous. That made us all feel so deeply sick," said Paula. "He seemed to get a kick out of *appearing* generous, because it made him seem like a big man about town. But *pretending* is worse than not giving at all.

"My parents were such good people. They didn't need dinners and flowers. They valued honesty more. I know they would have been just as generous if he had just explained that he was drifting and penniless and in need of help. But he couldn't do it—appearances were more important to him. His actions show that," Paula said.

Bud was angry. Charlotte was devastated.

"My parents were not naïve. They knew that there was evil in the world. But it hurt them to discover it in their own home, smiling to them at breakfast," Paula added.

But in the following days they had more unsettling news.

Frank had been spending a lot of time with Paula's brother, Bubba—John M. Parks Junior—and one of Bubba's best friends, Tommy Trebitz. To the young and impressionable teens, the older pilot with the Impala convertible was a smooth cat.

"The three of them would hang around Baton Rouge together," recalled Paula. "Bubba really idolized Frank."

They were sickened to discover that Frank had also been stealing from Bubba's small savings account.

"That was really pretty low. To find out that Frank was even stealing from my little brother who looked up to him and thought he was his friend was terrible," said Paula. "One minute Frank was posing for photos by his fancy car with his arm around my brother, the next he was forging a $50 withdrawal from my brother's savings account. That was a lot of money back then."

But it didn't stop there.

While Abagnale had been tooling about with Bubba and Tommy Trebitz, he had made his way into the offices of a small local business, Dooley and Son. Tommy's dad Al Trebitz was a senior manager with the fire safety equipment company, and they would often hang out there. Al Trebitz had no idea that his son's new friend had been rifling through their desks, helping himself to some company checks from the office.

This was how Abagnale had managed to secure an apartment in the Broadmoor VIP complex. He used one of the checks—for $312 ($2,200 today)—as a deposit.[95] He had only been there for a few days when he was arrested.

"My parents had to cope with the added guilt that they had let this common thief into our community. They were so grateful that Reverend Underwood acted when he did," said Paula. "Otherwise who knows what this creepy character with a pilot's uniform in the trunk of his car would have done next."

The house key that they had given Abagnale was never recovered. They changed their locks immediately. It was not until four days after his arrest—the first day of Mardi Gras—that Charlotte finally reached her daughter on a layover in Washington, DC. Her distress on the call was palpable.

"Nobody wants to be right about something like this. Mamma was so upset that she had not listened to me," said Paula, "but I was just glad it was over."

But it really wasn't.

\*     \*     \*

Frank Abagnale was sitting in the Baton Rouge jail while Lieutenant Thompson and Sergeant Sanders were investigating his local crimes and looking for other outstanding warrants for crimes in other jurisdictions.

Within hours the detectives had started taking witness statements from banks and local businesses who had cashed his bad checks—including the traumatized Parks family.[95]

Lieutenant Thompson had also contacted the police in Westchester County, New York, where Abagnale claimed to be from. He spoke to Larchmont-Mamaroneck's Chief of Police,

James J. O'Brien. That's where Abagnale's mother lived. It was soon learned that the man with the costume had previous arrests for stealing cars, writing bad checks and parole violations.[95]

Forgery and theft were added to his arrest report. It was a pretty open and shut case. As a repeat offender, many times over, Abagnale was looking at serious time—a ten-year sentence, perhaps. By then, it was clear that Abagnale had lied about his age, and he was really a few weeks short of twenty-one years old. With parole, he might be out of prison by the time he was actually thirty years old.

Abagnale knew this. He also knew he needed a good lawyer. And bail would be good too. So, with one of his phone calls, he decided to call Bud and Charlotte for help!

"Can you imagine the gall of it?" said Paula, still amazed by his audacity in calling the very people he had stolen from. It was Charlotte who answered.

"She was shocked enough just to hear Frank's voice again," said Paula. "Then he lied again and told them that there had been some misunderstanding about a vagrancy charge, and he wondered if they might pay his bail—and secure a lawyer for him!"

He did not appear to realize that they had already discovered the entire ruse and knew that he had been stealing from them. That Charlotte had paid for her own flowers! Needless to say, Charlotte Parks' generosity had run out.

"She could hardly believe the nerve he had to ask them for more money. It was just another selfish, thoughtless act," said Paula. "Completely crazy to think that my parents would not find out pretty quickly, if they hadn't already. To me it just shows how desperate he must have been."

The man who later claimed to have been a millionaire twice over by the time he was twenty-one could not afford a lawyer.

His filthy-rich uncle Roy in Miami was a real person—a household name in south Florida finance. But neither he nor anyone else was rustling up money for bail or a sharply dressed lawyer. Instead, he would have to make do with a court-appointed defense attorney—possibly one working out of the back of a nail salon. Dennis Whalen got the job.

The office of the district attorney in Baton Rouge—which is to say, the very people Abagnale would claim as "colleagues" in the grand illusion he and Spielberg sold a few years later—would be those handling the case against him.

"We didn't know then that the specter of Frank Abagnale would return to haunt us years later, and we would have to live with the years of watching him becoming ever more famous with his lies," Paula said, remembering how upset her parents had been when they first saw Abagnale appear on Carson's *The Tonight Show*.

"We all thought it was utterly outrageous when Frank later claimed he worked as a lawyer with the Baton Rouge Attorney General while still in his teens," said Paula, remembering how the family relived their frustrations almost ten years later, when Abagnale reappeared in their living room, this time on television. "We tried to contact the media to set the record straight, but they just didn't want to know. That just made my parent's pain and frustration worse."

In a bizarre twist, the forgery and theft prosecution was led by Baton Rouge Assistant District Attorney (ADA) Ralph L. Roy. He was still working alongside ADA Kenneth C. DeJean in the Baton Rouge offices a decade later when, prompted by Abagnale's *The Tonight Show* appearance, the Baton Rouge Attorney General and Louisiana Bar Association were turning over their offices trying to prove that Frank Abagnale or "Robert Conrad" had never worked there as a lawyer in the late 1960s.

Mr. Abagnale *had* been there in 1969—but sitting in one of their jail cells instead! If only they had looked in their criminal records instead of their employee records, they would have seen his name in plain sight. ADA Roy could hardly be faulted for not remembering the Abagnale conviction. In the ensuing nine years, Roy handled dozens and dozens of high-impact trials, including death penalty cases. This case was certainly not high profile—it did not stand out.

The story of the swindler's visit to Baton Rouge would certainly stand out one day, but only after it had been rewritten by Hollywood screenwriters and scrubbed of the truth that he ripped off a small business and destroyed the trust of a generous local family.

In yet another bizarre twist, both Bud Parks and Kenneth DeJean had separately called NBC in 1978 to dispute Abagnale's nationally televised claims that he worked in Baton Rouge. But both calls were ignored. The Parks family could have given ADA DeJean the information he needed to pursue a line of inquiry that would have debunked Abagnale's claims with absolute finality. A circle of truth could have been completed.

"People need to understand that there was another layer of pain, and that was the pain of watching someone who has hurt people you love get away with a grand hoax and then profit from it," Paula said. "There's nothing funny about that."

> *There is no greater agony than bearing*
> *an untold story inside you.*
> Maya Angelou

History may have been very different if someone had only listened to the Parks' story. In their possession were letters that would have cast a very different light on Abagnale's past. His previous incarcerations were still unknown, even to the detectives investigating his case in Baton Rouge. But the series of letters, written by both Abagnale himself and each of his parents, reveal the truth.

The letters contain information that the author has since verified through public records. They reveal where Abagnale was in the period immediately preceding his first encounter with Paula on the Delta flight from New York to Miami. Remarkably, Abagnale had just been released from Great Meadow Correctional Facility, a major prison in Comstock, New York, on December 24, 1968.[99] This was only a few days before he first met Paula, the smell of fear still on him. For most of the previous four years—almost the entire time he claimed to have been traveling the world as The Great Imposter—Frank W. Abagnale Jr., was behind bars.

# CHAPTER 10
# Escape from Angola

*The conditions at Angola shock the conscience. The worst prison in the nation.*
Judge E. Gordon West, 1975

Frank Abagnale was still sitting in his Baton Rouge jail cell planning what was soon to become his greatest escape. That is, he was doing everything he could to escape entry into the Louisiana State Penitentiary, commonly known as Angola. It was easily the most notorious prison in the United States. With almost certain conviction in Baton Rouge, that was where he would be heading. Abagnale knew prison life well. He had only been released from the Great Meadow Correctional Institute in Comstock, New York, about seven weeks before this latest arrest. But Comstock was not Angola. The prospect of a looming ten-year sentence in Angola must have been chilling.

In 1969, conditions in Angola were horrendous. There, Southern hospitality took a very different form. Solitary confinement for extended periods was common and involved being placed naked in a small cell without a bed, fed once at 4:30 a.m. and again at 3:00 p.m. That feeding was only a slice of bread, a teaspoon-sized serving of turnip greens and a glass of water.[100] The daily per-prisoner funding of Angola was half that of the national average.

Although best known for its violence (dozens of murders, hundreds of stabbings each year[101,102]), hard labor, decrepit buildings and understaffing, Angola was a place, at that time, where a significant percentage of the *inmates* actually ran much of the daily operations.[103] Incredibly, about 240 of Angola's 4,000 convicts were armed with shotguns and sidearms, supervising the other prisoners engaged in hard labor! These convict guards were also responsible for record-keeping, inmate testing, and new prisoner intake interviews.[104] What could possibly go wrong?

The true depths of Angola's depravity would not be addressed until December 1970, when five ex-Angola prisoners filed a lawsuit concerning the archaic use of convict guards.[105] Even after years of reform talk, hardline Louisianan politicians worried that it would become a "country club." In 1975, after so-called reforms, that "country club" still had eighteen murders and 173 stabbings. In 1969, the odds of a 21-year-old Yankee dandy surviving years in Angola unscathed were not good.

\*      \*      \*

In the Baton Rouge jailhouse, Abagnale was still unable to post bail. Four days after his arrest, detectives had returned to interrogate the prisoner. Lieutenant Thompson's file entry on February 18 indicated that this visit was a response to a letter from Abagnale.[95] "The accused had sent a note to officers from the jail—that he wanted to speak to us," wrote Thompson.

Frank Abagnale wanted to talk, and talk some more. The case file of the interview records a conversation in which Abagnale spoke at length to Lieutenant Thompson and Sergeant Sanders— about how he had met Paula, how he had followed up the invitation to Baton Rouge, how her parents had arranged for him to be a house guest, and how they had believed he was a pilot and a social worker.

But Abagnale would not admit to stealing or forging any checks from either the Parks family or from Arthur Dooley and Son. He said his lawyer told him not to admit that. However, he did admit having *possession* of the checks. He also admitted *cashing* the checks with Tommy Trebitz, but with the full permission of the Parkses, he said, who had called the bank and sent him to make the withdrawal. All lies. He even had the gall to say that he had given the withdrawn money to Bubba.

Yet, after this denial, Abagnale changed his account again. Lieutenant Thompson amended the record to show Abagnale had relented—adding that "the accused stated that he knew he was guilty and asked to see the district attorney so he could go ahead and plead guilty to all he is charged with."[95] The same day, Thompson added additional witness statements and a note that the Sheriff's office would be adding additional stolen check charges to the indictment.

With a strong case building against him, Abagnale appealed to Reverend Earl Underwood for help.

Despite the fact that the pastor had turned him in, Abagnale knew that the reverend was sympathetic to his situation. So, who better to advocate for him? The reverend was a highly respected figure in the Baton Rouge community; a good word from him could have a powerful influence on any judge at sentencing.

> *I have always found that I had to be a fake*
> *to find someone who cares.*
> Frank Abagnale, letter from prison in Baton
> Rouge, 1969[106]

\* \* \*

Reverend Underwood visited Abagnale in prison to offer pastoral care to the troubled prisoner. Abagnale appealed to the reverend's sympathies and implored him to act on his behalf. The reverend agreed to act as an intermediary between Abagnale and the Parks family, as his main victims. Abagnale agreed he would express his remorse and his desire for reform in the form of letters, so these could be shared with the Parkses, and potentially the court.

"I love those people [John and Charlotte Parks] like my own mom and dad," Abagnale wrote in one of those letters. "They treated me with more love than I ever received before. God knows I'm sorry and I'll never forget what I did to them for as long as I live."[106]

He said he would also ask his own parents, Paulette and Frank Sr., to each write to the reverend to express their support for leniency so Frank Junior could receive the help he needed and make amends.

And so, after the visit, on the morning of February 19, 1969, Abagnale wrote a four-page letter, beginning with his gratitude to the pastor.[106]

"I first want to say how grateful I am for your kind visit," wrote Abagnale. "I felt kind of lost at first, with no one to turn to ... I'm so sorry for misleading you. I meant no harm."

He wrote at length about his repentance and his desire for reform—all the things that would touch the heart of any caring person.

"I was sincere in what I wanted to do. I love kids and hope they will never have to go through what I have been through. I'm 20 years old, I have gray hair, ulcers, and I feel about 50 years old. Life is becoming a blank for me. I want help ... I need help. I want to be able to live a normal life. I want very much to go to college ... I wanted very much to attend LSU ... But again, I realize that I have problems, and they must be cured first. I belive [sic.] I can overcome [them]," wrote Abagnale.

"I have been looking for help for five years," he went on to say. "I'm not scared of prison Rev. Underwood, but I'll only come out the same in ten years. I need help and I want it very much. I have lost five years of my life so far, 15 to 20 [years old], and I know I may lose ten more ... I cannot afford to go to prison again."

Abagnale went on to describe the long hours sitting in his cell contemplating his life and his fate. He described how he would look out the window and ponder why he had ruined his life. He also described how much he loved Baton Rouge and that he had wanted to stay in such a beautiful city.

"I came to Baton Rouge and I loved it, I loved its people, I fell in love with a girl here. This I lost. All this, I knew I was going to lose," Abagnale lamented.

"But I must understand this mental problem I have. I don't ask for your help. I beg for it," he wrote, with double lines firmly scored under each of the final four words.

As agreed, Reverend Underwood contacted both of Abagnale's parents. He also hoped that any supportive words from them would also help the Parks family understand the situation. Abagnale's parents were already divorced by that time, so he asked each of them to write letters of support. And they did.

They separately described a very troubled young man living in a fantasy world, who showed very little self-control, and a compulsion to break the law. It is not clear if Frank had specifically asked his parents to emphasize his need for psychiatric help as a means to support his defense, but both of them took that position.

Paulette Abagnale wrote with thanks in advance to the reverend as he considered advocating for a psychological approach.

"He is in dire need of help, I mean psychiatric help," she wrote, "as he seems to have a compulsion to write checks and is unable to stop. He has spent three years in Great Meadow Correctional Institution in Comstock, New York. Two years the first time, [he] came home and was writing checks a week later, spent another year in Comstock and was writing checks again three days after his release. I am mentioning this so you would get a picture of what his behavior has been like."[106]

In that one letter, Paulette destroyed the false autobiographical narrative her son would one day invent for *Catch Me If You Can.*

Paulette expressed her thanks for the kindness and comfort that her son Frankie had found in Baton Rouge. She obviously had no inhibitions about the truth concerning her son's whereabouts, and his years in confinement. She went on to write that she had tried to get psychiatric help for her son in New York but had not been successful, and he was "just getting worse." She still believed that psychiatric treatment rather than prison time was in Frank's best interests, and she prayed that Reverend Underwood would succeed where they had not, thanking him for the kindness he had shown her son, even though none of the therapists she had enlisted were helpful thus far.

"I feel you are my son's only hope now and hope and pray you might succeed in getting him psychiatric help in an institution," wrote Paulette. "I am very grateful and relieved that he is not completely alone."

Frank Senior, Abagnale's father, made a similar appeal, about his adult son.

"My son is mentally sick," he wrote.

But Frank Sr. also blamed himself for the actions of his

wayward son.

"Neglect and indifference to the problems of my son in his early youth are my sins. [Frank Jr.] lives in a world of grandeur, trying I believe, to emulate his father who likewise believed that the world owed him a living without the effort and discipline required to achieve it," wrote Frank Sr. He also made clear that his son's emotional problems were apparent over a decade earlier, before Frank Sr.'s marital breakup with Paulette. He also urged that Frank Jr. was in "desperate need of psychiatric treatment" rather than prison.[106]

Frank Sr. indicated that he wanted to come to Louisiana to see his son and appeal for leniency and psychiatric help, but that he could not afford it.

"I wish I could make this plea in person," he wrote, "but finances will not allow it—I am at present a mail handler at the New York Post Office Department. I would further appreciate knowing what else I can do from this distance." He also added that his own mother, Frank's grandmother, was gravely ill in hospital.

Frank's parents were each genuine and sincere—both at a loss for how else to help their delinquent son. Curiously, Frank Jr. did not seem to know his mother's home address. He had given Reverend Underwood an address c/o Dr. J. Carlucci of Post Road in Larchmont, New York. When Paulette left Abagnale's father, she had, according to Frank Jr., gone to dental hygienist school. She worked with dentist Joseph Carlucci, and subsequently fell in love with him. Although Abagnale would go on to say, on occasion, that his mother had never remarried,[107] records show that Paulette did marry, and that Dr. Carlucci was Frank Abagnale's stepfather.

Reverend Underwood visited him several more times, and Frank Abagnale Jr. wrote more letters, including a final plea to the Parks family.

"There are no words to express how ashamed and sorry I am," Abagnale wrote. "I cannot ask for forgiveness and I guess I just deserve the ten years you promise me. However, I want you to please understand that I have no control over what I did. I love you all very much and the last thing I want to do is hurt one of you. I'll never forget what I did. I think of that 24 hours a day. I'll be sorry for the rest of my life . . . You people have showed me more love in six weeks then I ever saw in my lifetime.

"Even though I will go to prison, every cent I owe you will be repaid. I will have to live with what I have done. That to me is worse than any jail. I'm sorry. God is my judge," he finished.[106]

Image of one of the letters that Frank W. Abagnale sent from the prison in Baton Rouge, March 1969. (Courtesy of the Parks family archives.)

But Bud and Charlotte Parks were unmoved. When Paula read the letter, she didn't buy it at all.

"I didn't believe a word. He had been playing the reverend's sympathy, but it wasn't working on us. My parents had been played once already, and it seemed obvious Frank was still doing it," she said. "It was more self-serving manipulation, designed to tug on the heartstrings. He was pulling out all the stops and—you have to admit—he was good at it. My parents were such kind people, but they didn't want him to get away with it. If he did, where would it end?"

Abagnale was seeking compassion. Yet the man who had pretended to be a social worker displayed very little compassion in his public views on crime and punishment a just a few years later—despite having been in that very predicament himself. Instead, he advocated for expanding the prison-industrial complex. In 1982 Abagnale had this to say to a crowd of law and order, hang 'em high bankers: "I'm a strong believer that we need mandatory prison sentences for certain crimes. We need more prisons. Prison is punishment; it is the deterrent."[108]

But in 1969, Angola looming, he appeared to have a wholly different perspective.

\*     \*     \*

Abagnale was scheduled to appear in front of District Judge Donovan W. "Mickey" Parker. Known for his conservative values and firm views on petty crime, his nickname among convicts was the "Hanging Judge." Mickey Parker's successful campaign motto for the elected position of judge was "I Believe in an Honest Day's Work for an Honest Day's Pay."[109] It was a slogan that did not bode well for a grifter like Abagnale.

On April 11, two months after his arrest, Abagnale and his lawyer, Dennis R. Whalen, decided to take a different approach—insanity. They made the submission to Judge Elmo E. Lear, who was temporarily covering for Parker.

Whalen contended that he and his client "believe that because of mental aberrations manifested in the conduct and character of the defendant, the ends of justice require that a sanity commission be appointed to inquire into whether or not defendant was legally sane."[110]

Since Judge Lear was a man who adhered to process, he agreed. Lear ordered Baton Rouge's official physician, Dr. Chester A. Williams Jr., and his deputy Dr. Russell M. Coco, to secure an independent expert opinion through what was then known as a Lunacy Commission. The panel was not intended to determine whether or not Abagnale fit the criteria for the dark triad—the criminally sinister combination of narcissism, psychopathy and Machiavellianism—they simply had to determine whether or not he knew what he was doing when he committed the alleged criminal acts.

It did not take long for them to make an assessment.

The day before his twenty-first birthday, the Lunacy Commission ruled that Frank William Abagnale was indeed sane. In a letter dated April 26, the physicians wrote that "after an examination it is our opinion that Frank Abagnale is able to distinguish between right and wrong, is able to assist counsel in his defense, and understands the magnitude of the charges."

The Lunacy Commission concluded "Frank Abagnale should be returned to court."[111] And so, he spent his twenty-first birthday in jail.

"I have not seen the spring or summer since I was 16," he wrote shortly beforehand, conceding how much of his teen years were spent in confinement. He also lamented his lost love in Baton Rouse, presumably Paula's cousin. "My futures never last long," he added.[106]

\*   \*   \*

On June 2, 1969, Frank Abagnale appeared before the "Hanging Judge" and pleaded guilty to forgery and theft. Mickey Parker now held the fate of the convicted felon in his hands. For similar crimes, Parker was known to dole out five, ten, fifteen-year sentences. Melvin White would know. Parker had given the twenty-six-year-old Baton Rouge resident four years for only *attempted* burglary. Worse still, Parker was known for having a special dislike for recidivists. The deck was stacked against Abagnale. Angola seemed inevitable.

But Abagnale still had one trump card—Reverend Earl Underwood. And he had played him well. It was one of the most pivotal moments in Abagnale's life, and Reverend Underwood was the man who changed everything.

"Your [sic.] a wonderful person Reverend Underwood, and God knows how badly I need someone like you," wrote Frank. "Your [sic.] the first one that's ever given me a ray of hope, that I may get the help that I so much want and need. I pray to God that you will show me the way, I pray to God that Mr. and Mrs. Parks will find forgiveness in their hearts."[106]

Convinced that Frank Abagnale was deeply sincere about wanting nothing more than psychiatric help, the reverend worked behind the scenes to rescue Abagnale from Angola—and possibly even saved his life. There is little doubt that had Abagnale been sentenced to a decade in Angola, his life would have been very different.

Instead, on June 17, 1969, the day of sentencing, Judge Parker did show uncharacteristic leniency. First, he ordered that Abagnale be given the psychiatric treatment that he so desperately claimed he craved. Second, he diverted the thief from prison. Parker sentenced Abagnale to twelve years total for the theft and forgery convictions. But instead of Angola, Parker sent the grifter to supervised probation. In the annals of Parker's rulings, it was a miracle.

The soft sentence was in no small part due to Reverend Underwood's kind words. Judge Parker also ordered that Abagnale provide restitution to his victims. He was then placed under the supervision of probation officer James H. Craig and ordered to appear at the Baton Rouge Mental Health Center (BRMHC) at 655 North 5th Street.

The order stated that Abagnale was to "follow the advice of their physicians and continue to receive treatment from a psychiatrist as long as the psychiatrist or the BRMHC deems it will be of therapeutic value during period of probation." The arrangements for BRMHC treatment were ordered to be initiated in no less than thirty days. Restitution to the victims would be processed under the direction of Abagnale's parole officer.[112]

\* \* \*

It was the summer of '69. Men the same age as Abagnale were dying in Vietnam. The lunar module Eagle would soon be landing. And Frank W. Abagnale Jr. had the chance of a new life in the city he claimed to love.

In his 1980 book, *Catch Me If You Can*, Abagnale briefly pays homage to an unnamed pastor who had persuaded him to help build "several children's playgrounds in blighted areas of the city" and "other urban youth projects." He wrote that "for the first time in my life I was giving unselfishly of myself, with no thought of any return, and it made me feel good." But, then Abagnale added that:

"A sinner toiling in the vineyards of the Church, however, no matter how worthy his labors, shouldn't put in too much overtime."[87]

And, that was it. Abagnale left town. He missed his probation appointment in late July. He skipped out on the psychiatric help he had claimed he wanted so badly—that he had so desperately begged for.

State of Louisiana probation officer Jim Craig informed his bosses that Abagnale was missing, and the case subsequently found its way back to Judge Parker. However, it wasn't until September 15 that the judge issued a formal bench warrant.[35] [113] [114]

Just as Paula predicted.

"Three things were learned quickly in Baton Rouge in the summer of '69," she said. "Frank didn't love Baton Rouge that much. He had no interest whatsoever in psychiatric care. And he played Reverend Underwood's heartstrings like a bayou fiddle. Actually, there's a fourth thing too—he wasn't at Woodstock either, because now we know he had already moved on to his next victims."

By August 1969, he was in Sweden—already ripping off several cars and stealing from yet another family man, or two.

"I wanted his address real bad," said Bud Parks, referring to Frank Abagnale when he became famous and claimed on TV that he had never done anything to hurt any families.[35] Charlotte Parks never really recovered.

"Our mamma's nickname used to be 'Sparky' because she was such a livewire. So full of energy and zest for life," recalled Paula fondly. "But Sparky had lost her spark—and she never got it back again," she added with a sigh.

Her brother Bubba agreed—their mother was never the same again. Reverend Underwood was also devastated. Not just from the terrible humiliation, but from the disappointment—he had truly believed in Frank.

"He never paid back a cent," said Paula Parks. "It wasn't about the money, it was about doing the things that he had pledged to do—it just proved that all the things that he had said in his letters were meaningless. Frank threw the opportunity we offered him in our faces. He made everything worthless."

With the reverend as an unwitting accomplice, Frank Abagnale had made a dramatic escape from Angola. But he had also escaped from his promises.

> *I never committed a violent crime and never, ever ripped off any individuals. I don't feel any guilt now because I paid back all the money.*[115] [116] *I returned all the money I stole. I was under no legal obligation to do so.*[61] *No one is out one dime because of the crimes I executed 20 years ago.*[62]
> Frank Abagnale, 1982, 1987, 1989

Mark Zinder, while working as Frank Abagnale's booking manager, circa 1980.
(Courtesy of the Mark Zinder collection.)

# CHAPTER 11
# Fantasyland

*That night, Walter Cronkite ended the news by saying how
I was the youngest master thief ever wanted by the FBI,
and the youngest man ever sent to federal prison.*
Frank Abagnale, in a speech to
college students, 1981[117]

"Wake up, Z! No sleeping, Z!"

Frank Abagnale was once again elbowing his agent Mark Zinder in the ribs as he dozed against the cabin window of the airplane. By 1980, they only flew first class or, if need be, hired private jets. The champagne was flowing, but Mark was exhausted. Abagnale usually kept him up half the night, so catching a few moments rest before the next event was more appealing to Mark than the exotic menu.

Working with Abagnale was certainly exciting, but it also had its downsides.

"He always woke me up," recalled Mark Zinder. "He never seemed to sleep, and he hated to see me sleep—especially when we were flying. It was as though he never stopped performing and always wanted an audience."

Abagnale's best-selling autobiography *Catch Me If You Can* was out, and business was booming. His event calendar was booked solid, and they were constantly on the road. Money streamed in and out, with no shortage of lavish dinners and luxury hotels.

"Frank was spending money left, right and center. When we went out to dinner with a group, he didn't ask what we wanted, he just ordered everything on the menu," said Mark.

"We lived out of fancy hotels. But the weird thing was that he always wanted to share a twin room with me. Then he would invite groupies back at night and kick me out of the room. He could have easily afforded his own room, but he seemed to enjoy pushing me around and impressing me with his after-hours exploits and much more."

This had become the routine. Another day, another jet plane. And Mark was living in Abagnale's dream.

\* \* \*

Houston was home base for Abagnale's vast operations. Space City. Mission Control. A place where moonshot dreams become realized. Mark Zinder had been lured there at the invitation of Abagnale in the summer of 1980, and it became his home too.

"I was a wide-eyed 23-year-old. Ambitious and hard-working, with a keen eye for the type of talent that could fill up university auditoriums," Mark recalled. "I admit I was naïve, probably too trusting, and willing to take people at their word."

Mark was a graduate of the University of South Alabama. He had been offered a full scholarship to return to undertake a Master's degree and become director of student activities—based on his outstanding success in marketing and promotion as an undergraduate. He was selected to represent the university in a "Who's Who Among Students in Colleges and Universities"—an honor that earned him eight job offers on graduation. But it was New Line Presentations in New York that hunted him down while vacationing with his family in Florida.

"New Line were having a party and invited me," recalled Mark, "but it was really an interview. They liked me and offered me a job as an agent. So, I had to make the very hard phone call to turn down the university offer. Then I headed to the excitement of New York."

New Line Presentations (NLP) was the special events arm of the better-known film production studio, New Line Cinema, currently owned by Warner Brothers. The presentations branch had connections to celebrity talent. In particular, NLP was a leader in securing university bookings for talent of various kinds, including Frank Abagnale.

But his first fateful encounter with Abagnale had been two years earlier, just before Mark Zinder's senior year in college. Mark had been heavily involved in campus activities since his sophomore year, sitting on the committee responsible for bringing engaging speakers and performers to the campus. He worked closely with the director of student activities.

In August 1978, several weeks before his senior year was due to begin, Mark made his way to the International Platform Association (IPA) annual meeting in Washington, DC. The IPA annual convention was a renowned gathering of world-class public speakers, many of them discussing the next big idea. It was like a TED conference before TED was a thing. The place to watch the already and soon-to-be famous. A once-a-year Woodstock for public speakers.

"As a speech communications major with a minor in theater, I simply had to be there," said Mark. "The university had encouraged the trip. I had to scout and preview talent and decide who to spend my budget on, who to bring to South Alabama over the next year. It was fun and exciting, but there was a job to be done."

Every year the IPA meetings promised household names peppered among unknowns with exciting potential. The '78 meeting was no different. The sixty-two speakers included senators, congresswomen, generals, syndicated columnists, celebrated speechwriters, major TV broadcast news personalities, the U.S. Secretary of Health, Education, and Welfare, and an address from President Jimmy Carter. And among that impressive lineup was a relatively unknown speaker—Frank William Abagnale—an ex-con who advised businesses. He was certainly a gimmicky outlier.

"I didn't know what to expect, but when Abagnale took the stage at IPA, I was in awe," Mark said. "He so deftly described his daring capers. Physician. Lawyer. Professor. Pilot. Millions in bogus checks. One of the most wanted men in the world, eluding all authorities through a five-year on-the-run crime spree! Now turned good guy. By then, he been on *Tonight* with Johnny Carson, the *Today* show, *To Tell the Truth*, and several high-impact talk shows—which all added to his credibility."

Given the institutional legitimacy of the IPA, its prestige and social cachet, the accomplished people at its podiums, Mark had no reason to question the legitimacy of the speaker they had handpicked.

"The story certainly sounded incredible, but I never doubted for a second that most of it was true," Mark said. "There was no way, I thought, that the IPA would let a con man penetrate its ranks unless his story was true."

As soon as Abagnale had wrapped his speech, Mark went to introduce himself.

"I told him that his story would be a huge hit on American university campuses. At that point he was delivering his speeches mostly to financial institutions, chambers of commerce, business associations and the like," said Mark, "but I knew the college lecture circuit was considerable and lucrative—and I told him so."

Indeed, at that point Abagnale was working a narrow field, epitomized by regaling captains of the agribusiness and feedlot industry at their annual galas. The cattle and poultry bosses would name their "Man-of-the-Year"—then settle into their banquet to "Hear Frank Abagnale, the World's Greatest Con Artist!"

The con man told Mark it would take $750 to book him at his university. Mark was responsible for a hundred thousand dollar budget (almost $400,000 today), but he did not say that.

"Perhaps he was trying to test me, figuring I'd balk at such a figure," said Mark, "but I saw his eyes light up when I told him that the fee was no problem, that I had a significant budget to bring in talent, that I paid some celebrity acts more than that."

Mark had Abagnale's full attention. The con man grinned.

"Then I told him there were nearly a thousand affiliate schools in the National Entertainment and Campus Activities Association, each with similarly large budgets," said Mark, as Abagnale grinned some more. The biggest, cheekiest grin imaginable, Mark thought. Like Seuss's Grinch when he got his "wonderful, awful idea!" to raid Whoville.

Looking back, a vision of the Monopoly man running away with sacks of money comes to mind. But in 1978, Mark was elated. With Abagnale's contact info in his hand, they parted ways. Walking out into the streets of the nation's capital, Mark could feel possibility in the air.

Back in Alabama, Mark told his committee and the dean about Abagnale's act. The administration was more than a little dubious. Not about the veracity of the claims. It was a question of whether he provided a positive, empathic and pro-social message. What was the overall message for young minds? They were naturally concerned about glamorizing crime and questioned whether

Abagnale's message was a good fit for the university mission or the intent of student activities.

"I reassured them that the overall message was one of redemption, or at least it could be, and that he was working intimately with top-flight businesses and law enforcement agencies," said Mark. "I told them I would make sure that he included a cautionary tale against a life of crime."

The administration trusted Mark, and they moved forward with the booking.

"I worked with the best graphic designers on campus and marketed the heck out of the event," said Mark. "When Abagnale showed up for his lecture it was standing room only."

As promised, Abagnale came up with a college-appropriate moral for his story.

"If you are eighteen, be eighteen. If you are twenty, be twenty. Don't try to be someone you are not," was the message that Mark recalled. "Frank went on to say that he could have been any of the people that he pretended to be if he had stayed in school. 'Stay in school and become the person you want to be,' he told them."

The administration loved that.

It was a raucous night, and the students mobbed Abagnale after he put the microphone down. Mark Zinder recalls that it was like a scene from the '70s and '80s when a professional sports team won a championship title and the fans stormed the field. They were clinging on him, asking him to sign autographs on paper and portions of anatomy. The showman sought Mark out afterwards.

"I could get used to this," he said, clearly reveling in the adoration of his new young fans. "I love those posters you made," he added, referring to Mark's marketing materials.

"I told him those posters and other campus-wide marketing

materials were key," Mark recalled. "That's why students filled the seats and stood two-deep along the walls as he spoke."

Although Abagnale had a glossy press booklet, he didn't have support for on-site marketing. He was used to merchant associations, chambers of commerce and banks shepherding groups into confined spaces for dinner or near-mandatory lectures. But colleges were different, Mark told him. Pre-internet, there was literally and figuratively an art to highly competitive campus marketing.

It was something Mark Zinder had a knack for. An announcement for an engaging speaker or performer could easily get lost in a sea of corkboard ads for used roller skates and Atari game cartridges. Mark had seen other promoters try their hand, bringing in well-known talent, but theaters would be near empty if the message didn't get out to the students.

Abagnale seemed impressed.

"I boldly told him that I could replicate this night's success on other college campuses. What he witnessed on this night could be mushroomed all over the land."

"I'll tell you what," Abagnale replied, "if you make any college booking for me, any booking over a thousand dollars, you can keep the rest."

For the rest of the school year, that was exactly what Mark did. Abagnale's speaking schedule filled up. Sometimes Mark was there with him on campus. Sometimes he worked the marketing from a distance. The love for Abagnale was immense. Not just the smitten students. Administrators contacted Mark with letters and calls of appreciation. It had been an enormous success for Mark and helped pave the way for his prestigious post-graduation position with NLP in New York.

\* \* \*

Mark moved to New York in the summer of '79 to start his new life in the metropolis. Every weekday he took the Long Island Railroad to the NLP offices at 575 Eighth Avenue in Manhattan. Suit and tie. Another worker bee trying to make it in the urban honeycomb.

Frank William Abagnale was already one of NLP's clients—largely because Mark had connected Abagnale with NLP while he was still a student.

"In a sense, he was already my client when I started at NLP," said Mark. "It was a great way to start because from my experiences in college, I already knew I could book him solid." And book solid, he did. In the autumn of 1979 through spring 1980, The Great Imposter's calendar was full.

On January 15, 1980, Mark drove down to Auburn University in Alabama to meet up with Abagnale before one of his gigs. A chance to visit home and catch up with friends.

"My good friend from high school, Fran, was a senior at Auburn studying graphic design and exceedingly talented," said Mark. "She had gone above and beyond with the marketing materials to make sure it was a full house. Which it was."

Abagnale told his tales. One student asked him which was his the most enjoyable imposter scam.

"The airline pilot," responded Abagnale without hesitation, "because of the women!"[118]

Abagnale played the Casanova and routinely said he was single. Even local journalists reported on his bachelor lifestyle.

"I don't drink, smoke or gamble. I'm not married, and I just enjoy traveling," said Abagnale in 1980 to a 500-strong packed house, according to the *Albuquerque Journal.*[119]

"He has never been married because he could never find a woman that would trust him," wrote journalist Debi Schmoyer several years later, after taking notes during another of Abagnale's performances to college students, at Northern Arizona University.[57]

Mark was unaware that Frank William Abagnale had been married the whole time. Actually, since late 1976, or that he already had children.

"I had no idea, at least not then. He told me he liked to unwind and connect with students after the talks. Pick their brains. Learn about student life," recalled Mark. "He said he was lonely, and it was difficult to find women to converse with. Especially being out on the road so much. He wondered if I knew any female students that would like to meet him."

But Abagnale had specifications. "They have to be really thin," he told Mark.

"I thought that was weird," said Mark. "Honestly, I just thought it was some kind of joke."

Mark had already introduced Abagnale to his good friend Fran. He wanted to make sure the con man knew that her design skills and marketing efforts were such an important part of the success of the evening.

"I really just wanted Fran to get the credit she deserved," Mark said. "Frank seemed to like her, and I did not think more about it."

Mark recalls he had to get back to work, so he didn't stick around after the show.

"I never knew what his intention was," he added.

But when Mark next spoke to Fran on the phone, she did not seem happy that he had left her with his client. She did not say what had happened after Mark left, but there was no mistaking that she was no fan of the showman. Whatever happened, Mark said Fran avoided talking about that night, even when they later married. Decades later, this took on a new significance for Mark when Abagnale stopped him in the airport and asked about Fran. Then oddly wanted to apologize to Mark without explanation.

\*　　\*　　\*

Abagnale's book release was scheduled for around September 1, 1980. It was originally planned for earlier in the year, but the manuscript needed work. He had big plans for the launch, and so did his publisher, Grosset and Dunlap. They needed a booking agent they could rely on to pack his speaking schedule and ensure book sales. Abagnale knew that Mark Zinder at NLP was largely responsible for his robust college calendar and a growing wallet—but he was looking to cut the large commissions he was paying NLP.

While on a trip to New York in the spring of 1980, Abagnale stopped by the sixteenth-floor offices of NLP and asked to see Mark in private.

"I was wondering if he was hand-delivering me a bonus check for all the extra bookings I had brought him," said Mark.

But Abagnale was empty-handed. Instead, he had a pre-packaged idea.

Once they had settled in a private meeting room, Abagnale started the conversation by noting his displeasure that NLP was taking thirty-five percent of his speaking fee. If a party booked Abagnale through NLP typically for $2,000 per engagement, he would get $1,300. Then he turned the conversation to Mark.

"What's your net?" he asked, wanting to know Mark's cut of NLP's thirty-five percent. It was clear that he was working out some sort of angle.

"I'm not sure I would've answered that question with any other client, but he had a buttery smooth way of extracting what should have been personal information. So I told him—eight percent."

"Come work with me," said the grifter. "I will give you a base salary and twenty percent per booking. Move down to Houston. The rest of 1980 and all of 1981 are going to be huge!" he exclaimed. "The book is close, and I've signed a Hollywood film deal with Bud Yorkin Productions. Think about what we can do over the next five years."

And then he was out the door.

"I really didn't need to think about the offer that hard. I called him within days after the meeting and told him I would accept," recalled Mark. "The New York scene, it's commute, record crime, and the daily grind wasn't for me."

Houston sounded really appealing. So did the excitement of working with an emerging star adored by so many. A man with a redemption story. A man of decency, working for the good guys.

"I've also been a magician since childhood, but the work with New Line and then for Frank Abagnale didn't happen by magic. It was through hard work and determination. Clichéd, I know. But true," said Mark. "And, as I accepted the offer, I really did feel that there was magic in the air. I had no idea I was about to enter fantasyland!"

*    *    *

Mark happily left New York, and briefly went back to stay with his parents for a few weeks in Tennessee as he planned the big move to Houston. Mark had started going out with a young woman when Abagnale made a brief visit there, and he invited Abagnale out with them. Big mistake. His client worked his charms like magic that night, with talk of Hollywood movies and riches beyond imagination. Mark's date was enthralled. They had only dated a few times, and it was not serious, so Mark was not too upset when she left with Abagnale instead.

A few weeks later, when Mark called Abagnale's Houston office about arrangements, he made a passing comment to the "reformed" con man's secretary, Kelly Welbes.

"The girls really like Frank," he observed at some point during their conversation, based on his recent personal experience. He had spoken to Kelly on other occasions to make bookings and arrangements while he was at New Line. It seemed innocuous enough, and he didn't think of it again.

But the next time Mark saw Abagnale, he got a friendly schooling. The conversation started while they were sitting in Abagnale's car. The older man pulled out his wallet to show Mark a picture of a small child. Mark was confused. After an awkward few moments of dead air, he told Mark it was his child, and he was married to the child's mother, Kelly.

"I had no idea that Kelly was his wife!" said Mark. "I was stunned for sure."

Mark had not seen the syndicated articles written by Soll Sussman and Stan Redding over three years earlier. They had featured photographs of Kelly Welbes, back when having a wife was useful for Abagnale's credibility. At that time, she was reported to have completed her master's thesis based on her husband's life story. Abagnale had clearly been downplaying this aspect of his biography since then. Even a decade after Abagnale started his shtick in Houston, members of the media simply referred to Kelly Welbes as Abagnale's secretary, making no marital connection.[62]

Abagnale made it pretty clear that Mark's discretion was expected.

"He always spoke in a soft, mild-mannered fashion, making you feel you had done something really wrong, and feel doubly worse for doing it," said Mark, who knew he was being warned never to do anything like that again. "That was the first time I felt I was put in my place. But it wasn't the last."

In 1980, Houston was at the high point of its opulence, as described in a recent retrospective by the *Houston Chronicle*: "Sleek company cars plied the streets of the city. Membership at tony golf clubs soared. Corporate jets stood at the ready to whisk executives to anywhere in the world."[120] Migration from the northern United States of was immense and housing was in great demand.

By the beginning of June, Mark had secured a two-bedroom apartment in Houston. He really only needed a one-bedroom, but it was all he could find in a pinch. However, the second bedroom soon turned out to be a valuable asset.

"As soon as I got a mattress and a phone, the next order of business was to get over to the offices of Frank Abagnale and Associates," said Mark. "Based on what he had told me, and others, I had high expectations."

Mark had already heard Abagnale publicly announce that he had forty-three employees working in his Houston and Denver offices and that the company was making four million dollars a year from consultancy.[121] He also said he had a fleet of nearly two dozen company vehicles.

The young promoter broke out the Houston street atlas and followed the directions to Frank W. Abagnale and Associates, as relayed by his new boss.

"Based on his descriptions, I guess I was expecting central operations to be within a 25th-floor suite of a glass tower cohousing big oil companies and rocket designers—or at least *something* like that," joked Mark. "But I got a rude surprise."

Instead, Mark pulled up in front of a nice, but not exceptional, suburban Houston residence. Frank W. Abagnale and Associates, it appeared, was little more than a post office box and a home office. It was also the first time he met Frank's wife, Kelly.

"At that stage, they seemed to be working out of their kitchen, since that's where we held our meetings on that day and many others," said Mark, who tried not to show his utterly deflated feelings. Given that there was so much at stake, he needed to confirm the arrangement before making a commitment.

They went straight to talking turkey. And it was quickly apparent that Kelly was the one making financial decisions. She was the one who presented the new offer.

"It seemed he'd shredded the deal we made in New York. Actually, it was more like he had amnesia," Mark recalled about the meeting.

"Didn't we shake on twenty percent?" Mark insisted.

"That's not how I remember it," Abagnale disagreed.

"What about the base salary, then?" Mark asked, presuming Abagnale was cutting the commission back by five percent to accommodate a salary.

"What salary?" Abagnale replied. He wasn't joking.

But Mark was not having it. He had left his job in New York based on what he thought was a good opportunity. What they were offering was not worth pursuing, and Mark made that clear.

"We went back and forth but I held my ground," recalled Mark. "They finally agreed to honor the original agreement— with one carrot on the stick—a $5,000 bonus ($14,000 today) if I could book him fifty times in a twelve-month period," recalled Mark. "I am sure Kelly didn't think I could do it. That many engagements in one year is a *full* calendar for *any* speaker. I was proposing that I would do fifty in *addition* to what he was already doing himself."

All Mark needed was a challenge and some goalposts. Now he had both. And he would deliver. With Abagnale's fees increased from $2,000 to $2,500 per event.

The only sticking point was exclusivity. Mark wanted it. Abagnale, which is to say Kelly, refused. So there was nothing stopping other agents from cold-calling venues and brokering engagements for Abagnale directly. In the end, Mark got all his other conditions, but not that.

Kelly wrote up the contract.

"I remember it looked very professional like an attorney had done it," Mark recalls, "But what I really learned that day was who I was really dealing with. Frank was the smooth-talking salesman, but Kelly ran the business."

That night Mark Zinder looked more closely at the flamboyant signature on Frank W. Abagnale gold-embossed stationary, wondering if it was all show. Looking back, the tip-off should have been that the address of both the Houston and Denver offices on all of the high-grade stationery was the same Houston post office box. Forty-four employees? Four million dollars in corporate income?

"Now it seems so obvious that it was pure fantasy. On one level, I was giving him the benefit of the doubt—after all, he said he was working for the FBI, so I assumed that the subterfuge was some kind of front that I no business asking about. But, at the same time, I have to admit that I was naïve and far too gullible," said Mark.

When Mark signed on, it was agreed that Frank Abagnale and his newest associate needed a proper war room, a place to strategize. That was when they did secure some high-end office space. Spacious and modern.

Mark went to work and quickly filled Abagnale's diary—on a clear trajectory to delivering his promises. The lack of exclusivity remained a source of frustration for Mark. There was nothing stopping other agents muscling in on a sure thing. And they did.

"Although Frank would let other agents book him and liaise

with the venues, I still had to handle all the contracts and travel work," Mark said. "It didn't matter how many times I explained this to Frank—he wouldn't give me an exclusive." It meant more work for Mark but still did not stop him from reaching his targets.

Around the time of his move to Houston, Abagnale had another job for Mark. He presented his agent with a roughly printed first draft of the manuscript of *Catch Me If You Can*.

"This is my life," said the man who told everyone he was "The Great Imposter."

"He told me to study it. Memorize it. And check for grammatical errors," Mark recalled. There was no mention of checking for *factual* errors.

"So, I went through it all for him. I thought he was just shirking the hard work," said Mark, "But as an early school dropout, perhaps grammar was not his strong point."

Mark did wonder about the content, which seemed to focus more on Abagnale's sexual conquests than the entertaining storylines Mark was more familiar with from his talks. He could not help wondering what Kelly thought, but she gave no hint of disapproval. It did showcase his impersonations, and although it left Mark wanting for details, it certainly reinforced his persona as The Great Imposter.

"In the early days he used to tell his college audiences that the movie *The Great Impostor* was based on his life," said Mark. "People believed it and perpetuated the myth for him. Even years later I heard people who had admired Frank repeat this claim to their friends. They didn't know the real story—I certainly didn't."

Indeed, at least one reporter even recorded the absurd claim that the movie *The Great Impostor* actually *was* "based on Abagnale's life on the run."[122]

Nobody seemed to realize how utterly impossible this was.

Not least because the Hollywood blockbuster, starring Tony Curtis, was released in 1961—when Frank Abagnale was only thirteen years old. The movie was based on the actual life of Ferdinand "Fred" Demara—a remarkable *true* story about a man who had been largely forgotten in the decades since. Anyone who did know it would certainly see the similarities with the man who had started his career as The Great Imposter before Abagnale was even born.

*Those who imitate produce imitations, second-rate, often exaggerated versions of the real thing.*
Professor Gerard DeGroot[123]

It was some years before Mark looked more deeply into the story behind *The Great Impostor*—long after he parted ways with Abagnale. He went to his local library to find a copy of the original best-selling book—the true story of Fred W. Demara Jr.—published in 1959. Written by biographer Robert Creighton, it had formed the basis of the Tony Curtis film by the same name.

As soon as he started reading, Mark realized its significance. Demara's incredible story had many strange parallels with Abagnale's unverified tales.

In the years after World War II, Demara had successfully assumed a series of stolen identities—including a Navy surgeon, a schoolmaster at an elite high school, double enlistments in both the Navy and Army, graduate of a law program, assistant warden at a Texas state prison, a Trappist monk, and PhD psychology professor at two colleges, among others.[124] [125] [126] [127] [128] [129] Demara was clearly enormously talented, and his motivations were neither fame nor fortune. In fact, he went on to become a church pastor.[130]

One huge difference from Abagnale's story was that Demara's audacious activities were verified by authorities and captured in real-time, as they unfolded, in the national press.[124-129,131] Abagnale's were not. When Demara's ruse as a professor of psychology at St. Martin's University in Washington was unmasked, the university spokesperson seemed disappointed. "The students were enthralled [by Demara]. The man has a wonderful personality. All the students were going to become psychologists," he said.[132]

Demara always underscored that a good imposter knows the burden of proof belongs to the skeptic. He also shared a few tips on his success posing as a teacher. "I just kept ahead of the class. The best way to learn anything is to teach it," said Demara.

That sounded very familiar to Mark. Abagnale would repeatedly say almost the exact same thing—that when he posed as a professor at Brigham Young University, he "just read a chapter ahead of all the students."

"I immediately recognized that from Abagnale's press kit," said Mark. "By the time I read about Fred Demara in *The Great Impostor*, I already knew that Abagnale had made up most of his story. The similarities, though, were rather striking. Perhaps that was also why he eventually stopped drawing people's attention to that movie. Instead, he started telling his audiences that he had made TV appearances on *Hill Street Blues, M\*A\*S\*H, Hart to Hart,* and *The Rockford Files*."[57]

And then Mark recalled how, when the credibility of Abagnale's claims had been challenged, the con man had said, "Well, if I impersonated The Great Imposter, doesn't that make me the greater imposter?"

Abagnale had certainly known about Demara when he first embarked on his storytelling campaign. He even made the comparisons himself in his early interviews.[23]

Demara's story would have certainly been wonderful inspiration for any imaginative teenager sitting in a New York prison for much of the 1960s.

> *In prison, we used to sit around and say "do you believe how stupid some of these people are?"*
> Frank W. Abagnale[133]

Frank Abagnale (left) with Phyllis Diller and Mark Zinder,
circa 1980. (Photograph courtesy of the Mark Zinder
collection.)

# CHAPTER 12
# Insatiable

*Being an imposter is a tough habit to break.*
Fred W. Demara

Abagnale's campaign as the greatest imposter was about to go into overdrive. With the launch of his book in 1980, one of the main items on Mark Zinder's agenda was a strong marketing plan—and eye-catching promotional materials. For that, he turned to high school friend Fran, the graphic design aficionado. She still had to complete two semesters at Auburn before receiving her degree. But Mark asked her if she would come down to Houston and help him out over the summer.

"To my delight, Fran agreed," Mark shared recently. "She was not wild about Abagnale, but she wanted to help me out. Having that second bedroom for her worked out perfectly."

In June 1980, Fran moved in with a few belongings, intending to stay only for about ten weeks. But that plan soon changed when Cupid struck. Their platonic relationship grew into true love and romance over the summer.

"I distinctly remember how cut up I felt when I saw that Fran was packing her belongings to head back to Alabama. So I asked if she would consider staying in Houston," said Mark with a grin. "I was over the moon when she said yes. One year to the day after she moved in for her temporary stay, we got married—on June 13, 1981."

As the summer of 1980 ended and *Catch Me If You Can* was released by Grosset and Dunlap, Mark and Fran both realized the possibilities that surrounded them. They carved out plans to rent a van and drive all over the eastern half of the United States. But not on a sightseeing tour.

"We hit the autumn regional conferences of the National Entertainment and Campus Activities Association," said Mark. "These were the meetings where university-based leaders in campus activities would sign on speakers. And we promoted the dickens out of Frank W. Abagnale and his new book."

Driving thousands of miles on a shredded-shoestring budget, Fran and Mark lived hand-to-mouth, camping along the way. It paid off in spades. They were barely back in Houston when Abagnale's calendar started filling up with campus bookings.

Life was good. Fran was creating phenomenal promotional material, Mark was booking the Greater-than-Demara Imposter and collecting new clients in Houston and beyond.

"Together, we didn't have a care in the world. Houston was a boomtown, and Fran and I were living the American dream."

Then the con man called Mark back for a meeting.

"In his kitchen, Frank told me he wanted me to travel with him for all the college gigs. "You know," he said, 'to make sure everything was smooth with the on-site affairs,'" recalled Mark. "I was honored. I thought that he really liked me. This great man, about ten years my senior, so worldly, was taking me under his wing.

"Fran was not entirely thrilled," he added, "but she agreed. We both thought it was the best move—so of course I said yes."

\*    \*    \*

Cue the music! A dramatic fanfare announces the star before he bursts into the spotlight!

*"Rich Man . . . poor man . . . beggar man . . . thief . . . Ladies and gentlemen, Frank Abagnale!"* the recorded announcement already has the young starstruck audience spellbound before he even speaks. It is the same routine each time and never gets old.

"He paced the stage with restless animation, the young college students followed his every gesture and anecdote with enraptured attention that approached envy," wrote one reporter who witnessed the pageant in Arizona. "But they turned hushed and pensive when he spoke of the dues he paid for his criminal ways."[134]

Indeed, out on the campus tours, Abagnale followed the advice Mark gave him.

"Make sure that you deliver a clear message that a life of crime isn't a glamorous one, I told him. I was still getting some feedback from university deans that there was too much glamorization and not enough of a cautionary tale," recalled Mark.

Some had complained that about eighty percent of the talk was about braggadocio scams with little concern for the victims. Abagnale had already insisted that he didn't believe that he had really hurt anyone in his years as an imposter.[72] So, believing the gist of his story, and that his scams were youthful indiscretions with neither harm nor malice, Mark recommended that his client make all that much clearer in his marketing materials:

"At 16, I thought I was smarter than the rest of the world—that the rules didn't apply to me. I want young people to know about the mistakes I made, not because I am proud of them, but because that knowledge will help them to make better decisions than I did," Abagnale reassured his audiences in a formal quote added to his promotional brochure.

Many of the speaking gigs were block-booked within geographic regions, so naturally Abagnale was flown first-class from location to location. He told his audiences that his consulting firm, Frank Abagnale and Associates, was now making over $10.5 million a year and listed number thirty in the Fortune 500.[116, 135] He even told them he traveled in his own Lear jet![135] Mark had certainly not seen any evidence of a Lear jet, although they did hire one on occasion.

Although he could see his client was prone to reckless exaggeration, Mark accepted it as part of the flamboyant showmanship. Until recently, Mark had not even heard the claim that there were over a hundred workers with the firm. It made him laugh.

"Well, other than Kelly, I never saw any sign of the other ninety-eight employees in the years I worked there. They sure must have kept a low profile," Mark joked, before adding deeper reflections.

"Looking back, I still find it hard to explain to people," he said on a more serious note. "The whole thing was so surreal, and I have to admit that I was under his spell—even if I didn't realize it at the time. I know that almost everyone else he met was too, but that doesn't make it any easier to justify why I let myself be so willingly pulled into his world."

And what a world. It was also hard not to be carried along the endless wave of action and excitement.

"To be honest, we were so busy I didn't have time to think that deeply about it," Mark added. "Like everyone else, I still believed the core story that formed the basis of his book."

Event after event. Adoring crowds. Limousines. Clubs. Only the best hotels. All the jumbo shrimp you could eat. And his diamonds were usually on show.

"[His] gabardine pants [are] lined with silk, silk shirts painstakingly embroidered with his signature and a stickpin and a ring of white gold and diamonds proudly shaped into his initials," wrote one reporter.[134]

No expense was spared—that was why it was so strange that Abagnale wanted Mark to room with him.

"I know how strange it sounds now, and even I wonder why I went along with everything," Mark admitted recently, still feeling guilty, not only that he had been drawn in by the con man, but that he had actively promoted him.

"He always called me 'Z,'" he added.

Whenever Mark heard that, it was like a bell to Pavlov's dog. He would feel his heart sink.

"I can't remember exactly how many times I heard him call 'Z'—even in the middle of the night—which was his one letter message for me to disappear to the lobby while he entertained women in his room," Mark recalled. "Of course, I never witnessed what went on behind closed doors. He may have just been talking shop—but I doubt it."

One early incident captured how it would go for the rest of the tour. They had just arrived back from the evening speaking gig to find a young co-ed sitting outside the hotel room door. It was around nine p.m.

"Z," was all Abagnale said, nodding his head to the side. Just the one letter.

"I knew that meant I had to disappear," said Mark. "Which I did. About an hour later, he found me in the lobby."

No sooner had they got back to the room when someone else knocked on the door. Another woman. This time someone from the meeting, as Mark recalled. Abagnale had called her and asked her to meet him for a drink.

"Z," he said again.

"Close to midnight, he once again found me in the lobby. Back in the room, I started drifting off. But before I could, Abagnale opened up the bedside table housing the Yellow Pages. I heard the tapping sound of fingers on the pushbutton phone," Mark recalled recently, still with disbelief.

"How much for a date?" inquired the con man. "Okay," he said as he provided the hotel name. "Make sure she's thin," Abagnale added. Evidently, an escort was on her way over to the hotel.

Or maybe she wasn't. Maybe Abagnale was speaking into a dial tone. Perhaps it was all a show. Whatever the case may have been, Mark was told to get dressed and leave the room with that one spoken letter—Z. Abagnale laughed as he closed the door behind his agent. For the third time in four hours, Mark was back in the lobby. Maybe Abagnale just chatted with the women about his escapades, role-playing doctor and attorney general. Mark doesn't know.

"It speaks volumes that he couldn't just get his own room, because he wanted me to witness all this," said Mark. "He needed admiration like a drug. And having it from the girls wasn't enough somehow—he seemed to have such a low opinion of women. Why else do it? But it might also have been some sort of power trip, just so that he could kick me out. Like dunking me in the pool."

At the time, Mark admits he did not appreciate these undercurrents. He was more flattered that the older man had taken him under his wing and into his confidence. Their tour was a raging success, and if his client needed to kick back after a hard day's work, it seemed like a small price to pay at the time.

It was the '80s. An era of not so guilty pleasures. Bawdy talk and raunchy behavior were the norm. From frat houses to Wall Street, it was understood that boys would be boys. Abagnale would also play to these appetites in his audiences, be they boorish bankers, businessmen or college students. Usually, the women in his stories came off second best.

> *I'm not impressed by today's tomes on women's rights in*
> *the bedroom. When Henry Ford invented the Model-T,*
> *women shed their bloomers and put sex on the road.*
> Frank W. Abagnale, 1980[87]

Abagnale's tale about a prostitute with a cashier's check was a fan favorite. It was really a variant of an age-old joke: "Hey, did you hear about the guy who used a bum check to pay for a call girl? They both got screwed!" But he dressed it up. He told crowds it really happened to him in Miami when he was nineteen years old while staying in the penthouse of the famed Fontainebleau Hotel. The mayor of Miami, according to Abagnale's retooled story, had taken a shine to him and invited him to a grand party. That's where he met the twenty-four-year-old top fashion model moonlighting as a call girl and claimed that he deliberately overpaid her with a hot check so she would give him change in cash.[136]

And as he told the story in the 1980s, he looked every bit the believable business executive. Appearances were everything in adding to the convincing façade. The new veneer of sophistication was as important as the stories.

"Frank W. Abagnale can afford $400 [$1,200 today] blue, pinstriped Yves St. Laurent suits and $75 custom shirts . . . on the cuffs of Abagnale's shirt, there embroidered in gold thread for another $60, is his signature," wrote one journalist.[137] "Sporting a gold monogrammed ring, shiny black boots and just the right amount of gray hair to convey that 'man of the world look,'" said another[136]—all adding to his dazzle. The three-piece suit was a new kind of uniform that convinced men and women alike.

He'll tell you himself. "I always like to dress well. That's why I was a success at sixteen. That's why I'm a success today."[138]

Mark would marvel at how, while entertaining small groups of men over lunch or dinner, Abagnale often bragged of being the world's greatest cocksman. The old-boy backslappers from chambers of commerce and financial intuitions loved it. It is not hard to see the echoes of what Evel Knievel's agent, Shelly Saltman, had said about his client.

"Other men live out their fantasies through Evel Knievel," Saltman had written about the biker con man, "Evel is the personification of machismo, and even when his fans doubt, even when it's their wives he talks about [in his sexual conquests], they want to believe."[14]

It made Mark wonder how many of Abagnale's claimed conquests, and the Z-to-the-lobby excursions, were actually the wives and co-ed daughters of those businessmen and chamber officials he so entertained.

More than once, Mark was present when Abagnale heard a good story that would later work itself into his routine if it played well. Like any entertainer, when things no longer played well, he would drop them from his set.

Abagnale certainly had plenty of opportunities for dalliance.

"I tried to keep it all at a cognitive distance, but that was increasingly difficult," Mark said. "He asked me to put his name on my mailbox because he was giving *my* home address to women he met on the nationwide tours. He wanted to make sure he got all his fan letters, and his wife didn't. From college co-eds to older women in high finance and business, his appetite knew no bounds."

Mark didn't open Frank's mail, but he was still privy to the contents—like it or not—because Abagnale delighted in reading many of the letters aloud.

"He wanted me to know, I suppose, what a great manly lover he was, how desirable he was, and that, in his view, almost every woman alive wanted to be in bed with him, whether they would admit it or not," Mark recalled.

"One particular letter is burned into my mind. It was from a woman who initially shunned his advances. Recently divorced, she'd now regretted turning him down, she wrote. Then she went into dramatic detail concerning all the fantasies she would fulfill."

Of course it was possible that the letter was from a jealous husband testing Abagnale!

"Z to the lobby" became standard fare on the road.

"I never asked any questions about what went on behind closed doors. He told me he was the great Lothario. Who was I to doubt it? Whether all of Abagnale's boasts to me about his sexual conquests were real or fabricated, I will never know. That he was propositioning women is not a matter of debate. That much I witnessed. Plus, numerous women told me so, including women I knew quite well," added Mark. "In any case, I told him I wanted my own hotel room, but he still insisted we bunk together. And he made it clear he was the boss."

When the first edition of *Catch Me If You Can* was published, Abagnale was incensed because the publishers had inadvertently added a comment on the back cover that threatened to ruin his bachelor image. Underneath the staged photos of Abagnale in various imposter roles, directly under the photo of him with Johnny Carson, it stated that "Abagnale now lives with his wife and daughter in Houston, Texas."

"It was an error, because he didn't have a daughter—at least that I knew of. He had two boys at that point. But that was not why he was incensed," said Mark. "The real reason he was so upset with the Grosset and Dunlap screw-up was the bit about him being married."

But the grifter had a clever solution. Abagnale had rolls of promo stickers made up. They were oval-shaped and ideally fitted to cover that inconvenient error.

"He kept them in his briefcase, ready to add to his books before signings and events," said Mark. "Frank smiled when he told me he didn't want anyone to think he was married. Those specially treated books might be out there today, floating around used book dealers and eBay."

Somehow, he still cultivated a playful, boyish charm. At the end of one of his speaking events, one Colorado journalist reported seeing Abagnale leaving the seminar with two women. He overheard their conversation.

"Do you ever con anyone anymore?" one of them asked Abagnale.

"No, I'm a good boy," replied the con man, as they walked out together.[139]

\* \* \*

Despite all the time they spent together, Abagnale remained an enigma to Mark.

"I traveled all over North America with him, slept in the same room, flew in the same jets, dined and partied with him, met celebrities with him, sat in on his talks, critiqued them after, and spent countless hours by his side. Yet, I never really knew Frank Abagnale the way that friends know one another," Mark reflected. "He was so evasive about his family, his schooling and his past. On one hand, he seemed to know everybody, and yet, at the same time, nobody really knew him. He seemed to be friendless. Everything was at the veneer level. He loved to have people around him all the time, but everyone was kept at arm's length."

Mark Zinder certainly admired Abagnale's remarkable ability to be high functioning on just a few hours of sleep in a given twenty-four-hour period. No drugs, no booze. He just didn't like being alone—like the rooming together and waking Mark up whenever he nodded off on the plane—there was always that regular elbow in his side accompanied by the familiar and playful "Hey, Z. No sleeping, Z."

Still, he was so charming and funny. And he was indefatigable and kept up with a demanding schedule, being on time and delivering on cue—a dream client in that regard. He was the ultimate road warrior. He never called in sick. Never mailed it in. He always showed up. Well, almost always. But we'll get to that.

\* \* \*

Abagnale had long been talking up big plans for a major motion picture, but this seemed more serious after his book was released. He had already signed a movie concept deal with Bud Yorkin Productions in 1979. To this day, a copy of that original option to the literary work sits in the United States Copyright Office. It was signed, dated and notarized by Abagnale on September 3, 1979. One year *before* his autobiography was formally published. Although Abagnale had already contracted with a publisher, Grosset and Dunlap, the title of the not-yet-written book hadn't been decided upon. So, when Yorkin signed on, the working title was *The Thirty-Foot Con and other Swinging Swindles: The Frank Abagnale Story*.[140]

But Abagnale's grand tales of movies had been invented long before this. Even before his big break on *To Tell the Truth*, he was already telling grand tales about his bio-pic movie. In March 1977, at a local meeting of the American Business Women's

Association in Galveston, he informed the crowd that MGM Studios had just wrapped production on a film about his life—and that the movie, *The Skyway Man*, would be in theaters the summer of '77, starring Dustin Hoffman, Charlton Heston and Cybil Shephard.[141] Shortly after that, in May 1977, Abagnale added that "he feels good about Hoffman playing him because of the actor's intensity."[17] There was no end to the fabrication.

Even after the book *Catch Me If You Can* was released, the word on the street in Los Angeles was that screenwriters and producers really didn't know what to make of the autobiography. Moviegoers would need to see a more sympathetic character. For now, that seemed to be a job too hard. Reading about the escapades in a book or listening to Abagnale on stage recounting his daring tales was one thing, but it would take screenwriting contortions to translate his autobiography into a story of a loveable, relatable character.

Since signing with Yorkin, Abagnale was rebuilding movie hopes and promising his crowds that the film was already in the final stages of production with Dustin Hoffman. But these exaggerations led to some embarrassment when the *Chicago Tribune* and later the *Arizona Daily Star* fact-checkers reported that both Yorkin and Hoffman denied that any film was even being contemplated at that stage.[92, 142]

Abagnale was growing frustrated. And so was his audience. The speaking circuit was an oval track with return visits to various locations, and the movie claims were a liability. Even those who loved the con man would ask about it.

"Hey, you said the film from Columbia pictures was supposed to be released last summer," Mark remembers one young man saying.

"In a moment of brutal honesty, Frank approached me for advice on what to say about the upcoming movie," said Mark. "I was genuinely confused. At first, I was not sure what he was asking. Up to that point I thought that there *was* a movie. I was just his booking agent and assumed that his literary agent was handling everything else."

Presumably, after finding the advice he was looking for, Abagnale did come up with a clever, well-calculated retort—that he was personally putting a hold on the film because the studios were making his life far too glamorous![121]

So, at least at that stage, despite Abagnale's ongoing hints, an actual movie deal was off the table.

*   *   *

Still, 1981 promised to be an even bigger year. As fireworks rang in the New Year, Abagnale and his agent geared up to crisscross all over the United States. In the months that followed, Mark Zinder never once tired of hearing Abagnale's lectures.

"I honestly enjoyed each presentation as much as I did years earlier, in 1978 at the IPA," he said. Although the routine was tightly scripted, a Hollywood-like monologue repeated over and over in each new city and college town, it never got tired. "It was like an amazing Groundhog Day, every day. Never boring."

And Mark really relished the work. "Other than being sleep deprived and sent to the lobby a few too many times and having to listen to his exploits—real or not—it was such an incredible time," he said.

He had never worked so hard. Fran mainly worked behind the scenes on their promotional materials, while Mark was on the road with Abagnale.

To build Abagnale's profile and bookings even further, Mark invested heavily in the National Entertainment and Campus Activities Association (by then renamed the National Association for Campus Activities—NACA) annual convention. This nationwide gathering was being held right in their backyard—just three hours away in San Antonio.

"Fran and I put in the hard work to land Abagnale a speaking gig at the convention. She was an amazing copywriter, and we delivered a really sleek presentation for the application, along with great testimonials. It paid off. He was the chosen one. He was given the center stage Showcase Lecture followed by Ralph Nader!" said Mark. It was huge.

On April 19, 1981, Abagnale walked out onto the NACA stage to a packed audience and entertained the heck out of them. Because of the meeting format, it was abbreviated to thirty minutes, shorter than his normal lectures to commerce and campuses.

"But that was good because it left the audience all wanting more! Abagnale was a hard act to follow—even for Ralph Nader," said Mark. Thanks to Mark's two-page insert in the conference program, anyone interested in booking his client knew exactly how to do so. Everything was in place at the booth to take bookings.

"It was a busy five-day convention, but by the end of it I had already lined up a full schedule!" Mark was jubilant, unaware he was about to learn that his services would no longer be required.

\* \* \*

Unbeknownst to Mark Zinder or Frank Abagnale, a criminal justice professor, William "Bill" Toney, had driven down from Nacogdoches, East Texas, for the event. Some of his students had told him about the growing popularity of Abagnale's work on crime prevention. Indeed, the campus activity committee was planning to book the reformed con man for an event later in the year—at the Stephen F. Austin (SFA) State University in Nacogdoches, Texas. As a widely respected orator and expert in the field of himself, Toney was keen to hear Abagnale's lecture. But after hearing Abagnale speak, the professor had other ideas.

*     *     *

Oblivious to the secret campaign that was about to develop in Nacogdoches, Mark was elated with how things were going. Houston was booming for both Mark and his client. He thought there was no better time to approach Abagnale about the agreed-upon bonus.

Fifty completed gigs had come and gone. Mark waited until the fifty-third booking was done and made his move.

"We were in the office in Houston. Frank was in a particularly good mood that day, so I asked him about the agreed bonus check," Mark recalled.

"What bonus check?" he asked.

"You know, we agreed that once I hit the target of fifty bookings I would get $5,000," Mark said, adding, "A deal is a deal."

"He stared at me like I had just landed from Jupiter."

"Nah," Abagnale said, "many of those bookings weren't at premium rates. They were 750 and 800-dollar jobs. We agreed on fifty 1000-dollar jobs."

Mark insisted there was no stipulation in their agreement about the booking fee. "Each of those fifty-three bookings were cleared by you," he said. "You gave me the go-ahead for each one, regardless of whether it was $750 or more."

"Nope," he replied. "Bring me fifty premium bookings, and then let's discuss your bonus later."

Mark was in shock. This was a guy who would walk into a

boutique men's suit shop and spend money like there was no tomorrow. High-end silk-lined trousers? "Give me six pairs," Mark would hear him say. He was also with Abagnale just weeks earlier when they walked into a Houston hi-fi shop. "What's your most expensive stereo system?" Abagnale had asked and barely waited for the response before saying, "That's the one I want." He walked out with a Bang and Olufsen top of the line stereo.

And now here he was playing cheap on my bonus, thought Mark.

"You can cheat on other people, like your wife, but you can't cheat me!" said Mark, throwing caution to the wind. "You're such a con man," he said in disgust and walked out for some fresh Texan air.

Evidently, Frank William Abagnale, self-proclaimed con man, didn't like being *called* a con man by his agent. Bizarrely though, he later sued a newspaper[143], reportedly for saying he *wasn't* a con man, but just a pretender—he claimed that asserting he *wasn't* a con man was damaging to his reputation!

The next day, Mark walked into the offices of Frank Abagnale and Associates and found an envelope on his desk. Everything on the desk had been pushed to the sides so the envelope would be noticed. It was a letter of termination. Pack up and get out. But it also included a check for the $5,000 bonus. He was glad that he had stood up to the con man.

\*   \*   \*

The termination stung Mark—mostly because his client had broken their deal. Overnight he went from jet-setting to waiting tables while he rebuilt the Mark Zinder Agency in Houston. The rent had to be paid, but they were in good financial shape. The work with Abagnale had been lucrative. Their agency still had other clients, including the Amazing Kreskin, and before long their phone was ringing again with other interested clients. Fran brought her award-winning graphic artistry to the table—it was a great partnership. The big upside of losing Abagnale as a client was spending more time with Fran.

"Life was actually really good," said Mark, "Houston was a boomtown at the time. We had time to travel and hang out at Houston's Comedy Workshop."

By day, they would build the business, and at night Mark would also work his own show as a magician at local clubs.

"That was a form of meditation for me, and I also met a ton of aspiring performers," said Mark. Then he got the call from the Comedy Workshop—the hotspot for comedians and improv actors. Word had traveled, and they wanted the Mark Zinder Agency to represent their comics. They were also looking for a part-time manager, and Mark secured that salaried position. It was the perfect hangout and an ideal platform for promoting many of the emerging stars.

The Comedy Workshop was gaining a national reputation as the only serious comedy club on the Sunbelt, and *the* marquee club between Miami and Los Angeles.[144] Mark Zinder quickly rebuilt his career with Fran's help.

"I later heard through the grapevine that The Great Imposter's bookings had tanked after he canned me," said Mark, "but I really didn't think about him at the time. I was looking forward, not back. Things were going well, and I really didn't think of it that much."

Then there was an unexpected call.

"Out of the blue, he called and asked me if I wanted to buy his office furniture," said Mark, who then wondered if Abagnale had fallen on hard times. "It was a little unexpected, but I told him that I did have budget earmarked for an IBM Selectric typewriter."

Abagnale was keen.

"He told me I could have all the old furniture I had used in his office—a mahogany desk, and matching credenza, leather office chair, art, couch, rug, and an IBM Selectric typewriter—all for $500," recalled Mark.

Mark thought that was even more strange. He wondered if Abagnale remembered that Mark was *with* him when he purchased all the furniture originally and that it cost more than $5,000.

"I said I'd be right over!" laughed Mark, who still uses the beautiful desk and credenza today—a lovely set of classic contemporary furniture. He picked up the load with barely a backwards glance.

Months went by.

In early 1982, Mark was alone when he heard a knock at the door. He ran downstairs, expecting one of his clients from the comedy club had stopped by to visit. When Mark swung open the door, he was completely surprised by who he saw.

"Well, look who it is," were Mark's first words before he even said hello.

There stood the so-called world's greatest con man.

"I was thinking that we might want to work together again," said the perfectly smooth gentleman, affable and sincere as always.

Mark didn't ask why or what for. He was building a successful talent agency, and here was successful talent. One with a proven track record, a guy who shows up. If Abagnale had come back, hat in hand to his old agent, looking for work, Mark did not need to think too deeply about it.

"As far as I was concerned, it was a business deal," he said. "I had not paid much attention to what he had been doing the past year but heard he only had one college gig in my absence. Frank knew he needed me—and it seemed that he realized the value of what I brought to the table."

It was decided.

"But I only agreed to take him back on the condition that I had an exclusive—which he had always refused in the past," said Mark, "He agreed on the spot."

What Mark had been hearing about Abagnale's career was correct. He even conceded that bookings were way down, especially on college campuses.

"He also said he missed me," recalled Mark. "I know it seems ridiculous and naïve, and in hindsight—he was probably just playing to my ego and my emotions. But at that stage his opinion still meant something to me. I still believed in his remarkable story—that he had pulled off those daring ruses, that he never hurt anyone, and had paid everyone back. I also knew he could deliver for audiences—night after night—like no one I had ever seen."

And so, the Mark Zinder Agency was officially representing Frank William Abagnale once more. Fran had her reservations but agreed that it was the best thing for the agency.

\*     \*     \*

All the while, they were oblivious of the storm that was brewing just two hours to their north in Nacogdoches. The professor from SFA State University was engaged in some deep research. And he was about to mount a piercing assault on fantasyland.

Jan Hillman, sportscar enthusiast and proprietor of the car lot in Klippan, Sweden. One of Frank Abagnale's victims in Europe, he says he is still awaiting restitution.

# CHAPTER 13
## Euro Trip

*"That man still owes me money!"*
Jan Hillman, Klippan, Sweden, 2019

Jan Hillman remembers it well. Now eighty-one years old, he still lives not far from the small village in Sweden where Frank Abagnale stole from him, and others in their community. In fact, one of the very first things Mr. Hillman said—when the author contacted him for comment in late 2019—was that Abagnale still owed him money. With fifty years interest! Abagnale had never repaid what he stole, from any of them. He had ignored the restitution ordered by the Swedish court.

After Abagnale fled Baton Rouge, Louisiana, in the summer of 1969, Mr. Hillman was one of his next victims, but he was certainly not the last.

Knowing that Judge Parker would issue a bench warrant for skipping bail in Baton Rouge, leaving the country was a logical move for 21-year-old Abagnale.

It would not have been difficult for Abagnale to reach Europe—especially by dusting off another airline costume. That summer, Pan Am began offering bargain-basement deals to employees of competing airlines like Delta or TWA—seventy-five percent off a seat to Europe. Qualification for the deal was easy. Simply fill out a not-difficult-to-find Interline Request Form and add the signature of a supervisor. It was unlikely that Pan Am would take the time to verify every signature from other airlines. It would have been a simple escape for any convict with a penchant for pilot costumes and forgery.

While nearly half a million of his contemporaries converged on a field in upstate New York, celebrating peace, love and music, Abagnale was on a very different mission—in Europe. By the end of August, Abagnale had already stolen cars and cashed a series of counterfeit checks, mostly in France and Sweden.

He first came to the attention of authorities in Sweden.

The first bad check in Sweden was recorded on August 9 in Norrköping, a modest-sized Swedish city just an hour south of Stockholm. There he stole US$233.60 using a forged check at the Enskilda Bank—some folding money (around $1,500 today) for his summer fun. Five days and five hundred kilometers later, he passed another phony check for US$386.33 (around $2,500 today) at the Skandinaviska Bank in Åstorp, in the south of Sweden not far from the ferry crossing to Denmark.

From there, Abagnale made his way to the nearby small town of Klippan, about fifteen minutes by car from Åstorp. In Klippan, he kicked around the small-town streets applying his charm to impress and befriend locals, just as he had done in Baton Rouge.

He befriended a mechanic there by the name of Arne Hansson. Like Paula's parents, Hansson had welcomed him and let him stay at his home.

Abagnale needed more folding money, so he targeted Hansson's boss, gas station manager Harry Andersson.

Although they knew him only briefly, Andersson and his wife Doris quickly became very fond of the pilot. Doris in particular seemed to like him as a son, as Paula's mother Charlotte had, at least in the beginning. Abagnale was there for a week and many others welcomed him, offering up Swedish hospitality, most with good English.

On August 19, Abagnale wrote a check for $289.38 (around $1,900 today) and convinced Andersson to give him Swedish currency in exchange. The next day Andersson took the check to the Swedish Handelsbanken in Klippan, where he received cash for the check—at this stage, the bank had not yet recognized the fraud by forgery.

When Abagnale eventually arrived on Jan Hillman's small used car and auto repair business on August 22, no one had been alerted to the dirtbag criminal in their midst.

\*   \*   \*

It was a late summer day in Krika, a small village on the outskirts of Klippan. An overcast Friday afternoon. The mid-60s high temperature was starting to recede. Even in August, it can get crisp in Sweden.

Fifty years later, Jan Hillman still recalls the scene with clarity. He was closing up his auto repair shop when the American drove onto the lot in a damaged blue Fiat. The stranger wasn't alone. He was traveling with two young Swedes, a man and a woman. But it was the American that did all the talking.

He said his name was Frank Abagnale. A TWA pilot.

"He was dressed in a beautiful uniform," Hillman said.

The American pilot explained that he needed new wheels. Hillman saw that the blue Fiat was pretty badly damaged in the rear. It had a French license plate on the back. Then the pilot asked Hillman if he could rent a car from him while his vehicle was being repaired.

Hillman had no reason to suspect that the blue Fiat didn't belong to the pilot. That it had been unlawfully taken from a Frenchman. He also had no reason to suspect that he was dealing with a felon who had broken the terms of his probation in faraway Louisiana. Hillman was a kind and trusting man, a gentle Swede who had no reason to question the authenticity of the man or his uniform.

The American surveyed the dozen or so used cars on Hillman's small lot. There wasn't a wide selection, but the sporty Volvo Amazon 122S naturally stood out to Abagnale. It looked like a hybrid of a Rolls Royce and an Aston Martin. Royalty and intrigue. Perfect for a pretender. Low miles, only two years old.

Hillman offered the American to take it for a short test drive.

His customer said he liked the Volvo but needed more time with the car. More time to think about it, he told Hillman. The man stressed that it wasn't about the money—he was a well-compensated pilot and held a steady and prestigious job with a major airline—he just needed to make sure the car was right before he signed up.

It was by now Friday evening. Could he have the car over the weekend, the American asked. Could he finalize the deal first thing Monday morning?

It seemed reasonable, especially as he planned to leave the Fiat in the workshop for needed repairs. The American did look older than his actual age, later discovered to be twenty-one, and Hillman thought he seemed trustworthy. His two Swedish traveling companions added an extra level of reassurance.

And so, Hillman agreed. He even called his own auto insurance company to place an out-of-Sweden driver on the plan. He did not suspect that the car would not be returned, even less that the flashy American customer would appear on a game show called *Truth* just a few years later claiming, "I never actually stole anything."

Neither the pilot nor the car returned to Hillman's lot on Monday.

And on Tuesday, Hillman learned the vehicle was on a ferry to Denmark.

Before Abagnale left Klippan, he had the audacity to return to visit the gas station manager Andersson and his wife, Doris. There, on Tuesday, August 26, he was brazen enough to ask Andersson for more cash. The con man offered a check-like document as collateral—asking Andersson not to cash it straight away. Then he disappeared.

When Andersson attempted to cash the check, he learned it was worthless. Anderson also then discovered he was on the hook for the first bad check and had to repay that amount to the bank—bearing the costs personally. Doris was extremely distressed when she heard that Abagnale had lied to them and stolen from their family. They never forgot it.

By Monday afternoon, Hillman reported the car stolen. He also called his insurance company.

Abagnale crossed into Denmark by ferry—taking Hillman's Amazon 122S with him. It was actually one of his young traveling companions who alerted Hillman. The Swedish lad who was with Abagnale on the car lot had started to suspect something was not right with the American and called Hillman to warn him that the car was being stolen.

The youngster also told Hillman the American wasn't really who he said he was.

"I told him to grab the keys from Abagnale if a moment presented itself," recalled Hillman, "but it was too late."

Hillman called the Danish authorities.

"Yes, they saw the car," he said, "but they told me they couldn't act unless the Swedish police called them first." By the time the Swedish police had sent the alerts, the car and its driver were gone.

And so, Abagnale returned to France with the stolen Volvo Amazon, making his way south to Montpellier. Abagnale had a penchant for college towns, and everyone knew Montpellier was and still is a city of students, an epicenter of American cultural exchange programs. But the Volvo was now a liability—with its Swedish plate L15565, the Volvo stuck out like a sore thumb in the south of France. And so did the American.

It was only a matter of a few weeks before he was arrested in France. Abagnale's future claims that he eluded authorities for months and peppered Europe with millions of dollars in phony checks "like confetti"[145] are pure fantasy. He was apprehended swiftly by the French and also arrested in absence by Swedish authorities in September 1969, only two weeks after Judge Parker issued his bench warrant for the missing convict. The Swedes initiated extradition from France but agreed to wait for Abagnale to first answer his French charges.

For his French crimes, touching on four articles of French law including theft and swindling, Abagnale got off lightly. Records from the French National Archives show clearly that his sentence was only "quatre mois de prison"—just four months.[146]

Abagnale entered the Perpignan prison on October 3, 1969, and his maximum stay, according to the logbooks, would have been until February 3, 1970. However, in contrast to his autobiography, wherein he claimed "horrible treatment in Perpignan prison ... six months in that hellhole,"[87] he left Perpignan on January 9, 1970, after serving only three months.

From Perpignan, the car thief was then transferred to Montpellier city jail, where the Swedish extradition process began.[146] His time in France could not have been more different from how he described it years later. In his fabricated *Catch Me If You Can* accounts, he claimed he was only in France because he had grown weary of his life of crime in America, and retired to a quiet life in the French countryside: "I gave it all up. I moved to a small town in southern France called Montpellier. I bought a small house, nothing extravagant, and a little Volvo."[68]

Looking through the smoke to the tiny embers of truth, it was the "little Volvo" Abagnale had stolen, not bought, from Jan Hillman, that quickly led to his apprehension.

\*    \*    \*

Hillman was one of the first to learn his car was discovered over one thousand miles away, in Montpellier, France. "I got the call only a very short time after I reported the car stolen," he said. It still had the Swedish number plate on it. One of the windows was smashed. But it was drivable.

"This guy clearly had problems driving. Both of the cars he stole, the Frenchman's car, and my car, were damaged," said Jan Hillman, who once raced sports cars as a hobby. But the onus was on the Swedish small business owner to sort out the logistics of its retrieval. Hillman also had to repair the damages to the rear right-side door and replace the window. And he kindly repaired the stolen blue Fiat so that it was drivable for the Frenchman Abagnale had stolen it from. The Frenchman was in the same predicament. Which is to say, he had to take time off and sort out the transportation of his car, thousands of kilometers from Sweden back to France. Time. Cost. Frustration.

Hillman was looking forward to seeing the man again in court. When Abagnale was extradited to Sweden to face charges, he would be there to see it.

None of these people appreciated the later depictions of *Catch Me If You Can* on the silver screen in 2002—all fun and games. No victims. No damaged or discarded property. No small businesses and individuals picking up the pieces. No harm at all—with poor, misunderstood Frank Abagnale as the only victim. Hillman couldn't even bring himself to discuss the farce of a Broadway "musical."

On March 5, 1970, Abagnale was in front of a Swedish judge. He had his day in court. It was only days after the extradition. Hillman was right there to look him in the eye. Swedish authorities had no shortage of evidence: Hillman's car, the bogus checks, and several witnesses. Arne Hansson, the mechanic and metalworker who invited Abagnale into his Klippan home, was a government witness.

Since Abagnale has long claimed that during his "six months" at Perpignan prison he was essentially starved by his French jailors, losing eighty-nine pounds while laying around in pools of his own urine and feces,[45, 147, 148, 149] the author asked Hillman about the grifter's appearance in court. Abagnale has stated publicly, including in his Talks at Google[107] and the PBS WGBH gala lecture,[150] that he had entered Perpignan prison at 198 pounds and left the prison at 109 pounds for immediate extradition to Sweden. He doesn't produce any records to back up the claim. Rather, Abagnale says that "Spielberg told Barbara Walters" he [the filmmaker] went to Perpignan, had a poke around the old prison records, that he had found some logbooks and was able to personally confirm the astonishing weight loss.

The Perpignan (and other penitentiary) records are actually held at the French National Archives, where this author obtained the available documents. As explained by Archives officials, weight is considered health-related information, and under no circumstances would they have divulged prisoner weight, even if they had it. No one could simply have a wee look through old health records. Setting that aside, the claimed weight loss doesn't even pass a rational sniff test. A 6-foot tall man, 109 pounds at discharge? That's only about fourteen pounds more than Irish hunger striker Robert "Bobby" Sands' weight at his death in Belfast in 1981. Sands was on a zero-food hunger strike for approximately ten weeks when he died. Blindness had already set in well before then.

If the bold claim is true, if Abagnale was essentially starved to near-death during his twelve weeks in Perpignan, Hillman would surely have been shocked at the sight of a skeletal Abagnale, forty kilos or so lighter than the uniformed man on his car lot just months earlier.

"He looked exactly the same, just no longer in his beautiful uniform. Certainly, his weight appeared no different," Hillman told the author recently, "The only difference I saw was that he was not as happy and cheerful!"

The Swedes are not punitive. On March 26, Abagnale was found guilty of gross fraud by forgery, and they handed down the sentence—two months in Malmo jail, deportation and an eight-year ban from re-entering Sweden. Two months!

One additional key component of the court order was that, upon release, Abagnale would be required to pay back Andersson and Hillman—with interest to accrue at five percent per year on any outstanding balance after March 1970. Abagnale has never repaid either of the families, they told this author decades later.

"So, he owes us quite a bit now!" said Hillman, wondering what Abagnale would have to say about how five decades of interest have accrued.

Like Jan Hillman, Andersson also still lives in Klippan, and is now ninety-two years of age—Andersson said Doris, who died not long ago, never forgot what Abagnale did. Just like Charlotte

Parks, Paula's mother, Doris Andersson felt the betrayal when Abagnale's actions were later glorified.

Neither Andersson nor Hillman were aware that Abagnale was back in Sweden recently, boasting, which is to say lying, to media that he had paid everyone back[151]. If they knew they would have had something to say about it.

Swedish TV host, Fredrik Skavlan, did ask a question that appeared to make Abagnale flinch.

"How do I know that everything you tell me now is true?" asked Skavlan in 2014. The grifter seemed really taken aback by the question.

"Oh, it's been documented for so many years and written, and, ah, as you know it's been a book, a movie, a Broadway musical and now a very popular television show in America," replied the con man, "Ah, so, it's been researched and documented so many times."[151]

A Broadway musical as proof that the tales are real? Skavlan asked a vital question, and Abagnale called on works of fiction and entertainment as "documentation" of his life—all vastly different from the truth of public records.

\*     \*     \*

On the Swedish taxpayers' krona, Abagnale instructed his court-appointed lawyer Elsa Kristiansson to fight the deportation. Unlike other characters in his autobiography, her identity was not disguised. The records show the appeal wasn't directed at the paltry two-month prison term or the restitution to his victims—which he ignored anyway—but against the deportation order. Abagnale liked Sweden. He wanted to stay. That much about his autobiography appears true.

But from that point on, Abagnale's autobiographical claims depart from all reality. He claimed that a dozen nations wanted to get their hands on him, but a corrupt Swedish judge saw to it that the nations seeking justice would be ignored. Abagnale says he was whisked away from Swedish prison to the fancy home of this local judge. They had tea together, according to his book. The swooning judge hatched a devious plan to thwart extraditions to Italy and elsewhere so that the grifter could avoid brutal prison conditions. The fictitious judge conspired with local contacts in the American embassy to revoke Abagnale's passport and thus, according to the wacky tale, somehow make him immune from the multinational extradition requests. It's a tale that defies all known facts, logic and law. And if, as Abagnale claimed, more than twelve separate nations had filed extradition papers in his name, at least some of those extradition documents would still exist.

*The* [Swedish] *judge liked my talent and intelligence.*
Frank Abagnale, 1981[152]

In reality, both the Swedish lower court (on March 26, 1970) and appeals court (on May 14, 1970) arrived at the same decision: Deportation to the United States. There was no mention of any hungry-to-extradite nations in or around Europe in the complete (unredacted) documents from the Swedish National Archives. But such a tale would be good material if someone, let's say at a kitchen table in Houston, circa 1976, wanted to create an illusion of multinational desperation and large-scale efforts to exact justice on an international fugitive.

Kristiansson's appeal was only delaying the inevitable. The appellate court denied the grifter's wishes. They ruled that since Abagnale had no connections whatsoever to Sweden, and that due to the nature of his crimes, he was highly likely to "continue criminal activities here"—the deportation order was upheld.

Attorney Kristiansson had until June 11 to provide any compelling evidence that could convince the court to overturn their decision and allow Abagnale to become a Swedish resident. Otherwise, Abagnale was to be put on a flight back to his home in New York. And soon enough the liar was on his way back stateside.

> *Escape would have been easy . . .* [but] *never entered my mind. I loved it at Malmo prison. One day, to my astonishment, one of my victims* [bought me] *a basket of fresh fruit and Swedish cheeses. I had really conned that kid. I had made him my friend, in fact, even visiting his home in order to perpetrate my swindle.*
> Frank Abagnale, 1980[87]

It is not clear what grain of truth was buried in these words from the grand hoax of his autobiographical accounts. But none of the locals the author contacted felt any such admiration or sentimentality for the convict. None. On the contrary, they think America is a bizarre place where adults that steal, lie and fabricate grandiose tales become the subject of tap-dance numbers on Broadway.

There was no extradition ordered by the U.S. government, as Abagnale occasionally claimed.[45,72] There was no documentation that American law enforcement had any involvement, or that INTERPOL had placed him on an unsubstantiated "Master Thief" list, as he also claimed.[28, 153] He was simply deported in 1970 and was not welcome to return to Sweden for at least eight years.

*They put me on board a flight to New York. The FBI*
*asked to come* [to Sweden] *but the Swedish government*
*said, "no way." The FBI said, well, he has no violence on*
*his record I'm sure he'll be fine on the plane. Shea was*
*waiting ... and of course, next day* [the] *front page* [of
the] *New York Times,* [was] *Skyway Man Disappears*
*at 30,000 Feet.*
Frank Abagnale, 1982 [68]

There was no reason that Atlanta-based FBI Special Agent
Shea would have even heard of Abagnale at that point—and
certainly no reason he would be waiting for his return to the
United States. It would be several months before Abagnale's
activities would finally come across Shea's desk. And although
Shea was one of the FBI agents involved in Abagnale's
subsequent arrest in Atlanta, the years-long cat-and-mouse FBI
chase depicted in *Catch Me If You Can* was fiction, as we will see.
It never happened.

Still, it is likely that Abagnale thought his deportation might
trigger a warrant check when he arrived at JFK airport customs
and immigration. The terrifying prospect of re-appearing before a
very disappointed Judge Parker—having skipped bail and so
blatantly abused a rare moment of leniency—would have been
daunting for anyone. But in 1970, without a readily accessible
nationally coordinated databank, it was more likely that U.S.
citizens with warrants in local jurisdictions could pass
international borders without detection. Even to this day,
American tourists arrive home with local warrants unflagged at
airports. Abagnale's Louisiana warrants would not have been
discovered without much deeper layers of inquiry.

None of this fits the narrative of a man wanted by
INTERPOL who claimed, "I'm one of only eight men since 1902

given the classification of Master Thief, today I'm only one of two still living."[154] To explain why he had been neither accompanied during his deportation nor immediately apprehended at his JFK destination, Abagnale needed to create a story. He needed a magnificent Houdini-like escape.

The tale he decided upon wasn't a very good one.

In the early versions of this story, he told audiences that "he knew from co-pilot experience that a man could raise the toilet, go through the opening, and leave the plane through the space below. He ran across the runway, climbed a fence and caught a cab," as journalist Will Hundley wrote after sitting in on a lecture in 1978, two years before Abagnale's autobiography.[155] When he first started assembling his grand hoax in Houston circa 1976, it was also a tale he relayed to journalist Soll Sussman, the man who first gave the grifter syndicated coverage.

Abagnale repeated this story for many years until the film was released in 2002, at which point expert aeronautical engineers proved the tale to be impossible.

By the time his autobiography had been published Abagnale upped the ante on the JFK escape caper and was describing dramatic scenes at the arrival gates—flanks of FBI agents and media thronging in anticipation of his arrival—with the sensation captured in the next day's headlines "Skyway Man Disappears at 30,000 Feet," he said[117]

But such headlines were conspicuously absent from all major newspapers—a search of thousands of newspapers across the entire nation found no mention of Abagnale or an escaping Skyway Man at all.

At that point, Abagnale was not of any great interest to the FBI. Stealing cars and forging personal checks were largely in the domain of local authorities. In reality, no one appeared to notice

Frank Abagnale's return to the United States—there were certainly no reports of it at the time.

> *Con artists sell only one thing their entire life and that's themselves. A con artist is a man who believes when you impress people you intimidate them and that when you intimidate people, you have them at their mercy.*
> Frank W. Abagnale, *Kansas City Times.* 1981

> *I was actually just arrested once in my life, when I was 21 years old.*
> Frank W. Abagnale, Talks at Google. 2017

# CHAPTER 14
## American Pie

*Pan Am estimates I flew two million miles for free in two
years, in eighty-six countries around the world.*
Frank Abagnale 1986[154]

Pan Am never estimated anything of the sort. Ira Perry, *The Daily
Oklahoman* journalist, confirmed that.[56] But, when Abagnale
returned to the United States in 1970, after his one-way flight
from Sweden, he did indeed run a very short-lived, small-scale
scam involving Pan Am checks. It lasted only a matter of weeks,
and only earned him a grand total of $1,448 . . . and sixty cents. A
far cry from the millions he claimed to have swindled from Pan
Am. He was apprehended quickly. Back in custody within around
ninety days, there was no time for him to fly two million miles—
the equivalent of circumnavigating the entire globe around eighty
times.

But this small-time scam in the late summer and early autumn
of 1970 formed the basis of the grand hoax that would follow.
These would be the ninety days that ultimately underwent a
metamorphosis into the legend of *Catch Me If You Can*. He finally
stepped on the trip wire that drew the attention of the FBI.

When he returned to the United States from Sweden,
unexpectedly a free man, 22-year-old Abagnale went back to

doing what he knew best—traveling the country and forging checks. With no sign that the officials from Baton Rouge knew his whereabouts, he was careful to avoid Louisiana and Judge Parker all the same.

By late July 1970, Frank was hanging around another college town—this time Durham, North Carolina, home to the University of North Carolina. The university was in summer session when he arrived. He may have missed out on the Woodstock festival the previous summer, but the movie was on the big screen at the Janus Theatre, held over for its fourth month. And, on display at the local planetarium, was a big chunk of moon rock brought back by Neil Armstrong. But Frank Abagnale may have had no time for these distractions. Emboldened by his by previous efforts, he dusted off his airline uniform routine once again and wrote the first of only ten Pan American Airlines checks.

This time, instead of forging a simple personal check, he dressed one up and gave it the appearance of a Pan Am paycheck. Using typewriter print, check #108 was signed by Leo C. Huff and made out in the amount of $108.16 to first officer Frank W. Abagnale. It was cashed in Durham on July 31, 1970, and drawn on Bank of America in New York.

Unlike his previous forgeries, this was a paycheck, so it would inevitably make its way to New York and to the attention of Pan American Airlines. This took a few weeks but eventually triggered the attention of federal authorities. Finally, Frank William Abagnale was noticed by the FBI. But the "master thief" who, for some odd reason, used his real name on the phony paychecks was not at large for long.

Abagnale moved on to Dallas. On August 3, he went back to the well for slightly more—but still a modest amount of only $191.16. Once again, he created a Pan Am check that would also be drawn on a non-existent Pan Am account at the Bank of America in New York, this time signed by fictitious Pan Am executive Lane C. Hail. Abagnale favored the middle initial "C" for the executives who "signed" his checks. Interestingly, all ten of the Pan Am checks were made out with differing dollar amounts, but always with an added sixteen cents.

It was another six weeks before he tried to cash another Pan Am forgery. In the meantime, he was still trying to cash personal checks and getting the neatly pressed Pan Am uniform out of his trunk for other reasons.

Over the summer and fall of 1970, Abagnale was witnessed wearing his airline costume at several college campuses, trying to impress co-eds and anyone else who crossed his path.

\* \* \*

Retired pilot and ex-CIA operative Captain Paul J. Holsen II remembers him very well. He had a front-row seat to Abagnale's campus activities in Arizona, 1970, and has written about it on the University of Arizona website, and in his own published memoirs.

Holsen was a student at the University of Arizona when Abagnale arrived on the campus. Unlike most of his fellow students, Holsen was a little older, already married with children and had been a pilot with Air America before enrolling. Highly personable with marketable credentials, Holsen was interested in securing a good job in commercial aviation after graduation, so it was logical for the university placement officials to alert Holsen that a Pan Am pilot was conducting interviews for flight crew. Even though the Pan Am man had told them he was recruiting for stewardesses, there might be an opportunity to talk with him and learn more about getting a spot with the prestigious carrier. Holsen was definitely interested.[156]

"On the day of the interview I arrived to find a line of beautiful girls. I was the only male," recalled Captain Holsen, who waited as the Pan Am pilot called each candidate individually. When it was Holsen's turn, the Pan Am man seemed confused and explained that he was looking for female stewardesses, not pilots.[157]

"I did not know that pilots did this," said Holsen as he took a seat opposite the man in the Pan Am uniform.

"Not only am I a pilot, but a doctor too," explained Abagnale. "I do everything. Interviews and physicals."

Holsen thought this was all extremely odd. But still took the opportunity to share some of his own flying experience with the man be believed to be a fellow aviator.

"Want to see my pictures taken inside a 707?" asked Abagnale with photographs in hand. Even more strange.

"But he was a good talker," Holsen recalled years later. "He was impressed with my flying background and said I should call Pan Am's headquarters in New York so they could make arrangements to fly me up for training after graduation."

Abagnale gave him a number in New York but said he should wait for three weeks before calling. Holsen waited patiently as requested. But when he finally called Pan Am, they had no knowledge of him or the recruiting pilot. He finally got through to someone who told him to expect a call from the FBI.

"I was surprised to be told that an FBI agent in Tucson would call me," said Holsen. "Agents came the next day and showed me pictures of the pilot who interviewed me and asked if I recognized him."

Holsen confirmed it was Frank Abagnale.

"The agents told me he has stolen the uniforms and credit cards," he said. "Worst yet, he was not even a doctor but did all those physical examinations on the girls."

Paula Parks was shocked to learn this recently.

"I know that I should not be surprised, but the idea of the young students being physically examined by him under false pretenses is just terrible," she said, "it is so disturbing."

\*    \*    \*

The University of Arizona[56] was not the only place Abagnale tried this. He also made an appearance at the Arizona State University in Tempe.[158] University officials confirmed that he approached them to arrange a fake Pan Am recruitment event—promising to invite young women to Los Angeles at some point for further talks. But both the University of Arizona in Tucson[56] and the Arizona State University[158] indicated that Abagnale's "recruitment" efforts that summer failed. None of the women went anywhere, and his depictions[72,87] of them traveling across Europe as stewardesses were wholly untrue.

> *Each one was an outrageous flirt, and I of course, was the*
> *prince of philanderers, and when one of the girls was*
> *inclined to make a sexual advance—and each of them did*
> *on several occasions—I was hardly prone to fend her off.*
> *But I managed.*
>
> Frank W. Abagnale, commenting on the co-eds
> he claimed to have recruited for Pan Am, 1980 [87]

Again, Abagnale did not appear to know that the highly coveted Pan Am Jet Clipper  program,[64] which recruited young women from North American universities for a summer dream job of international travel, had been discontinued the previous year, in 1969.[65]

*   *   *

It was not until September 13 that Abagnale tried to cash his third Pan Am check in Southern California at the San Diego Hilton hotel. This time the check was signed by Tom C. Homing and drawn on Chase Manhattan Bank in New York. It was made out to first officer Frank W. Abagnale in the amount of $128.16.

By then, six weeks after receiving the first two forgeries, Pan Am was fully aware of his paycheck scam. The airline's fraud prevention manager, Maurice J. Fitzgerald, was already on the case. Fitzgerald's impressive resumé included service in both World War II and Korea. He was a retired army colonel and New York City Police sergeant before he secured his position at Pan Am. Fitzgerald immediately determined that Frank W. Abagnale was not a Pan Am employee—and contacted the FBI.

That was when FBI Special Agent Joseph Shea—the partial basis of a fictitious character portrayed by Tom Hanks in the movie *Catch Me If You Can*—most likely first came across Abagnale. Shea was part of the team who began investigating the 22-year-old for check fraud, but he did not chase Abagnale for years, nor for millions of dollars, as the movie suggests. And Shea certainly wasn't chasing him throughout his teenage years, as Abagnale continues to insist.

Emerging reports of a fake Pan Am recruiter on college campuses no doubt helped close the net quickly on the imposter.

*   *   *

On the move to avoid detection, Abagnale left San Diego and went straight back to Texas. This time to Houston, the city he would later adopt as his home. Once there, he cashed two more Pan Am checks, one for $98.16 and the other for $96.16. According to the report later submitted by FBI Special Agent James E. Kiel, Abagnale was in Houston for the week of September 14 to 19.

Contrary to his proclaimed ethical code of only cashing checks with big corporations, he targeted a family-owned laundry and dry cleaning shop. On September 17, one of his unsuspecting victims was forty-seven-year-old Mary C. Wooding at Pilgrim's Laundry, working away in a dry cleaner sweatbox on a ninety-six-degree day in Houston.

Special Agent Kiel also spoke to another witness, Imelda Dykes, who had seen Abagnale in Houston. The FBI agents had easily identified Abagnale because of his stupefying move of making forgeries in his real name. They were chasing a goofball, not a top international master thief. His criminal history and mugshots were secured immediately. Public records confirm that in Houston, Dykes identified Abagnale from a series of photographs.

But Abagnale had already zig-zagged back toward Arizona. In early October, he was again witnessed trying to recruit young women in his pilot's uniform on a college campus.

Once in Tucson, Abagnale stayed at the Executive Inn at 333 West Drachman Street. It was a low-budget hotel that boasted a gift shop, a coffee shop and a direct-dial telephone and radio in each room. There was also a sparkling swimming pool. Abagnale checked into room 238.

The hotel had recently installed waterbeds in select rooms and the Howard Trio was playing an easy rock-jazz medley in the hotel's Fiesta Lounge during the week of Abagnale's stay. The scotch and soda crowd leaned in. All perfect for a bachelor first officer on a layover.

On his way out the door on October 3, Abagnale hit his next mark—sixty-year-old hotel clerk Isabella Metzinger. Checking out, he suggested that his Pan Am check could cover the room. Isabella obliged. This was his largest Pan Am check, for $221.16. Once again signed by Tom C. Homing and drawn on the Chase Manhattan Bank.

This particular check is publicly available—front and back—in the National Archives. Not because it's special, like Armstrong's lunar rock, but simply because that's where federal crime documents eventually end up. What was likely a Pan Am model kit decal has been peeled off. Even to an untrained eye it does not look very sophisticated. In upper-case type the lettering for Chase Manhattan Bank, with its 299 Park Avenue address is crudely lopsided, not running square to the edges of the check. The background embossed lettering for "Pay to the order of" is clearly from a standard-issue check. The typed details of the payee—his rank, his name, and the amount—each appear separately added, and not in line with each other as expected with a typed document. The check numbers on the right are in typical bank MICR font, whereas the routing numbers on the left appear to have been added with a typewriter. But the impressive American eagle and star-spangled banner on the left side provide a likely distraction.

One of the few Pan Am checks cashed by Frank W. Abagnale. This was cashed for $221.16 in Tucson, Arizona—the other nine checks on record were for less than $200. (Courtesy of the National Archives and Records Administration.)

When the FBI interviewed Isabella and her son Michael Metzinger, who was the assistant manager at the Executive Inn, they also showed them a photo of Abagnale. There was no hesitation. They each positively identified the man in the photo as the one who'd ripped off their hotel.

Abagnale had already made his way back to San Diego to the El Cortez Hotel and Convention Center where he passed his next Pan Am check for $162.16 on October 7. The 250-room El Cortez Hotel was bustling with professionals, well-heeled tourists and convention attendees. The Starlight roof restaurant and Skyroom cocktail lounge were still a huge draw, and husband and wife musical act Bobby Sherwood and Phyllis Dorne were featured in the lounge that week. In 1970, when the phony Pan Am pilot graced the premises, the hotel was enjoying the last of its glory days.

Joan Bridges, a young clerk working in the El Cortez office, was his next mark. She cashed the $162.16 Pan Am check signed by Abagnale's "boss," Tom C. Homing. When the FBI interviewed Joan and placed FBI photo 279-205-F among a group of others, she had no difficulty pointing directly to Abagnale. The man in photo 279-205-F was the fake Pan Am employee. But again, Abagnale was in the wind.

> *I'd never been arrested and mugged and printed, so I didn't know if Frank Abagnale was a wanted man or not.*
> Frank W. Abagnale in his 1978 promotional brochure, commenting on being a hunted man as a Pan Am pilot.

For the next two weeks, things were strangely quiet. No Pan Am checks. Then pop, pop, pop. Three in one day in Provo, Utah, on October 24, 1970.

Downtown Provo was busier than usual on that brisk autumn day. Tens of thousands of spectators funneled into town to watch Brigham Young University's competitive homecoming parade before the university's highly anticipated football game against Utah State University. The parade included over a hundred different units, including marching bands, elaborate floats and the like, all vying for prizes. With countless out-of-town visitors, it would have been a good opportunity for someone trying to pass bad checks.

And he did. Abagnale targeted one of Provo's beloved small businesses, Leven's of Provo, a men's clothing store with quality goods at discount prices. When the grifter walked through its doors at 116 W. Center Street, on the busy Saturday, the shop was celebrating fifty-seven years of business. Salesman Carl W. Reed turned Abagnale's bogus $181.16 Pan Am check into cash.

On the same day Abagnale made his way to a Provo camera and optical store owned by 41-year-old Ernest Melvin Hales. Another small family-run business. Inside the small retail shop at 66 North University Avenue, Abagnale handed Hales a phony

Pan Am check in the amount of $97.16. Hales cashed it.

Finally, Abagnale hit up the recently opened Safeway in the Mountain Shadows shopping plaza. The assistant manager Dan Kallas accepted a worthless Pan Am check made out to First Officer Abagnale. The phony pilot walked out the doors at 25 South State Street with another $164.16. Twenty-nine years old, Kallas, a BYU microbiology student who had worked his way up from bagger to assistant manager, was left holding the worthless bag.[159]

Meanwhile, it seems, Abagnale still had time to stop into Ferrel Massey's portrait studio in Provo to pose for some photos in his Pan Am uniform. Chubby, he certainly did not look as though he had emerged emaciated and skeletal from a French hole just months earlier weighing 109 pounds. Indeed, he appeared much heavier than he was in Baton Rouge, a year and a half earlier when photographed by the Parks family posing as a TWA pilot. He was also growing in some sideburns, which he didn't have in 1969.

But Abagnale had already passed his last fake Pan Am check.

There were just ten checks. And the grand tally did not even reach $1,500. There was no years-long cat-and-mouse chase between the FBI and the grifter, as depicted in Spielberg's film. He had a ninety-day run on his Pan Am checks. The unsophisticated game was up almost as quickly as it had started.

Ten years later, Abagnale told crowds of adoring students a very different version of events—that he had fooled the FBI for years and that Special Agent Shea "was going crazy" at his uncanny ability to evade capture. He claimed that Shea specifically requested the courts that he should be housed in the inescapable Atlanta Federal Penitentiary. It was, according to Abagnale, the last straw for Shea when he quickly made a daring escape. Abagnale claimed Shea was so exasperated that he gave up and retired two weeks after the escape.[152] In reality, there was no escape from the Atlanta Federal Penitentiary, and Shea retired almost seven years later, on December 31, 1977.

*　　*　　*

On November 2, 1970, eight days after passing checks in Utah, and only three months after the first Pan Am check was cashed in Durham, Frank Abagnale was apprehended in a low-rent motel situated between Smyrna and Marietta, Georgia.[160] In Cobb County. The very same place where he later proclaimed himself to be chief of pediatric residents!

On that drizzly day in suburban Atlanta, the *Marietta Journal* had an interesting horoscope for Abagnale, the Taurus man. Not only did it appear to portend the imminent events that would unfold that day, but also perhaps the fantastical journey to Hollywood.

"You will be restricted in certain work you do," it predicted, but no matter. "Be patient, your finest efforts will bring like returns," the horoscope advised.[161]

Post-arrest, Abagnale was hauled from Cobb County over to downtown Atlanta where he was arraigned in front of U.S. Commissioner Frank A. Holden. Commissioners like Holden absorbed the workload from overwhelmed federal judges. They were authorized to hold a defendant or set bail. Commissioner Holden initially set Abagnale's bail at just $5,000. The initial charge involved the Pan Am check the grifter had cashed out of state, in Tucson.

Again, this went completely unnoticed by the media. There was no mention of his arrest in the press at all. Recall, he regaled early-1980s crowds about how Walter Cronkite announced the news! If the man, eventually to be celebrated at highbrow galas as a "brilliant young mastermind of international deception and fraud,"[150] had finally been caught, why did no one from the media notice or care?

And, in particular, why was there no news in Cobb County that their former chief of pediatric residents had been taken down by federal authorities in their own backyard? If Abagnale's now celebrated narrative is to be believed, this would have been sensational news—not just locally but far beyond.

It was not until almost three weeks later that the *Arizona Daily Star* made minor mention that the man who had been harassing female students on campuses had been apprehended. This news was buried back in Section D of the paper. Federal authorities in Tucson were drawing up their charges and had informed the *Star*, which reported "Fake Recruiter Charged" with a short arrest notation. That was it.

According to Abagnale's own narrative, he should have had many medical colleagues at Cobb General Hospital ready to post his bail—after all, hadn't he been recently employed there in a leadership role, for nearly a year? On countless occasions Abagnale had described how he had lived in Cobb County for months before he was even hired at the hospital. He said he had become good friends with his neighbor Gordon a distinguished-looking fellow pediatrician.

"He and I became good friends," claimed Abagnale in 1977. "I started eating lunch with him at his hospital and people got to know me as Dr. Williams [and after a year] I became the most highly respected [doctor]."[162]

As Abagnale described the scene to an audience of bankers in 1982, "One afternoon he [Dr. Gordon] came up and he said 'Listen, what are you doing next Friday? I'd like you to come to the opening of Cobb County General Hospital in Marietta. It's opening day and I'd like you to come with me as my guest. It's an all-day affair, eight to four, a doctor's luncheon, I'd like you to see the new facility.' I spent the whole day at the hospital. I met everyone. Orderlies, nurses, department heads, administrators, everybody," he added, going on to describe how this set the stage for his employment as their pediatrician. "I stayed there one year. Twelve months, five nights a week."[68]

He also told the same group of bankers that "a news reporter named Ken Dickinson for *The New York Times* researched the story" and corroborated it. Abagnale loved to name drop America's paper of record. Moreover, Abagnale told them, Dickinson thought the imposter was so clever to have chosen Georgia, where his consultancy role wouldn't be scrutinized due to convoluted medical laws.

However, "Ken Dickinson" of *The New York Times* appeared to be as mythical as Abagnale's tenure as a pediatrician at CGH. Just like his term as a top-flight lawyer in Baton Rouge—where in reality he was picked up for vagrancy.

\*     \*     \*

In the real world, no one was bailing out Frank W. Abagnale from Cobb County jail. He was incarcerated there for three months, awaiting his federal trial in 1971. To be sure, he did escape from a local jailhouse for a couple of days in early February, slipping past the deputies in a booking room while they were processing paperwork. He fled to New York, where he was swiftly apprehended. The New York authorities held him for around six weeks while waiting for his transfer back to Georgia, and it is not clear if either of his parents visited him in the New York jail. On March 30, 1971, he was delivered back to the custody of authorities in Atlanta, Georgia.

J. Owen Forrester was the Assistant United States Attorney

who prosecuted Abagnale's case. There was never any doubt about the outcome. Forrester had the checks and there were plenty of witnesses. In Atlanta, Abagnale pleaded guilty to the charges of the ten Pan Am checks and the additional escape charges.

"I was convicted on $2.5 million dollars' worth of bad checks," he recently told a style writer—invited to his South Carolina mansion to talk up the craftsmanship of his compound for a lifestyles-of-the-rich-and-famous exposé.[163]

But the facts and the court records wildly contradict his storyline today.

On April 29, 1971, Abagnale was sentenced to ten years in federal prison for the forgery cases in Arizona, Texas, California, North Carolina and Utah. He also received a two-year sentence for escaping from Cobb County jail. He was remanded to the federal penitentiary in Petersburg, Virginia. Frank W. Abagnale was back in prison, yet again. But he served little of the sentence behind bars. Sentenced under U.S. code 18:4208(a)(2), he could be paroled at any time without a minimum amount of time served. Abagnale underwent some federal psychiatric "treatment," after which, on March 9, 1973, Louisiana dropped its warrant on Abagnale and agreed that he could be continued on supervised probation.

By early autumn 1973, he was a man about town in Houston—where his pilot uniform made yet another appearance.

\*    \*    \*

On June 20, 1979, less than a decade after his arrest there, Abagnale made a brazen return to Marietta, Georgia. He was invited there by the Cobb County Chamber of Commerce. They were an influential group who had once been engaged in helping

to plan the construction of the Cobb General Hospital—
Abagnale told them all he worked in the community as a
pediatrician. No one questioned it. Tickets to hear his lecture at
the Cobb County Civic Center were just three dollars each and it
was a sell-out.[164]

Not long after the event, he had the audacity to claim that a
few of his old medical colleagues showed up at his talk and that a
good time was had by all.

"Nobody had any hard feelings," Abagnale smiled when
pressed on whether his old medical mates were still carrying
wounds about his year-long ruse. He continued to double down
on the fantasy.[145]

Abagnale later gave crowds mesmerizing alternative facts[68]
with regard to his work at CGH. He said that not long after he
quit the job, the FBI visited CGH to investigate the imposter.
The CGH administrator "almost threw 'em out" because
[Abagnale] couldn't be an imposter, no, he "was one of the finest
residents we've ever had!" Abagnale also told his audience that
after visiting the hospital, the FBI got a tip he was in Baton
Rouge, Louisiana, so they sent his photo down to none other
than AG Gremillion's office. The attorney general's office in
Baton Rouge was shocked, he said. "This picture you sent, Frank
Abagnale, this is Bob Conrad," and they wanted to know why the
FBI was looking for their former colleague and attorney! "He
worked for you?" asked the FBI, according to Abagnale's hoax.
To which the attorney general's office responded, in Abagnale's
words, that not only did he work there, he was "a helluv-an
attorney!"[68]

All fantasy.

By 2002, Abagnale was commanding a lecture fee of
$15,000—on the eve of the release of *Catch Me If You Can*, the
film.[165] A far cry from his meager earnings from the Pan Am

check scam that he used to build his reputation as a con man and master thief. In total, the Skyway Man's official haul from ten Pan Am checks over a twelve-week period was only $1,448.60.

| | | | |
|---|---|---|---|
| Durham, NC | July 31, 1970 | $108.16 | Unknown |
| Dallas, TX | Aug 3, 1970 | $191.16 | Unknown |
| San Diego, CA | Sept 13, 1970 | $128.16 | Hilton Hotel |
| Houston, TX | Sept 17, 1970 | $98.16 | Pilgrim's Dry Cleaning |
| Houston, TX | Sept 17, 1970 | $96.16 | Unknown |
| Tucson, AZ | Oct 3, 1970 | $221.16 | Executive Inn |
| San Diego, CA | Oct 9, 1970 | $162.16 | El Cortez Hotel |
| Provo, UT | Oct 24, 1970 | $182.16 | Leven's Men's Clothing |
| Provo, UT | Oct 24, 1970 | $97.16 | Hales Camera |
| Provo, UT | Oct 24, 1970 | $164.16 | Safeway |

It was all a mirage. When the so-called genius and master thief was sentenced to prison for his crimes against Pan Am, there was *no* mention in *any* newspaper that extensive research could find—and the author searched every major database.

> *The New York Times wrote a syndicated column about*
> *me for over five years* [and] *referred to me as*
> *the Skyway Man.*
> Frank Abagnale, 1984[76]

The *New York Times* never did anything of the sort.

But Frank Abagnale continued to spin his Pan Am story. More than twenty years later, he was still claiming to have cashed millions in checks and traveled millions of miles for free. In 2010, to a large PBS WGBH gala audience, he said, "Pan Am says they estimate, that between the ages of sixteen and eighteen, I flew more than a million miles for free and boarded more than 250 commercial aircraft in more than twenty-six countries."[150] The details may have not-so-subtly changed over the years, but the story is the same. And just as false.

Even today, Abagnale often makes claims indirectly by humbly telling his audiences that "people say" how amazing he is, or, as in this case, "Pan am estimates" how impressive his cons were—like a magician suspending disbelief by creating false sources of validation.

Abagnale even hijacked the term "Skyway Man."

This was a term that was already widely used in 1970 for altogether different reasons—for real plane hijackers. In that era, around the time that Abagnale was deported, there was a spate of hijackings, with literally dozens of Skyway Men reported between 1970 and 1972 in the United States alone. As one major media editorial described such hijackings and airborne extortion at the time, "Foiling the skyway man is a job demanding cooperative action by pilots, airlines and governments . . . this is a jet-age problem that Congress has been pursuing at horse-and-buggy speed."[166]

Over the decade of Abagnale's real but unknown crime spree, he appeared to be collecting ideas and shiny fragments like a magpie. What may have started as a nest to shelter him from reality eventually grew to consume the truth—a bizarre repurposed collection of other people's stories, gargantuan exaggerations and pure fantasy.

Frank Abagnale would soon become famous for what he didn't do. But when he walked out of prison in 1973, he was still a stranger to the world.

Camp Manison, Houston, Summer of 1974—staff and camp counselors. Frank Abagnale appears on the top row (4th row, 2nd from the right). Others who contributed their memories to this story include Morris Fuselier (next to Abagnale, right end of 4th row), Kevin Gallaugher (4th row, 4th from the left), Jan Jackson (3rd row, 2nd from the left), Paul Foreman (3rd row, 3rd from the left), Curtis Clarke (2nd row, 3rd from the left), Katy Thorpe (2nd row, 4th from the left), and Margie Madona (2nd row, 5th from the left). (Camp photograph and list of names provided courtesy of Margie Madona.)

# CHAPTER 15
# "Houston, We Have a Problem"

*Do you hire a car thief to tell you about mechanics?*
*Of course not. It does not make sense, and neither does*
*what this man is doing.*
Former FBI agent Gene Stewart, Assistant Special
Agent in Charge of the Atlanta division,
commenting on Abagnale's claim to expertise,
1978.[56]

In his 1973 memoir, *Return to Earth*,[167] Apollo 11 astronaut Buzz Aldrin described how politicians, the rich and the famous, jostled for one of only 500 VIP invitations to the launch of NASA's moonshot. On July 16, 1969, each of the three moon-bound astronauts were permitted to invite around twenty-five people to the historic event. And on Aldrin's list was a dear personal friend, Tom Manison.

Among the American and international elite gathered at Cape Canaveral, it is likely that no one other than Aldrin knew Tom Manison. But in the Houston suburb of Friendswood, everyone knew the big-hearted man, affectionately known as "Uncle" to the broader community. He was a military veteran, superintendent of schools, a city councilman, and board member of the local soil and water conservation district. But he was best known and loved as the proprietor of Camp Manison.

Camp Manison was the epitome of America's mid-to-late twentieth-century summer camp culture. Situated between Houston and Galveston, and just minutes away from NASA's Mission Control, the lightly wooded green patch was the place to be for awe-filled summers. Swimming, archery ranges, athletic fields and bridle paths, along with rustic cabins, bunkhouses, a western barbeque hut and a dining hall punctuated some 175 acres of wilderness.

Buzz Aldrin had a great sentimental attachment to the camp. His kids enjoyed wonderful summers there, and he later joined the camp's board of trustees. That's how the second man to walk on the moon got to know Tom Manison.

"The summer camp was a source of much pleasure to my family," wrote Aldrin in his memoirs.

Uncle Manison and his wife Marjorie worked tirelessly to maintain the treasure of Friendswood, a summer camp where kids could be kids and thrive in nature. Each summer they would employ dozens of counselors, usually college students, to help with activities and supervise the youngsters. It was a strong community. Many of the counselors had their own fond childhood memories of Camp Manison and returned year after year. And many stayed in contact long after. The camp buzzed with laughter and joy for fifty years until it finally closed in 1997. Today, its treasured lands have been infiltrated by retail. McDonald's, Pizza Hut, Popeye's and a Player 1 video game outlet now sit on the site where the children used to play in nature—in a sadly ironic reflection of what has been lost with modern progress.

Yet the spirit of Camp Manison lives on. Even today, fond memories are still traded by former attendees and camp counselors on websites devoted to the much-loved camp.

However, only a few know what happened there in the summer of 1974—when Frank W. Abagnale Jr. arrived at its gates.

Those events have been carefully omitted from the con man's autobiography and the film. But they are still very much alive in the memories of the team of then college-aged counselors who worked alongside him that summer. Not to mention the public documents which chronicle his exploits while there, and in the period just after. Many of those former counselors were pleased to add their memories to this book. It was the author's privilege and pleasure to meet with them in his travels across Texas and Louisiana. This was a conversation that brought some of them back together for the first time in many years.

*   *   *

In the mid-summer of 1974, Camp Manison was at its zenith. And that is when a pilot turned up offering to work with the kids. Curtis Clarke and Kevin Gallaugher were there when Abagnale arrived at Tom Manison's office. The boys from Louisiana were just eighteen years old at the time, working the camp counselor gig before heading to college. They are still friends today, and there was plenty of side-splitting laughter and knee-slapping when we all caught up at Curtis's Cajun restaurant in Austin to reminisce recently. Almost fifty years later, they remember it like it was yesterday.

It was late in the evening and the two friends were just arriving back at the camp after a few hours off duty. Manison was in the main office when the pair checked in to register their return. He had company. A man dressed in a pilot's uniform—white shirt with epaulets, standard-issue slacks, black shoes and a blazer with ringed sleeves slung over one arm.

Their boss was extremely excited to tell them about the new

recruit. He didn't know that wickedness had just slithered into Camp Manison, as it had to the loving home on Woodhaven Drive in Baton Rouge, and the string of places in between.

"Manison was all aflutter and clearly smitten with the new guy," said Curtis, a warm and colorful character whose French heritage is now echoed in his musketeer-like appearance. He described how Manison could barely contain his enthusiasm as he introduced the new addition—a furloughed Delta Airlines pilot looking to help a good cause during his forced break.

"Yeh, he was totally intoxicated," agreed Kevin, a still handsome architect in Austin. "The pilot told us he was on sabbatical and wanted to give back to the community. Manison just loved that. He was raving at what a good role model it would be for the kids at camp."

Strangely, the pilot had decided to wear his uniform. Even though he was on sabbatical. The surprised Louisiana boys looked on as Abagnale did the talking.

"And he wasn't just any pilot! He told us that he was president of the pilot's fraternity," said Curtis with a smile, and his distinct Cajun accent. "We were definitely impressed—at least to begin with."

Of course, Abagnale did not mention that he was still on parole, just released from federal prison in Virginia several months earlier. It is not clear what brought him to the tranquil forest camp in the shadow of NASA's Mission Control, using essentially the same old ruse he had tried in Baton Rouge—just a different airline this time. He was clearly still looking to fulfill his mission to work with kids—just as he had told Reverend Underwood and the Parks family in Baton Rouge five years earlier.

By the time Kevin and Curtis arrived at the office, Abagnale had already convinced Tom Manison to take him on at the camp for the summer. There was a lingering gasoline crisis in early '74 and many airline pilots had been furloughed or redeployed, so this may have seemed plausible to Manison. All the same, it certainly was odd work for a Delta Airlines pilot, furlough or not.

The camp had an impeccable reputation; so did Tom Manison. As part of a Texas government panel that shaped tighter regulations of summer camps, he advocated for higher levels of supervision and numbers of camp counselors per child. He was a stickler for the health and safety of camp guests.[168,169] Like so many others, Manison was initially unsuspecting of the personable pilot. This was before the days of mandatory checks on anyone working with children, and Abagnale appeared to have excellent credentials and references. His resumé, of course, carefully concealed the true facts.

Manison was almost apologetic when he offered the pilot a position, because his duties as a general gofer and errand man would be pretty menial. But Frank Abagnale accepted without hesitation and was also given a place to stay and three meals a day as part of the deal.

Years later Abagnale would tell packed audiences that his road to redemption had begun immediately after his release from federal prison "in 1974" (although already known to be living in Houston in 1973)—working in fast-food restaurants and supermarkets to get a fresh start.[148,170] At least in the early versions of his story, he said he worked for the Texas-based Pizza Inn franchise followed by an entry-level job at one of Weingarten's Houston-based supermarkets.[171] He lamented that on each occasion he was fired when they "discovered his past" despite being a model employee.[171]

In more recent versions of his life story, he claimed that he was directly paroled from Virginia—plucked out, like a prized cockerel—on condition that he conduct free anti-fraud seminars and workshops for bank tellers.[172]

"The government decided to parole me on two conditions," Abagnale announced when *Catch Me If You Can* was released. "One, that I go to Houston—where I had never been before—and two, that I go to work helping the government deal with these crimes, by educating law enforcement agencies about how to deal [with] forgery and counterfeiting."[173]

But obviously, Abagnale *had* been to Houston before. It's where he ripped off Mary C. Wooding in the sweaty heat of Pilgrim Laundry in 1970. Moreover, nobody at Camp Manison saw any evidence that Abagnale was a "crime fighter", cleaning up Houston in collaboration with law enforcement agencies. Quite the opposite. In fact, his next actions demonstrated he was still operating on the *wrong* side of the law.

Abagnale's parole officer was surely unaware that his charge had secured himself a full-time gig at a children's camp and was already falsifying his identity by impersonating a pilot—or presumably he would have acted. In the epilogue of his autobiography, Abagnale makes brief mention of two parole officers without mentioning either by name. When he was first paroled to Houston, he said he was met by a "hostile, antagonistic, antipathetic and hard-nosed" parole officer who held a particular disdain for con men and believed Abagnale would soon reoffend.[87]

That first parole officer appears to have been either clairvoyant, or more likely, a good judge of character with an understanding of the true meaning of a "low criminal threshold."

\* \* \*

Abagnale went straight back to his usual routine. He started by befriending a young man who would unwittingly facilitate a plan to refine his airline masquerade. This time his mark was camp counselor Morris Fuselier III. Morris was a twenty-two-year-old teacher and artist, and like Curtis and Kevin was also from southern Louisiana. Morris led the arts and crafts activities that summer, and had even painted and decorated the new designs on the Camp Manison buses and vans.

Indeed, one of Abagnale's main duties was as the primary driver of Manison's fleet of old vehicles—including the Manison Day Camper bus. Manison may have assumed that the pilot would naturally be good at driving buses as well—but that did not prove to be the case. Swedish car enthusiast Jan Hillman could have told him that.

There were more than one hundred children, aged between six and sixteen, staying on-site at the camp for the summer. But there were also around two dozen kids from the surrounding area who traveled in and out each day. It was Abagnale's job to shuttle those children back and forth around Houston—no doubt providing an opportunity to impress them with his stories as a pilot along the way.

The Louisiana boys explained that Tom Manison used to source old buses at auction from Texas Corrections—so just months out of the federal pen himself, Abagnale was driving retooled prison buses. They enjoyed the irony.

"The old prison vehicles were painted camp green, but some still had the old bars and mesh screens," said Curtis. "We had no idea at the time, but I guess it was thrilling for Frank to be on the other side of the barrier for a change!"

From pilot to kid's bus driver. If Manison and his team of counselors thought that was odd, most agreed they would have been even more surprised to discover that their new bus driver was a convicted felon—a man who had spent most of the previous decade in prison, with some half-dozen separate jailhouse experiences over a ten-year period. Not a lot of opportunity to polish his bus driving skills!

There were around forty summer camp staff including counselors who supervised the children and ran a wide range of camp activities each day. Most were only in their late teens and early twenties, and about half were young women. They all wore matching green and white uniforms. The men had white T-shirts with forest-green trim, emblazoned with the Camp Manison logo, and matching green shorts. The women wore sleeveless V-necked shirts, but their green shorts were much shorter.

Frank Abagnale can be seen smiling in the back row of the official Camp Manison staff photo taken in 1974—standing next to his new friend, Morris "Moe" Fuselier III. By then, at the age of twenty-six, Abagnale was already looking husky and sporting a combover.

One of the camp counselors, Margie Madona, kept the photo and shared it with the author. She also shared her first impressions of the new recruit.

"I had an uneasy feeling about him from the beginning," admitted Margie, who was also thrilled to reconnect with the group after so many years. "My spidey-senses told me to give him a wide berth—and I am glad I did."

The staff quickly got to know each other. The camp was enormously popular. A fun summer working environment. Everything revolved around outdoor activities, group games, shared meals and social activities for the children. It was an equally social environment for the staff, and many developed lasting bonds. Even after forty-five years, it is clear that many of the friendships and memories still thrive with great fondness among all those contacted for this book.

Abagnale was quick to join in on camp activities, and most of the staff counselors were naturally curious about the older pilot.

"We were all fascinated by him at first because it was strange to have someone with his credentials working with us," said Paul Foreman, now a seasoned insurance defense attorney in Lake Charles, Louisiana. "Of course, we now know it was all a scam—it is amazing how the story he tells now completely bypasses the events of 1974."

The Delta pilot continued to regale them all with his stories. He explained that he was really at the camp as a special consultant to Tom Manison because of his extensive industry leadership experience.

Although Abagnale spent more time with the slightly older counselors, including Morris Fuselier and his high school and college classmate Paul Foreman, he seemed far more intent on impressing the much younger teenage counselors—and showing off to the women.

"Many of us were in our late teens, and he was almost ten years our elder, so we definitely saw him as a bit of an outsider because of that," said Kevin Gallaugher. "But he seemed so desperate to belong, and he was trying *way* too hard to impress us all. It started to get weird after a while."

Abagnale made it clear to all the Louisiana boys how popular he was with the ladies. They all recalled how Abagnale flirted with the young female counselors. Sometimes excessively. But it seemed that the women were less easily impressed than the men. They tolerated him at first, but their patience began to wear thin before long.

One way that Abagnale tried to ingratiate himself with the young women was to chauffeur them in the evenings to enjoy Houston's hottest nightclub scene. Among its small fleet, the camp also had an old eight-door Checker Aerobus airporter stretch limousine—an elongated version of the classic New York yellow cab. Another of Manison's auction purchases. The faded classic had once epitomized the heyday of 1960s airline travel but was badly in need of new paintwork. It also featured the kids' camp logo on its fading patina. By day, the enormous limousine was sometimes used to transport camp kids. But by night, Frank Abagnale had other plans for it.

"The limo was so massive that Frank could take most of the girls to the Houston strip in the evenings for a good time," recalled Curtis Clarke. "That certainly increased his stock for a while."

Even now, he and the others still find it amusing that the guy pretending to be the pilot was chauffeuring an airporter limo filled with women at night. He wasn't even a good driver. The boys heard Abagnale smashed the gearbox on at least one of the camp vehicles that summer. There is no indication that Abagnale ever wore his uniform when he was driving. But it was still quite a scene when nearly a dozen beautiful young women emerged from the converted airport limo—with the trying-hard-to-be-hip ex-con driver in front, on the other side of the mesh grill separating the driver from his passengers.

Actually, it was exactly the same kind of Checker airporter stretch limousine that appears in a fictitious airport scene in the movie *Catch Me If You Can*—in the film a teenaged Abagnale arrives in an eight-door Checker limo with eight recruited women posing as Pan Am stewardesses to help him evade the FBI. That never happened, but like so many of his fabrications, his illusions were often built on other memories. The grain of truth was vastly different from what grew from it.

To impress the Camp Manison counselors that he was "the man," Abagnale would take them from one Houston club to the next—always picking up the tab. The legal drinking age was eighteen at that time, and the group could run up sizable tabs. But Frank would take care of it.

Kevin Gallaugher went along for the ride one night.

"Frank told us not to worry about money, everything was on him," said Kevin. "Our first stop was a Middle Eastern restaurant with a mesmerizing performance by a traditional musician and a belly dancer," he added, recalling his amazement. "I was barely out of school, and it was one of the first times I had been out drinking. I had never seen anything like it. The exotic dancer was definitely erotic in my youthful, inexperienced eyes."

After dinner, Frank gathered up his contingent of happy campers to continue their itinerary of Houston nightlife, stopping at a series of bars and popular nightspots.

"We'd all drink one beer, and then Frank would shepherd us off to the next venue," said Kevin. He recalls that Abagnale pulled out a credit card each time he picked up the tab.

"He must have spent hundreds of dollars," said Kevin. "It was a lot of money back then, especially to us at that age. But we figured he was a pilot and could afford it. We certainly thought he was generous but still strange that he was spending so much when we didn't really even know him."

On the way home, Kevin decided to sit up close to the pilot. To be friendly and find out more about him. But, despite all his bragging back at camp, Abagnale didn't have that much to say. Nothing of any depth. Especially when Kevin tried to learn more about his work with Delta Airlines, the pilot's answers seemed strangely vague.

"I remember wondering why he seemed to avoid wanting to talk about the life of a pilot," Kevin added. "To be honest, for all his efforts, he just wasn't that interesting."

The women had humored the charming pilot at first, but it was not long before they started complaining about him. Some said he was pushy. By the end of the summer, one young woman in particular had developed a very strong dislike and distrust for

Abagnale. It ended in an altercation. And threats.

That woman was Jan Jackson, from Texas. She was a skilled horse handler who was overseeing the trail riding at the camp. At the beginning of summer, she had rolled into the camp driving a marine-blue 1967 Corvette. Her father, Bill Jackson, was not far behind—with her horse and trailer in tow.

"It was a sight to behold," said Paul Foreman, who described how everyone had stopped in their tracks to stare at the woman in the coveted '67 Vette. Paul had quickly become friends with Jan. She had a warm but strong personality and did not suffer fools gladly.

"I vividly remember borrowing Jan's Corvette for jaunts into Houston to see my fiancé and hugging the I-10 curves near downtown," Paul said. Jan, who he had just met, was a good sport about letting him drive her Vette, he added, laughing that Morris, a childhood friend would not let him drive his "Z-car"— a Datsun 260Z.

Jan Jackson was not at all impressed with Abagnale's stories.

"We thought he was totally creepy," Jan recalled, with much the same impression of the pilot as Paula Parks had several years before. "He was so arrogant. He acted as though he was the hottest thing, a gift to all women."

In a stranger-than-fiction coincidence, Jan's father was in the airline fraternity. He was a pilot, a captain for none other than Delta Airlines! William Franklin "Bill" Jackson was a veteran who had served in the Army Air Corps during WWII. He worked with Delta until he retired in 1982, after thirty years of service. It's very likely that Bill Jackson and Paula Parks—both working for the same airline in the southern United States during the same time span—crossed paths unawares.

Jan Jackson, camp counselor at Camp Manison, daughter of real Delta pilot who challenged Frank Abagnale's story in 1974. Pictured with her 1967 Corvette (top) and her horse (bottom).

The odds that Frank Abagnale, pretending to be a Delta Airlines pilot at a Houston-area kids camp, would have a co-worker there whose father was a real Delta Airlines pilot seem infinitesimally small. Indeed, among seventy million adult males in the United States in 1974, there were only three thousand pilots and co-pilots working for Delta Airlines nationally. Many worked out of Miami, Atlanta and New Orleans. It would have hardly seemed credible in a Hollywood script!

"Right from the start Abagnale wanted all the women to know he was special and that he was recruited as a high-level consultant for camp operations because of his experience with Delta," said Jan. Yet, in the day-to-day camp life, the Delta man's "consultancy" seemed to only consist of running mundane errands and acting as a chauffeur. A water boy of sorts.

Jan was dubious and wrote to tell her father about the furloughed pilot working with them. Frank's arrogance was one thing, but there was something sketchy about him as well.

She wondered if her father knew him.

*   *   *

It was not long before Abagnale asked his new friend Morris Fuselier for a special favor. Morris was a skilled graphic artist, and Abagnale wanted to take advantage of Morris's fine-grained skills. He explained to Morris that, as president of the Delta pilots club, he had some ideas for improvements to the employee identification cards. Abagnale said he had some concepts running through his mind, including several innovative changes that might make the ID cards more secure. It would be great, he told Morris, if he could mock up some ideas for Abagnale to pitch when he returned to full-time work at Delta. Paul Foreman also confirmed hearing this conversation.

Given that it was just for a mock-up design, Morris didn't see the harm and said he was happy to help his new friend. Then

Abagnale suggested that they drive to a hobby shop in nearby League City. Paul came too.

Morris was not really sure why, but Abagnale picked up a medium-sized model of a Delta Airlines aircraft he said might be useful for getting the logo right. They also went to a print shop in the industrial area of East Houston for additional materials.

Next, Abagnale arranged for a new ID photograph to be taken. Curtis was along for the ride that day, and recalls thinking it was more than strange that they did not go to a local portrait studio for the headshot—they assumed that he was trying to avoid paying studio prices. Instead, Abagnale insisted that they go to local county administrative offices. When they got there, Abagnale brazenly mooched a free photo on a background normally used for employee identification cards—all to make it look as authentic as possible for his presentation, he told Morris.

Then it was time for Morris to apply his skills to generate a newly styled identification card. It looked good. He added Abagnale's photo. To complete the picture, Abagnale suggested that they carefully remove the small-scale decal from the model plane and affix it to the mock identification card.

Morris was pretty happy with his handiwork and hoped it would do the trick for what Abagnale needed to show his colleagues at Delta.

"Abagnale had several prototypes in mind," said Paul, "but Morris used his own creativity." Hindsight provides focus. It wasn't really about creating a newfangled card at all. "We now know as Moe presented his original ideas, all of the changes Frank suggested were actually to steer Moe to replicate an actual Delta ID. Frank didn't need Moe's creativity—he needed Moe's artistic hands-on production of the 'prototype,'" remarked Paul.

"Of course, I had no idea what he *really* wanted it for," said Morris recently, when he was contacted by the author. He also had no idea who Abagnale really was. Nor did Morris suspect he was working at the behest of a known felon.

Morris recalls that he then went with Frank to the County offices with the final artwork. Once there, Abagnale convinced them to use their machine to refine the artwork, eliminating all the cut-and-paste edges. Serious gall to have the County do his bidding. From there, they made one final stop at a print shop and ran it through a basic laminating machine. That's how he got the final ID card.

"That ID card was likely much better than any employee ID card at the time," he added, recalling his work with pride and affection. It looked very official.

Abagnale was very pleased too. It looked real. Likely far better than anything Abagnale—who later described himself as a "master forger"—had ever created himself. And it would come in very handy. Certainly not model behavior for someone later claiming to be paroled to work for the FBI or any agency promoting crime prevention.

"He was actively running a scam in the summer of '74, and using young naïve Louisiana boys to help him," said Paul with wry humor. "Over the years, I have thought about Frank and his sanitized movie story, especially after seeing him pontificating on national news outlets and writing in AARP [American Association of Retired Persons] publications about how to avoid being scammed. The story the world hears takes a wide detour around the truth—we know different."

Paul is referring to his one-time campmate's recent appointment as an AARP "ambassador" advocating for the elderly and the retired and protecting them from fraudsters.

\* \* \*

Captain Bill Jackson of Delta Airlines was immediately suspicious. The letter he had received from his daughter Jan did not add up. Delta was the only major carrier *not* to furlough pilots during the fuel-crunch of 1974. An odd claim, then, for a man to say he was a furloughed Delta pilot. Odd like everything else about the story.

It was almost five years since Abagnale had been placed on TWA's list of undesirables for loitering in airports and cashing bad personal checks. Paula Parks, who was still working as a Delta flight attendant, was unaware that the man who had stalked her was up to his old tricks again.

Bill Jackson started asking around at Delta Airlines. And the answer was clear. His suspicions were correct. Delta Airlines quickly confirmed that Abagnale was neither a current nor a past employee. He was a phony.

\*     \*     \*

Meanwhile, Captain Jackson's daughter Jan was taking things into her own hands. She and the other young women didn't trust Abagnale. They had just about had enough of the pilot's constant bragging and over-the-top flirting.

"He was so arrogant and so conceited, we decided to teach him a lesson," said Jan. "So, seeing he thought he was so hot, we decided to cool him off—literally!"

A large bucket of cold water seemed to be the ideal remedy.

They decided to play a harmless prank on Abagnale, to send a clear and symbolic message. "Most of the girls were in on it," camp counselor Katy Thorpe recalled recently.

"It was around six in the evening by the pool," recalled Curtis Clarke, who was watching on with the others as the women executed their plan. "The young women kept Frank engaged in conversation, distracting him while Jan snuck up from behind."

Jan made her move and had the great satisfaction of dumping the better part of a five-gallon plastic bucket of cold water over the crown of the "special consultant."

The girls burst out laughing, but Frank did not. Although it was harmless poolside horseplay, something was seething beneath his surface.

"He was so angry. Furious. It turned dark quickly," Jan recalled. "He physically threatened us. He had something in his hand and I thought he was going to lash out with it," she added.

"You don't know who you are messing with," Abagnale growled at them. He was soaking wet. And a large flap of hair was dangling down on one side of his head. In the shadow of NASA's Space Center, the pilot on "sabbatical" had landed hard.

"Actually, we *didn't* know who we were messing with," said Jan, still amused at how they had ruffled his combover. "We had no idea at the time that he had been in the federal penitentiary only months before. We were young and didn't think too much about his physical threats. But the mask was off. He showed what was beneath his smooth exterior."

"I was also surprised by his reaction," agreed Katy Thorpe. "Sure, not everybody would laugh it off, but his reaction was well outside normal. He was enraged."

They all watched as the grifter stomped off in a dark rage—perhaps a rare moment of comeuppance for the man who loved to connive, trick and play others for fools.

"He was clearly incensed," agreed Curtis. "It must have really got under his skin because he packed up and left the camp. We never saw him again after that."

When Mark Zinder heard about the incident recently, he was immediately reminded of Frank's reaction in another Houston pool only a few years later. Did the memory of poolside humiliation at Camp Manison trigger the same silent rage that Mark had been so surprised to see the day he had dunked Frank?

Abagnale appeared to sense that the game was up. None of the counselors knew what he was *really* up to at that point. But he always seemed to know just when to leave.

\*   \*   \*

Tom Manison had other more serious concerns of his own. As part of Abagnale's duties at Camp Manison, he had been entrusted with camp valuables and equipment. He also had access to money, cameras and art supplies. Manison had frequently asked Abagnale to use the camp van to run errands for him. He also entrusted him with cash and even asked the helpful pilot to take valuables to Houston and sell them on at least one occasion.

Valuables began to disappear. Supplies were missing. Cameras gone. There had also been a series of car break-ins. Was the temptation too great? Manison finally suspected there was something off about the pilot and approached Morris, who appeared to be Abagnale's closest friend.

Manison told Morris that the grifter had sold camp cameras and pocketed the money. That's not all. According to the camp owner, their furloughed pilot was fueling up the camp vehicles with what Abagnale claimed to be his own credit card. Tom was reimbursing him in cash. But Manison had just discovered that the credit card numbers actually belonged to the camp, so he ended up paying for the gas twice!

Morris was also starting to wonder too. He had just discovered that some of his own valuables and property had also been stolen. Manison had already confronted Abagnale, but he had denied it and insisted that someone else had stolen the items. But Tom Manison wasn't buying it.

Around the same time, they got word from Jan's father, Captain Bill Jackson—the *real* Delta pilot. It was official. Abagnale, the man who once had a penchant for giving out fake flowers, was a fraud.

This additional incriminating information made the camp thefts feel even more disturbing and sinister. More than just insult to injury. What else had Abagnale been up to while he had been driving their vehicles around that summer, they wondered? But the grifter was already in the wind.

They called the police immediately.

*    *    *

Tom Manison first reached out to an old friend, Constable R.L. "Robbie" Weyer. The wily cattleman with the ten-gallon hat was the constable of Precinct 6 covering Friendswood, League City and Dickinson. Weyer was an elected law enforcement official—and soon to be a man with a mission. Manison explained his suspicions about Abagnale. As Weyer began to investigate the thefts and the series of recent car break-ins, the likely culprit was immediately obvious. He alerted the Friendswood Police Department, where detective Jimmy Sprague and Sgt. Keith Still took over.

Abagnale was tracked down and arrested on August 29, 1974. This time his arrest did make the local papers, but only as a common thief alleged to have stolen art supplies and cameras from Camp Manison.[174] There was no mention of any master thief or master forger by the *Friendswood News*. Stealing from a much-loved kids camp run by one of the community's greatly admired figures was not a good look.

Both Morris Fuselier and Tom Manison filed charges against Abagnale. Morris was shocked and disappointed after helping

Abagnale and being a friend to him over the summer. But loyalty to Tom Manison was foremost. Nobody wanted to bring embarrassment to the camp or its proprietors. And so, the events of 1974 were largely not openly discussed again—until people were contacted for this story. Indeed, many of the other counselors were not even aware of Abagnale's arrest or the charges. Even now, it is clear how much everybody wants to honor the memory of Camp Manison.

If Abagnale's account of his "hostile" parole officer's predictions is true[87]—that he had a low threshold to reoffend and would be unable to stay straight—this also proved accurate. He had not been able to keep out of jail for long. Yet again.

Frank W. Abagnale, one year later (summer of 1975), shortly before he is accused of stealing by yet another employer (Aetna Life and Casualty). Identity of companion withheld and purposefully obscured by author. Image used with permission of Nona Tell.

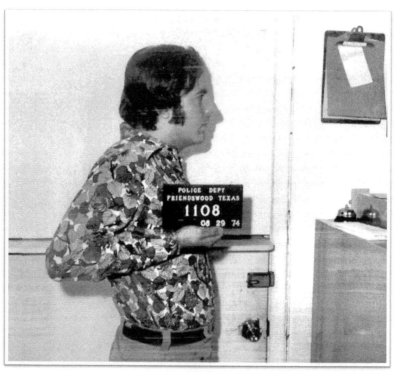

Frank W. Abagnale, aged 26, arrested in Friendswood, Texas, August 1974.

# CHAPTER 16
# A Woman's Touch

*Women were my only vice. I loved women.*
Frank Abagnale, 2002[175]

Mitch Wright was the chief of police in Friendswood in 1974, and even in his old age he remembered the case. Not because it was a particularly remarkable crime—it certainly wasn't—but because the convict later became so well known as the subject of *Catch Me If You Can*. Wright died in 2016 at the age of ninety-two, but a few years before his passing he was interviewed by local teens who were collecting stories from Friendswood's most-notable people.[176]

He recalled the break-ins and the events at Camp Manison, '74—but one thing stood out. Wright told the students that he remembered a very beautiful woman yelling at the arresting detectives, demanding Abagnale's release, adamant that her man couldn't possibly be a criminal!

\*       \*       \*

After his arrest by the Friendswood PD, on August 29, 1974, Abagnale was booked and fingerprinted—his mug shots show him sporting beefy sideburns and a vivid multicolored shirt patterned with a busy forest-leaf motif. The police made note of the twenty-six-year old's "receding hairline" among his distinguishing features.

He was arraigned in front of Galveston County Justice of the Peace, William T. Fuhrhop. Since Abagnale was charged with a lower-level felony, it was handled in the North County Office Building in Dickinson. Justice Fuhrhop was no hanging judge. Quite the opposite. Among a sea of conservative Texas judges with authoritative style, the grifter was matched up with a liberal Democrat who did not favor harsh punishment.[177,178] Abagnale looked set to land on his feet, yet again.

He pleaded not guilty. Bail was set. From there, he was transported to the Galveston County jail to await trial. He sat in the cells for a day or two and was interviewed again, this time by the Sherriff's Office, on August 31, 1974.

Unlike his arrest in Baton Rouge, this time he did find someone willing to post his bail—it appeared to have been paid by the beautiful and mysterious young woman described by Chief Wright.

Perhaps most interesting, on Abagnale's official paperwork with the Galveston County Sheriff's Bureau of Criminal Investigation there was a line for "spouse" information, should there be one. He did have one, at least according to the record. "Jennie" was listed on that line—sharing his address at the British Inn Apartments, 8901 Braesmont Drive, in Houston. The other biographical information entered on the official documents—his mother's Algerian heritage, his claim to time in the U.S. Navy and where his siblings resided—all proved accurate. But it is not clear if, or when, Abagnale had married in the short time since his release from federal prison.

In any case, the real name of the stunning blond living with the husky "camp consultant" at the Braesmont address—in apartment 274—was Jennie. Not originally from Houston, she hailed from another city in Texas and was a student at a Houston-area university when she met the grifter. She is retired now and still lives in Texas. To protect her privacy, her last name has been intentionally withheld by the author.

Morris was stunned to learn about Jennie. Abagnale had never mentioned a wife. Or a girlfriend. Morris and his guy pals had no idea he was living with a woman in Houston. He had very much behaved as a single man all summer. Morris first saw a mystery blond, presumably Jennie, when she appeared with Abagnale in court. He and Tom Manison assumed Abagnale had convinced his romantic partner to bail him out.

The Louisiana boys might not have known about Jennie, but Jan Jackson sure did. So did other women counselors. They knew he had a girlfriend, if not a wife, which was another reason they had resented his camp-wide flirtation and decided to douse him with water.

On one of their excursions into Houston with him as their chauffeur, Abagnale had needed to swing by his apartment for something. Jan remembers walking into his really cool second-floor apartment with her friends. A nice place with a balcony overlooking the outdoor swimming pool. They were surprised to meet his girlfriend there. But not as surprised as she was to see them. Jennie seemed very displeased as a troupe of young women from the camp piled into her apartment.

"She was a strikingly beautiful woman with long blond hair. She seemed annoyed and confused," said Jan Jackson. "Definitely put out that we were there. I distinctly remember wondering why in the world such a beautiful woman would be interested in him."

Hearing this, Katy Thorpe only recently realized that she too had met the mysterious Jennie on one of their evenings on the town with Abagnale. Consistent with Jan's recollections, Katy remembered the beautiful blonde woman.

"Oh, yes! She was in the camp limo when we worked our way around the Houston clubs," Katy recalled. "But although she came out with us for the evening, we didn't really understand who she was. Or why her boyfriend was going to so much trouble to impress us. We didn't even know him. It was a lot of fun, a night to remember, but also quite weird."

Several others recalled that Jennie visited Camp Manison for a cookout and hung out there with some of the employees on at least one occasion. Morris and the boys don't remember Abagnale's companion. If they did see a glamorous model, perhaps they didn't realize she was dating their camp limo driver.

Abagnale also had several addresses during that period. He told the folks at Camp Manison he lived at the Frenchman's Creek complex at 7003 Bissonnet Street, in apartment 1822. That was also his listed address in the early 1974 Houston directory. It was a run-down place on a busy Houston thoroughfare—the kind of place where a twenty-something working in Montgomery Ward might live. But the address he gave the Sherriff was the upmarket apartment at 8901 Braesmont Drive that he shared with his "wife" Jennie.

The apartment was actually leased by Jennie's friend Nona Tell. They went to university together, although Nona had already graduated. She would let Jennie and Frank stay there. There was only one bedroom, and they slept in the living room when Nona was there. She did not see a lot of Frank, as he and Jennie would typically enter the apartment late at night and leave early in the mornings.

But Nona still has a half dozen of the lovely "thank you" cards that Frank left for her when they stayed. These are dated as early as October 1973, indicating the couple had been together for over a year by the time Frank's camp case was in the courts. Even though Nona only met Frank in person a few times, the grifter wrote as though she was his dearest friend. Strange. But she did not think too deeply about it. She recently shared the cards with the author, including the one Frank wrote on New Year's Eve of 1973.

"To a very beautiful friend," Frank Abagnale wrote to Nona in his characteristic script, mixing upper and lowercase letters as he did in the correspondence to Reverend Underwood and the Parks family four years earlier. "We both wish you a very beautiful New Year and thank you for being part of ours! Love always, Jennie and Frank."

Nona did not know too much about Frank. Apart from that Jennie said he was a pilot. Presumably he had his own residence, but it seemed more convenient for them to hang out at her place instead.

Eventually, when Nona moved out of the Braesmont apartment in mid-1974, she suggested that Jennie take it over. Frank was not far behind, and the happy couple set up house. They even got a dog—a Dalmatian—despite the "no pets" policy.

This was where they were living when Frank was arrested. Nona heard that there was some "trouble," but Jennie was reluctant to share any details. All Nona knew was that Jennie had to go down to Galveston to bail Frank out of jail. But the rest remained a mystery.

Although Jennie and Nona remained good friends for years afterwards, Jennie stayed mum about Frank—apart from the revelation that he was not a pilot after all. As far as Nona knew, the couple was never married. It is more likely that Abagnale nominated her as his "wife" on the Galveston County Sheriff's paperwork in 1974 because there was no other option to define his partner.

Whatever her reasons, Jennie appeared to be the one who made a financial investment in Abagnale's freedom awaiting trial. If so, she would have stood to lose a significant sum if he decided to take flight—as he had in Baton Rouge, five years earlier. The walls were closing in on the grifter.

*   *   *

Morris, who had gone back to his teaching post in Louisiana, returned to Galveston County in the fall for court proceedings. He climbed the steps of the imposing North County building wondering if Abagnale would show up, or if he had already skipped bail.

Abagnale did turn up in the court. And he was not alone. He appeared in court with a striking blonde woman. Morris was not sure who she was, but she gave every appearance of being involved in some way with Abagnale.

"Mostly, she looked extremely embarrassed," said Morris, adding that "she looked very unhappy, as though she did not want to be there at all." Morris had hoped this would be the last he would see of the thief who had stolen their memories of a happy summer. But the case was not resolved in the first hearing, and another date was set. Abagnale left the court with his female companion. Whether or not this was a formalized marriage, he gave their shared address while the case was being processed through channels. Once again, Morris traveled back to Louisiana without closure.

He certainly did not expect what happened next.

Being questioned by the FBI is a daunting prospect for anyone, no matter how innocent. When agents tracked down Morris, he was naturally stunned. When they informed him it was about Abagnale, he was far less surprised.

Their contact with Morris was in the months after Abagnale's arrest in Friendswood, but before the case had been resolved. The FBI wanted to know if Morris had crafted a Delta Airlines employee identification card in the name of Frank William Abagnale Jr.

"Of course, I told them that I did it," Morris recently recalled. He had nothing to hide and explained that Abagnale had misled him and engineered the whole episode.

The G-men explained that the forged card had recently been used by Abagnale in an attempt to flee the United States. They did not say why he was on the run. Morris wondered if it was to escape penalties from his ongoing court case.

Although Abagnale's charges were relatively minor, they were part of a long history of reoffending. The potential violation of his federal parole conditions was obvious. The evidence against him seemed undeniable and he had good reason to be concerned about the potential outcome if found guilty.

Morris immediately realized he had created the forged document used by a convicted felon to flee the jurisdiction. It seemed that Abagnale had been caught again. And given out Morris's name as part of one of his elaborate stories, possibly trying to deflect responsibility. At least that is how it looked to Morris.

"But I wasn't nervous at all," Morris recalled. "I knew I had not done anything wrong." He explained to the FBI that he had been deceived. And the FBI seemed to recognize this without much question. They were cordial and said they were only doing their job, pursuing facts.

They also volunteered that the main reason the card was recognized as fake was because the laminate had been tampered with, seemingly in an effort to get underneath and change the surname from Abagnale.

Morris was amused that it was the attempt to *alter* his handiwork that had drawn attention to the identification card rather than the quality of his unintended forgery. The FBI understood that Morris wasn't complicit. They confirmed that he was the one who had sculpted the identification card for the Houston man, Abagnale, and that was that.

It would have been ironic, thought Morris, if Abagnale had succeeded in fleeing the charges that Morris had bought against him, using the fake ID that he, the complainant, had made for him!

If Abagnale had used the ID at Houston Intercontinental Airport, it gives new dimension to one of the final scenes in Spielberg's film. Considered by fans to be the most dramatic of the entire movie, the already paroled Leonardo DiCaprio is seen walking down a long airport hallway. Although the storyline is altogether different from reality, "Frank" is dressed once again in a pilot's uniform. He is about to flee, with Tom Hanks' character FBI agent "Carl Hanratty" not far behind, depicted as the only friend "Frank" has in the world. The film set is nearly identical to the real-life endless walkway tunnel of Houston Intercontinental Airport, circa 1974. Is that a coincidence, or is it yet another grain of truth?

"Frank, nobody's chasing you," says agent Hanratty in the film—before he simply walks away, leaving Frank with the choice. Yet another grain of truth, likely built around Abagnale's next real-life parole officer, James Powell Blackmon, a compassionate man who almost certainly helped Abagnale reinvent himself.

Apparently, Jim Blackmon took over as Abagnale's second federal parole officer in late 1974 and is almost certainly the more "rational and unbiased" officer described in Abagnale's autobiography. The fate of the "antagonistic" parole officer is not clear, but the Camp Manison fiasco suggested that supervision had been wanting. A prominent and beloved Friendswood citizen had been embarrassed by the events, possible grounds for an officer to be reassigned or removed.

Blackmon was a deeply religious man with a master's degree in theology. He took a great liking to Abagnale, and it is hard not to see echoes of Reverend Underwood. With his wife's blessing, Blackmon even invited Abagnale to live with them—as a lodger in their garage apartment—not long after things went awry in Friendswood.

"I knew if I'm going to help him I've got to be right on top of him," said Blackmon in a rare interview years later, not long after the movie was released.[179]

"I definitely owe a great deal to Mr. Blackmon," wrote Abagnale in a letter of recommendation around the same time. "He saw in me what no one else saw."[180]

It is not clear if Blackmon was already involved in Abagnale's case by the time the FBI was investigating the forger's attempt to flee the jurisdiction using Morris' fake ID, or what role he had in ensuring the defendant stayed to face trial—but he certainly had a major influence in what was to follow after that.

\*　\*　\*

Abagnale was present in court again when Justice Fuhrhop made his ruling in the autumn of 1974. The camp bus driver, Fuhrhop decided, was indeed a crook. But the Justice was well known for his leniency. Very few of his cases were escalated to higher-level charges. More often than not, the Justice knocked his low-level felony cases down to misdemeanors and just dispensed fines.[177,178] So, once again, Abagnale looked set to skate through the system.

Fuhrhop ruled that Morris was entitled to restitution of $125 (about $650 today) for stolen goods. Morris wondered if he would ever receive what he was owed. Based on Abagnale's record, it was a realistic concern. Surprisingly, the restitution checks did start arriving. But they were not from Abagnale. Instead, Morris saw they were each signed by a woman and she did not share the name Abagnale.

Morris recently explained that for the next five months he received checks for $25 in monthly installments. He assumed they were from the beautiful woman who had appeared with Abagnale in court and named as his wife, Jennie, in the Galveston County jail records.

The Friendswood PD marked their case closed shortly before Christmas, 1974. Again, Abagnale appeared to get off lightly. Morris was possibly one of the only victims who was actually paid back for what was stolen—though even then, Abagnale appeared to have convinced someone else to pay his restitution.

It is also not clear how things ended between Abagnale and Jennie after his criminal case. Two years later, on November 3, 1976, Frank Abagnale took out a marriage license to marry Kelly Welbes, who he has oft-described since as "his first and only wife."

But at the very time Abagnale was contemplating matrimony to Kelly, Jennie was still in the turbulent financial wake of her relationship with the grifter. Court records show that Jennie was served with papers in autumn 1976—tracked down at her workplace by both Montgomery Ward and Spring Branch Bank—for long-outstanding credit card charges and an unpaid promissory note.

\* \* \*

Morris moved on with his busy life, although not without wondering what this character would get up to next. He did not hear anything more about Abagnale for about three years. None of the Louisiana boys knew what became of him. Word was that he was working as a carny, part of a small-time traveling circus in Texas and Oklahoma.

Then, at around 11:30 p.m. on April 6, 1978, Morris had a surprise awakening and discovered exactly what Abagnale was up to. He was just starting to doze off on his living room couch with *The Tonight Show* on in the background. When he heard Carson say the name Frank Abagnale, Morris sat bolt upright.

"At first, I couldn't believe it could be the same man," recalled Morris, hearing Carson announce Frank Abagnale and his antics to the world. But then Morris saw the shady driver of old limos and former prison buses, his one-time Camp Manison mate, walk onto the stage!

Turns out Abagnale was a carny in a different circus.

Morris immediately recalled how smooth and convincing the man was. It was really not so surprising at all. That guy could sell anything to anybody, he thought. And it looked like he was still doing it. But how on earth did he go from a sleazeball grifter stealing from older Louisianans and working at a kids' camp under false pretenses to instant stardom on the Carson show?

Jan Jackson never saw Abagnale on *Truth*, *Today* or *Tonight*. But her mother's sharp eye caught a newspaper article a few years after the grifter's unceremoniously wet departure from Camp Manison. "You're never going to believe this . . ." announced Jan's mother to her family when the man her husband, Bill Jackson, had revealed as a fake, became a media celebrity in Texas and beyond.

But when this author asked Jan if she or her father had ever been contacted by any journalists or any person related to the

*Catch Me If You Can* film, the answer was firm. "No, never," she said. Who was going to believe that he had been a bus driver stealing from a kids' camp?

Although Katy Thorpe did not particularly like the con man, she has followed his career ever since and was immediately appreciative of the fact that he was an even more impressive fake than the film portrayed—even though he had never done the things he made a living boasting about.

"I guess that means he has pulled off an even larger hoax and fooled the whole world," she concluded. Her father, now sadly deceased, was a career FBI agent. She regrets not asking him about his thoughts on the whole episode.

\*　　\*　　\*

By the time Abagnale appeared on *To Tell the Truth*, he had already made a return visit to the Friendswood community—not far from Camp Manison. This time, on January 27, 1978, he was invited as the keynote speaker at a gala dinner at the Friendswood Golfcrest Country Club. The *Friendswood News*, which had announced his arrest at the kids camp thirty-eight months earlier, headlined the big event—billing Abagnale as "one of this century's great imposters ... truly amazing man with an incredible story to tell."[181]

This time he made page one! There was no connection to Camp Manison '74.

At the Golfcrest, banquet guests sipped on cocktails and carved their prime rib, all for $15. They listened to the keynote speaker telling the most imaginative of tales—never suspecting that one of his most audacious feats was unfolding *at that very moment*. The man they were paying to admire had re-entered their community without them even realizing that he had been in their jail, masquerading in their community, stealing from their beloved kids' camp. They were part of the con, without knowing.

It was the ultimate sleight-of-hand, dealing from the bottom of the deck.

*   *   *

Abagnale has always been inconsistent and hazy about his path from habitual offender to habitual storyteller. Committing a fresh round of offenses at Friendswood's Camp Manison in 1974, while still on parole from his 1970 federal charges, could have drawn more significant prison time. But it didn't.

Having a sympathetic parole officer in Jim Blackmon made a world of difference as Abagnale set to start a new life.

"He did little odd jobs, working here and there," explained Blackmon in his rare interview with a local paper in Uvalde, Texas.[179]

But early in his tenure as Abagnale's parole officer, Blackmon received an unexpected call from his charge.

Without Blackmon's knowledge, Abagnale had already gone back to the activities he had told Reverend Underwood he wanted to do—to work with vulnerable children. And, as he had in Baton Rouge, he claimed to have a master's degree to secure a suitable post at a children's home. This time it apparently worked.

Decades later, he claimed he was at the Houston orphanage on an "undercover assignment for the FBI"[182]—which he was almost certainly not. He also indicated that this was where he met his wife, Kelly Welbes, who was also working at the children's home, pursuing a degree in child psychology. [182]

"I was working undercover in Texas in 1975. I met Kelly [Welbes] as part of this assignment. She was an innocent aside, and not part of the focused criminal operation. I immediately fell

251

in love with her. I did the unthinkable and blew my cover. I told her in honesty about my background."[183]

However, the orphanage "assignment" was purely of Abagnale's own making. We know this because Blackmon has described what really happened in Texas, circa 1975.

Abagnale called Blackmon to tell his parole officer the news of his latest employment. That he was already making good and working for the local children's home. The man of faith would surely be pleased with that. But, in yet another bizarre coincidence, Abagnale had apparently chosen the *exact* institution where Blackmon himself had previously served as superintendent! That also meant Blackmon was well acquainted with the regulations and job requirements.[179] Initially, Abagnale said that he was working as the "recreational director," and Blackmon was quick to point out that this was totally inappropriate. Even that job, he knew, required a degree. He told Abagnale to expect a visit because he was on his way over to the children's home to investigate.

Faced with the imminent arrival of his parole officer, Abagnale changed his story over the phone and conceded that he was doing more than directing recreation. But what he was *actually* doing was even more concerning.

"Well, I'm placing children in foster homes," Abagnale admitted, according to the parole officer.[179] Blackmon knew full-well that this required considerable training and an advanced degree, something Abagnale who only had minimal education, did not have. Blackmon wasted no time and went straight over to the home.

He arrived to find Abagnale ensconced in the children's home, in his own office decorated with photographs of his previous "career" as a pilot and a framed master's degree.

"Here's a guy knowing his federal parole officer is coming,

cool as a cucumber," recalled Blackmon.[179] He also explained that his parolee told him that he "had not forged any documents," but instead had asked his girlfriend, who was attached to a local university, to "make a diploma for him."[179] Had the self-styled "master forger" once again solicited other artisans to do the work?

"Nobody ever checked anything, it was so perfect," Blackmon told the Uvalde journalist in 2003. It is not clear if Blackmon really thought it was "perfect" or perverse at the time, but his comments three decades after the events may have been influenced by the positive reaction to the loveable character portrayed in a popular movie. According to folklore, employees at the children's home considered the con man to be "the best to ever hold the position he worked at." [179] None of those workers were interviewed for the story.

Nonetheless, Blackmon claimed he made Abagnale pack his things and "resign" immediately. In the aftermath of his fame, the magnitude of the original event appeared to have grown. Scenes of Nixon's farewell on the south lawn of the White House spring to mind—emotional co-workers, the helicopter, flashing of double-handed victory signs.

If it were the present day, an ex-con using false pretenses and a fake resumé to secure a job working with vulnerable children would almost certainly face multiple criminal charges. Just the fake degree alone in Texas is good for a $2,000 fine and 180 days in jail. But that's not a path the parole officer wanted to go down. Blackmon conceded that he shielded Abagnale from what would have been dire consequences.

"I was always rehabilitation-oriented with my clients," Blackmon told the journalist, explaining that he decided to give his "client" another chance and not report the incident through channels. He added that he kept a record of the incident as leverage and realized that Abagnale needed far closer supervision.[179] And so, he invited his charge to become his lodger. Abagnale was soon living in a garage apartment at the back of the Blackmon's place on Bobbitt Lane! What a deal—the professional-friend-in-the-guesthouse thing, two decades before Kato Kaelin. The Uvalde journalist did not query on what, if any, financial arrangements surrounded the lodging.

Recall, this was the time—as Abagnale later told audiences—that esteemed actor Dustin Hoffman was shadowing his every move, while filming *Marathon Man*, in 1975.

"He spent a month with me, watching everything I did," Abagnale said just a couple of years later.[17]

This "scene" takes on a dramatic new dimension, as we might now imagine the big con man entertaining the slightly built Hoffman in Blackmon's garage. Blackmon's garage!

In any event, Blackmon said he urged the con man to change his ways and claimed he was the one who landed Abagnale a job with a local security company, which set him on the path to establishing the Frank W. Abagnale and Associates consulting business not long after that. Abagnale has acknowledged that his parole officer allowed him to travel out of state for the tectonic shift in his life—multiple trips to Burbank to tell Carson his tales.[184]

It's little wonder that the *Catch Me If You Can* filmmakers acknowledged that Hanks' "Hanratty" character was a composite of agent Shea and "Abagnale's parole officer." We can safely assume this was not referring to his first parole officer. It is also much easier to imagine Abagnale calling Blackmon at the holidays—as DiCaprio phoned Hanks in the film—if not saying "pass the stuffing, please" across the festive table on Bobbitt Lane.

\*　　\*　　\*

In his own version of events, Abagnale approached the government to see if he could use his "past to make a living."

By his account, he spent most of 1975 involved in generating educational crime prevention materials, before the government granted him permission to do this commercially. He told journalist Casey Selix that he was paroled to Houston on condition that he engage in a form of schoolboy homework. Rather than writing ten thousand lines of "I will not steal checks belonging to older Louisianans," Abagnale said he was "required to write about the ways of con artists for government," wrote Selix.[133]

"First, the federal government allowed me to write training programs for federal agents and secret service agents at their training academy. Then they started letting me write policy and procedure to deal with forgery," Abagnale later told his audiences.[68] "This, I did for free for over a year."

In reality, Abagnale did finally land a decent job in 1975. He was hired by Aetna Life and Casualty—one of the largest companies in the nation. But it did not go well. Indeed, the company ended up suing him for check fraud—suggesting that he had failed to resist his old habits and had strayed, yet again, from the path of redemption.

According to court records filed in Harris County, Houston, Abagnale was sent to Hartford, Connecticut, to attend Aetna's training courses for new recruits. Like the tens of thousands of employees who flowed in and out of the company's highly regarded training, he was there as a student to learn basic business skills and the fundamentals of claims.

The court records also reveal that, while there in October of 1975, he cashed a series of four worthless checks at Aetna's HQ.

He used personal checks in his own name, written against a Great Southern Bank account that had already been closed. In each case, he added the name of one of the Aetna course instructors on the back of the $50 checks to add legitimacy. The checks bounced after he left Hartford.

Aetna may have been a $5 billion company at the time, but they were not prepared to let the $200 (about $1000 today) go. According to court filings, the company made exhaustive efforts to have Abagnale "pay off the debt in question and to make the worthless checks good, but to no avail."

Fortunately for Abagnale, Aetna did not pursue criminal charges. But they did eventually file civil charges (Case#304469) two years later in 1977—after Abagnale appeared on *To Tell the Truth*. Aetna lawyers alleged that Abagnale's efforts were a deliberate effort to defraud the company. The four checks were presented as evidence.

"The Defendant knew or should have known of the status of the bank account in question. The passing of the worthless checks in question constituted a fraud on the Plaintiff."

Whether Abagnale squared his debt with Aetna is unknown, but his employment there in late 1975 was certainly short-lived. Public records confirm he branched out on his own, and registered Frank W. Abagnale and Associates a few months later. In April 1976 he set up shop in a little den at 1770 St. James Place, Unit B-3, right next to James Furlan furriers.[185] His anti-crime seminars do appear to have emerged around this period. He was soon claiming to have had been "operating undercover" for several years.[29]

After moving out of Blackmon's garage, and a brief residence at 9600 Glenfield Court, the self-styled crime consultant was living next to the China Cottage buffet and the Bull 'n' Anchor Pub in the 600 block of the dilapidated Westbury Square shopping plaza. Dreamed up in the 1950s, Westbury Square was a fake Italian-style village with mixed retail and apartments. Its halcyon days in Houston were long gone. By the time Abagnale moved there, the complex was better known as *Wastebury* Square—a hangout for stoners who purchased supplies from its multiple head shops. It was a dubious high-crime neighborhood—so bad that a vigilante-like Westbury Neighborhood Watch Group emerged and was even featured in out-of-town newspapers.[186]

By then, Abagnale and girlfriend Kelly Welbes were very much established as a couple. She was from a much nicer side of town. The leafy, manicured section of North Houston. Their union marked a major turning point in his career. By the end of 1976, they had married and were living in the suburbs. His new wife seemingly played a major role during his transformation, appearing in his very early media appearances.[21,29]

Photographs of Kelly Welbes by her husband's side were featured in Sussman's and Redding's first reports outlining his elaborately reinvented life story. Even then, Abagnale claimed to have met her while posing "undercover during an investigation conducted by his security firm."[29]

"I was posing as a sociologist," Abagnale told Stan Redding of the *Houston Chronicle* in 1977 during his interview with the reporter who would also later write his autobiography. "We went together for six months, and I'd fallen in love with her before the case was wrapped up and I could reveal my real identity. She didn't mind at all. In fact, she wrote her master's thesis on me."[29] At most universities in North America, master's theses are copied and made publicly available should anyone wish to examine them. There is no evidence that Redding asked to see the thesis, which obviously would have been useful as he began to write a book on the subject.

"Now, that's a thesis I would like to read," Paula said recently.

In other recorded accounts, Abagnale recounted a different story. He told bankers he met his wife while working at a "grocery store in Houston, Texas," adding that it was in that context that "a young girl decided to become my wife. I was stocking groceries. I didn't have a dime to my name. I told her I had been in prison and that anyone could send me back to prison at any time. Yet, she became my wife anyway."[7]

Abagnale poses with his wife, Kelly, in *Texas*, the Sunday magazine of the *Houston Chronicle*, 1977. E. Joseph Deering/©Houston Chronicle. Used with permission.

If his unlikely claims to have been recruited to work undercover for the government are true, it was presumably after his arrest in Houston in late 1974, and his alleged mysterious dash for an international border—which prompted the FBI's visit to Morris investigating the fake ID card. Following his arrest in Friendswood, federal authorities were notified because a felony arrest could have jeopardized his federal parole. Indeed, former Friendswood chief of police Mitch Wright did recall the FBI took an interest.[176] Certainly, it seems miraculous that such a compulsive recidivist avoided a longer prison sentence, especially when he appeared not to have quenched his appetite for writing bad checks.

Others believed his claims to be working for the FBI were as flimsy as his claims to be working for other reputable organizations, such as Neiman-Marcus. As journalist Perry had discovered, Abagnale claimed he was "employed" and "saving them millions" after just giving a brief seminar in one of their local offices. A gross misrepresentation—like virtually all of his claims.[56]

"Frank Abagnale probably knows less about white-collar crime than most well-read 15-year-olds," said one of Ira Perry's sources in 1978, when the journalist shredded Abagnale's claims. In reality, the man who claimed he had gathered extensive expertise during years of successfully outmaneuvering the law had been caught easily time and time again—a dilettante who had signed checks in his own name and spent most of the time between 1965 and 1974 inside prison!

Perry did actually speak to Jim Blackmon in 1978, still Abagnale's parole officer at the time. Even though Blackmon had little to say to Ira Perry, he did let the cat out of the bag and conceded that most of the con man's audacious tales were untrue—although Perry indicated that Blackmon only made this acknowledgment indirectly.[56]

Abagnale's "undercover" claims certainly verged on the bizarre at times. He told one reporter, Holly Wood, that Texas

Attorney General John Hill had handpicked him for special undercover work. His assignment? To "cash as many checks as humanly possible" in three days, he said, and in the same period, to buy as much stuff as he could at various retail outlets using a credit card.[171] And so, with the Texas Department of Public Safety supposedly watching him, Abagnale claimed he secured the name of a deceased infant from old newspapers, which he then parlayed into a new birth certificate, credit cards, and a bank account.

He boasted to Wood that he was able to cash $58,000 ($260,000 today) in bad checks and separately purchase merchandise worth $42,000 ($200,000 today) within 72 hours. To what end? It was not clear. Law enforcement would already know how identities are stolen, checks are cashed, and credit cards are used. Not to mention the unnecessary logistics of truckloads of refunds and retail returns after the seemingly pointless record-breaking check-writing spree. Holly Wood never asked.[171] And neither did Hollywood.

There are also several odd observations that are difficult to explain.

The first was by Paula Parks in 1978. It was not long after she returned to Delta Airlines from maternity leave. She was passing through the crew lounge at Chicago International Airport when she was shocked to see a poster with a familiar face staring at her. There were five bold words emblazoned across it.

"HAVE YOU SEEN THIS MAN?" yelled the poster, offering a Delta contact phone number beneath it.

"I thankfully hadn't seen him, but I knew exactly who he was," recalled Paula, still surprised and annoyed that he could possibly still be up to his old tricks. This was *after* Abagnale had made appearances on national television claiming to have given up his old life.

Paula did not hesitate. She called the number.

"I told them that it was Frank Abagnale," she said. But what happened after that was really strange.

"I was immediately taken off my next scheduled run and directed to remain in the crew area," she remembers. "Not long after that, they put me on a plane and flew me back to Atlanta."

The FBI was waiting for her when the plane landed in Atlanta.

"I was taken into a secured room and questioned by the agents," Paula said. She was quite bewildered as they recorded her statement, including her account of Frank Abagnale from many years before, when he had tracked her movements under false pretenses, followed her from place to place, moved in with her family and stole from them.

"But they mainly wanted to know if I had seen Frank *recently*," she added. "Why the hell would they be asking that, if he was really working for them at the FBI?"

To this day, she is unclear what had prompted the call for information about "this man." Why was his poster there? She is positive about the date because there is no question about the timing of her son's birth.

The other observation came from Eugene Stewart, the former FBI agent who became Delta's vice president, corporate security. He was also the chairman of the security committee of the Air Transportation Association. When he was interviewed by Ira Perry in 1978, he stated that Delta was aware of reports that Abagnale had been impersonating a Delta employee in Texas and allegedly tried to pass bad personal checks while he had been on parole.[56]

Former FBI agent Eugene Stewart, Assistant Special Agent
in charge of the Atlanta division, Delta Airlines security
boss. Media release photo, 1973.

"We reported it to the U.S. parole authorities," Stewart told
Perry. "But they apparently declined to revoke his parole."

Stewart made it clear that airline security thought this lack of
action was odd. There was no explanation given. Abagnale's
parole officer, Jim Blackmon, would not comment further—apart
from his hints to Perry that many of Abagnale's talk show claims
were phony.

As former assistant special agent in charge of the FBI's
Atlanta division, Stewart would have known that the bulk of
Abagnale's public claims were fictional. Indeed, he was

262

supervising activities of FBI agents all across the East Coast at the precise time of Abagnale's fictitious cat-and-mouse story of eluding agent Shea.[78] It did not happen. And it was clear from his interview with Perry that Stewart knew that Abagnale's brushes with federal law amounted to little more than a handful of forged checks and transporting a stolen car over state lines.

A law graduate from Columbus School of Law in Washington DC, Stewart was a deep thinker, an intellectual, and highly regarded by the FBI. He was very much part of a storied family of agents, and when he retired—a few years after his interview with Perry—he was appointed president of the Society of Former Special Agents of the FBI.[77] Today, Stewart may have been perplexed by the ways in which many contemporary federal agents appear to look up to Abagnale with unearned admiration when facts in the public domain so clearly contradict the con man's claims.

Abagnale has continued to double down on this narrative that he was working for the "Bureau." However, Perry's inquiries in 1978 produced several former FBI agents, including those his own literary agent was herding clients toward, who were not able to confirm his claims. One even expressed frustration that his name was being thrown around for verification.[56]

*　　*　　*

It was around this time that Abagnale's new life story appeared to emerge. It is not clear exactly when the largely fake dossier was written, nor when the grand publicity plan was hatched. But this appears to come into focus between 1975 and 1976, shortly before he was married.

Around the time he established his consulting outfit in 1976, Abagnale had started giving talks to small businesses. And to high school students in the Houston area.[187] The latter talks were part of the distributive education program aimed at preparing students for the workplace through vocational competency training.[187] It seemed that Frank Abagnale was finally doing what he told Reverend Underwood he always wanted to do—working with kids and providing advice as a role model. This time, he claimed, it was as a service to the community with the blessing of his parole officer.

But only a few months later, at the end of 1976, Abagnale's resumé had been miraculously transformed. Ahead of his first major public event at McAdams Junior High School, he presented phenomenal credentials—claiming he had already lectured at Harvard Law School, the U.S. Treasury, Chase Manhattan Bank, Exxon Oil, the Los Angeles Police Department—and even Scotland Yard![188]

Was it all cooked up around the kitchen table? Or were there larger forces at play? Had someone powerful already seen something far more important—his talent for story telling? Or, more particularly, the potential he had for story *selling*? And, had they already had a hand in engineering his career? Was that how he had made his almost overnight transition from a completely unknown small-time criminal stealing from good Samaritans in Baton Rouge to Johnny Carson's hallowed couch? Did someone help fashion a new life story?

This appears to be exactly what happened, and as this author looked more deeply, some interesting connections began to emerge. But first, it is important to understand what really happened during his earlier years, from the age of sixteen, and why this was hidden from view. It contradicts the entire narrative of *Catch Me If You Can*.

\* \* \*

There is no question that Abagnale landed on his feet—time and time again. But there is no evidence that this was anything more than luck and happenstance. He had walked away from several potentially long sentences even though he was a known habitual offender and continued to perpetrate crimes of a similar nature. Many of his victims felt that the system had failed them— not just the ones affected by his *real* crimes, but those who suffered the perpetual frustration of being subjected to the *fabricated* stories he subsequently created. In that, the media and societal appetites were as much to blame for seemingly having no interest in the truth.

But none of this might have happened at all if Abagnale had not slipped through the cracks in the first place.

# Facts versus Fiction

| Timelines | Claims | Verified Facts | Facts versus Fiction |
|---|---|---|---|
| | | * Targeted individuals or small businesses | |
| **1964** (age 16) | **The Pilot** "When I was 16 years old I impersonated an airline pilot for Pan Am for 2 years cashed over $2 million in 26 countries" | Petty crimes in New York | Petty crimes reported, (1964-1965) * |
| **1965** (age 17) | | UNITED STATES NAVY | Stolen car, arrest in Eureka, CA (June 21, 1965) * |
| | | Multiple arrests in New York | |
| | | **Jail**, Eureka, California | Check fraud, arrest in NY, * (July 15, 1965) |
| | | **Jail**, Westchester, New York | |
| **1966** (age 18) | **The Doctor** Cobb County General Hospital, Georgia "At 18, I practiced medicine for about a year" | **Prison** Great Meadow Correctional Institute in Comstock, New York | Federal warrant for interstate transport of stolen vehicle, * (July 19, 1965) |
| **1967** (age 19) | **The Lawyer** Baton Rouge Attorney General, Louisiana "At 19, I practiced law for about a year" | Paroled to mother in New York, but reoffended immediately in Boston | Granted parole (May 19, 1967) |
| | | **Jail**, East Boston, MA | Larceny by forgery Boston, MA (July 19, 1967) |
| **1968** (age 20) | **The Professor** Brigham Young University, Provo, Utah "At 20, I taught 2 full semesters as a PhD" | **Prison** Massachusetts Corrections | Return to Comstock to complete sentence, released December 24, 1968 |
| | Retired to Montpellier, France, bought "a charming and gracious house" | **Prison** Comstock, New York | Theft and Forgery * Arrest in Baton Rouge (February 14, 1969) |
| **1969** (age 21) | | Lived with Parkses in Baton Rouge | |
| | | **Jail**, Baton Rouge, LA | Released on parole June 17, 1969 |
| | **Prison** Perpignan, France | France and Sweden | Theft and swindling (October 3, 1969) * |
| | | Perpignan **Prison**, France | |
| **1970** (age 22) | **Prison** Malmo, Sweden | Malmo **Prison**, Sweden | Fraud and forgery * (March 26, 1970) |
| | | Deported to USA | |
| **1971** (age 23) | | | Forgery (only 10 * Pan Am checks for total of only $1,448.60). Arrest in Cobb County, Georgia (November 2, 1970) |
| **1972** (age 24) | **Prison** Federal Correctional institution, Petersburg Virginia (12 year sentence) | **Prison** Federal Correctional institution, Petersburg Virginia (12 year sentence) | |
| **1973** (age 25) | | | Released on parole in 1973 |
| **1974** (age 26) | | Paroled to Houston, Texas (petty crimes, theft) | Arrested for theft * Friendswood Kids Camp in Houston, TX (August 29, 1974) |
| | Paroled to Houston, Texas, claimed to be working for the FBI | **Jail**, Galveston County, Texas | Violated federal parole? |
| | | Moved into parole officer's garage | |
| **1976+** (age 28) | Develops and promotes the "Imposter" narrative | | Defendant in at least * eight civil cases in the next decade |

# CHAPTER 17
# In Uniform

*Tomorrow's man in tomorrow's world . . . Opportunities*
*for travel and adventure are unlimited.*
*All yours when you GO NAVY.*
United States Navy 1960s recruitment brochure[189]

When he was sixteen years old, Frank Abagnale did wear a uniform. But it was a real one. In the United States Navy. He signed up just before Christmas in 1964.

Life in the Navy promised unlimited opportunities. Brochures from the 1960s inspired glamor and international adventure, covered with colorful artists' impressions of futuristic space-age technology and deep-sea exploration. Recruiting stations even used real-life curvaceous, bare-legged models to entice young men to "Join a Great Service." Scantily clad in naval-style tunics complete with shiny buttons and knee-high white boots, the smiling young women were posed in front of soaring rocket ships—no doubt inspiring thoughts of unlimited possibility in the minds of young potential recruits.

It is not known what inspired young Frank Abagnale to join their ranks. According to letters from both of his parents to Reverend Underwood, he was already a troubled young man in need of psychiatric help—support that his mother Paulette said they had tried to get him but failed. His father, Frank Sr., in particular felt that he had failed his son—a young man he felt had suffered emotional problems for years.[106] His parents had already separated, and his own letters to the Parks family and Reverend Underwood five years later, amid the sympathy ploy, likely still reflected the truth of his feelings.

"I love my mom and dad very much, and I know they love me, and their separation was a little too much for me to understand," wrote Frank.[106] "I don't feel sorry for myself, because God gave me free will, but I must understand this mental problem I have."

When Abagnale was a young child, the family did indeed live in affluent Bronxville, New York, at 27 Parkview Drive. Frank Abagnale Sr. had drifted between jobs—first as a print shop salesman and then as a factory worker at the Ford Motor Company plant in Edgewater, New Jersey—before he enlisted for service in WWII.[190] After the war, he secured a sales job at Gramercy Stationary, a well-established printing and engraving establishment at 284 Madison Avenue. He took out ads in the New York Athletic Club's magazine *Winged Foot*, making sure that members knew he was the go-to guy for all their printing needs.[191]

Frank Sr. purchased the Bronxville home in 1948, the year his son Frank Jr. was born.[192] As the leader of the New York Athletic Club Anglers in the 1950s, Frank Sr. regularly rubbed shoulders with prominent New Yorkers and arranged fishing tournaments in the United States and beyond.[193,194,195] But his fortunes began to change, and so did the health of his marriage. In May of 1956, Abagnale's parents made a move to legally split their home, dividing the ownership equally.[196] With divorce inevitable, the family home was eventually sold in June 1960, when Frank Jr. was just twelve years old.[197]

After the marital split, Frank Sr. left Bronxville. He moved around various locations in Westchester County, eventually settling in Mount Vernon.

The divorce was finalized January 20, 1964. Paulette did what thousands of New Yorkers did in the 1960s. She went to Mexico for a "quickie divorce." And like so many others, she selected "incompatibility" as the grounds on the documents. Typically, a New Yorker-Mexican divorce could be completed within hours and only cost $175—plus travel.

But less than three months later, it was Frank Sr. who married again. On the afternoon of April 10, 15-year-old Abagnale gained a stepmother. In a low-key ceremony in lower Manhattan, with Arthur J. Ryder of Croton, New York, as his witness, Frank Sr. formalized his romance with Westchester divorcée Lillian Mae Hecker. Fourteen years younger than Frank Sr., she was a receptionist at a local TV station. The newlyweds lived together at 122 Primrose Avenue in Mount Vernon.

Even before his marriage to Paulette ended, Frank Sr. described his son's emotional challenges, which were only worsened by the upheaval that followed.

"When I lost my home, I lost my life," Frank Jr. later explained in his own letters to Reverend Underwood and the Parks family.[106] The Navy may have looked like a good option for many reasons.

> *If I wanted to lay down a baby con, I could say I was the*
> *product of a broken home . . . but I'd only be bum-rapping*
> *my parents.*
> Frank Abagnale, 1980[87]

General recruiting guidelines for the Navy at the time listed a minimum age of seventeen years, and even then only with signed parental consent. Abagnale was only sixteen, so his route of entry is not entirely clear. The Navy certainly offered structure and discipline that may have been helpful to a wayward youth. Records do confirm that Abagnale was already known to authorities in Westchester, New York[198]. Before enlisting, "Frankie" Abagnale, as his mother called him, had already shown a proclivity for petty crime. He had been accused of ripping off small businesses, including a local dry cleaner who contacted his parents, insisting Abagnale repay what he had stolen—to no avail.[199]

It was a common practice for judges in mid-century America to show leniency to young offenders facing minor charges like theft, and offered the choice of military service instead of jail.[200,201] An easy choice for most at the time. Whatever his reasons, Frank W. Abagnale Jr., entered service with the Navy on December 23, 1964.[202]

But Abagnale's relationship with the United States Navy did not last.

He did not live the "Go Places, Do Things" dream offered by their bumper sticker slogan—at least not with the Navy. Abagnale parted ways with his fellow recruits on February 18, 1965. He was discharged from the Navy, just months after entering service.

Perhaps he decided to go places and do things on his own.

Within days of arriving back home, to 122 Primrose Avenue, in Mount Vernon, New York, Abagnale was accused of forging checks and stealing again. The local police responded quickly and arrested him for forgery on February 25, 1965, only one week after his naval discharge. Two weeks later, on March 11, he was arrested yet again by Mount Vernon officers. This time for vagrancy.

Back on the street and awaiting the outcome, Abagnale

initially remained in the New York area. He was known to hang out at the home of an Italian-American family on Jefferson Place in Tuckahoe. He was reported to be friends with the teen and young adult children there. Since 17-year-old Abagnale had never finished school and had a police record, regular employment proved difficult. But he did appear to have worked for a time at the newly opened Gordy's Steak House in Bronxville—"A Nice Place for Nice People" was their slogan.

But he soon decided to flee New York and went on another crime spree ahead of his departure. Again, his main targets were largely individuals and small local family businesses. This appears to be how he financed a transcontinental road trip from New York to California.

First, he needed a car.

At that point in his career, air travel did not appear to be part of his repertoire. Instead, he had his eye on a bright yellow 1965 Ford Mustang not far from his father's Mount Vernon home in Pelham, New York. It was a stand-out car and must have been hard to resist. The beautiful two-door 289 V8 coupe with a black vinyl roof was a popular car and is prized among collectors even to this day.

The car was recorded stolen on May 29, 1965. But he did not leave town immediately. The bold thief and his shiny Mustang were both seen on Jefferson Place, where he had been visiting his young friends.

Next, he needed folding money for the road.

He set his sights on a lovely stone-built service station alongside the leafy Bronx River Parkway near Scarsdale. The cottage buildings are still there today on the edge of the greenbelt carriageway, though now boarded up and in disrepair. But in 1965 it was a busy local business owned by Mamaroneck resident Thomas Russell. The stone station provided local and regional customers with gas, tires and breakdown services.

On June 2, just a couple of days after securing the prize Mustang, Abagnale pulled up at the Parkway service station. While owner Thomas Russell was otherwise engaged, Abagnale carefully helped himself to Russell's checkbook. Just as he later did at other small businesses, like Dooley and Son in Baton Rouge. Abagnale peeled back three blank checks belonging to the small businessman.

This is completely at odds with the "code of ethics" that forms the central moral core of the story he now tells of his early life.

"If I had walked into a dry cleaners and the register drawer had been open, I would never have touched the money. To me, that was stealing," he told the press decades later,[203] and is still claiming he has never stolen from individuals or small businesses.

The following day, on June 3, Detective Stephen Fischer of the Westchester County Police reported that Abagnale wrote a phony check in New Rochelle.[204] The 17-year-old subsequently cashed the checks from the Bronx River Parkway service station—for a total of $350 (almost $4,000 today). A serious felony charge, no doubt. He now had the dough for his cross-country road trip.

But before he left, there were reports that Abagnale passed a few more bogus checks at a series of other local businesses in the nearby village of Tuckahoe, including Victoria Laundry and Marcelo's Tailors. Frank Miller, the owner of Tuckahoe Camera, also filed a complaint. With that, the grifter was on his way west, all the way to the Golden State.

The following evening, on June 4, 1965, the Mount Vernon police went in search of the petty criminal as their key suspect for the allegedly stolen Mustang. But he had gone missing from his Mount Vernon residence.[199] They issued a bulletin to the surrounding towns, including descriptions of the fugitive and his stolen car. The six-foot-tall seventeen-year-old was described as wearing a black sports knit shirt, black trousers and loafers—classic beatnik attire worn by many young men in mid-60s America. The Westchester police also added a warrant for his arrest—for the significant sum stolen from the Parkway garage.

Someone, presumably his chums from Jefferson Street, told investigating officers that Abagnale was taking the Mustang on a southern road trip to Florida. Authorities along the East Coast were on the lookout for the vehicle. But it wasn't the Sunshine State he was headed for—he was going in an altogether different direction. Westward to the Golden State. But taking the stolen vehicle over state lines was about to add a federal offense to Abagnale's rap sheet.[205]

Abagnale had been on the road for little more than two weeks when he reached the idyllic if not sleepy fishing town of Eureka in picturesque Northern California. But, he had chosen exactly the *wrong* place to stop and likely had no idea what lay in store for him.

\*    \*    \*

The sun had burned off the morning fog, and Eureka was headed for its high of sixty degrees as Abagnale headed into town. Along coastal Highway 101, the Midway Drive-In theater was showing a risqué film called *The Farmer's Other Daughter.* Abagnale checked into the Imperial 400 Motel Inn at 1630 4th Street. Jim Bauer, the owner-manager of the two-story forty-three-room air-conditioned property, did not initially see anything amiss.

At first brush, Eureka probably looked like a good place to stay for a while. A quiet enough place in Northern California, a good distance from other regional cities. But in the same way Abagnale later found himself defying all odds by choosing sleepy Friendswood, where an actual Delta Airlines captain figured him out, Abagnale picked the wrong place in Eureka. It was home to one of the country's best-run police forgery units, headed up by 39-year-old Sergeant Fred Sonberg.

When Abagnale drove into town, his yellow Mustang sticking out like a sore thumb with its New York license plates, he probably wasn't aware that Sonberg was a legend in Humboldt County. The sixteen-year veteran of the Eureka Police Department had an uncanny knack for collaring grifters and check artists. Including those who were breezing through.

Four years before Abagnale arrived in the city, Eureka officials established a zero-tolerance attitude toward check fraud. Sgt. Sonberg had been tasked with heading up the fraud and check detail.[206] Sonberg gave seminars on white-collar crime to businesses in Northern California. He lectured merchants on bank routing numbers, correct dates and so forth. He showed films on shoplifting and encouraged local supermarkets to install automatic camera systems to photograph all those cashing checks.[207] He was doing all this for free, a decade before Abagnale began doing the same thing for big-league speaking fees.

In his lectures, Sonberg even used many of the props that Abagnale later appropriated. Like showing *actual* checks that had been cashed signed "I. Stuckyou," "Ima Crook," "Uve Ben Haad," and simply "Miss Dungeon."[208,209]

Sonberg also made very high-profile arrests for check forgery.

The most notable was the case of another Navy man—Marvin E. Lee. The AWOL Navy sailor was a notorious check forger who had been peppering the United States and Europe with phony checks for two years without being caught. An actual *Catch*

274

*Me* character, far more entitled to the moniker! But when Lee tried his hand in Eureka, his successful two-year run was undone.

Thanks to the system set up by Sonberg, local banks were primed for surveillance and monitoring for wanted check artists working their way around the country. Lee's routine, like that of virtually all check artists at the time, was to open a checking account with a small amount of cash, secure an immediate checkbook, then quickly write checks around town before moving on.

Lee wore uniforms from various branches of the military and used forged discharge paperwork to aid in his appearance of legitimacy when cashing checks, a key part of his success.

In March 1963, because of Sonberg's training, the United California Bank in Eureka alerted the detective when they suspected Lee had walked into their bank—he fit the profile of a man on a cautionary alert. Sonberg arrested him at a local motel soon after. In Lee's room they also discovered dozens of false identification cards, umpteen checkbooks and an instructional sheet! This how-to guide gave a list of pro tips on how to rip off banks using the three C's: calmness, courtesy and casualness, among other suggestions! And with this trove, police discovered a small wardrobe of military uniforms.

The man who had been hunted all over the United States, and as far away as Denmark and Iceland, was taken down in sleepy Eureka.[210,211,212] All others beware!

\*   \*   \*

Abagnale didn't stand a chance. He went to a local branch to open a checking account—a process that usually yields the aforementioned temporary checkbook from which a new account holder can start to draw funds. But the bank administrators were immediately suspicious and contacted Sgt. Sonberg's fraud and check detail with the Eureka Police. It was quickly determined that Abagnale had claimed to be a United States border agent when he checked into the Imperial 400 motel in a strange effort to secure a federal employee discount on his room at the hotel. Another dumb move. Because of this, the police alerted local FBI agent Richard Miller who also began to investigate.

They also issued a description of the highly distinctive car Abagnale was known to be driving—the bright yellow late-model Mustang with the word "Bandit" now stamped in large lettering on both front fenders. Not exactly a good way to blend in.

At some stage during his transcontinental adventure, the car had apparently been altered at a body shop. In addition to the word "Bandit" emblazoned along the side of the car, there was a weird emblem. It was an image of a masked man and a Derringer-type pistol firing several shots.[213] The car stood out so obviously it was a major factor in his rapid capture.

Special Agent Miller had spotted the distinctive car on Fifth Street but lost it in traffic. Miller radioed police headquarters for a roadblock in the vicinity and an all units broadcast. It was Sheriff's Detective Lee Templeton who spotted Abagnale soon after and brought him into custody—on June 21, 1965. Another Abagnale arrest by local law enforcement.

Among the items discovered in the yellow Mustang was a regulation police baton, raising concerns about what else the teenage fugitive had been up to on his travels.

Left: Frank W. Abagnale, aged 17 (in the squad car), when arrested in Eureka, California, June 1965. Right: Police inspecting the stolen car branded with "Bandit" and pistol motif. (Both photos Copyright 1965. *The Times Standard.* Used with permission.)

He was initially charged with impersonating an employee of the United States Department of Customs and Immigration.[198] Notably, his autobiography also took him to Eureka, where he claimed to have impersonated an FBI agent, escaping in the nick of time—but the reality is not quite as impressive or successful.

But he did make his first press appearance, including a photograph taken after his arrest, looking at the camera from the back seat of a squad car while being questioned. This made page 11 of the local *Eureka Humboldt Standard* on June 30, 1965.[213]

He was turned over to the U.S. Marshals and transported to Sacramento, where it was also determined that the car was stolen. This led to additional federal charges, including interstate transportation of a stolen car—VIN #5T07C157889, and NY plate WX 6944, for car buffs, or others who might wish to determine its fate.

The U.S. district attorney in Sacramento prepared to transfer the case to New York. The court had already contacted

Abagnale's father to make arrangements for his son's bail and transportation back to Mount Vernon, New York.[213] Frank Abagnale Sr. had made his way all the way to Sacramento for his son's court proceedings. By several accounts, Frank Sr. had hit hard times and could ill afford a significant bond, let alone the airfare. Court records show he now lived at 122 Collins Avenue in Mount Vernon. It was in the shadow of a spaghetti junction of highways, just around the corner from the recently constructed shopping mall called Cross County.

Bail was set at a single one-dollar bill, by the sympathetic United States Attorney, Cecil Poole. Satisfied with the token bail, he also agreed for Frank Sr. to personally accompany his son back east to New York, where the court proceedings would continue.[198] On July 6, Poole wrote to his New York counterpart that "the defendant will be returning to the East Coast in the company of his father who flew out here for the proceedings."

For reasons unclear, Abagnale has consistently maintained that he never saw or spoke to his father after he ran away from home at sixteen.[61,148,150] "Ever." He was emphatic. He said so on multiple occasions, including his oft-viewed Talks at Google, and even disputed a scene in the movie indicating that they had met again.[107] His disavowals are not true. This documented father-and-son reunion in Sacramento and cross-country return trip when he was seventeen contradicts that bizarre claim.

"If remorse and a guilty conscience of a father could somehow undo the sins of his son, I would gladly submit to the punishment I deserve," wrote Frank Sr. in a letter about his son sometime later, when Frank Jr. was back in jail again.[106]

On July 2, 1965, Abagnale was released on bond to Frank Sr. It was agreed that once back in New York State, the young man would live with Frank Sr. in Mount Vernon—also home to his eldest son, Frank Jr.'s older brother, Eugene "Jean-Paul" Francis

Abagnale.

This transcontinental flight may have been Abagnale's first taste of air travel, its glamor and its operations. A source of great inspiration. And quite an opportunity to gather information on airline processes—like deadheading, for example. Some are now speculating that this flight, likely on the government's dime, may have been the origins of his subsequent airline impersonations. Certainly, this dad and son trip would have made a great scene in Spielberg's film, but of course it was at odds with the constructed narrative of the grand hoax.

> *From the glacial age to the great age of atomic energy, con*
> *men have always found a way to earn a dishonest living.*
> *Beware of this newest type of confidence man ... the sharper*
> *who preys on the most up-to-date travelers in the Age of*
> *Air, the gentleman thief of the transcontinental airways.*
> Peter Beckett, *Con Men in the Atomic Age,* 1949[214]

\*   \*   \*

Back in New York, they were again a family divided. Frank Abagnale Jr. did not hang around his father's humble Mount Vernon abode—likely because the local police departments across Westchester County were looking to have a chat with him about the Bronx River Parkway checks. His mother, Paulette, was living only ten miles away in a more glamorous apartment complex. But Frank Jr. did not go there either. Instead, he made for the Town and Country Apartments on Mayflower Avenue in New Rochelle.[215] It was walking distance from Gordy's Steak House, which was celebrating its grand opening.

As well as his efforts to evade the Westchester County Police (then known as the Westchester Parkway Police), Abagnale appeared to have another mission. The ex-Navy man wanted to get back in uniform. The trip back from California did appear instrumental in transforming his career of crime—because very soon afterwards the police in Tuckahoe, New York, recorded one of Frank Abagnale's first documented appearances in a pilot's uniform.[199]

Had the inspiration come from his experience flying back from Sacramento? The Navy? Or by stories of the internationally hunted check forger Marvin Lee—the man who had been apprehended in Eureka with an array of uniforms to assist his scams and a list of instructions on perfecting a good con? Whatever the inspiration, within a fortnight of returning from California, Mr. Abagnale Jr. was seen wearing a pilot's uniform of his own.

We know that he had ordered some kind of uniform from the All-Bilt Uniform Company of 450 Sixth Avenue, Manhattan, the very same company that manufactured naval uniforms, airline uniforms, soda jerk's whites and what not. That uniform was shipped by first-class express postage to the address he gave them: Frank Abagnale c/o Gordy's Restaurant, 500 New Rochelle Road, Bronxville, New York. Abagnale was sure to be at Gordy's place for the pick-up.

An image of that very package, front and back, still exists on microfilm.[199] Although this packaging was empty when recovered among his possessions by the Tuckahoe police, it was almost certainly the airline uniform he was seen wearing shortly thereafter, and likely not a uniform with a soda jerk hat for flipping burgers at Gordy's Steak House.

Next, he was seen making several visits to a local tailor—Maresco's Tailor at 71 Columbus Avenue in Tuckahoe, where he used the services of expert tailor and proprietor, 75-year-old Ralph Maresco, a highly respected Italian immigrant. Presumably for minor alterations to his new costume. At the time, the basic airline uniform, supplied by All-Bilt, wasn't difficult to obtain. The tailoring and embroidering, even for legitimate pilots, was performed locally.

In the early 1960s, Tuckahoe, New York, also just happened to be the epicenter for production of airline wings—the custom badges and aviator pins that adorn uniforms. The Stoffel Seals company was less than a five-minute walk from Maresco's Tailor. It was the primary manufacturer of wings for the major airlines. Indeed, Stoffel held patents on airline wing making. Just the place Abagnale could have acquired the wings for his new uniform.

He was also making inquiries at an art gallery and lithograph maker near Fifth Ave Avenue in Manhattan, around the corner from Lenox Hill Hospital. We know this because he jotted down the details and the address on the back of the uniform package after it arrived at Gordy's. An art center was the kind of place that would be handy for someone trying to mint an ID badge.

It is not exactly clear where he first wore his newly tailored uniform and accessories, but there is a now-famous photograph of a young Frank Abagnale, apparently in uniform, posing with an airline stewardess against the backdrop of the New York skyline. He has the same appearance, age and build as when he was arrested in Eureka only weeks before.

Excitement may have been in the air for Frank Abagnale, but these precious days, working his grift at All-Bilt, Gordy's and the Tuckahoe tailor, would prove to be among his few remaining days of freedom for the rest of the 1960s.

On July 12, 1965, at 9:30 a.m., Abagnale was required to make an initial appearance before federal court in Manhattan on the stolen Mustang charges under the Dyer Act for interstate transportation of a stolen vehicle. He did appear and appealed to the court that he should be treated as a juvenile.

The date for the follow-up hearing was set for just a few days later. But he failed to show.

Missing again, a federal arrest warrant was issued on July 19, 1965.

The reason for his no-show was that the Tuckahoe police had already found the beatnik thief—he was back in custody again.[215] And when arrested he was not wearing his fashionable loafers and all-black attire—but a rather different costume.[199]

\*　　\*　　\*

After returning from California, Abagnale had successfully eluded the police in Westchester County for the first two weeks of July. Detective Sergeant Henry Norman of the Tuckahoe, New York, Police Department was diligently looking for Abagnale. Sgt. Norman would later become the first African-American police chief in Westchester County, and one of the first in the nation—with a plaque later unveiled in his honor in 2018. He was one in a long line of local law enforcement officers who quickly caught Abagnale, long before his capture by the FBI in November 1970.

Even before Abagnale absconded to California, Detective Sergeant Norman had been compiling evidence for a forgery case against him. Witnesses had reported seeing him driving his father's white Ford since returning to New York, but the police had not succeeded in locating him. They had already been watching the house on Jefferson Place in Tuckahoe, where Abagnale was known to visit friends, but Detective Norman had a new tip.

An informant told him that Abagnale had left some belongings behind at Maresco's Tailor shop and that the thief was very anxious to retrieve them from the premises. On July 15,

1965, Detective Norman was watching Maresco's, at 71 Columbus Avenue.

It was a stakeout.

On an exceptionally hot summer day, the detective sat patiently waiting, hoping the grifter would make an appearance. It was a solid lead. And it paid off. At 3:40 p.m. Abagnale was seen approaching the premises.

Bizarrely he was wearing a full pilot's uniform.

And he wasn't alone.

"The subject, when apprehended, July 15, 1965, was in the company of an airline stewardess," wrote Detective Sergeant Norman in his arrest report, "and [he] was attired in a pilot's uniform."[199]

The unsuspecting flight attendant was surely floored by the sudden commotion as the police swooped in to arrest her companion on the sidewalk before he even entered the premises. If she had high hopes for a relationship with the tall, dark and semi-good-looking pilot, they must have been dashed in an instant.

Abagnale appeared to have returned to Ralph Maresco's tailor shop to collect a black leather bag. A clichéd but essential accessory that would complete his pilot's outfit. Later, a search of the leather bag revealed some nondescript personal effects. But among them the detectives discovered one very odd item. Japanese-made handcuffs.

Also among the possessions recovered at Maresco's was the now-empty packaging from the All-Bilt Uniform Company that once contained a uniform. Two things are near certain. The first, that Maresco was tailoring Abagnale's new uniforms. And the second, that Maresco or someone else in the neighborhood had alerted Detective Sergeant Norman that the hustler was heading to pick up the items.

Abagnale had scammed many local stores in the area, seemingly even the tailor whose services he had used. Abagnale had passed Maresco a shady check for $40—it was drawn on a California bank. Despite his arrest in the Golden State, the young grifter had evidently kept a few checks from an account he opened while on his road trip the previous month.

Abagnale was placed under arrest and taken in for questioning. It was not clear what the young "pilot" was planning to do with handcuffs or the matching police billy club that had been recently recovered from the stolen Mustang.

Still wearing his uniform, he was initially processed at the Tuckahoe police station, where he told the police that he was employed as a trainee at Pam Am to account for the uniform and his visit to the tailor.

In the mid-1960s, scores of entry-level trainee positions were advertised by all the major airlines, calling for "neat and ambitious lads" eager for an airlines future.[216,217] No degree or experience needed! Most offered free travel as a glamorous perk even for ground staff, who also wore smart uniforms, similar to the aircrew.

"Flight privileges are yours if you're not afraid to meet the public," tantalized newspaper ads in the mid-1960s, "No degree or experience needed!"[216,217]

Perfect for someone with Abagnale's resumé. It was certainly a handy story for Abagnale to use as an explanation for his unusual attire. He had plenty to say and freely admitted to the forgeries.

"I admit giving checks to the Tuckahoe Camera Shop, Victoria Laundry and Maresco's Tailors," Abagnale wrote in his signed affidavit. "I know that I did wrong and I am willing to pay the people their money," he added.[199]

After making his full confession for the bad checks in

Tuckahoe, he was turned over to Detective Stephen Fischer of the Westchester County Police Department to answer the warrant for the larger sums stolen from the Bronx River Parkway service station. Still dressed in his Pan Am uniform, the fully costumed pilot moved from one stationhouse to another, and onward to the Westchester County jail. Quite a sight. He was already in custody in Westchester four days before he was due to appear in the Manhattan court on the federal stolen car charges.

In the face of overwhelming evidence, the Westchester County case against Abagnale for the Bronx River Parkway was wrapped up quickly. The hammer was dropped on July 22, 1965, just a week after his arrest. He was sentenced to three years for the forgery, to be served in the Great Meadow Correctional Institute in Comstock, New York—set to be confined there through July 13, 1968, unless paroled.

In the following months, other complainants stepped forward, including an innkeeper in Elmsford who claimed to have been scammed by Abagnale. But once informed that the grifter was serving a three-year sentence, the complainants agreed to drop their charges. Detective Sergeant Norman and the Tuckahoe police did the same. They had extensive evidence and a confession, but with the convict already heading for Great Meadow, justice was served, and complainants in Tuckahoe decided not to pursue all the additional charges.

But the still-pending federal stolen car charges filed in Sacramento had not been dropped. Abagnale had also signed a full confession in that case as well. Those charges had not yet been answered when he was transferred to Great Meadow for the conviction in Westchester, New York.

Abagnale's scheme to "take to the skies" in his pilot's ruse was foiled. It was over before it had even begun. There had been no cat-and-mouse chase. No "Agent Shea" on a five-year quest.

Detective Sergeant Henry Norman and the other local police had clipped his wings before he was even ready to take flight. No resemblance to the story that eventually appeared in Spielberg's film. But by then, lots of fantasy had been added in its stead.

Now he would have three years in Great Meadow to think over his thwarted plans.

\*   \*   \*

But two years later, on May 8, 1967, Abagnale was granted parole and another chance at freedom. The chance for a fresh start. Or to put his derailed schemes back into action.

His federal charges were still pending—but federal authorities knew he was under New York State parole supervision and agreed to the parole as they set a date for the stolen car charges. As a formality, U.S. Marshals officially arrested him at the Great Meadow Correctional Institute in Comstock at the time of parole and instructed him that the federal case was still ongoing. He was then released into the care of his mother, Paulette, on May 19, 1967.

That did not go well either.

"He came home and was writing checks a week later," his mother later wrote in exasperation.[106] And it was also not long before he was caught again. This time he was arrested in East Boston, Massachusetts, near Logan Airport.

It was on June 20, 1967, just weeks after being paroled and released into Paulette's custody, that Abagnale was picked up by Massachusetts State Troopers. Perhaps this was fodder for the story he later told Carson on *Tonight*—the fantastical tale of two buffoonish troopers who helped him with his payload in a quick-witted getaway at Logan Airport.

"They [two Massachusetts State Troopers] helped me get [the

stolen loot] out, load it into the car," he would tell Carson. But the cold reality is that the troopers arrested him close to Logan Airport for grand theft auto and two separate charges of small-time larceny by forgery.

He was sentenced to six months for the stolen auto. He was housed in the famous Charles Street Jail. On the larceny charges, he initially pleaded not guilty, and the case went to Superior Court in downtown Boston. Finally, on October 26, 1967, now nineteen-year-old Frank W. Abagnale entered a guilty plea in Suffolk, Massachusetts, Superior Court. He was given a suspended sentence of one year, two years of probation and ordered to pay restitution.[218,219] He had also violated his New York parole, and New York State parole officer Charley York also got his man for the parole violation. After serving a total of 128 days at the House of Correction in Massachusetts, just as his mother Paulette wrote in her letters, he was sent right back to Comstock, NY, on December 12, 1967.

Indeed, it was the letter by Paulette Abagnale in New York that initially led this author to the public records which burst the *Catch Me If You Can* bubble, once and for all. Those records revealed Abagnale was in Great Meadow Correctional Institute in Comstock and that there he stayed until his release on December 24, 1968.

But he showed no signs of reform after walking out of the prison gates.

"[He] was writing checks again three days after his release," his mother Paulette wrote not long afterwards.[106]

And within days of walking out of Great Meadow, Abagnale zeroed in on Paula Parks as she was simply going about her business on a Delta flight out of the Big Apple. When he boarded Paula's flight, he had still not answered his federal stolen car charges from 1965. He had slipped through the cracks.

\*　　\*　　\*

Importantly, at the time of his release from the facility in Comstock, the federal warrant was still active. Since Abagnale had already signed a sworn statement that he did, in fact, steal the car and drive it to Eureka in 1965, a quick disposition and sentencing seemed certain. However, this federal case had been incessantly delayed because of his other repeated offenses, and his incarceration by state-level New York authorities. Records show that federal authorities believed that Abagnale was still under the supervision of the New York State authorities, unaware he had been released.

It was not until January 27, 1969, that his federal case was reviewed. By that time, he had already commandeered another car and moved into the Parks family home, enjoying home-cooked meals and stealing from their checkbook.

Abagnale's file arrived on the desk of Assistant U.S. Attorney Leonard M. Marks, who went on to become an entertainment lawyer, representing the Beatles, Elton John, Billy Joel, Eddie Murphy and many others. On that day, Marks was under the impression that Abagnale was still under the tight supervision of the New York State authorities. So, he signed a *nolle prosequi*—the U.S. prosecutor's notice to abandon the case. Leonard Marks' action would still need to be confirmed by his boss. As an assistant U.S. attorney, he could only "recommend" the *nolle prosequi* in the Abagnale case.

The recommendation still had to go through channels and be decided upon by the United States Attorney for New York's Southern District, the famed Robert M. Morgenthau. But at no stage did anyone appear to determine the whereabouts of Abagnale. On February 27, 1969, Morgenthau signed the *nolle prosequi.* That made it official. Frank W. Abagnale was no longer of interest to federal authorities. By then he was already under arrest for serious crimes in Baton Rouge.

A federal sentence for his 1965 charges had just evaporated, likely without him even knowing it. He was also about to avoid another sentence at Angola for his crimes in Baton Rouge. A very, very lucky man. And his crimes would soon continue.

The *nolle prosequi* document did prove one other important point—that the federal authorities were *not* interested in Abagnale. He was certainly not wanted by *any* federal authorities. There was no ongoing hunt for the guy who later claimed, absurdly, that he was the youngest man ever to make the FBI's Top Ten Most Wanted list. A claim that was parroted by the movie studio in the days leading up to the release of *Catch Me If You Can.*

\*   \*   \*

At this juncture, it might be worth reflecting on the impossibility of his later claims—the grand hoax built in Houston. Taken as a whole, the real events between Tuckahoe, Boston and Baton Rouge mean that between the ages of sixteen and twenty, Abagnale had virtually no opportunity to do laps around the globe with Pan Am, or any other airline, and become a millionaire writing bad checks. The FBI was not chasing him. He wasn't working for nearly three years as a doctor, lawyer and professor. He wasn't, because he couldn't.

He had plenty of time to imagine it, though.

Essentially from June 21, 1965, to December 24, 1968, Frank W. Abagnale was, for the most part, behind bars. Before that, from December 23, 1964, through February 1965, he was in the Navy. The only exception was a brief parole in May of 1967 which led to almost immediate re-confinement in Massachusetts and another parole violation.[99] Again, after his release on Christmas Eve 1968, he was only free for about six weeks before he was once again confined in Baton Rouge between February 14, 1969, and June 17, 1969.

He was well and truly an adult for the subsequent crimes he committed—dressing as a pilot and passing Pan Am payroll checks—albeit only ten checks for $1,448.60. This also dissolves all ongoing claims that he was just a kid and did not know any better when he perpetrated all these crimes, or that if he started doing that at twenty-one, then he probably would not have done it.[32]

And then there is his curious claim that "I was actually just arrested once in my life, when I was 21 years old," as in his famous Talks at Google[107] and on many other occasions. Why? Apart from underlining his persona as a master thief who evaded detection, such a claim would also deflect any investigation of his *actual* arrest record with a long list of convictions. Those records, as we have proven, are the wind that knocks over the house of cards upon which the grand hoax is built. Everything caves in. By admitting he had been arrested—but only once—he likely dampened more critical investigation of his actual activities. Whatever his motives, there is no doubt that he has been successful in ensuring that his grand hoax has remained undetected.

\* \* \*

There was, however, one very curious event in 1968 while Abagnale was serving the remainder of his prison sentence.

Any serious researcher looking into Abagnale's life history to corroborate his claims would make an extensive search of newspaper records. Even diehard fans might seek out the countless newspaper reports he claimed had chronicled his international escapades in the mid-to-late 1960s. After all, he oft-claimed that there was a long-running "syndicated column in *The New York Times*" about him.[76] Researchers would not find much at all on any Abagnale over that period, apart from his arrest in Eureka, for car theft.[213]

But there was one rather strange report from another town in Northern California. Ukiah, California.[220]

Abagnale is not a common name, and the arrest of a young man by that name is obvious cause for interest. Especially when he gives his address as Larchmont, New York, the home of Paulette Abagnale. And especially when he is booked for "credit card forgery" and "unlawful conversion of a vehicle," a charge commonly applied when a rental car is not returned. What's more, the individual was posing as some sort of healthcare worker.

Importantly, the date of this newspaper report is April 1968. Records show that Larchmont's own Frank W. Abagnale Jr., was confined at the Great Meadow Correctional Facility at the time. But it is a curious story, nonetheless.

When the man was arrested in a local motel, he gave his name as Jean Francis Abagnale, according to the *Ukiah Daily Journal*. He claimed to be 25 years old and said he was a "therapist." He had arrived in Ukiah driving a '67 Pontiac Firebird. And he was with a child. [220]

"At the time Abagnale was arrested, he was accompanied by a seven-year-old Michigan girl," reported the local paper, also indicating the child's unsuspecting father in Michigan had just been alerted.[220]

"He [the father] had no idea as to his daughter's whereabouts until advised of Abagnale's arrest," the article reported.

Arrangements were made with the welfare department for the child's care in San Francisco until her father flew from his home in Jackson, Michigan, to reunite with her the following day. The father told authorities that he had given the man, who he believed to be a legitimate therapist, permission to take the girl east to New York City for treatment she required after a recent car accident. There was no explanation concerning how, or why, Abagnale and the child went in the opposite direction, and ended up 2,300 miles away among the California redwoods.[220]

Details of this case are tough to find. The identity of the Michiganders is concealed for obvious reasons, and it is not clear if the family pressed charges. That being the case, the person named as "Jean Francis Abagnale" was presumably released from custody. Today things would be different. The identity of the Larchmont imposter in Ukiah, also called Abagnale, is not mysterious—but this time it was clearly not Frank.

It is verging on bizarre that Larchmont, NY, an exclusive village inside the small town of Mamaroneck, seemed to have spawned another imposter. Whatever the case may be, Paulette Abagnale would have certainly received a steady stream of calls from law enforcement between 1965 and 1974.

*　　*　　*

It is not clear whether Frank W. Abagnale returned to visit either of his estranged parents or his three siblings when he was released from Comstock the day before Christmas, 1968. Or what spurred him to leave New York only days later. His mother said that he was writing bad checks just three days later. That would be enough reason to leave.

A decade later, long after his father's death, Abagnale would assure audiences that his parents were proud of him—and not at all disappointed in his career choice.[135]

"After all, out of four children, I'm the most successful one," Abagnale said.[135]

But his agent, Mark Zinder, saw a very strained relationship between Abagnale and his mother. He was with Abagnale around the time he made that statement about his family in 1980. In particular, Mark recalls the very cold reception Abagnale received when they visited his mother. They were passing through on a speaking tour, and Abagnale invited Mark on the drive up to see Paulette, who was still living in the Larchmont, New York, neighborhood, less than 20 miles north of Manhattan. It was a very strange visit.

"Frank was decked out in his finest clothes. Clearly dressed to impress," said Mark. "I knew his silk-lined pants cost $600 a pair. It was obvious that he was really trying hard."

By then, Paulette had met her new love, dentist Dr. Joseph Carlucci. Mark remembers visiting the nice residence. Paulette welcomed them politely but was guarded and reserved. Mark could sense the uncomfortable tension in the air.

Even at the time, Mark thought it was odd to see how little warmth there was between them.

"His mother was very cold and very standoffish," Mark recalled. "The conversation was so forced and strained. She did not seem pleased to see him. It felt weird and really awkward."

Abagnale talked everything up as usual. But Paulette did not look that impressed.

Frank's so-called "autobiography" had just been released. Paulette would have known it was almost completely fabricated. It sadly revealed that he had not changed at all. Her son was still living in a fantasy world. He was even duping his young agent, who seemed none the wiser. She certainly did not say anything to give the game away to Mark. Maybe she thought Mark knew the content was fantasy. Although the strange coldness of the interaction was obvious, Mark was oblivious to the deeper undercurrents at the time.

"In retrospect, I can see how Frank was trying to win her approval, but she was wary and did not seem to trust him," said Mark. "Now I understand why—knowing just how many times she had been called by the police, informing her Frank has been arrested yet again. Over and over. For ten years. She was probably still waiting for the next call. At the very least, she must have been expecting his latest ruse to be discovered."

Paulette had seen how easily Frankie's schemes had been discovered in the past. How quickly he had been arrested when he crossed the line of the law. She was likely anticipating the renewed embarrassment and inevitable exposure of his latest con. Perhaps she was just relieved that he had not yet crossed the line of the law again. Or perhaps she marveled at just how long Frankie had managed to fool people this time. But, at least from what Mark observed, Paulette did not seem particularly pleased or proud that day.

\*   \*   \*

All of these facts are contrary to the simple story the grifter later concocted. According to his autobiography, at 16 years old, in June 1964, he ran away from home. Soon after he was jetting around the world. In countless public talks, including WGBH and the recent Talks at Google, he said he had been attending the private Iona Preparatory School in New Rochelle, right through the tenth grade. This claim is listed on Wikipedia, so it is assumed to be true. Yet Frank Abagnale Jr. is nowhere to be found among the freshman and sophomore classes on inspection of the 1962-63 and 1963-64 Iona Prep yearbooks.

Perhaps the most famous Iona Prep alumni of the period is iconic musician singer-songwriter Don Mclean of *American Pie* fame. When this author recently contacted his management, Mclean who graduated in 1963, said he had no recollection of any Abagnale. It was not a large school, the kind of place where classmates would be known to one another.

\*     \*     \*

Although Abagnale had slipped through the cracks of the judicial system many times, that was nothing compared to the much larger cracks in public scrutiny that allowed the mythical stories he created to be celebrated and perpetuated. How could the grand hoax go unquestioned for so long—even when the truth was obvious?

*Beauty is truth, truth beauty—that is all*
*Ye know on Earth, and all ye need to know.*
John Keats, 1819

Frank Abagnale regales a packed house at
Stephen F. Austin University, 1981.
Image from SFA Stone Fort Yearbooks.
Copyright cleared, East Texas Research
Center, SFA University.

# CHAPTER 18
# The Tooth Fairy

*I have always found that I had to be a fake to find*
*someone who cares.*
Frank W. Abagnale. Letter dated March 2, 1969,
Baton Rouge, LA[106]

By early 1981, he was a sensation. Evel Knievel may have twice filled the Houston Astrodome and flown his motorcycle on occasion. But Abagnale was jumping his version of Mack trucks night after night, without fear of broken bones. His hunger for attention seemed insatiable, and so was the appetite of his audiences. Photographs in newspapers from the era show Abagnale surrounded with excited students—blissfully unaware that another group of students in Nacogdoches and their criminal justice professor were planning to take him down.

"By then, Frank must have been doing over two hundred lectures a year," Mark Zinder estimated. A good portion of Abagnale's lecture circuit was taking him to universities and colleges.[57]

Even before his book was released in 1980, aided by friendly Texan media, Abagnale could draw massive crowds—such as the 1,300 who showed up to hear him in El Paso, Texas.[221] But the book took things into overdrive.

"Large crowds weren't unusual," Mark explained. "Afterwards, he would be mobbed by college students desperate to get an autograph and a handshake."

At almost every talk, he would begin by saying something to make each audience feel special.

"I don't often talk about my life," or words to that effect, were Abagnale's typical opener, even though that is all he *ever* seemed to do! Then he would add something like, "I usually only take the podium to talk about technical procedures to stop white-collar crime, but tonight I have been asked to tell you something about my life." The audience immediately had the impression that they, unlike others, were about to get the low-down on a secret life. Many variants of the "I don't often talk about my life" theme can be seen today in countless recorded talks that have been uploaded on YouTube. Mark recalls that it created the illusion that Abagnale was up to his eyeballs in consulting work, and barely had time to talk to people about his life.

"But he said that almost every time—and then would always talk about himself," Mark explained. "It was a part of his routine. He was so busy giving pretty much the same talk that I saw no time for all the consulting he implied he was doing," said Mark.

In Abagnale's crazy maze of mirrors, the con man may have been confident in the knowledge that he *was* telling a half-truth when he said I *don't often talk about my life*—because most of it *wasn't* actually the true story of his life—as the group of criminal justice students from SFA State University in Nacogdoches would soon reveal.

Abagnale played up his role as a jet-set playboy and international man of mystery. And he always dressed the part. Whether it was a suit and tie for the bankers or a turtleneck for the students—he dressed with suave sophistication. Almost always with a jacket. And in his top pocket, what appeared to be an expensive pocket square was really a pair of women's silk panties.

The panties were part of one of his favorite stage routines.

"I'd never been arrested and mugged and printed," Abagnale would lie, explaining that frustrated federal authorities, those chasing him all over the land, had to resort to hand-drawn sketches for his FBI Most Wanted posters. Hand-drawn! He then told his audience how he loved to go into the Miami post office to check out the artist's impression of what they thought he looked like—which he claimed showed him impeccably dressed, with a colorful silk handkerchief in his breast pocket.[222]

So his audience of willing believers now had a mental image of young Mr. Abagnale admiring an artist's rendition of himself on the wall of a Miami post office. Next he would delight in pointing to the silk handkerchief in his breast pocket. Then beam as he pulled out a pair of women's panties—like a magician.

"Remember," he would remind his audience, "Everything is not what it seems."[223]

Indeed.

The men in the crowd especially would hoot when they saw him waving the silk panties in the air. Abagnale would stare at the panties.

"Makes you want to catch a cold or a flu," he would add.[224] He often admitted that women were his only vice—apart from crime.

Not everyone was impressed.

"The faces of the mostly female audience turned [red] when Abagnale drew from his lapel a pair of ladies underwear," wrote journalist Jim Schlosser on one such occasion, who was not impressed with the bawdy antics or Abagnale's portrayal of women, especially at an event where they comprised the majority of his audience.[62]

But mostly audiences lapped it all up. And still wanted more.

"There was no shortage of co-eds eager for Frank's attentions," said Mark, who was focused on trying to manage the ever-increasing demands of Abagnale's schedule, as they climbed from one jet to the next.

"I'm a non-conformist," Abagnale said at the time, reflecting on his popularity. "Everybody loves a rogue. Everyone, down to the most conservative individual, would like to have done what I did. But most people don't have the opportunity or the guts."[134]

Although not everyone was fooled, they seemed to be in a significant minority.

Like Paula, Doris Ashcraft saw through him immediately. The Houston-area resident certainly had her doubts and wrote to her local Baytown newspaper, expressing her concerns after seeing Abagnale regaling crowds at the newly opened San Jacinto Mall.[225] By the 1980s, the malls of America were social and cultural hubs. They were beacons of community activity, gathering places for teenagers and destinations for consumers of all ages—like the old Sherman Oaks Galleria made famous in *Fast Times at Ridgemont High*. Just the place for Abagnale to make appearances and sign and sell copies of *Catch Me If You Can* to passing shoppers ahead of his various speaking gigs.

In May 1981, learning that The Great Imposter was book-signing in the San Jacinto Mall, Houston-based KTRH radio held a live broadcast, and curious shoppers watched and listened as disc jockey Jim Taite interviewed the dazzling grifter. Doris Ashcraft was looking on. So was local journalist Chuck Raison.

"He entertained passers-by with his stories of younger years when he impersonated an airline pilot, a doctor, a lawyer, a college sociology professor and millionaire," Raison wrote dutifully.

The night deposit box out of order caper at Boston's Logan airport was a favorite with the crowd that day. The con man's tale was getting taller, and now the payload had grown to $32,000 in cash, too heavy to lift off the curb without the help of two Massachusetts State patrolmen.[226]

But Doris Ashcraft thought it was ridiculous.

"I wonder if Frank Abagnale is trying to con the public," wrote Doris, concerned about the perpetual mindless adoration.[225] Although Abagnale had expressed his apparent regret, his focus was on his *own* losses—lost youth and missing the prom, with no consideration of his victims.

"Does he really consider himself a loser? Will his story be a deterrent to white-collar crime?" Doris asked. "Ultimately, will Frank Abagnale be admired as a winner or scorned as untrustworthy?"

Why did so few see that the emperor had no clothes?

She ended by cautioning that Abagnale's story "presents an unscrupulous individual who 'won' in the beginning and in the end!"

But the emperor had nothing to fear. The evidence that supported Doris Ashcraft's correct intuition—provided by Stephen Hall in *San Francisco Chronicle*—was lost in predigital history.

Instead, the emperor's full glory had been just displayed nationally a month before. In another landmark moment, Abagnale had just graced the highly venerated pages of the *Weekly World News* on April 7, 1981. The famed black-and-white printed tabloid, once ubiquitous on the checkout racks of supermarkets and convenience stores, ran a full-page story on Abagnale's daring exploits. The Great Imposter article celebrated Abagnale's most outlandish claims yet—that his escape from the Atlanta Federal Penitentiary was a feat so rare, he said, that there was now a *plaque on the prison wall* to commemorate the event![227]

It was fabulous media exposure. *The Weekly World News*

enjoyed a circulation of well over a million in 1981, with headline stories including "Bigfoot Touched Me" and "Blazing UFO Blasts Town," so Abagnale's story likely looked to be one of the more highbrow legitimate items. When placed next to ads for slenderizing foil bodysuits and "UFO in China Linked with Pilot's Disappearance" in the same issue, the idea that the federal correction officers' union in Atlanta chipped in to buy a plaque to commemorate Abagnale surely seemed semi-plausible!

The checkout tabloid also included legitimate photographs of him appearing on *To Tell the Truth* and various talk shows, which no doubt added to the credibility. Mark had provided a panel of images from their press kit, which also included Abagnale's appearance on the *Toni Tennille Show* with actress Catherine Bach and, of course, on Carson's *The Tonight Show*.

But one real stamp of legitimacy had already been earned. *The Weekly World News* may have been a wink and a nod, but a speaking slot at the International Platform Association was a living certificate of authenticity. It was a major reason that few had questioned Abagnale's claims—including Mark Zinder.

\*    \*    \*

The International Platform Association (IPA) annual meeting was a highly prestigious national event of enormous cultural influence—as mentioned, it was the equivalent of an invitation to give a TED talk today. Even to be on that stage was a ringing endorsement. It usually also meant that "fame may be just around the corner."[228]

Abagnale had already given a talk at the IPA conference in Washington, DC, in 1978—where he originally met Mark Zinder. The IPA conference followed just a few months after his first appearance on *Tonight*. Perhaps merely sitting next to Johnny

Carson had been enough to score the prestigious podium spot at IPA.

Journalist John Walter had been on scene in DC for the 1978 meeting.

"When Frank Abagnale speaks of appearing on *The Tonight Show* with Johnny Carson, everybody quiets down and listens. He's made it! He's even going to sub-host for Johnny soon!" wrote Walter.[228]

Abagnale later claimed he was voted in the top five IPA speakers that year, although records show he did not make the list of top twenty speakers in the actual post-conference attendee survey.[229] No matter. Given the cultural influence of the IPA, how celebrated it was at the time, word traveled quickly—and fame and legitimacy did indeed follow.

"The IPA was such a big deal. That was one of the things that clinched it for me. Plus that he told everyone he worked for the FBI," said Mark. "In all the time that we were together—and we were together a lot—I never actually saw or heard him interact with the FBI on any level. But I heard him talk about it on stage—almost every day. And that had a big influence," he added.

The only direct interaction with law enforcement that Mark ever recalled was with Abagnale's parole officer.

"We were out driving in Frank's Mercedes when he unexpectedly pulled up outside a building without preamble and announced that we were waiting for his parole officer," Mark recalled. "Before the officer got in the car, Frank coached me on what to say if the guy asked me any questions."

The parole officer climbed into the convict's shiny Mercedes and the three men drove across Houston. It was likely not every day that the parole officer was picked up in such style. What a scene.

Mark had no idea why Frank had deliberately brought him

along to meet his parole officer without prior explanation. At the time, the encounter fit Abagnale's narrative that he was working at the behest of law enforcement to make amends—this appeared to be his handler. In hindsight, Mark suspects his presence was to add legitimacy and impress on the officer that Frank was gainfully employed.

The identity of this parole officer is not clear, as Jim Blackmon had retired from that role in 1979. Although the officer almost certainly had full knowledge that his parolee's claims were fabricated, lying to audiences was not against the law. Abagnale certainly had made a giant leap from his days at Camp Manison in Friendswood, on the south side of town just a few years before.

"It's only with hindsight that many of these things make more sense," said Mark. "There were so many clues in plain sight—but he usually had an answer for everything."

Like the dossier used in the press kit. There were so many signs that it was faked, but it was easy to find reasons for the little things. Still, there were some things that Mark Zinder felt more uncomfortable with than others. Like the so-called real photos of Abagnale masquerading in various professions.

"I actually took some of those," said Mark, pointing to the image of the college professor in Utah, "because he told me he did not have the originals. We just needed some visuals. No harm in that, he told me."

No one seemed to notice that Utah college kids were dressed in fashions at least a decade ahead of the time. In all the photographic images, even those of imposter events he claimed occurred in the mid-1960s, Abagnale sported the same generous sideburns that had not made their wide cultural appearance until the 1970s.

It wasn't as though Abagnale didn't still openly bend the rules occasionally, but he always made it seem like harmless fun. He had a fake police badge and used it. Sometimes to get around traffic tickets, nothing serious. He even admitted as much to audiences. Just a lark. Mark saw it too. Abagnale even told a story that he pretended to "arrest" a man trying to sell stolen stereo speakers, so the man would hand over the "hot" merchandise before making a run for it, leaving the goods with Abagnale. He laughed as he confided with audiences that he had not lost his touch.[134]

"I put a lot of it down as part of his performance act. Maybe I just didn't want to think about it. Everything was going so well," said Mark.

But it was Abagnale's high-profile IPA appearance that had cast the most long-lasting shadow of legitimacy for Mark. That IPA appearance had also caught the attention of someone else who was far less impressed—military veteran and former law enforcement officer, Professor William Toney in Nacogdoches, Texas. And he smelled something sour.

\* \* \*

In 1981, 68-year-old professor, William "Bill" Toney, may not have been among the million subscribers reading the *Weekly World News* stories of the "Zombies of Horror Castle" and "The Great Imposter" in the 1981 April issue. But he had already started clipping and collecting a large amount of other more legitimate material on the self-styled imposter. These items, and everything else he discovered on Frank W. Abagnale Jr., all found their way into a large accordion file.

Bill Toney was a professor of criminal justice in Texas's public university system at the Stephen F. Austin (SFA) campus in Nacogdoches. He was in the U.S. Army in his youth and re-enlisted in the U.S. Navy during World War II. Toney had decades of experience in law enforcement. He had been a high-ranking federal officer in the United States customs and immigration border patrol service, a probation officer for the state of Texas, and a licensed private investigator.

He was a straight shooter in every sense. Literally. He won national marksmen contests and officiated at the 1984 Olympic Games. But he was also a highly respected figure in his community, a man beyond reproach.

Like Mark Zinder, Bill Toney was a huge fan of the IPA annual conference. He attended on a regular basis and was also an invited speaker himself. His experience in law enforcement and the justice system made him highly skeptical of Abagnale's claims.

But then came the last straw.

On November 17, 1981, the cockerel strode onto Toney's turf. The students may have been delighted, as Abagnale took the stage of the SFA University's Grand Ballroom in Nacogdoches, but Toney was not.

Abagnale regaled the crowd of young SFA students with his usual tales and bravado. He even threw in one of his favorites—the "panty trick"—pulling a pair of women's panties out of his top pocket and waving them proudly on cue. For the con man, it was just another day, another fistful of dollars. But for Bill Toney, the performance only reinforced the professor's concerns about Abagnale's credentials as a top "crime consultant"—and his doubts about Abagnale's legitimacy in general.

Critical appraisal was part of Professor Toney's 1981-82 academic curriculum, as one of the country's top criminal justice degree programs. He challenged his students to differentiate between facts and falsehoods. He encouraged them to consider that in both criminal justice and popular culture, things are not always as they appear to be—whether on the street, the courthouses, or in corrections, credulity is a dangerous thing.

Several of Bill Toney's students had asked him if they could receive course credit for attending Abagnale's lecture. This was not an uncommon request at the time. Indeed, students from a wide range of institutions would attend Abagnale's lectures and take notes for assignment credits. Since Abagnale professed to work for "the Bureau," he appeared to be a well-placed authority and role model for students on the value of integrity. Even high school students attended Abagnale's lectures to learn about marketing skills.[230]

Left: Frank Abagnale waving a pair of women's panties during a lecture to students at Stephen F. Austin (SFA) University in 1981, Nacogdoches, Texas; Right: Criminal justice professor William "Bill" Toney—former federal officer and private investigator —lecturing at SFA University. (Images from SFA Stone Fort Yearbooks, Toney Family Archives. Copyright cleared, East Texas Research Center, SFA University. Prof Toney photo credit, J. Stotts.)

"On that score, he was an ideal candidate," joked Mark. "His ability to market himself was phenomenal, long before I came on the scene. Of course, marketing was not what he was formally lecturing on."

Bill Toney was not impressed by the request to include Abagnale in his course materials. But he saw an opportunity. The fair-minded professor offered a compromise and set his students a new assignment. They should indeed attend Abagnale's lecture, take notes, and study everything he said in detail. Then they should apply critical appraisal and research every statement the self-proclaimed con man made.

Frank William Abagnale, said Professor Toney, was an ideal case study. And so he challenged his class to verify The Great Imposter's claims. It became a shared task. The students became more and more enthusiastic as they realized what they had found—or more particularly, what they had *not* been able to find. Professor Toney also assisted with working the phones and requesting public documents.

By the middle of 1982, Toney and his band of students had been unable to corroborate any of Abagnale's wild tales and found multiple sources who debunked most of his claims. They even used federal court records to challenge Abagnale's wild exaggerations about the numbers of forged Pan American payroll checks.

The students were chomping at the bit to share their findings, and Toney had the perfect forum. The IPA—the platform that had helped Abagnale make it in the first place.

Bill Toney had been invited to give his own talk at the 1982 International Platform Association in Washington, DC. This seemed the most impactful way to get their message out. He had his students' full blessing. And he would give them full credit for the work. It was decided.

The IPA was a forum for truth, which had somehow got hijacked along the way. It was time to set things right.

And so, the well-respected professor took the stage at IPA in August 1982 to discuss the veracity of Abagnale's claims—and raise concerns that they had all been hoodwinked. He destroyed Abagnale's tales, line by line.[231] The evidence he presented to support the work included new sources his students had uncovered, as well as ground previously turned over by Hall and Perry in their still overlooked efforts to debunk the con man.[48,56] While Toney had not located all of the available federal court records, he found enough to know that Abagnale's conviction was based on low dollar amounts in bad checks, not millions.

Toney explained how his students had called representatives at the large corporations Abagnale claimed were paying him ten million dollars a year in crime prevention, including Sears, J.C. Penney, Chase Manhattan Bank and American Airlines.[231]

"None said they were," said Toney, "although Abagnale made that claim in a speech at many colleges."

The IPA could maketh, but it might also breaketh, and Toney and his students hoped that this might put an end to the clearly false claims, not just about the con man's past, but also his false claims about the present.

By that time, the spielmeister con man's reputation was of legendary proportions—it was no small feat for Toney to attempt to debunk the myth. Abagnale was even already featured in *academic* textbooks. The educational publishing house, Scholastic Books, published a book called *Great Imposters* in 1982.[232] Alongside dozens of known historical figures, were the claims from Abagnale's press kits and autobiography—merely condensed and included as fact. Sensational claims in the *Weekly World News* are one thing, but once Scholastic Books and criminal justice textbooks reprinted falsehoods, efforts to disabuse deception became exceptionally difficult.

Bill Toney and his students had presented the truth on a platter. They had started a serious ripple that was about to hit Abagnale and his young agent, Mark Zinder. Although the story was picked up by sections of the press over the summer of 1982, the effects did not really start to reverberate until the academic year started again in the fall—when the college campus speaking events ramped up again.

*     *     *

Over the summer, unaware of Toney's campaign against his client, Mark Zinder had already planned a massive campaign for the National Association for Campus Activities (NACA) conferences. That included regional NACA promotional events and a string of bookings across college campuses, culminating in the high-profile annual NACA conference, which was to be held in Baltimore on February 17, 1983.

Abagnale was set to be one of the top-line keynote speakers at these events. It is difficult to overstate the reach and impact of NACA. By 1982, the organization maintained a thousand university and college members, with over six hundred associated firms representing some of the best in entertainment, recreation, performing arts and fine arts. With millions of dollars on the line, as well as stardom potential, scores of aspiring entertainers and their agents would clamber to NACA every year.

Careers could be made through NACA. Linda Ronstadt had shot to stardom after the NACA 1971 annual conference, for example. Mark Zinder knew the power of NACA, and it was a core part of the 1982-1983 strategy for Abagnale and Associates.

Most universities invested heavily in campus activities with large budgets, as Mark had administered for the University of Southern Alabama when he had been a student. Regional colleges would join forces at the convention and block-book talent to save money on travel and expenses. Most performers would drop their one-event prices significantly if schools banded together and block-booked several dates in the same geographic area. Lilah Lohr, a journalist for the *Baltimore Evening Sun*, described the frenzied level of NACA buzz over peddling and pushing talent each year: "[Days of] non-stop showing, selling and signing culminates in nine hours of razzle-dazzle trading that would put the commodity futures market to shame as bidding schools form cooperative buying blocks and dicker over dates and dollars," she wrote.[233]

It had seemed like a sure thing for Abagnale and the Mark Zinder Agency—or so Mark thought.

He had even already secured a conference booth for Baltimore—which would be not far from the internationally famous talent agency International Creative Management representing Linda Ronstadt, and the elite Hollywood-based William Morris Agency. It did not come cheap.

"I had already personally invested $20,000 of my own funds in the event," said Mark. "and I had to take out a loan to do it."

Because Abagnale and Mark's other major client, The Amazing Kreskin, was regularly filling up large venues, Mark was easily able to secure a $15,000 ($40,000 today) bank business loan for the Mark Zinder Agency. It had seemed a pretty sure thing, and Mark was expecting a strong return on the investment.

"I then put up $5,000 of my own cash to seal the deal," said Mark, "which was basically every nickel I had to my name."

\* \* \*

As the new academic year ramped up, so did Abagnale's college circuit keynote events. Mark attended many of his lectures, and it was vital for him to attend both regional and national NACA conferences, to showcase several of his clients and lock in signings for more events into 1983. By now, Abagnale was one of the top-billing speakers at these meetings.

At that point, Mark had not heard any of the rumblings after Toney's IPA expose and Abagnale never mentioned anything. So, when he went to set up his booth for a regional NACA event in Texas that fall, Mark was unaware of Bill Toney's findings, or that his client's credibility was in serious question.

There were a number of students on the showroom floor helping to set up before the official opening of the NACA event. But there was a small group of four poking around Mark's booth, showing particular interest in Abagnale's promotional materials complete with glossy images of his many TV appearances and select newspaper features.

"Is this Abagnale's booth?" asked one, although the answer was obvious.

"Yes, it is," Mark replied. "I'm his agent," he added, assuming that they were looking for autographed materials like so many others. But they had an altogether different agenda.

"Have you heard?" asked that same student.

"Heard what?" Mark replied, wondering where this was going.

"Oh, nothing," was the response.

"No, no, no—you started, so please finish," Mark insisted, asking once more for them to explain themselves. But he already had a very uneasy feeling.

"I really shouldn't say," said the student, who actually looked quite pleased to say, "but, don't you know that Abagnale is a fraud?"

"What do you mean?" Mark said, confused by the uncharacteristically hostile attitude to his client, who was usually a fan favorite with the students.

"His story isn't true. He's conning everyone!" exclaimed the student, no longer pretending not to be excited.

Mark had come face-to-face with some of Toney's students

from SFA State University. The student gleefully explained how they had researched Abagnale. How they had discovered that many of his claims were not true. How they worked with Professor Toney. And how they were looking forward to their professor confronting Abagnale with the evidence. They couldn't hide their enthusiasm.

A different student had picked up one of the glossy 8x10 photos of Abagnale.

"Believing in Frank Abagnale is like believing in the Tooth Fairy," he said, tapping his forefinger into the con man's eyes. "You, sir, are representing the Tooth Fairy!" he exclaimed as they all burst out laughing.

*"Actually, I haven't changed. All the needs that made me a criminal are still there. I have simply found a legal and socially acceptable way to fulfill those needs.*
*I'm still a con artist.*
Frank W. Abagnale, 1980[87]

# CHAPTER 19
# The Truth Affidavit

*The man is not an imposter, he is a liar.*
Kenneth C. DeJean, 1981 Assistant District
Attorney, Baton Rouge[114]

As the students drifted off chortling to each other, Mark just stood there dazed. He was left wondering if they were playing some kind of crazy prank. They were certainly cocky but did not seem to be joking. His mind was momentarily lost in the crazy maze of mirrors—wondering if he had been on the wrong side of the truth without realizing it.

Bill Toney had been on the same speaker circuits with Frank Abagnale before, and their paths had crossed tangentially through the same crime prevention programs. And based on what the students had just told him, Mark realized it was well within the realm of possibility that Toney might plan to continue his truth quest publicly on the NACA stage. He had to find Abagnale to let him know that they were on the warpath. And to find out what was going on.

But Abagnale was nowhere to be found. A no-show.

Mark's most reliable client just hadn't turned up. No explanations. Mark had no idea where Abagnale was. He started dialing Abagnale's office every ten minutes but got no response.

Mark could only assume that his client was avoiding a confrontation and wanted no part in a faceoff. But was that because he had no interest in debate? Or did he actually have something to hide? At that point Mark had no idea. Abagnale must have known that trouble was brewing but clearly decided not to tell him.

Mark soon learned that Toney's revelation at IPA had already started filtering out to some university campuses in the autumn of 1982. Those that had lined up Abagnale for speaking engagements were already rethinking the decision. Some passed on the con man. Others with impending, already-booked lectures pondered other options. But the Abagnale sideshow was still in demand—some wanted to listen because of the controversy, others just wanted to listen.

The University of South Carolina had a novel idea—a truth affidavit. They asked Abagnale to sign an official document attesting to the truth of the content of his lecture—a simple request for a now reformed con man.

The school officials even gave Abagnale an out.

Even if he did not sign, the scheduled speech could still proceed with his agreed $2,500 speaker's fee. In that case, the university would require a pre-lecture announcement to audience members. They would be informed that Abagnale "had not promised *to tell the truth.*" Quite similar to the way major social media outlets today place labels over videos, tweets and posts with dubious content.

In a strange, ironic symmetry, the last four words of the proposed pre-lecture disclosure—*To Tell the Truth*—conjured echoes of the first truth affidavit that he had "signed" on the television show of the same name, five years earlier. But this time he was faced with a real document from an academic institution rather than a light-hearted performance on a game show.

Abagnale refused to sign it.

Insulted, he canceled the event.

It was a slap in the face, he said. The press reported that the con man speaker was retreating "under fire."[231]

"He was not taking my calls," said Mark recently, "and I was quickly losing confidence in the confidence man."

\*     \*     \*

Within two weeks, Abagnale had also canceled his highly marketed gig at Georgia Southwestern State University. It was to be a lecture in the university's Jackson Hall, as part of its prestigious Autumn Convocation Series. Mark was hearing from his college contacts and getting increasingly worried about his client's future on the college circuit, not to mention the serious implications for his own business.

In a letter to Georgia Southwestern administrators, Abagnale wrote he was canceling "because a presentation at a college opens me up to a great deal of unnecessary controversy." This raised clear questions in the press about the veracity of the claims in his book *Catch Me If You Can* as well as all his lectures.[231]

Not long afterwards Abagnale announced he was canceling *all* university talks indefinitely. Had he jumped the shark? Would he disappear into the Texas sunset? Start painting limited edition artwork, like Evel?

We know that's not what happened.

As Abagnale was threatening to close down his entire college circuit, the con man came up with a new narrative and a new excuse—which was a clear attempt to place himself back on the high ground.

"[My cons] are not something to which young impressionable minds should be exposed," Abagnale wrote in the letter canceling all his college speaking engagements. The report in the *Columbus Daily Enquirer* was clearly cynical. In his litany of boastful exploits, he had never previously shown any concern about sharing his exploits with students.[231] In fact, that's how it all began. He had been doing it since at least 1976! Why now, just when his claims were imploding, did he suddenly consider "impressionable" minds?

Reporter John Dagley wasn't buying it. When Dagley phoned Abagnale directly for a comment, the con man would not concede he had engaged in deception about his imposter claims but spoke in suggestive generalities.

"As one gentleman said to me, 'If you didn't do all these things, and you've made all this money you've made in advances, royalties and speaking engagements, then you are in fact the greatest con man,'" Abagnale said to the reporter.

"As he was talking over the telephone," Dagley wrote at the end of his article, "it was impossible to tell if Abagnale was smiling as he said that."

Was the con man finally telling the truth? Dagley may have thought so. And appeared to want his readers to know it, too.

*   *   *

Mark did not know he was dealing with recurring behavior. Abagnale had been careful to downplay any bad press he'd had in the past. No one seemed to recall the negative reports by Hall and Perry, several years before. Mark had still been a senior in college and did not even know about it. Nor did he know that this was the third time that Abagnale had canceled speaking engagements when the heat was on—only to return to the limelight when things cooled off. He had done so after Hall's piece in the *San Francisco Chronicle*[53] and after Perry's in-depth

317

article in *The Daily Oklahoman*.[85]

Abagnale simply made a temporary withdrawal from the trouble zone and moved on to where negative press had not penetrated. But he had always miraculously bounced back. And would do so again.

In fact, there were bookings in other venues, despite the college cancellations in late 1982. Abagnale was still popular with bankers and business backslappers. Toney's message had not really touched that world.

On Thursday, December 9, 1982, he entertained a crowd of almost 1,200 at the San Antonio Convention Center. It was the annual holiday banquet of the Greater San Antonio Chamber of Commerce. Evidently, there were no impressionable minds that needed shielding there. And everyone seemed oblivious to the college campus firestorm. Abagnale had them hollering with laughter—especially with his story of how he scammed the hooker with a bad check.

"I never did get a chance to ask her if she thought it was worth it," he chuckled.[234] He often claimed that he had given back every penny of the 2.5 million dollars he took through his con games but joked that the hooker was the only exception.

The adoration of a crowd filled with members of San Antonio's elite seemed to be a soothing balm.

"He had hardly missed a beat," said Mark.

In January 1983, Abagnale was still thrilling crowds as they dined on smothered steaks and pecan pie at a Louisiana Chamber of Commerce meeting where he was reported to "steal the show."[235] He was equally well-received in Tennessee, where he "fascinated audiences."[236] There was no mention of the controversy he had left behind in Georgia and South Carolina. Evel was back on his bike!

On the back of a series of highly acclaimed gigs with the

chambers of commerce crowds, Abagnale was riding high. Mark wondered if Abagnale was already missing the adoration of the young female students who mobbed him on the college circuit. The bankers and businessmen did not give him quite the same reception!

But word had traveled quickly along the vast networks of North American college campuses. In early 1983, the University of Michigan newspaper also wrote a piece about Toney's findings and reaffirmed that Abagnale was quitting the university lecture circuit.

"The cancellations came after William Toney, criminology professor at Stephen F. Austin University, in Texas, told a Washington audience that Abagnale's a bigger imposter than thought," said the report. The piece cited Toney's research outlining Abagnale's false claims of having passed as a doctor, an assistant attorney general and a college professor.[237] It was quickly becoming evident that Abagnale's claims were all foam, no beer, all icing, no cake. Groups were taking notice. People were talking.

Mark had admitted to reporter John Dagley that he was becoming increasingly troubled by his doubts about Abagnale's veracity, and that he had lost personal credibility himself for promoting Abagnale. His comments had appeared in the *Columbus Daily Enquirer*, along with reports of his lost commission money for the engagements Abagnale had already canceled for the year.

"I myself don't know what's true and what's not," Mark had told Dagley.[231] He suspected that Abagnale would not like that. At all.

\* \* \*

Psychologically shattering as the revelations were, Mark's

immediate thoughts had been for his other clients and his livelihood. Mark knew his reputation was at stake, and he needed to pull the plug on the shady con man. The Mark Zinder Agency had other clients. The Amazing Kreskin could not afford to be associated with this drama, and neither could the band of emerging comics he was representing. The thing about being a talent agent is that when things go sour with one act, it can have a catastrophic domino effect.

There was no denying Professor Toney's file of facts. The Great Imposter was, in fact, a not-so-great pretender. Mark could no longer represent the Tooth Fairy. He needed to resolve the situation and his commission, and determine if there would be any consideration of the substantial investment that he had made to promote Abagnale at the NACA conference before the wheels fell off on the college circuit.

"I must have called his office a dozen times," Mark said. "I was relentless until he finally took my call."

By then, all Mark was interested in was the truth. All thought of their financial arrangements was secondary—he wanted to know if Toney's students were correct in their assertions. He will never forget the conversation that followed.

"I know," was all Mark said to his old client when he picked up the phone, testing the water, but clearly inferring that he knew about Toney's report.

Abagnale's response was equally direct.

"I know you know," was his cool and calm confirmation.

So simple and to the point—and all the more shocking.

There the conversation took a brief pause. It seemed the con man was mulling his next chess move. Mark was waiting. Perhaps for some resolution to their financial arrangements. Then he said something that shook Mark to his core.

"Listen to me carefully, Z," Abagnale said very slowly and

deliberately. "It will only cost me about ten thousand dollars to make this problem go away."

And with that, the line went dead. He had hung up. Leaving the words permanently branded in Mark's memory.

"It is hard to fully explain how terrified and broken I felt in that moment. There was something about it that shook me to my core," Mark admitted recently. It went far beyond the obvious threat—Mark also felt a mask had slipped.

"I had spent years with him, day and night, without a real sense of who he was beneath the veneer. In that moment, even on the phone line, I felt something more real than I ever had before. And it was like a punch in the gut," he said.

Mark reflected that in all the time they were together, Abagnale was almost always even-tempered. Rarely emotional. Rarely phased by anything. If something did annoy him, he was very controlled about it.

"The guy had nerves of steel," recalled Mark, "It was rare to see anything shake Frank. He was so calm, and that is what made the apparent threat even more real and more sinister."

Mark's first concern was the threatening tone. He had been under the man's spell for so long and was worried about what he might be capable of. There were a few ways of interpreting Abagnale's final comment. He wasn't clear if Abagnale was referring to him, Toney or both of them. Mark was worried either way.

"We were clearly both 'a problem,'" Mark said. It certainly sounded more like a bid for ten grand worth of cement boots, rather than an offer to settle up with his agent so that the grifter could consolidate his debt!

Thankfully Abagnale had never shown any violent behavior. Mark was unaware that his ex-boss had been previously arrested with a police baton and sophisticated handcuffs among his possessions. But Mark did remember how Abagnale had pulled a gun out from under the driver's seat in his car as they were driving around Houston one day. He waved it around.

"Don't worry, Z, it's not real," he had grinned.

Nothing seemed real anymore, except the fear.

\*    \*    \*

Genuinely fearing Abagnale, Mark immediately went to look for help and advice. He made a beeline for a cop he knew from his time at the Comedy Workshop. The patrolman was with the Houston Police Department and had a moonlighting security gig at the neighborhood comedy club. He told his officer friend what happened—how Mark's former convict client had said he could make his "problem go away" for a price.

The patrolman immediately put Mark in touch with the Houston Detective Bureau. The detectives interviewed Mark. They showed empathy but did little to allay his anxieties. He was even more worried by their response.

"Abagnale served time in prison, and you make friends in prison," one detective told Mark. "I would take him seriously."

Looking for some reassurance, Mark asked what he should do.

"If I were you, I would get out of town and wouldn't tell anybody where you are going," the detective said.

"That's not something you ever forget," said Mark. "I was already stunned when Abagnale made his veiled threat on the phone. But then to have a detective tell me to get out of town—it was getting worse. Like a western movie. Get out of Houston, Texas. That made it very real to me. The hole kept getting deeper."

The detectives told Mark that they were well aware of Frank Abagnale and knew his criminal record—although they did not tell Mark he had been arrested in Galveston County just a few years earlier for stealing from the Friendswood kids camp. They did tell Mark to call them if there was any threatening communication from his now-former client.

Although Mark was released from his contract with Abagnale, it took much longer to recognize his emotional entanglement and release himself from that. His wife Fran was a great support, and he began to appreciate why she had been so wary and suspicious of Abagnale.

"Then I gradually also began to realize how I had been a captive to his manipulation for so long it had become normal to me." Mark recalled that it took a long time to undo the ramifications of his cult membership. "The only way I can describe it is like Stockholm syndrome, but somehow more sinister. I was very young and genuinely admired him. The irony is that I really believe that *he* was the one who was emotionally lost and needed my constant attention and admiration as a compass."

\* \* \*

Mark still went to NACA in Baltimore as he had planned in February of 1983. He set up his booth and worked the floor, but Abagnale was no longer his client. He still had the Amazing Kreskin, a world-renowned mentalist on his books. Arguably more famous, Kreskin was amazing for much more than just his ability to blend showmanship and science.

"He was and still is an amazing human being. A class act through and through," said Mark. "I also represented rising stars in the word of comedians. Which was exciting because this was the halcyon days of lucrative comedy clubs."

But all of a sudden Houston wasn't looking like the city of big dreams. The illusion was shattered. Mark felt ashamed of being burned twice by the con man, but it was the apparent threat that made him want to get the hell out of rocket city. Fran wanted out, too.

Two months later, in April of 1983, Mark landed a secure job in the financial industry, working for Dean Witter. The Amazing Kreskin and Phyllis Diller provided him with impeccable references. Both knew he felt tarnished by his experiences with the not-so-great imposter. Mark still has copies of those references. Given what he had just been through, they both emphasized his honesty.

"Mark Zinder is an absolutely straight, honest, upstanding young man," wrote Diller.

"He is a remarkable young man who I feel can be highly trusted," wrote Kreskin.

Fran and Mark jumped at the opportunity to move to Tennessee when Dean Witter had an opening in their Nashville offices. Over the next few years, they chipped away at their debt and started raising a family.

\* \* \*

Still in their early twenties, they made a fresh start together. Many wonderful things. Eventually, though, cracks began to appear in their happiness together. After they eventually separated, Mark always wondered how much their experiences with Abagnale had clouded their relationship. The con man had affected them both. And Mark knew it may have run deeper and darker than he had suspected. He recently explained that Fran would never share the all details of why she detested Abagnale so much. And he understood that may have been because she knew how just much Abagnale had affected him.

Mark went on to have a highly successful career. After working in prominent positions for global organizations, including as national spokesperson for Sir John Templeton and the Templeton Group, he became a successful public speaker in his own right. He rarely ever mentioned Abagnale, and few people knew of that aspect of his past.

"Mostly, I put Frank Abagnale in the rear-view mirror," said Mark, "but there always seemed to be something to remind me, especially after the movie eventually came out."

In time, Mark put a framed photograph of Abagnale on one wall of his office, and one of Sir John Templeton on the opposite wall.

"I would tell people I had worked with clients on both ends of the ethical spectrum."

The episode faded like a strange dream in a twilight zone. But somehow the shadow still lingered, mostly only at the edges of Mark's awareness. It was hard to be completely free of the apparition, especially in the following decades of Abagnale's expanding international fame. He kept coming back like some invincible zombie, only stronger each time.

Toney and his team had succeeded in pulling back the curtain—for Mark and for anyone who cared to listen. The college circuit certainly took it seriously. But it barely penetrated the world at large. And people would soon forget, as Abagnale had always predicted. Mark never would. Neither did Toney. The former professor, lawman, parole officer, licensed private investigator and marksman continued to stuff an accordion folder full of information he collected on Abagnale.

Toney's family recently informed this author that the professor remained forever irritated by the federal agents who appeared to enable Abagnale as he continued to sell his falsehoods over the decades—through either silence or overt admiration. It is not clear whether Toney was ever aware that former FBI special agent in charge Eugene H. Stewart shared his views, but there is little doubt it would have soothed Toney's frustration at the seeming lionization of the small-time grifter. Stewart essentially forewarned that a parasite can cling to a healthy host; that intelligent, well-meaning agents could unwittingly be used as shills for a commercial enterprise.

After Toney's death in 2010, his documents on Abagnale remained in storage for years. The bulging accordion file was still in the family home for his daughters to discover as they sorted through his possessions in 2019.

*We do not see the minds that we hurt when we publish falsehoods, but that does not mean we do no harm.*
Professor Timothy Snyder, *On Tyranny* (2017)

# CHAPTER 20
# Family Man

*We live in an extremely unethical society. There are no*
*ethics taught at home or in school . . . this generation*
*thinks it's OK to lie, cheat and steal.*
Frank Abagnale, 2018[238]

Bill Toney had delivered some heavy blows while Abagnale was
playing rope-a-dope, just trying to make it to the bell. As he
staggered back to his corner, handlers applied petroleum jelly.
Lackey bankers and soft media rinsed his cuts, sponged him
down, and applied ice. He retreated to the sanctuary of willing
believers.

While Professor Toney won the 1982 bout, we already know it
wasn't a TKO. Abagnale would live to fight another day.
Eventually, Spielberg would sculpt him into the heavyweight
champion of the world. But that would be many years yet. Too
early to run the champ on Santa Monica beach with Apollo
Creed, or pipe "Gonna Fly Now" through the Kenwood
speakers. He needed to retreat from the ring for a while.

Abagnale drifted away from the national stage and into venues
where he was still welcomed and surrounded by sycophants and
fawners. There were certainly ongoing appearances in chambers
of commerce and businesses. But there was a clear decline in his

media profile. Mentions of Frank Abagnale in national newspapers dropped by seventy-five percent in 1983 compared to the previous year, according to several major databases. By 1984 he was barely mentioned.

There were also plenty of lawsuits on the horizon. Bill Toney. Mark Zinder. And at least two other parties were about to sue him.

In 1983, Bill Toney decided to take a new tack to challenge Abagnale's veracity. He had tried academic channels. Tried a public forum. And tried to alert media as best he could. But this had failed to inspire any "Ron Burgundy" characters in colorful plaid to jump out of local "Action News" vans and confront Abagnale getting into his luxury sedan at a strip mall. No tough questions through the con man's window as he tries to speed away. Nothing like that.

So, Professor Toney was resorting to legal avenues to try and compel Abagnale to answer questions about his past, and his claims—in court. Toney drove over to 1432 Shelton Drive in his hometown of Nacogdoches, Texas. There, he saw a trusted advisor—well-known attorney Tom Rorie. Together they prepared to file a civil suit for damages in the Harris County Courts.[239]

Through the court, Toney and Rorie filed interrogatories—questions that the defendant, Frank Abagnale, was required to answer and sign under oath.

He did not comply. Officers of the court trod a well-worn path to Abagnale's front door, serving writs that were mostly ignored. And so Toney and Rorie filed a Motion to Compel Answers. But again, he refused to abide by the court order. He also failed to make an appearance in person, or by counsel, when Toney filed a Motion for Sanctions for willful failure to comply with the court's requests. But Toney kept coming after him.

It was a battle Abagnale could not win—against the truth and public records. Abagnale's usual response was to run. He also had others bearing down on him.

With a likely dive in his income from speaking events, times may have been tight. Abagnale had been asking people in the local community for large amounts of money.

"Abagnale had even asked my parents to invest in his business," recalled Mark. "Tens of thousands of dollars. I am so glad that they were suspicious and decided against it. But I am sure others did."

Mark suspected that there were likely to be a number of people pursuing Abagnale for money he owed them. He, for one, was never fully compensated for his losses.

Indeed, Abagnale had secured sizable amounts from at least two separate investors—including a Houston pediatrician and, separately, the wife of a senior law enforcement official. Abagnale and his wife had signed and notarized promissory notes to each investing party. And the repayments were due—$20,000 apiece (about $50,000 today) plus significant interest. It is unknown how many others signed and notarized similar agreements.

Records show that both the doctor and the law enforcement official's wife filed independent lawsuits.[240,241] They asserted that repayments were not received on the due date, and it wasn't until months went by without repayment that they finally resorted to legal channels.

Abagnale had already faced a series of lawsuits by then, including the case filed by Aetna Life and Casualty, among others. This also included individuals who claimed he had failed to repay borrowed money. Like Warren Adams Jr. of Houston, who sued Abagnale (Case #335181) for failure to repay a personal loan for travel expenses amounting to $1,000 (about $4,200 today). Mark Zinder also filed a suit for his losses. The pressure was on.

The regular appearance of officers of the court at Abagnale's front door may have been one good reason that he prepared to sell his residence on Thornvine Lane—and leave Houston. At least that is what lawyers reported in the civil court documents filed in Harris County.

Learning he was on the move, urgent writs were issued by the court on behalf of those seeking to recover lost investments. The court recognized the immediate danger if the defendant and his named business, Frank W. Abagnale and Associates, removed all their assets from the state of Texas "and none will be left to satisfy their obligations to the plaintiff."

But when officers attended the house on Thornvine Lane, the one-time base of Frank W. Abagnale and Associates, a new owner answered the door. Abagnale had already taken up a new residence in Tulsa, Oklahoma.

\* \* \*

Many months later, Abagnale did dare to venture back into Texas for several speaking engagements. On November 21, 1985, he was at the Westin Galleria Hotel in Houston about to speak to the American Banking Institute. His reputation in those circles was unsullied, and he was expecting an enthusiastic reception. At 9:10 a.m., a man approached him as he was readying himself to address his audience. Perhaps he thought it was an admirer about to ask him to autograph the papers in hand. But as soon as the man spoke, his purpose would have been made clear.

"You're served," was the likely announcement of the court process server.

Not such a welcome reception after all. And probably not something he would have wanted his audience to know about. A subpoena over a promissory debt. The plaintiff's team had noted in court records that the con man would be visiting the Westin Galleria—the hunter being hunted, a downside of advertising speaking events.

Just a fortnight later, on December 4, 1985, he was at Angelton High School, forty miles south of Houston. It was a relatively low-key event, but before he could regale his small crowd, another process server struck. At 2:15 p.m., right inside the high school hallway, Frank had papers served on him again. Another plaintiff. Another promissory debt.

The records don't show the ultimate outcome; that is, whether or not the unpaid debt to either party was recovered. However, the motions show that the Default Judgment of the court was in favor of the plaintiffs and that both plaintiffs were still looking for their unpaid dough years later.

Around that time, in Harris County, he had more than five separate lawsuits against him. Some dragged on for years. In April of 1985, Bill Toney and Frank Abagnale reached a compromise and entered into a settlement agreement—so Toney did not pursue his action further. The terms of this agreement remain confidential. Abagnale never answered his vital questions.

*    *    *

All the while, Abagnale was rebuilding in the background, ready to gradually return to the lucrative spotlight. Abagnale was remarkably tenacious. In 1985 he re-entered Mark's sphere in Tennessee, thankfully at a distance. He was a keynote speaker at the Tennessee Governor's conference on tourism and featured in the Sunday papers on September 15.

Mark Zinder had moved to Nashville by then and saw the specter of Abagnale rising before him from the Living Section of the *Tennessean*, right there on his living room table. Mark could see Abagnale was still peddling the same story that Toney had already debunked. Making his false claims of professional impersonations and scoffing about it.

"People didn't check my credentials, didn't check if I was a doctor. It only would've cost 22 cents, 13 cents [in postage] back then," the *Tennessean* reported Abagnale saying while recounting the laziness of the personnel professionals who hired him for his year-long job as a physician. Mocking people who didn't check his background to a reporter who wasn't, you know, checking his background. So rich. But what concerned Mark the most was Abagnale's comment that he would "probably open a Nashville office in the next couple of years."[242]

From anyone else, this continued audacity would be hard to believe, but Mark knew Abagnale.

"The guy has no conscience," said Mark, "he was still telling bald-faced lies. And the media weren't interested in veracity. And that just enabled and emboldened him more."

In fact, Mark had already tried to contact the media to raise his concerns.

\*　　\*　　\*

Mark Zinder had gone straight to CBS—to Philip Scheffler, famed documentarian and senior producer at *60 Minutes*. The top-ranked program in investigative journalism would surely be interested in the truth behind the man who had claimed to be one of the greatest criminal masterminds in modern history. Especially when those claims had been shown to be false.

On September 24, 1984, Mark had written a letter to Scheffler at CBS. Although Mark was concerned that he might look like a disgruntled former associate, there were plenty of other sources and legitimate evidence that could be the clear basis of a serious investigation. Toney's damning report had been one thing, but it was without the reach to counter the Abagnale legend, still hanging in the public arena after appearances on *Today*, *Tonight*, and his best-selling book in wide circulation. The slippage of truth and justice as the glue in American culture was a much bigger societal issue, and that needed to be addressed.

Mark also wondered if *60 Minutes* were even aware that they were featured in Abagnale's boastful capers.[243] He had often claimed that *60 Minutes* newsman Dan Rather accompanied him into a Chicago bank with hidden cameras and recorded Abagnale cashing a $50 check written on a cocktail napkin after he stepped out of a Rolls Royce.[244,245]

"I did get a call back from someone at CBS," said Mark, although he could not recall their name. "We spent a few minutes on the phone, but I could tell there was no real interest. They said that they would get back to me. But they never did."

In the years that followed, it was difficult to see Toney's efforts evaporate into the ether as the Abagnale juggernaut began to gather momentum again. Mark could only imagine how Bill Toney must have felt. Mark was frustrated with CBS at the time, but that would be nothing compared to how the media as a whole would eventually assist Hollywood in elevating Abagnale to the upper stratosphere.

By then Abagnale would be taking potshots at CBS, even mocking their top anchorman Dan Rather and his team's failure to fact check spurious memos concerning President George W. Bush's service in the National Guard.[246]

"If my forgeries looked as bad as the CBS documents it would have been *Catch Me in TWO DAYS*," Abagnale scoffed.[246]

*   *   *

Over the next decade, his popularity steadily regained momentum. Once again crisscrossing the United States on lecture tours, he even eventually returned to the college circuit. But he largely refused to take interviews or questions from the press—journalists were told that quotes must only come from his lectures.[62] He had made exceptions for the likes of Johnny Carson in the past—but had not been invited back for many years.

His book, *Catch Me If You Can*, hung around. By 1989, he had sold 3.5 million copies—at least by Abagnale's estimate—bringing in lucrative royalties.

He had also continued to leverage this in Hollywood, continuing to sell the option for movie rights—actually over and over again.

"They [Yorkin and Hollywood collaborators] gave me a $20,000 option on a $250,000 purchase," said Abagnale, who explained that they purchased the rights for one year, with the option to renew for a second for another $20,000. And they did. But Yorkin never progressed with the movie. So Abagnale was $40,000 richer and retained full rights to shop the project to another group each year. Which he did—for about a decade.[247]

"It was the biggest racket in the world," guffawed Abagnale, and he continued to shop his option every year, until finally in 1990 when, if his account can be believed, one studio purchased it outright for $250,000.[247]

Abagnale continued to tease audiences with talk that his film was in production, but nothing materialized. He had been telling crowds that filming was underway as far back as 1977, so long ago, in fact, that the idea of Dustin Hoffman playing Abagnale no longer seemed plausible. After the release of the 1986 mega-hit *Top Gun*, Abagnale began claiming that Tom Cruise[62] had replaced Dustin Hoffman[17] as the lead! His fans seemed to tolerate the ongoing disappointment, though some among the press were more cynical.[62]

All the while, Abagnale continued to promote his story at banquets and other keynote events—retelling his narrative almost word for word, as evident from recorded speeches throughout the 1980s and early 1990s.

Crowds still enjoyed seeing him produce women's silk panties from his jacket pocket.[223] He enjoyed injecting bawdy innuendo, as he often did when introducing his story as a pediatrician in Cobb County.

"I'd have been a gynecologist, but at eighteen I didn't know any better," he would say.

Addressing the chamber of commerce crowds in flyover states, he brought a jingoistic message, underscoring religion and the devastation of divorce.

"Every night during the crime spree, he thought of his parents. His experiences [of his parents' divorce] taught him to value country and family above everything," reported another front-page story celebrating his character.[248]

But he still maintained his bachelor-style swagger, publicly stating that he was unmarried—as he did when he told the American Institute of Banking in 1987 that he "never had children or a family."[249]

\* \* \*

But that changed by the mid-1990s. America was now on a family values kick, especially within the conservative circles that offered the reformed con man a steady spot at the podium. The silk panties gag and tales of ripping off a hooker were no longer testing as well with audiences. So Abagnale made his transition

335

from playboy bachelor to virtuous husband and father—a family man.

His core fantasies of being a grand imposter, with years-long work as a doctor, a lawyer and a professor, as well as a five-year-long chase by stupefied federal authorities, were still in place. Those lies he shared liberally. He still referred to himself as one of Interpol's most sophisticated criminals who had paid back all the stolen money. But now the hoax was framed within a larger tear-jerking saga of redemption and model family values.

The media picked up on the transition. Journalists listened as he peppered his stories with a new kind of reform—showing how he was also "a confirmed family man."[250] By 1995, headlines even underscored the point for him—"Ex-Con Artist Prefers Family, Fatherhood over Fraud" said one in Utah.[251]

His wife of twenty years, Kelly Welbes, had featured in his very early press[23,29] but had been conspicuously absent since. Now it was time for his wife to re-enter his narrative, even if only generically.

"Success has absolutely nothing to do with money," he advised his audiences. "Being a man has nothing to do with achievements, skills, professions. Nothing. There is only one thing that makes a man, a man. And that is that he loves his wife. He is faithful to his wife. He is loyal to his wife," he added somberly.[7]

"You show me this man, and I don't care what he does, who he is, what he's been, and I'll show you a real man," said Abagnale, playing to the importance of family values. "I've done a lot of things in my life, but I assure you, I have done nothing greater, nothing more rewarding, nothing more worthwhile, than simply being a good husband, a good father."

And his final words left his audience in no doubt. "And what I strive to be every day of my life, is a good daddy."[7]

It was definitely a narrative shift, and certainly a dramatic departure from the behavior that Mark Zinder had observed on the road with Abagnale when he had been no less married. Mark did wonder if the leopard had really changed his spots, or if this was another marketing strategy. But it seemed to work.

From his new seat of respectability, Abagnale was ready to comment on many of the ethical and moral failings of modern society, taking his opinions to the international stage.

"We don't teach ethics at home, we don't teach ethics at school," Abagnale opined to Australian journalist Judith Heywood while lecturing on social decay and the erosion of integrity. This, almost in the next breath after his usual self-serving fictitious claims about the $2.5 million dollars he stole in the 1960s on his five-year crime spree, while circumnavigating the globe, outpacing his pursuers, and posing as a pilot, a physician and professor of sociology.[252]

In March 1999, he went after President Bill Clinton, as he faced impeachment for lying under oath about inappropriate behavior toward his intern.

"Young people in our country see a president who has cheated and lied and got away with it," Abagnale told the press in a public statement, as he called for teaching more ethical behavior across modern societies.[252]

For anyone who was aware of Abagnale's true history—like Bill Toney and Ira Perry, and like his many victims—the magnitude and dimensions of the hypocrisy of such statements must surely have seemed momentous. Not to mention Mark Zinder, who'd had to listen to Abagnale boasting of his own extramarital exploits, night after night.

But the family man was there to stay.

"Success has absolutely nothing to do with money," he would remind his listeners when lecturing about family values and the importance of being a good husband. "To those many men in the audience, I'm afraid that this is a lesson most men never learn," said Abagnale.[7]

\*   \*   \*

Abagnale had remained in Tulsa, Oklahoma, and appeared to be enjoying a quiet family life between his speaking events. The shadow of his detractors in Texas and his negative press had essentially disappeared. There was little aftermath. They seemed to have given up or been forgotten.

He appeared to have found a perfect balance—enough fame to ensure a steady stream of engagements, but not too much that it would thrust him back into the spotlight of far greater scrutiny. By the late 1990s, with speaker fees of a reported $15,000 for special appearances, and his book royalties, he was in a good position to look forward to a very comfortable and peaceful retirement. He just had to maintain that sweet spot.

In the meantime, he also enjoyed playing the role of statesman. His views on ethics and reform eventually made him a presumably suitable candidate as an ambassador for the American Association of Retired Persons (AARP).

He used his new soapbox to share his views on the criminal justice system and continued to take a hard stance on crime, showing little sympathy for young offenders as he called for mandatory sentences and harsher punishment. Although his credentials were based largely on being a reformed criminal and former inmate, his platform gave him a louder voice than scholars with a fact-based understanding of the philosophical and procedural differences between the retributive style of the American prison system—an overstuffed dumping ground for a mental health crisis—and the vastly different but more successful

Nordic approaches that are shown to return prisoners to being productive members of society.[253] Ironically, Abagnale had experienced both American and Swedish prisons and had clearly preferred the latter.

But he continued to promote misinformation on a topic on which he did not hold the facts. He claimed that the harsh conditions in French prisons were an important and effective deterrent:

"Americans could take a great lesson from the French. In France, they spend less than $500 a year to house an inmate. Less than one percent ever go back once they [prisoners] have been there," he lectured to a crowd of bankers in 1994. He made a similar claim in the 2002 *Catch Me if You Can* movie book.

In reality, France had, and still has, one of the highest recidivism rates in the world, with almost sixty percent reconvicted within five years.[254,255] Moreover, the per-prisoner spending in France is virtually identical to that in New York. But audiences seemed more likely to believe the man "who had been there" than the facts—especially when he described conditions that rivaled those in *The Count of Monte Cristo*.

"It measured five by five by five feet and had a bucket in it, and that was all. ... They never once opened the door," Abagnale often told his listeners, describing his French cell and how he was only fed on scraps of bread. "When the bucket [of urine and feces] overflowed, it got all over the floor and it burned ... After a while it got to be a foot deep, and I had to sleep sitting up."[148, 256]

He was also very careful to contextualize his own criminal past as that of a wayward kid who knew no better. He had long claimed that he committed his crimes as a juvenile. But in his growing role as a mature father figure, this was an ever more important part of his narrative. Not only as justification but for the lessons that he could provide for young people. As always, he gave clear timelines about his alleged crimes to reinforce that he was only a juvenile—all very different from his *actual* criminal record, which documented arrests well into his mid-twenties.

"[I'm] the only teenager still ever put on the FBI's Ten Most Wanted list," he would say to emphasize the point. "The one and only."[7]

But he wasn't on such a list, ever.

If the FBI had a *least* wanted list, he may have featured, thought Paula Parks.

"I only wish they had 'wanted' him a bit more," she said with a wry smile.

\* \* \*

By the late 1990s, it was twenty years since he had started telling essentially the same story at almost every event. He still told his audiences in different towns that he had been asked to "just take a moment to talk about my previous life" as though it was a special event, rather than actually repeated countless days in a given year.

There was always the illusion that he was an unwilling narrator, only responding to public demand—when in truth, as Mark Zinder knew, he had carefully constructed the story and the promotional machine that sat behind it. It was yet another dimension of the false narrative—that he was a reluctant participant in his own fame—that it was all created by others.

"When I came out of prison, I was ashamed of what I did. I felt it was something that should never be discussed again," Abagnale said, as though he had not been actively promoting it for years. "But the media thought otherwise. Books were written, movies will be made. People have always had this fascination."[7]

In time, Abagnale would invite selected writers to his grand mansion to admire the architecture and photograph the décor for glossy magazines. Between the well-worn anecdotes, such as how he had hoarded two million in unspent cash as a teen, he would talk about his love of family. Very much a man of culture, he would speak of his fondness for exquisite crown molding, his grandfather clock collection, and the contents of the fine bookshelves in his living room—an amassment of his own "tell-all" autobiography, *Catch Me If You Can*, including dozens of editions translated into foreign languages.[163]

His audiences were convinced. Perhaps he had told the story so many times that he believed it, too. Life was good. It was over a decade since Bill Toney had tried to derail him. The real story of Baton Rouge seemed forgotten, as were his escapades at Camp Manison. No one was asking difficult questions. The threat of greater scrutiny and exposure had passed. All would be well—if he didn't draw too much attention to himself again.

*Just remember, it's not a lie if you believe it.*
George Costanza, *Seinfeld*, 1995

Director/producer Steven Spielberg (holding cigar, on left)
and Frank W. Abagnale at the *Catch Me If You Can* London
premiere after-party on January 27, 2003. (Copyright 2003.
Getty Images. Used with permission.)

# CHAPTER 21
# Limelight

*He wouldn't go into a mom and pop store and rob the guy
that, you know, only made fifteen thousand dollars a year,
and that, to me, in a way, is kind of a hero.*
Leonardo DiCaprio on the real Abagnale, 2002.[257]

Fans were thrilled! The movie of *Catch Me If You Can* was finally happening. Some had been waiting for twenty-five years! Abagnale had been promising that Hollywood was making a movie about his life since 1977. But this time, when Abagnale announced that Steven Spielberg had just finished the script in 1999, it appeared to be true.[252] It was a surprise even to Abagnale.

Indeed, he did not appear as excited as might have been expected. Actually, he did not seem pleased at all. And some in the media noticed this.

"The one person who was not happy that the movie was finally being made was the older and wiser Abagnale," wrote one journalist.[258]

"To suddenly be confronted with a massive new interest in the escapades of his youth is a shade uncomfortable," wrote another reporter after contacting Abagnale. "He says he has put his youthful indiscretions behind him, started a business and raised a family."[259]

"My neighbors don't even know who I am," said Abagnale, "they just see me as the guy washing his car in front of the house on the weekend, working in the garden."[258]

For those who did not know how he craved the spotlight, he could easily be cast as a reluctant and reclusive hero who had turned his powers to good. And this is exactly the line that he played.

"I was not very happy about it," Abagnale admitted, "I didn't really care to have a movie out there exploiting my life as a teenager or glamorizing my life as a teenager."[260]

Not happy about exploiting his life? In 1979 he optioned his autobiography to Bud Yorkin Productions. He signed a document that gave the filmmakers "the exclusive rights to exploit said literary work by any means or medium!" Not to mention that Abagnale's *actual* life as a teenager, largely in the New York prison system, provided little to exploit and little to glamorize.

Still, it was a logical explanation, and few questioned it. Without knowledge of his real "youthful indiscretions" or his subsequent ongoing fabrications, it would appear the most likely explanation for his discomfort. But for a man whose lies had been unmasked before, there were far more significant concerns about exposing his grand hoax in a far greater public spotlight than when it had been uncovered by Bill Toney, Ira Perry or Stephen Hall. Anyone who had elaborately assembled a big-top hoax beyond anything P.T. Barnum ever dreamed up would surely be terrified at the prospect of a collapse.

Abagnale had no control of the situation. He had sold the rights.

"It was out of his hands," it was reported, and into the hands of Spielberg, Hanks and DiCaprio. All that Abagnale could do was to sit back and wait for the results. A meeting with Spielberg was said to have put his mind somewhat at ease.[260]

The man who had once imagined seeing Dustin Hoffman and Tom Cruise as himself on the big screen was also not so sure about the choice of Leonardo DiCaprio in the role.

"Abagnale, 54, who has a wife and three children, says he was a little concerned when he heard DiCaprio would portray him," reported *USA Today*. "The reformed criminal wasn't sure moviegoers would buy DiCaprio as a pilot simply because the heartthrob put on a uniform."[261]

It had taken screenwriter Jeff Nathanson three years to translate—which is to say, contort—Abagnale's autobiography into the Spielberg script.[262] But it appeared he had finally succeeded in capturing the "sympathetic soul of a gifted grifter."[263] Once dubbed an "unfilmable book," it had been a challenge for others to create a charming but likable character with a believable story. This contributed to why it took twenty years to translate the autobiography into a film.[264] Bud Yorkin Productions had previously described the story as "so convoluted and fantastic that [they] had to tone down many of the episodes in his life just to make a story believable."[142]

The choice of DiCaprio as the "baby-faced con man" helped audiences fall for the charm of the feel-good narrative.[263] There was a narrow path between glorifying crime and creating a character that people could identify with. The final result was a movie that portrayed an amusing adventure, full of seemingly victimless crimes—apart from the hooker he bilked.

"I was worried about how sympathetic we should make him," Spielberg admitted.[260] He also admitted he had softened the con man's image, promoting the angle that his criminal behavior was related to his parents' divorce. "I wanted to emphasize in the picture and always remind people that Frank was doing this [his crimes] for a reason," the director said. "He wasn't just doing this because he could, he was doing this because he was perhaps trying to get his mom and dad back together again."[265]

Keep in mind that Abagnale's father had already remarried in 1964. Not to mention that he was working his pilot grift and arrested at Camp Manison long after his father's death. Spielberg reportedly kept Abagnale in the loop throughout the production, faxing the shooting schedule to his home each night.[260] Abagnale and his family also spent time on set—he even scored a cameo role. He played a French gendarme who arrested "Abagnale" and snapped on the handcuffs after slamming DiCaprio onto the hood of a police car.

Soon enough, Abagnale was full of praise for DiCaprio's talents and portrayal.

"He's an absolutely incredible actor who took the role seriously," he said of DiCaprio. "I lived with him. He learned all my mannerisms."[261]

And DiCaprio was also impressed by Abagnale.

"Frank Abagnale is one of our great actors," said DiCaprio. "His stage, though, is the world."[260]

In an interview on ABC's "20/20 Investigates" DiCaprio shared some of Abagnale's tales with host Barbara Walters, reinforcing a narrative of harmless pranks and victimless crimes, as "kind of a hero."[257]

Walters' 20/20 Investigates did no real investigating that night, and instead buttressed the wholesome ethics of Abagnale's character. Like so many before her, the former journalist presented his false claims as fact. The hoax seemed to be in no danger of discovery. DiCaprio told her that Abagnale's most outrageous scam was convincing eight college co-eds to spend a summer traveling through Europe posing as his flight crew— using them to sneak past the FBI to leave the country.[257] Except it didn't happen.

In the lead-up to the high-profile movie release, there had been no way to predict what kind of new scrutiny Abagnale might attract. For anyone else, this would have been terrifying. Standing on the threshold of such unimagined fame was one thing, but for Abagnale there was also a tremendous new level of risk—and possibly the unbelievable thrill of taking the hoax to a whole new level. The middle-aged man and all of his imagined identities danced together on the ultrathin lip of an active volcano. The lava of hot truth percolated below, out of sight to most, but could he keep his feet? What a rush.

*   *   *

In Baton Rouge, some folks already knew the movie was coming. Actually, two years before the movie was due for release, Paula Parks and her family were contacted by a journalist. No one remembered his name, and they were not even sure he was from their local paper. He told them that production of *Catch Me If You Can* would begin in mid-2001, and wanted to get their reaction.

"We were all furious," Paula said recently, "especially my mamma. We had not heard much about him in recent years, and this news just opened old wounds. But by that point, what we were most upset by was the pure gall of it all—not just that he was still getting away with his lies, but how much he was profiting from it. A Hollywood movie was taking it to a ridiculous new level. It was utterly outrageous."

The Parks family had already seen a report in the Baton Rouge *Advocate* that referred to their ordeal. So, they knew that local journalists were certainly still aware of them. Their encounter with Abagnale was hardly a secret, and his less-than-savory activities were not hard to find if anyone wanted to look.

Indeed, Smiley Anders, local columnist for *The Advocate,* had written a short column entitled "The Big Con" in August 2000, reminding his readers of the "facts versus fiction" issue, including Abagnale's wild claims of working in their midst as a lawyer in Attorney General Jack Gremillion's office. Smiley underscored that "they had never set eyes on the guy."[266] He did not mention the efforts of Assistant District Attorney Kenneth C. DeJean to set that record straight. But he did state why Abagnale had indeed been in Baton Rouge in the winter of 1969. He was in jail—for stealing from the local family who had offered him a place to stay. Smiley finished his article by mentioning Abagnale's multiple prison sentences, including a few years in a federal reformatory— where he supposedly received psychiatric treatment. He also corrected any notion that Abagnale was then a juvenile.

"We were glad to see that. We were getting pretty sick of him using his age as an excuse," Paula said. "He was definitely no teenager. And his long criminal record should have thrown cold water on at least some of the claims in his book."

Smiley had not talked to their family for the article. They assumed that he had his information from the original 1981 *State-Times* article by Fayette Tompkins, who had interviewed them back when Abagnale was first promoting his book.

But someone in Hollywood seemed to take an interest.

"Not long after, we had a call from another journalist, at least we *thought* it was a journalist. They implied that someone in Hollywood was testing the water to see if we would 'cause any problems' for them when the movie came out," said Paula. "It wasn't clear what that meant exactly. But that 'someone' in Hollywood must have known that Frank was in jail here in Baton Rouge, and not a lawyer as he claimed. Or why would they be asking?"

For years, the Parks family has wondered about the real reason they were contacted. To assess the risk? Damage control? It was clear that someone, somewhere, was well aware of their story and his real criminal record—perhaps with full knowledge that Abagnale's story was largely a hoax.

"We made it pretty clear how we felt," said Paula. "But obviously we were of no great threat or concern, and we never heard another thing until the movie came out."

\*     \*     \*

But Paula's family were not the only ones stunned by the news. Mark Zinder had arranged to go out to dinner with a very good friend from high school, who had since become a respected member of the Hollywood community—nominated for an Academy Award no less. His friend Alan (not to be confused this author) was dating a documentary film producer and journalist at the time. They were both already seated at the restaurant when Mark arrived. Mark recalls the conversation well.

"So, they are making the movie," said Alan, even before the formalities of introducing his girlfriend. He knew Mark's history with the grifter and his feelings about his former client.

Silence.

"They're making the movie," repeated his friend, who had heard the news along the Hollywood grapevine. "DreamWorks. *Catch Me If You Can* is finally in production."

"Alan, I don't want to talk about it," said Mark, who had suddenly lost his appetite.

But Alan persisted, drawing it out, with dramatic effect.

"Soooo, they are making the movie," Alan clearly *did* want to talk about it.

His journalist girlfriend was already intrigued. She could immediately tell there was something significant lurking under the exchange and wanted to find out more.

"Alan, you tell her," Mark said, giving in to the tide of the conversation.

And Alan delighted in doing so. The journalist was spellbound as Alan explained that Abagnale was Mark's former client, as well as going into the deeper story of the con man.

"He didn't tell her everything, but he made it clear that Abagnale was still conning the world, and that most of his stories were bald-faced lies," said Mark.

She was stunned by what Alan had to say. She also saw a big story. And she wanted to write it.

"Yeah, right," said Alan, "and you are going to shut down Steven Spielberg's movie, one of the most powerful men in Hollywood? Your story would never see the light of day!"

"I also told her that others had tried," Mark said recently, recalling this conversation, "but their voices had been no match for Abagnale's story, which always seemed to dominate in the press and suck oxygen away from any attempts to get the truth out. I had even tried myself."

It was such an important story. And it needed to be told. Mark wanted the truth to come out and would have been overjoyed to see her write it. But he also wanted her to realize what she was up against first, and that her efforts might be in vain. He already knew that it could be soul-destroying.

"It has been hard enough to get traction without a movie," Mark had explained to his friends, "what chance would we stand against the massive DreamWorks media machine behind Spielberg?"

And that was the end of that.

\* \* \*

The sixty-five million dollar movie opened to rave reviews.

350

And was certainly a huge hit with audiences around the world. Overnight, the legendary story took on a new life of its own and extended its global reach. Today, there are few who have not heard of it.

"It's the perfect mid-20th-century victimless caper," wrote one reviewer, describing the con caper as the "real thing."[267]

"An achingly nostalgic trip back nearly four decades," wrote another. "A sweet-hearted con man can get away with just about anything . . . in the modern cynical new century, one can easily be forgiven for rooting for that mild-mannered swindler."[263]

The movie premiere was held at the Fox Westwood Village Theatre. Ten years earlier, almost to the day, *A Few Good Men* had premiered there, where Jack Nicholson introduced that most famous of lines to the world—"You can't handle the truth!"

On this December night, in 2002, Abagnale shuffled along the red carpet with the stars of the show, rubbing shoulders with the Hollywood elite. A dream had come true.

Also on the red carpet was a rather bewildered 83-year-old Joseph Shea, the former FBI agent who had been briefly involved in Abagnale's very short-lived Pan Am check scam. Even as the paparazzi were popping their bulbs at him, they were clearly wondering who he was.[268] Having an authentic retired FBI agent on the scene certainly added an air of legitimacy, even though the character played by Tom Hanks was fictitious.

Shea would have known that the story Abagnale had been telling publicly for years did not bear much resemblance to the reality—no 17,000 checks for $2.5 million in twenty-eight countries, chasing a slippery "juvenile" for five years. But it was Hollywood after all, and fiction, exaggeration and hyperbole were expected. Just ten Pan Am checks for $1,448 over three months at twenty-two years of age, as records clearly show, would not play so well. But that small caper did provide the minuscule grain of truth for the grand hoax.

"He never hurt anybody," the former FBI agent was quoted as saying.[31] And maybe that was what he truly believed.

It is not clear if Shea knew that Abagnale was claiming that the agent was his "boss" for a decade.[150] He was an exceptional agent who barely knew the grifter. Following his fleeting involvement in Abagnale's 1970 arrest, Shea did not actually see the former fugitive again until years after he retired from the FBI. Shea was working on more serious cases in Atlanta, while Abagnale was working his nutty grift at Camp Manison. None of this fit Abagnale's tale that Shea "supervised" him for ten years as a condition of his release.[150]

The actual Shea-Abagnale reunion occurred in the 1980s, long *after* he started his nationwide publicity tours. Abagnale happened to be speaking at a convention of FBI retirees in Kansas City. Abagnale was the one who sought out Shea to shake his hand.[268]

But on this night in Hollywood, carried along on the current of paparazzi and the spectacle of the red carpet, there was likely little opportunity for more than small talk. Who can know what unspoken knowledge passed beneath their exchanges when Shea and Abagnale saw each other amid the seething excitement at the premiere? Shea died two years later, at the age of eighty-five[269] and Abagnale has continued to exaggerate their relationship since.[203]

"Joe [Shea] never had a son. He adopted me in that role," Abagnale opined recently. "He personally came to see me, he personally worked the [federal prison] release deal. Joe Shea gave me a second chance."[183] This bromide seems more reminiscent of the father figure who *did* visit him in prison and helped work a release deal—Reverend Underwood in Baton Rouge.

Audiences and critics had plenty to say about how much they enjoyed the "bright, bouncing romp of a film."[270] But it took a little longer for Abagnale to provide his response and talking points, possibly waiting to see the general reaction.

"I needed a day or two of lying in bed, looking at the ceiling, thinking every scene out," he told one reporter a few weeks after the screening.[259]

Indeed. We can only wonder how much he was admiring the portrayal of his fiction, and how much he was wondering whether the people who knew the truth would come forward in protest. Did he wonder what they would think if they saw the film? The Parks family in Baton Rouge? Morris Fuselier? Mark Zinder? Bill Toney? Ira Perry? Stephen Hall? Jan Jackson? "Wife" Jennie? Jan Hillman? And the many others who knew his troubled past was far, far different from the film. For a man who was so admired for his fearless lies, perhaps reality was the one thing that gave him the chills.

He could only wait and see. In the meantime, he could control his own narrative. And he responded to the press with a series of talking points that signaled virtue and acquired wisdom—including the message that crime does not pay.[259]

"In the end, there's redemption," he concluded in his takeaway messages, "because this is a great country where everyone gets a second chance."[259]

He had already commented on the general accuracy of the film.

"I would say that 90 percent of the film is accurate," Abagnale had stated,[271] adding that he thought it was actually *more* accurate than his own autobiography.[272] Despite the fantastical nature of his escapades, most of the media seemed to accept it at face value—including Pulitzer-Prize-winning journalist and film critic Roger Ebert.

"That this story is true probably goes without saying, since it is too preposterous to have been invented by a screenwriter," Ebert gushed when the film premiered.[273]

Several brave journalists went against the grain and saw through the contortions required to make a celluloid hero and a victimless romp. Like Manohla Dargis, who questioned Abagnale's sincerity.

"An amicable cheat, he led a charmed life of victimless crime. Or so he has vigorously maintained in the years since," wrote Dargis. "If it's difficult to buy Abagnale's claims that none of the clerks or tellers he gulled landed in trouble, it's even harder to resist the fantasy of the guy that gets away with it with a wink, a smile and no bloodshed."[274]

Of the film itself, the journalist's criticisms were directed more toward the interpretation than the veracity of the content. "Where DiCaprio and the film run into trouble are the director and screenwriter's efforts to wring deeper meaning out of Abagnale's exploits, which is when the quicksilver turns to lead."

BBC journalist Sarah Montague was one of the few members of the press who tried to pin Abagnale down after the movie release, challenging him on her aptly named *HardTalk* show. After listening to Abagnale say he was concerned that filmmakers might glamorize his life, Montague seemed unconvinced. "You say you don't want to glamorize it, but the nature of the film, it does, doesn't it? You are played by Leonardo DiCaprio, for God's sake," she pushed. His response was to talk about how people just love the story, how many copies of his autobiography he sold, and its lasting popularity.

Abagnale told her, "I wasn't willing to steal some individual's money from them, or their life savings. I had certain limitations that I wasn't willing to go over that line." As he spoke of his regret and his reform, Montague appeared to question his sincerity, pointing out how much he seemed to be enjoying the celebration of his story, including all the things that had come from it.[275]

"Was it a victimless crime?" she pushed him, interrupting his milquetoast monologue.

"Victimless in that there were no individuals that I ripped off for money, nobody's personal money that I took," he responded, adding that, "I think there were people that [sic] feelings were hurt, that were deceived, girls I met, people I dated, things like that, but eh, other than that, that's all there really was to it."[275]

Montague didn't press on the veracity of his larger tale, but she did extract important information concerning his narrative about victims, or the lack thereof.

But even today, with the *HardTalk* interview now on YouTube, willing believers direct their outrage at Montague, "that woman" as they call her, in the comments section—complaining that she was judgmental and rude as she dared to ask their hero tough questions, interrupt him and corral him back from his deflections.[275]

Few others were as critical. Most interviews were marshmallow-soft and did not challenge the narrative or its creators.

Although the film version took artistic license to compress time, rolling the FBI agents into one character, and painting an idealistic view of life in the mid-to-late 1960s, Spielberg was quick to allay doubts about the truth behind the events portrayed.

"Every scam he pulls in the movie is what he pulled in real life," Spielberg said.[276] But what was he basing that on? For those who were familiar with the con man's real life, or even Perry's reporting, this is absurd.

Spielberg, described as the most successful filmmaker ever, had an obvious level of admiration for Abagnale. He even described his own teenage efforts as a con artist—pretending to be a young director on the Universal Studios lot before he even graduated high school. At seventeen, Spielberg said he marched into Universal Studios wearing ill-fitting business suits and carrying his father's briefcase. He put his name on the door of an empty office—Steven Spielberg, Room 23C—so he could rub shoulders with producers, directors, writers and editors. It was a harmless lark all born out of his "love of cinema and wanting to see how movies were made," Spielberg said.[260]

It was a great story—Spielberg had made his teenage dreams a stratospheric reality. His imagination had come to life. And thanks to Spielberg, so now had Abagnale's. The *National Post* aptly described *Catch Me If You Can* "as the story of two very famous con artists linked on and off the screen by mutual desire to pull the wool over people's eyes."[260]

Still, the movie opens with a disclaimer that it was only "inspired by a true story," leaving the apparent creator of that "true" story—Frank W. Abagnale—to defend its veracity.

* * *

The movie did bring handsome rewards at the box office—with early profits estimated at over $350 million. One report described Abagnale's frustration over the film, adding that it was unlikely that he would see a dime of the movie profits beyond the relative pittance earned when he sold the story years before.[272] But a new edition of his book was released by Broadway Books as part of the massive surge in publicity—with direct benefits in book royalties, speaking engagements and consultancy. His by then deceased co-author, Stan Redding, was still acknowledged as an author on the cover—but only in small print.

Although Redding had died in 1987, he was about to return to Abagnale's post-film narrative.

*   *   *

In the months after the release of the movie, Abagnale could be sure that more and more of the people he had crossed would hear about it. The trail of his real crimes and low-grade grift had been as long and as wide as the imagined version he had created in the autobiography hoax—so was the potential fallout. There was no way of predicting which of his nemeses might return, or where or even when.

*   *   *

Martina Smalley was a retired detective who had worked on forgery cases at the Gainesville Police Department in Georgia. When she watched the movie in 2003, she remembered Abagnale—specifically in regard to an unsolved forgery case.[277] She had been one of the first female officers in the department, and primarily worked on forgery cases after she made detective in 1978. Smalley recalled the biggest case of her career. It was in June of 1981.

This was actually during Abagnale's so-called life of reform, as he was traveling the nation with Mark Zinder, giving lectures on crime prevention to colleges, businesses and banks. After the film was released, Smalley contacted staff writer Christina Correll Griggs at the *Gaffney Ledger* in South Carolina with the story of her strange encounter with Abagnale shortly after the 1981 crime.

Someone had stolen checks from the offices of two doctors and an attorney and deposited them into a checking account under the name of a fictitious business at the local First National Bank. The person subsequently withdrew around $30,000 (close to $100,000 today) in cashier's checks.

Around the same time, Smalley read in the newspaper that

Frank Abagnale was in the area and would be giving a seminar in Gainesville on fraud prevention. His pedigree as a forger and white-collar criminal caught her attention—not just as an expert who might help solve the crime, but also as a possible suspect. And so she attended his seminar.

Afterwards, she introduced herself as a detective and said she would like to question him in relation to a case she was working on.

"He agreed, [but] on the condition that the interview take place in his hotel room," Smalley recalled.[277] She did go to Abagnale's hotel room later, but in the company of another officer.

Abagnale was extremely charming and not in the least defensive. He did admit to being in Gainesville before, and conceded that he did visit the First National Bank three or four times. But he evaded almost every other question she asked.

"I tried to watch his demeanor," she told the reporter, "but he was so good at it I couldn't pick up on if he was lying."

"You think I did it, don't you?" Abagnale asked her, she recalled.

"Yes, I do," she replied.

"But you can't prove it," was his cocky answer.

He flirted with her effusively, complimented her clothes, and her brown eyes and even asked her out to dinner. Not long after he left town, the detective received fresh flowers and a package at the police department. Shades of the behavior directed at Paula Parks, in Miami, 1969. The package included his book, which was inscribed with a message: "If you were chasing me, I would have given up!" he had written, alluding to his challenge in *Catch Me If You Can,* and signed the note "Love, Frank W. Abagnale."[277]

He also wrote a letter to the chief of police, George Napp, to say how fortunate the police department was to have such a smart detective. He complimented her on her interviewing skills and said how impressed he was. Smalley always felt the charm was intended to discourage her from pursuing the case, and the letter insulted her intelligence.

Abagnale was apparently already known to the president of First National, who had invited him to speak to bankers from across the state on how to protect the customers from check fraud. The bank president, according to the newspaper report, eventually admitted that he thought there was a good possibility that Abagnale had opened the bogus accounts at the bank.

"In my heart of hearts, I knew he was guilty, but I couldn't prove it," the retired detective said to the *Gaffney Ledger* in 2003. She said that they never had any solid evidence, but it continued to haunt her to that day.[277]

When Mark Zinder heard about the report recently, he chuckled and said that the flirtatious hotel room encounter that Smalley described with Abagnale sounded very typical, but he never saw any evidence that Abagnale was up to his old tricks.

"I don't recall the incident specifically," Mark said, "but the charm offensive certainly captures exactly what he was like. He would invite people to his room for meetings—especially women—and I would know. But I never heard or saw anything to do with bad checks. He was making so much money on tour by then, he really didn't need to do that."

The case in Gainesville was never solved, and it was a cause for much local speculation after the publicity of the movie—but there was no evidence that Abagnale had anything to do with it at all. It is also worth pointing out that during this time there were more than a few cases of young people who took to forgery and financial crimes *after* listening to an Abagnale lecture and reading his book.[278,279]

There were likely to have been more people contacting the

media with stories about Frank Abagnale, descriptions that never made the press. Paula Parks can attest to that. She had contacted NBC yet again after the movie in 2003—wanting to tell the real story of what he had done in Baton Rouge after he appeared on their network again—but they would not pursue it.

"Once the movie was out, I hoped that it would invite more serious questions, and the media would look into his *actual* story, and the claims that he was *still* making," said Mark. "Now that the spotlight was on it, I hoped that there might be more scrutiny, and someone might succeed in getting attention where I had failed." At that point Mark Zinder had never heard of Paula Parks.

\*    \*    \*

In Los Angeles, Bob Baker and Rachel Abramowitz were among the few journalists who did take up the challenge of investigating the underlying veracity of Abagnale's autobiography. If the movie was based on the book, they needed a closer look at the book.

Their efforts soon revealed how shady and shaky it all was. They even dusted off Stephen Hall's 1978 piece in the *San Francisco Chronicle,* which was the first recorded effort to debunk the story that became the basis of the book. Like Hall, Baker and Abramowitz concluded that there was little evidence to support the book's claims.

They wrote up their assessment, including the damning report from Hall, in the entertainment section of the *Los Angeles Times.*

"A teen con man's tale was impossible to verify, even before it got the Hollywood treatment," they wrote, adding that this lack of veracity applied to "most of the intriguing claims in both the book and the movie—all of which Abagnale says are true."[262]

"Frank Abagnale Jr., won't give details," wrote Baker and Abramowitz under the accompanying photo of the silver-haired statesman. "He feels it is unfair for people to challenge his veracity."

Unfair?

They reported how Abagnale had pivoted whenever previously challenged, simply repeating that he had intentionally used incorrect names. When asked specifically about the accuracy of the film, he again said that it was more accurate than the book.

"But in the final analysis, only I really know," he added.[262]

Public records say otherwise.

Extensive documentation in many jurisdictions across the United States, Sweden and France clearly destroy claims of accuracy regarding both the book and the film. However, none of this information showing his *actual* whereabouts was in the public eye at the time. Everyone was still following the misdirection of the magician, or looking to verify the *false* image.

While the rest of the media had generally been playing up the unbelievable but "absolutely true" tales of Frank Abagnale,[260] Baker and Abramowitz's story did hit a seam. There were still more questions about the believability of many aspects of the story. But the very fact that Hollywood was now involved had shifted the emphasis from accuracy to entertainment. Taking liberties with reality is part of the art. Specific digressions can be accepted within creative license but dilute the larger question of the veracity of the overall story.

Scriptwriter Jeff Nathanson's words are telling.

"Nobody really cares about having to know exactly what happened," he wrote after transforming Abagnale's autobiography into Spielberg's script, "Focus on what's true and what's not true [is] very hard for me after spending all these years on it, because it sort of deflates the effort we've all been making."[262]

Presumably, the "nobody" Nathanson referred to didn't include those excised from "exactly what happened." It certainly didn't mean everybody who is a nobody in Abagnale's narrative.

One journalist, Andy Seiler, wrote a comical account of the convoluted contradictions in the "real story of a true fake" designed to deliberately leave the reader lost in a house of smoke and mirrors of "different kinds of truths."[264]

"People want to know what is real or not in the movie," Jeff Nathanson told Seiler, "But I did not view this material as historical. This is the life of a con man—and only he knows the truth of it."

But maybe not. Seiler discovered that was not necessarily true either.

"You get to a point in your life," Abagnale told him, "where you go, 'I don't remember what I did.'" Maybe Frank Abagnale, now in his early fifties, who long boasted he had an IQ of 140 and a photographic memory, could not tell anymore. He didn't remember. But forgetting about almost three years in Comstock and a subsequent half-year in Baton Rouge jail? That's not like forgetting if he flipped burgers, waited tables, or parked cars at Gordy's Steak House in 1965.

Certainly, Abagnale was starting to distance himself from his own autobiography. Despite the considerable artistic license taken with the film, Abagnale continued to maintain the movie based on his book was more accurate than his own book.

The reason? Because he didn't write it!

At least that is what he then began to say.

# CHAPTER 22
# Puppet Masters

*Get your facts first, then you can*
*distort 'em as much as you please.*
Mark Twain, 1890[280]

Stan Redding had been an award-winning journalist with the *Houston Chronicle* for a quarter of a century before he met Frank Abagnale. Since joining the paper in 1951, he had covered many high-profile stories, including the assassination of President John F. Kennedy, the Jack Ruby trial and many others. Recognition for his work included several prestigious Headliners Club awards for investigative journalism, and he also received two Pulitzer Prize nominations early in his career.[281,282,283] In essence, a good investigator and a good storyteller.

For a young man like Abagnale, who had not graduated high school, and whose writing skills were known to be lacking, the local writer and journalist would have been an excellent choice as a skilled biographer.

Indeed, Abagnale's story was not the first that Stan Redding had magically translated into the written form. And Abagnale was also not the first Houston criminal whose story of reform Redding had brought to life. Freddie Gage was a one-time Houston teen gang leader who embraced religion and reform to become a prominent community leader, and eventually one of the leading Baptist preachers of the late twentieth century.

In the space of two years, 20-year-old Freddie Gage had skyrocketed from hoodlum to fiery evangelist.[284]And Stan Redding co-authored the autobiography, *Pulpit in the Shadows*, that told Gage's story—a book that provided a platform of formalized legitimacy and celebrity for the rest of Gage's career.[285]

Had Redding seen the same potential to amplify Frank Abagnale's story to an even greater level than Freddie Gage's? And, if so, when did he see it?

Following the premiere of *Catch Me If You Can* in December 2002, Abagnale developed a convenient solution for the problematic aspects of his autobiography. He deflected the blame for any misinformation, or outright disinformation, onto his book's co-author, Stan Redding, who had died fifteen years earlier. For the benefit of the skeptical minority, he distanced himself by saying that the 1980 autobiography had been largely engineered by his long-deceased co-author Redding.

"He was a great storyteller," said Abagnale in 2002, "and I always felt he embellished a lot of things, he exaggerated a lot of things, he overdramatized some things."[264]

Redding, he claimed, had interviewed him for four days, eight hours a day, and then went off and wrote the book on his own. But still, Abagnale was not specific about what was embellished, what was exaggerated, what was overdramatized, or what had been completely made up.

"That was his style and what the editor wanted. [Redding] always reminded me that he was just writing a story and not my biography," said Abagnale. "This is one of the reasons that from the very beginning, I insisted that the publisher put a disclaimer in the book."[262]

The disclaimer warned the reader that all the names, dates and places had been changed and that all of the characters and some of the events had been altered. Together with the admitted exaggerations and embellishments, how can the statement on the front cover of the book—*This is the true story of Frank Abagnale*—still be true?

Even the *Houston Chronicle,* the very newspaper Redding worked for, described him as "a rough-hewn raconteur, an indefatigable teller of tall tales," in his 1987 obituary.[286] Fellow Texas journalist, firecracker Molly Ivins, was more candid when she described Stan Redding as one of the "biggest liars" the state had ever produced.[287] Ivins, who worked at the *Chronicle* in her early career, never shied away from taking on the good ol' boy clubs in Texas.

Critics of his previous book, *Pulpit in the Shadows,* were less than enthusiastic about his style, voicing their discomfort over the "monotonous montage of mellifluous metaphor perpetually proffered by reporter Redding, who seems, at times, to have become mesmerized by the marvelous movement of his own language."[288]

Redding's colorful Texan style is very much evident in *Catch Me If You Can,* as should be expected. But so is Abagnale's voice—along with the same core elements of the story which he was *already* on record telling, since at least January 1977—the pilot, doctor, lawyer, professor, daring airplane toilet escapes, and the $2.5 million in checks.[23] The very *same* narrative structure and the timelines were all clearly in place in January 1977, almost four years *before* the book was published. And equally untrue.

Interestingly, in the very early report by Soll Sussman, one of the first on record, Abagnale was already referring to himself as the "Skyway Man," and comparing himself to Ferdinand Demara, The Great Imposter. He was already making appearances at school banquets talking about playing it straight.[23]

"I didn't want to be known the rest of my life as a great con artist," he told high school students in 1977. "No one remembers Ferdinand Demara, The Great Imposter, and no one will remember me."[23]

So where, and when, did the grand hoax begin?

And who was the mastermind behind the story that formed the basis of the publicity, the events, the talks, the book and everything else that followed?

Even when the story first emerged in the press in January 1977, it was already a fairly sophisticated and structured narrative—with suspense, intrigue, feel-good moments, complex thematic elements with an overall premise of reform. Long before the book was released, the narrative of Abagnale's revised life story had already been strategically restructured and embellished with distracting detours around calculated omissions—unlikely to be purely the product of a high school dropout and runaway thief, no matter how convincing a liar or huckster he might have been. That much of Abagnale's protests about not writing the book can be believed.

On the surface, Redding and Abagnale first appeared to meet for an interview that was published in the *Houston Chronicle* Sunday magazine in June 1977. That would have been a logical point for Redding to be inspired by the raw, real-life story of a wayward youth who had already started turning his life around. So inspired, in fact, that he simply wanted to write a book and tell it to the world. But that is not what happened.

Redding did write an in-depth interview with Abagnale for the *Houston Chronicle* in June 1977.[29] It was a lengthy article, complete with a full set of sleek, professionally produced photographs of Abagnale in "action"—performing medical exams, examining x-ray films, and exuberantly jumping with fistfuls of cash. While the latter was acknowledged as a promo shot, *Chronicle* readers were informed that the medical photographs were all taken while he was masquerading "as a consulting pediatrician at a Georgia hospital" in the 1960s. Yet he looked strangely more like Elvis in 1976 as he played his last show in Houston—bloated, thick-necked with heavy sideburns. In fact, the supposed "1960s teen" Abagnale looked virtually identical to his 1977 *Chronicle* photograph with wife, Kelly—and even looks to be wearing the same wedding ring.

The article was carefully laid out as a detailed summary of Abagnale's life and exploits as an imposter, much as they later appeared in the book. The carefully engineered, complex plot could only work with false claims, fictionalized events, crucial omissions, and bogus timelines. All of which were in full display in Redding's *Chronicle* article. Contemporary linguistic scientists have a name for deliberate omissions and the desire to not want to know certain facts, lest they disturb the narrative applecart. They call it strategic ignorance.

It is easy to believe that Abagnale made up a story to hide his lengthy arrest record and his three-year prison stretch in Comstock, New York—which would have immediately undermined the construction of the hoax. But it is very hard to believe that Abagnale had created a narrative of this sophistication *entirely* on his own. There is no question that he was a decent orator. Abagnale could voice a convincing grift, but Redding's material had the markings of a Hollywood script—with many of the elements of what it would eventually become.

A clue also sits within Redding's *Houston Chronicle* article.

Another figure makes an appearance. A former producer and director for both MGM and Columbia. A man with a lot of connections.

\*　　\*　　\*

In 1976, inside a nondescript office building at 5333 Westheimer Road, Houston, the boss at Langlois Communications already knew Frank Abagnale's story well—he helped bring it to life. Leo Langlois, the proprietor of this small film company, had a nose for opportunity. Although Langlois had done some peripheral work with MGM and Columbia in his younger years, he was mostly an adman. His life's work had been in award-winning advertising and branding, marketing and promotion—described by historians as one of America's great "hidden persuaders."[289]

By the time he met Abagnale, sixty-year-old Leo Montreuil Langlois had dabbled in a bit of Hollywood filmmaking, but his post-war resumé was built within the lofty tiers of mid-century-modern American advertising. He worked in the executive suites of marketing giants, such as Campbell-Ewald and Clinton E. Frank Inc. Before branching off onto his own, he was a senior vice president of Houston's AV-Corp, a small entity with massive government contracts. In addition to filming NASA's Gemini and Apollo programs, including Aldrin's moonshot, A-V Corp were separately contracted by NASA to "sell" the space program to a weary public increasingly concerned about the financial cost of space missions. They knew that what we now call "brand journalism" and "content marketing" were the keys to swaying public opinion. Producing a wide variety of public affairs films, astronaut biographies, management briefing films, and the like, Langlois and his team quite literally "sold the moon."[290]

Leo Langlois was an accomplished propagandist.[289] In fact, he had a hand in the famously wacky atomic-era *Duck and Cover* film that taught kids how to dive beneath their desks in the event of nuclear Armageddon. With the growing reach of television as a medium for mass marketing and social narrative, he had moved over to a small filmmaking company. There he had leveraged multiple contacts to break into government training and public service films.

And so, it is curious that within months of appearing in court for his crimes against Tom Manison, Abagnale had found a second Houstonian who had a front seat to the Apollo liftoffs. Perhaps less surprising, Abagnale's relationship with Langlois was also doomed to end in the courts.

For a guy with more than a working knowledge of how Madison Avenue sells dreams, and how government agencies and established institutions need attractive narratives, Langlois must have seen the tremendous potential in Abagnale—the 28-year-old Bronx man who had arrived in Houston via Perpignan prison. It is not clear whether Abagnale and Langlois first crossed paths during the development of crime prevention public service videos—which they are known to have produced together—or whether Abagnale first came to Langlois's attention through other channels, such as Aetna or the local talks Abagnale was giving to anyone who would listen.

But in Redding's *Chronicle* article Langlois was introduced to readers as a reputable source to vouch for Frank Abagnale. Langlois' MGM and Columbia pedigree, which Redding name-dropped into the Abagnale feature, provided a very meaningful endorsement. But it is highly likely that Langlois helped engineer the puff piece in the first place.

"Frank has to be one of the greatest hoaxers of modern times," Langlois said in Redding's 1977 *Houston Chronicle* article. Given that Langlois Communications were under contract to commercially promote the "life history of Frank W. Abagnale Jr." and given the efforts made to rewrite that history, it is hard to believe that Langlois did not know the true significance of describing his client as the greatest hoaxer. "For sheer audacity, he ranks with Ferdinand Demara and Stephen Weinberg," added Langlois.

Redding reminded his readers of the once-famous but now forgotten feats of Ferdinand Demara—who had successfully posed as a Royal Canadian Navy surgeon, doctor of psychology, a law student, a school headmaster, a college professor, a Trappist monk and even an assistant warden of a Texas prison—all verifiable. Similarly, Stephen Weinberg, who penetrated the White House on a ruse to be invited for lunch with President Warren Harding—but is best known for posing as the Romanian ambassador to the United States. The new-generation imposter Frank W. Abagnale was in good company, although Demara and Weinberg had been driven by self-aggrandizement, not profit, and neither had greatly benefited financially from their ruses.

But Langlois Communications had different plans for Frank Abagnale.

In 1977 Langlois announced he was negotiating a potentially lucrative movie-book package deal on Abagnale's exploits with his associates in Hollywood. Redding featured this information in his thinly veiled advertorial on Abagnale. But failed to mention that it was he, Redding, who was in the process of writing that book! In other words, Redding was leveraging his position as a journalist with the *Houston Chronicle* to write a trumped-up promo article about the imposter, taking quotes from the adman working on the movie-book deal, and neither mentioned that Redding stood to profit as the author, if they could sell the story!

America, the beautiful.

Langlois, like Redding, had seen the potential of what Abagnale was selling. What's more, it is hard to imagine that the award-winning creator of entertainment and marketing materials did not have a hand in creating the impressive new version of the story of Frank W. Abagnale Jr. and the campaign behind it.

Abagnale, and his new story, had been transformed into a highly marketable commodity—as history would soon show.

And Americans would buy anything. They were already buying pet rocks by the millions. Pet rocks! Two and a half tons of ordinary rubble sold around that time. Neiman-Marcus was peddling them in Texas, and the "inventor" was on Carson's *The Tonight Show*. Twice. The cultural scaffolding was already in place for another easy sell.

The only wrinkle was the *real* story, which, if revealed, could unmask a very different man with very different lived experiences. In order to construct and protect the Greatest Hoax on Earth from discovery, every effort was made to conceal reality, employing all the tools that "hidden persuaders" can employ—distraction with glamorous fantasy, wild entertainment and the touch of legitimacy that comes from a good book with a reputable New York publishing house.

\*   \*   \*

Although Redding's *Houston Chronicle* feature article had the appearance of an in-depth investigative report researched by the staff writer, it was essentially the fabricated narrative of alternative facts created to sell a reconstructed version of Abagnale's life—with all the notes that would capture public interest and imagination.

The benefits were mutual. Most of Redding's *Houston Chronicle* promotional article was subsequently used and credited in Abagnale's own promotional material—that is, it was reprinted almost word for word in the famous sixteen-page dossier used as part of his press kit. To underscore, the same dossier that Ira Perry determined was filled with falsehoods, and a press photo of young women at their Pan Am graduation ceremony, included an

371

acknowledgment that its content was largely based on Redding's article and reproduced courtesy of the *Houston Chronicle*! For his part, Redding was set to write what could be a best-seller. And the chances of that happening were more significant with Langlois involved.

Public records in Houston's Harris County Courts show that Redding almost certainly communicated with Abagnale and Langlois long before he promoted him in the pages of the *Chronicle*. But we will get to that.

First, we know that at least one article much earlier in 1977, from an independent source, recorded Abagnale saying Stan Redding was already writing "a book on him." And that the book would be released as early as July 1977.[17] Much else of what Abagnale said at that lecture—including how Dustin Hoffman spent a month living with him during the filming of *Marathon Man*—was clearly fabricated. But Abagnale's mention of Redding by name, just weeks after the McAdams cafeteria launch-pad gig, demonstrated he knew of the local storyteller. Most likely as part of the movie-book publicity campaign that Leo Langlois was already working on.

Was Redding provided with an agreed-on narrative to work into the book? How much did he know? For seasoned journalists, there is a greater expectation for scrutiny and verification. They are held to a high standard of truth and trust. But in his *Chronicle* piece, which is to say, Abagnale's Magna Carta, Stan Redding had not shown *any* visible effort to investigate the claims. Instead, he had acted as Abagnale's stenographer, adding his own flair to the narrative. Stephen Hall and Ira Perry clearly showed that even under a tight deadline, journalistic rigor is possible. Under their scrutiny, Abagnale's tales fluttered apart like dandelion seeds in the wind. They made quality journalism seem easy. By comparison, Redding's work looks like quackery.

Of course, the narrative contains small pieces of Abagnale's actual story, that only he could have provided, dramatically refashioned and sewn together with fantastical yarn to create a new patchwork figure, one that bears no resemblance to the original. A fabrication of more fiction than fact.

Plans for the book with Redding lasted, but the relationship with Langlois did not.

In 1978, Langlois Communications filed a civil lawsuit against Frank Abagnale—suing for their creative intellectual property. Meanwhile, Abagnale continued to pursue a book deal with Grosset and Dunlap and a movie deal with Bud Yorkin in 1979.

Although the reason for the rift between Abagnale and Langlois was not clear, the Langlois lawsuit is in the public domain. It indicates that the communications company had generated an extensive marketing platform, and instructed Abagnale to turn over all materials created, including those that were designed "to commercially exploit the 'life history of Frank W. Abagnale Jr.' whether by books, articles, or other written materials, or by film, videotape, slide/tape, film strips, records, or other audio-visual material," dating back to January 1976.[291] Perhaps it should have been more correctly stated as the "historical fantasies of Frank W. Abagnale Jr."

This dates their relationship to around one year *before* Abagnale gave his first major public address at McAdams Junior High, and around the time the grifter was still living in his parole officer's garage.

Langlois, the hidden persuader with government ties, had been making films under the auspices of a shadowy spin-off company called "Langlois Security Teachings." One of the documents filed in the lawsuit against Abagnale made reference to a "Confidential Memorandum" belonging to Langlois Security Teachings. Langlois convinced the judge to issue a protective order sealing the contents from public view. And both parties agreed.

The lawsuit demanded Abagnale return a video Langlois produced called *Catch Him If You Can*. *Him*, not *Me*. Importantly, Langlois also demanded records pertaining to the earliest agreements between none other than Stan Redding and Abagnale. The civil case dragged on for many years before reaching an undisclosed resolution.

Whatever the cloak-and-dagger operations of Langlois Security Teachings might have been, the filmmaking wasn't the stuff of the Academy. The Langlois "educational" film of Abagnale—seen walking down a grand staircase in a mansion as he begins a day of grifting, tooling around Houston in an Olds Cutlass Supreme, eating ice cream as he cases out a supermarket, and sniffing around the Houston Galleria for a mark—is the type of material that would have ended up on the *Charlie's Angels* cutting room floor. Still, it was all about connections, and Langlois had those.

Any contribution that Langlois Communications made to the early development of Abagnale's marketing does not appear in Langlois' posthumous career credits. But within months Abagnale had gone from speaking at local high schools to appearing on national television on *To Tell the Truth*. Langlois' many connections to television media in 1977 would have been a great asset in engineering Abagnale's rapid rise in fame. In those early days of 1977, while handlers knowingly or unwittingly built up the imposter hoax, Abagnale was already making sure that crowds understood his crimes had no personal victims.

"No one was hurt directly by what I did," he said.[292]

He was tracting from podium to podium, his homilies making converts from the masses in business and banking. Although discussions about a movie had started, the book remained an important step in building legitimacy and celebrity. As Redding had achieved for Freddie Gage. If stories are bound and sandwiched between a hardcover emblazoned with the two words "true story" and a New York publishing house stamp, it is much easier to believe.

When the first edition of the book was released in 1980, Abagnale confirmed it was to gain credibility because even some former clients didn't think his stories were legit.[293] Ahead of the launch, Abagnale told a crowd at Elmira College, in upstate New York, that *Catch Me If You Can* was "90 percent true," and only ten percent fictionalized.[294] He also informed his willing believers that he went to extraordinary lengths to track down all his victims. In Brownsville, Texas, one journalist recorded his claim that he spent $75,000 (about $250,000 today) just to find them. But, he said, some refused payment because they didn't want to pay taxes on the money![133] Other reporters were told similar tales. "I had to hire a law firm. They went back and researched all of the [crime-related] documents," he said, adding that "the only person not paid back was the hooker."[163]

None of the victims this author spoke to, or their families, reported that they were even approached, let alone compensated.

Abagnale made no public protests about the accuracy of Redding's presentation of his story then. The journalist and professional storyteller had found a man with a story to tell, and a talent for selling it. It was still a symbiotic relationship. And it proved *very* beneficial. Fueled by a showbiz-friendly media, the book was a runaway success, rapidly reaching the top ten best-seller lists—outselling non-fiction books by Nobel Prize-winning economist Milton Friedman and self-help guru Wayne Dyer.[295,296]

There is no question that it was a shared venture. It had to be. It may even have become difficult for Redding and his pal to dissect the parts of the Frankenstein creature they had sewn together with grains of truth from Frank Abagnale's real life—and there were many—and favorite fragments of other stories they had both collected along the way. All with the certain assistance of Langlois, a proven puppeteer and propagandist. There is also little doubt that together they had created a monster with a power that no one had fully anticipated.

Had Redding taken advantage of the naïve man in Abagnale? Or had the young opportunist taken advantage of a once-respected journalist? Redding proved himself to be a man willing to bend reality to greater effect than any Hollywood screenwriter might have done. Either way, the effect was grand. And they may not have cared. For the longer they dwelled in that land, the harder it was to leave.

There can also be no doubt that Abagnale was a more than willing and foolhardy engineer of his story and his fate. His talks are so filled with layers of such excessive and redundant fabrications that they even seem to threaten the legitimacy of the core narrative, whoever created it. But somehow their Frankenstein creation always prevailed and kept growing despite the occasional threat to its protagonist. It wasn't true, but it was becoming real.

For years afterwards, the lawyers for Langlois, Abagnale and their associated parties would continue to fight over who created the story that had been sewn together by Redding—and who owned the rights to commercially exploit the life history of Frank W. Abagnale Jr. The truth may never be fully known. At the dawn of the post-truth world, they were fighting to claim ownership of a true-life story that wasn't even true! Pulling at the parts of their much-loved Frankenstein as it continued marching on regardless.

Hired flack Marjel DeLauer brought the curious creature to the tawdry heights of *The Tonight Show* lot in Burbank,

California—demanding allegiance to Abagnale's maxim, otherwise she wasn't going to give anyone "a damn thing." And almost exclusively, the media obeyed.

With the eventual help of Spielberg's Hollywood in 2002, their creature had taken on a new life of its own. With a wonderful, luminous and shining purity. The growing creature now had a handsome face. It looked invincible.

*   *   *

When Frank Abagnale was arrested in the shadow of his exploits at Houston's Camp Manison in 1974, it was just over two years before he announced Redding was working on a book. At that point, writing a book had not seemed on his agenda. It was certainly not mentioned to those closest to him at the camp while he was driving the faded limo and patinaed prison buses. He was still fighting with his decades' long compulsion to break the law—and had failed—jeopardizing his parole.

Whatever the exact course of events in rebuilding his identity, it was a miraculous transformation. And a highly successful one. There can be little doubt that he had a guiding hand. Or two. Or more. His new bride, Kelly Welbes, had also been at his side in 1976. She had also featured in his first major press materials portraying him as a reformed man. They were photographed together in several major articles before she retreated behind the stage—she was referred to in media as his secretary and executive assistant, and would become the vice president and comptroller of Frank Abagnale and Associates.

*   *   *

The more we have learned about the real life of Frank Abagnale, the more we have come to marvel at how quickly he turned it around. He may have stayed on the right side of the law doing it, but he has not stayed on the right side of the truth. If he had, it would have been a true story of redemption—not fabricated and hollow.

The real story of Frank Abagnale has become a remarkable one and may yet be one of true redemption. We may wonder what would have happened if Stan Redding had written a true account, and if the grifter had been able to tell it. But it may not have been as exciting or as fun, for Abagnale or his audiences. The sentimental among us may wonder how much of a prisoner Abagnale has become of the fabricated story, one that has become harder to escape with each telling.

We might again remember the true story of the man holding tightly to the railing on the bottom of the hot air balloon basket, rising rapidly from the ground; the higher it goes, the harder the fall.[6] Fear keeps him holding on, even with the prospects of ever-worsening consequences. But now, in Abagnale's case, we might also wonder whether he was there, at great heights, entirely of his own accord.

"I used to think of Frank as a wolf in sheep's clothing—one that had been continually fed by the media," reflects Paula. "The more you feed the wolf, the more he eats the sheep. But I am beginning to see how trapped he is in the lies. Now I wonder if he is really the boy that cried wolf. Whatever he says now—I am not sure anyone will believe him—nor should they."

Perhaps that means that others must now tell the story, release the truth and free all those bound by the lies—including Frank Abagnale.

\* \* \*

As time wore on, the film version of the story supplanted the book for Frank Abagnale—and almost everyone else. It gave him a far grander platform to stand on. Monumental. And it was associated with great men, of more glorious pedigrees than Redding. Now he was standing next to Steven Spielberg, Leonardo DiCaprio, Tom Hanks. Men of great social importance who stand as living statues of success. The story was alive in a new form that was so loved that it would be immortalized. Through DiCaprio, he had been recreated as an innocent. It was a good story, a true story that did not even need to pretend to be *really* true. But for the real man, for anyone, there must be a real story. And Abagnale was rewriting his again.

By 2014, he was claiming that he had almost nothing to do with the various retellings of his life—not just the movie, but even the best-selling book it was based on! He said so in a keynote speech at a national conference of CPA practitioners in Long Island, New York. Columnist Claude Solnik was there for the *Long Island Business News*.

"Abagnale described how his life story had become a commodity and an industry—and how the story had been changed through the years," wrote Solnik.[297]

At the same event, Abagnale also claimed he was barred by the courts from making any money through the various retellings of his life.[297] This is simply not true. Not to mention that he *had* profited from millions of book sales and sold the rights to the movie many times over. He went on to say that he didn't even work on the book and that Stan Redding "wrote the book without talking with him."

"He was a police reporter who kind of wrote it with his own research," Abagnale said to the roomful of Long Island CPAs, "But the book was published with my name on it."[297] Funny though, on the inside cover, his autobiography is registered as Copyright © 1980 by Frank W. Abagnale Jr. and the Library of Congress placed his work in their Biography category. To the CPAs, he added that Redding wasn't the only person to create a work based on his life without consulting him. "When Spielberg made his movie, he got most information from FBI agents, I had very little to do with the movie. I don't know that the [FBI] would have let me talk with them [the filmmakers]," Abagnale said. Solnik reported that Abagnale claimed Spielberg didn't speak with him until after the movie version of *Catch Me If You Can* was completed.[297]

This is utter nonsense. Abagnale can be seen in file footage on set during the filming—laughing it up and talking with Spielberg, Hanks, DiCaprio and the gang—as seen even on the *Catch Me If You Can* special features DVD, commonly sold as a two-disc set. What's more, Abagnale appears in the film playing a gendarme!

Abagnale had sold the rights to the story of his life many times over, and it wasn't even true. He seemed disgruntled that others were now retelling it and cashing in—more than he ever likely had. Yet, despite his protests, he still continues to give keynote lectures recounting the same anecdotes he has shared for decades, much as portrayed in the book and the movie, from what he continues to call his true-life story. There is often still a big stack of *Catch Me If You Can* books at his signing table.

\* \* \*

Whatever fallout Abagnale had been anticipating after the film was released, he must have been relieved. Apart from the very minor media skirmishes, the press reports were generally very good. The film was incredibly popular—and still is. Although reference to Stephen Hall's 1978 debunking had made a momentary reappearance, it cast no more than a brief shadow which faded quickly. No one looked any more deeply. And none of the souls he had crossed had yet emerged from the darkness he once cast across their lives. At least none the world listened to or seemed aware of. Perhaps they still lay at the corners of his awareness, as he did in theirs.

Years passed. A decade. Another. The radiant creature of patchwork lies had lived and thrived, spawning a billion-dollar industry. The enterprise became affectionately known simply as *Catch*. As its puppet masters were fighting over who owned it in court, the beast had gently broken away from its strings. A dazzling story growing with new life. Beautiful falseness now turned to legend the world over. And no one really cares. Except those still trapped in the knowledge of truth, hoping that the world will one day be ready to hear—and this time listen.

*Relevant truths have many enemies. The easiest thing in the world is to douse the truth with so much confusion and noise, that its light is made invisible to the world.*
David L. Katz, MD, 2020

# CHAPTER 23
# That's Entertainment!

*What afflicted the people in* [Huxley's] *Brave New
World was not that they were laughing instead of thinking,
but that they did not know what they were laughing about
and why they had stopped thinking.*
Neil Postman, 1985, *Amusing Ourselves to Death:
Public Discourse in the Age of Show Business*[298]

The theater lights begin to dim, quieting the chatter of an audience anticipating the big story about to erupt on stage. It is the 2011 premiere of *Catch Me If You Can*—the musical!

The streets outside the Neil Simon Theatre in New York are decked with dazzling signage to herald *Catch* as "The best new musical on Broadway," which promises "a genuine jolt of pleasure," complete with "high spirits and higher legs!"

And, apparently, early-peek audiences are not disappointed with the performances, because enormous posters are applauding it as "Terrific! Fabulous! Absolutely Marvelous!"

Sounds of a roaring jet can be heard as an overhead announcement is playing—welcoming the audience to Miami International Airport—moments before an actor playing young Frank Abagnale bursts onto the stage, with a troupe of FBI agents giving chase. As they try to arrest him, he protests—he wants everyone to know something.

"I think they should know who I am and why I did it," cries Frank.

"This is one of your tricks!" yells FBI agent Hanratty, as he calls for his men. "You're not going to fool me again, Frank, like you did in that hotel room in LA. You're not putting on a show for these people."

"A show?" Frank looks at the audience and smiles. "A show!"

With a great fanfare of finger-clicking and hand waving, Miami International Airport transforms into a lavish backdrop complete with tuxedoed orchestra atop a flashy bandstand.

"My name is Frank Abagnale Junior—and this is *my story*!"

Time is suspended as the audience is transported on a delightful musical romp across decades to re-experience the story already familiar to most through the now-legendary Spielberg movie, this time told by an affable protagonist with jazz hands.

The rest of the stage saga unfolds in Frank's supposed teenage memories, as he shares the stories of his young life with the audience.

A pageant of color, action, singing and dancing before they finally return to the scene where they began—in Miami International Airport—the place where *in reality* he first began pursuing flight attendant Paula Parks with chocolates and flowers, following her from airport to airport, making her feel stalked, before moving in with her parents and stealing from them. Quite a different story from what has just unfolded on the stage.

\*    \*    \*

*"There was a time when people must have lived lives before*
*they could sell them . . . before they could persuade or*
*induce the world to buy or read their stories.*
S.T. Wallis, 1855[299]

A Broadway musical . . . based on a movie . . . based on a book . . . based on a story . . . that had never been verified . . . about a man that nobody really knew at all . . . plumped and puffed after a talk at a junior high school cafeteria in Dickinson, Texas. Forty years of marketing and soft media in the making.

The theater production of *Catch* officially opened on April 10, 2011, to mixed reviews. Many felt it did not translate well as a musical and that the creators had been challenged by dated content and failed to deliver a likable protagonist. All the same, it was nominated for four Tony Awards in 2011, and Norbert Leo Butz won the award for best performance by a leading actor in a musical.

And in the audience that night at the Tony Awards was the *real* Frank Abagnale Junior. What must it have been like to watch his creation celebrated on stage? Too bad Redding, a man described as one of the biggest liars in Texas history, and Langlois, one of America's most hidden persuaders, weren't around to see it all. The strange twist of events that had taken his *real* life from the Bronx to Broadway was more dramatic than the movie or the stage production. He had nothing to do with the musical production and told his audiences that he had not even been consulted.[297] In fact, his only credit listed on IMDb is as an "audience member" at the 2011 Tony Awards for the nominations.[300]

As the performance toured the country, some of agent Shea's retired FBI colleagues proudly attended the production. One, who really didn't know Abagnale, provided a pre-show talk about the con man. Another was photographed at a show with his autographed copy of Abagnale's book, flamboyantly inscribed to "One of the guys who finally caught me, My Best, Frank Abagnale." It all reinforced the long cat-and-mouse FBI-chase narrative . . . the one that had never taken place.

In reality, it was the many *local* law enforcement officials who had been catching the fairly inept criminal who mostly used his real name. Time and time again. With due respect to the FBI, Abagnale's story from 1964 to 1974 had little to do with them. It was the local police in Eureka, Mount Vernon, Tuckahoe, Westchester Parkway, East Boston, Baton Rouge, Montpellier, New York, and Friendswood who had put the cuffs on Abagnale—but were never acknowledged. An inconvenient truth. For sure, Spielberg's image of guys dressed up in suits with thin ties and fedoras chasing their man is way cooler.

Abagnale continued to misrepresent his relationship with FBI Special Agent Shea as a "father figure" who had taken "a special interest" in him over his teenage years, during the fictitious pursuit[203]. All completely at odds with the facts. He nonetheless ingratiated himself with Shea's family after his death, and he even took some of them to the Broadway premiere of the musical.

"They loved it," Abagnale told reporters, "We all had a wonderful time."[203]

When Paula Parks had first heard about the swinging-sixties musical, she immediately thought about how horrified, sad and frustrated her parents would have been. She has not seen the play and says that she never will.

"I thought the world had finally gone completely mad," she said. "We may have truly arrived in a post-truth era where people can't tell fact from fiction. But a Broadway play? Singing and dancing to celebrate a liar who still denies his past? You can't make that up!"

She had no resentment toward those behind the Broadway production.

"They based it on the Spielberg movie," she said. "Who can blame them for building on the big-dollar brand of the Spielberg film? I just wish that it had never even got that far ... that someone with both clout *and* conscience had put a stop to this madness much sooner. They sure wouldn't listen to us."

It has been hard for Paula to reconcile the character that had been created by Spielberg with the *real* character she knew—the man who had been, literally, creeping around her parents' house, manipulating their sympathies, and Reverend Underwood's, without showing the slightest conscience. He had abused their trust, not only with his thievery, but afterwards when they had tried to help him avoid prison and get psychiatric help.

"I wonder who would play Reverend Underwood and the Hanging Judge if they ever remake a film or a play about the *actual* real story." Paula shook her head. "It is one thing to get away with the original lies, and the ongoing deceptions, even to this day," she said, "but for him to sit and watch people celebrate it on Broadway unaware ... most likely enjoying his biggest con yet ... Enough is enough. It's time to wake up!"

When Mark Zinder got wind that the high-kicking chorus pageantry was about to arrive on Broadway, he felt much the same. Hyping the life of a fraudulent fraudster in a song and dance routine was elevating the story to new heights of ridiculousness.

"It was a bridge too far," said Mark, who also refused to see the play or the movie.

He was almost amused to hear that some critics were actually disappointed that the musical format "diminishes the cleverness of Frank's cons" such that "all the terrific show-stopping song and dance numbers interrupt our appreciation of Frank's conning skills."[301]

"We see him more as a womanizer than a con man," wrote disappointed critic Tom Williams after seeing the musical production.[301]

"Well, perhaps the musical was truer to reality than they realized," chuckled Mark in response to that point. "But there is no doubt that he *is* really a con man. He conned me. He is *still* conning the world. Right now," he said. "I am still struggling with the guilt that I played any part in his story. And, when I did wake up, that my efforts to stop it came to nothing."

Has the Frankenstein creation, affectionately known as *Catch*, finally crossed the line? Has its form become so overstuffed and over-botoxed as to become so truly ridiculous that its beauty is fading? Is the world ready to see what lies beneath the pretty patchwork of lies?

Sometimes things have to go to ridiculous extremes for the world to finally open their eyes to reality. This whole enterprise was very deliberate from the beginning. He might not have done it alone, but Abagnale was at the center of it.

"The biggest help Abagnale ever had was actually from the willing press," said Paula. "There have been exceptions, of course, some who asked difficult questions, but affectionate media is what really sold it all."

There is no question that the media had a major role, if not *the* greatest influence, in making Abagnale what he is today—not just by what they *did* in promoting him, but arguably more through what they *didn't* do, by failing to investigate him. With very few exceptions, journalists across the nation, and eventually the world, simply repeated the con man's own talking points. Even as he *told* them he was a con man! A con man! It is astounding that so few made the effort to look behind the curtain. Complicit through complacency. Or had they just been dazzled by the flim-flam, as they had been with Evel Knievel?

"It says more about where we are as a society," said Paula. "That the lines between truth and fantasy are so blurred that we can't tell the difference, and if we do see the difference, we too often prefer an entertaining lie."

\*     \*     \*

*The minimal, and perhaps most important, task of journalism in any well-run polity is to prevent lying with impunity. News organizations accept this responsibility, but for a generation or more have demonstrated a lack of capacity to fulfill it.*

John Nerone, PhD, Professor Emeritus, University of Illinois[302]

Rather than ask real questions, the media have helped put a con man on the world stage. And in the 1970s, no stage was more powerful than Johnny Carson's at *Tonight*. Indeed, he was commonly considered the most powerful man in the nation—even more powerful than the president.

"The Johnny Carson show is really a religious ritual," said Susan Margolis, author of *Fame,* in 1978. "He is like a priest to us, and I think the person who appears on the Carson show is ushered into fame the way people are ushered into marriage or baptized. Fame in some very hidden way seems to promise immortality."[303]

Television critic Robert Metz described Carson as arguably the greatest mythmaker in American history. *The Tonight Show* was considered to be "the seedbed of our contemporary mythos, our American dream" and had created and developed larger-than-life personalities more than *any* other communications vehicle.[304]

"Almost no one in show business will criticize Carson," wrote Metz, "and then only when the speaker is strictly off the record. For if a court jester becomes king—with more power than a potentate, more wealth than a Woolworth—who will dare to warn the jester that he's become a fool?"

And was Johnny Carson a fool to let Abagnale onto his stage? History would suggest so. Once on his set, Abagnale made a complete fool of Johnny. And the fool created a new prince.

It was not only the reach of *Tonight,* which was transmitted into fifteen million homes every night, it was the oxygen of Carson's name for the flames of publicity. The almost supreme power of deciding who the next American hero should be.

And in modern times, that supreme power has shifted.

To Google Inc.

Now, the most powerful kingmaker and breaker is a media company with a global reach far beyond anything even conceivable in 1978. The company owns YouTube and holds approximately 90% of the global search engine market. Along with most other major tech organizations, Google Inc. has made a commitment to reduce the spread of false information on the internet.[305] Such steps to shine light on fake news are laudable.

*We need to work hard to make sure that the digital revolution does not turn into a dystopian nightmare, a world in which anything goes without proper scrutiny and knowledge is re-imagined as an opinion based on an ever-spiraling loop of repetition of information that has never been properly checked.*
Prof. Andrew Hadfield, University of Sussex, 2020[306]

So, when Frank W. Abagnale walked onto the stage at the Google Campus in 2017, it was very much the modern-day equivalent of Johnny Carson almost fifty years earlier.

To be invited to speak at the Talks at Google series was one of his most significant endorsements yet—especially as the company stands for promoting *truth*. The Talks at Google podium is, according to the company, reserved for "the most influential thinkers, creators, makers, and doers." The unspoken blessing was enormous, not just for the full auditorium at Google the day it was recorded, but for the global audience of seven million people (and counting!) who have viewed it since.[107]

This would have been his best opportunity yet to tell the truth. The actual truth. And set the record straight. It would have been an incredibly terrifying but an extremely powerful thing to do. To say he had had enough of lying. To say he was out. To leave with the truth out in the world. He probably would have got a standing ovation. He would have owned it and transformed his own story.

But that was likely not even a consideration.

He did what he always does—repeat his litany of falsehoods. The fabric of truth was cracked once again. Abagnale conned Google Inc. and their young employees. An enthralled group of young and impressionable fans looked on—unaware that they were a new part of the multigenerational con.

The same stories were reconjured. Strangely never old after fifty years. He still mentioned that he'd worked as a pilot, a doctor, a lawyer. Although more specifics were obscured than in his early versions, he still mentioned, by name, that he had worked with Attorney General P.F. Gremillion in Louisiana for a year practicing law—the place where, in reality, he had been picked up for vagrancy and convicted for stealing from the Parks family.

He did curiously revise his account of the impossible escape from an aircraft toilet which appeared in his book, and countless early accounts—including the first 1977 articles that featured his wife. But he had been heavily criticized for the impossibility, especially after it appeared in the film. He naturally passed it off onto Spielberg's imagination.

"I escaped off the aircraft through the kitchen galley where they bring the food and stuff onto the plane, and [in the film] they had me escape through the toilet," Abagnale told the Google audience, "and [while watching the film] my wife kind of looked at me and said 'You didn't go through the toilet did you?' and I said no I didn't go through the toilet."[107]

But it is hard to imagine that his wife Kelly Welbes would be so surprised by Spielberg's toilet escape scene, unless she had never read her husband's own autobiography or listened to his lectures over the years—it's right there in the book, and there are countless recordings of Abagnale describing the toilet escape. It would also mean she never read Sussman's syndicated newspaper article or Redding's landmark *Chronicle* feature from 1977—although she was present in the newsroom and photographed at her husband's side.

The Talks at Google event was an enormous success, prompting great applause and more than eight thousand comments on YouTube, mostly positive, about his talent and strong moral character.[107] Would they still say that if they knew he had been lying to them? Some actually might. That is the attraction—people are impressed by a good con. Even if it is on them. That is post-truth in action. And that's entertainment.

Abagnale had now fooled the most powerful company in the world—what was he planning next?

*So the greatest liar has his believers; and it often happens*
*that if a lie be believ'd only for an hour, it has done its*
*work* . . . *falsehood flies, the truth comes limping after it; so*
*that when men come to be undeceiv'd, it is too late; the jest*
*is over and the Tale has had its effect* . . . [truth
following lies is] *like a physician who has found out an*
*infallible medicine, after the patient is dead.*
Jonathan Swift, 1710

\*     \*     \*

"Unreality" is a new and threatening menace. In 1961, Daniel
J. Boorstin described modern Americans as the most *illusioned*
people on Earth—the first people in history to have been able to
make their illusions so vivid, so persuasive, so realistic that they
can live in them.[307] The making of illusions has become the main
business of America—manufacturing news, entertainment,
products, gadgets, adventures, celebrity and even artificial heroes.
We can fabricate fame. But making someone famous does not
make them great.

"We can make a celebrity, but we can never make a hero,"
wrote Boorstin, ". . . we confuse [celebrities and heroes] every
day, and by doing so we come dangerously close to depriving
ourselves of all real models."[307]

Since the 1970s, our ability to manufacture celebrity has shot
into overdrive, and with it our ability to manufacture truth, with
fading awareness of what is real and if it even matters. Now, the
21st-century post-truth crisis of misinformation has been
described as "the major moral crisis of our times."[308] It has
become the norm to share fake news even if known to be false.
Repetition brings the illusion of truth. Each exposure enhances
the likelihood that falsehoods will be deemed true. It breeds

familiarity and trust. The scientific research confirms, quite literally, that "if people are told something often enough, they'll believe it."[309]

Now, we have reached a new and stranger state of affairs. The public has woken up in shock, only to discover much of the new media is no longer providing unbiased facts at all. Now alternative facts are currency—and consumers must decide which version of reality they want to tune into. Polarizing talking points have become expected and tolerated. The truth and ethics have been lost somewhere along the way.

But there is an optimistic side of the ledger—we crave truth. It has an important social function. A glue that holds us together as a functioning whole. It keeps us grounded in a shared reality. It curbs tension and anxiety while providing large-scale unity. Collectively, we understand this. We've begun to see that truth is under assault on a large scale that has passed a certain tipping point, and now we respond as if a virus has invaded our collective social body. We know it can be life-threatening.

Being awake is the first step toward change. Recognizing the implications of the post-truth crisis is important for meaningful change to begin—be this by calling out specific cases of deliberate deception and injustice, or shedding light on the wider societal implications of allowing misinformation to go unchallenged.

The role of an honest media is more crucial than ever. Their power to shape, and reshape, the narrative of our reality is unparalleled. Media power has shifted from broadcast news to a much larger online universe. Amid the noise of social media, the need for clarity and truth is even greater. Correcting public misinformation by closer scrutiny of those seeking power and influence has never been more important, whether a presidential candidate or a con man from the Bronx. It doesn't matter how morally flamboyant that person appears to be. If they are standing on a soapbox constructed by lies, then we should know the truth.

> *The making of illusions which flood our experience has become the business of America . . . demanding more than the world can give us, we require that something can be fabricated to make up for the world's deficiency.*
> Daniel J. Boorstin, 1961[307]

\* \* \*

Now anointed by Google Inc., the sky has no limits. Abagnale continues to sell his story at packed venues across the nation. The enthusiasm of his audiences is undiminished. Neither is his irresistible urge for spouting outrageous alternative facts.

"I have turned down three pardons from three sitting presidents of the United States," he announced at Google[107] and to other audiences since, "because I do not believe, nor will I ever believe, that a piece of paper will excuse my actions."

It is perhaps stranger that he has never been challenged in all the years of saying this.[310,311] No reporter had ever asked which presidents had offered such a gift, only to be rebuffed by the con man. It's worth pointing out that unwanted scrutiny invited by the lengthy Office of Pardon Attorney process would almost certainly reveal his hoax. Plus, a federal pardon would have no bearing on his state-level crimes. It would only pertain to his federal case—little more than a thousand bucks worth of Pan Am checks. Not something he would want revealed. But, like so many other outrageous statements, no one appeared to question that he had refused three presidents.

The bolder the lie, the less it is questioned. We need to re-examine the classic features of mythomania, the scientific term for repetitive fabrication.

Psychologists have studied mythomaniacs for over a century. They are individuals who provide imaginative tales, often with contagion-level appeal. Their fluency of speech is both persuasive and seductive. Indeed, many political, corporate and religious leaders have mythomaniacal tendencies which make them so effective in recruiting followers.[312]

"The true mythomaniac constructs a coherent story— coherent for himself at least—that he tries to make others believe. He ends by believing in his own fabrication, and this is the measure that those around him believe it. He is a gambler who doubles his wager every time he sounds a note of credibility in others," wrote Marcel Eck, MD, who explained that mythomaniacs will not stop lying out of a desire to be truthful. They will only stop a lie when they think it no longer has any interest. Or if they are found out.[313]

Like the airliner toilet escape.

"He will then construct a new fabrication," Eck added.

Bizarrely, the desire for attention is so great, they will implicate themselves in crimes, even if it's not true.[313,314] Material profit is often a factor, but not always. The compulsion appears to far outweigh the risks of being caught.

Abagnale's grandiose untrue claims were not limited to his talks.

Mark Zinder recalls the first time he realized that the con man might still be making up tall stories. They were with famed actress and comedienne Phyllis Diller in Los Angeles, not long after Abagnale had recruited Mark.

"I remember the first time I saw him get caught in a lie," said Mark. "We were in LA, visiting Phyllis Diller, a new friend of Frank's. They were on *The Tonight Show* together."

Mark showed a photograph he still has of the three of them. The lovely and dazzling Phyllis Diller is flanked by both young men. Each is wearing an open-necked shirt with wide pterodactyl wing-sized collars flaring out over the jacket. Frank's jacket is embroidered with the letters "FA," and Mark recalls that his cuffs were always ornately embroidered with his flamboyant signature. With monogrammed cufflinks. Frank is smiling broadly at the camera and also has what appears to be a silk handkerchief in the pocket.

"Frank told Phyllis Diller that he had not just one Rolls Royce, but a *fleet*," said Mark. Abagnale had bragged about having a warehouse full of cars to Mark as well—each with license plates personalized with his initials.

"We then went out for drinks, and on the way back, Phyllis asked Frank if he would drive her car—a Rolls Royce! Frank got behind the steering wheel but clearly couldn't figure out how to drive it," recalled Mark.

Frank appeared to have no idea how to even start the car! Shades of Camp Manison when he screwed up the transmission of the old prison bus.

"It was pretty embarrassing," said Mark. "Phyllis had to tell him. He was having the hardest time just trying to figure out how to release the brake. I was in the back seat, bewildered."

So many of his lies were pointless and even trivial.

Even Mark only learned the full truth of Abagnale's *actual* true-life story from this author, now a new friend, as we discussed the content of this book, *The Greatest Hoax*. He was stunned to discover that Abagnale had been easily caught by authorities in the United States and abroad, and had been in confinement for almost all of his late teenage years.

"Now I see Abagnale's story like P.T. Barnum's mermaid on display. Patched together bits of a large fishtail sewn onto a primate body," said Mark.

"I can't believe that this is the guy who has been selected as an ambassador for the AARP, our nation's advisor to senior citizens, advising them how to avoid shysters and protect themselves from by scammers—when *he* has been the one selling a $17 paperback with his made-up stories," Mark added. "But standing up at Google—that really takes the cake."

\*　　\*　　\*

Debunking Abagnale is no mere act of academic fancy, nor just an effort to correct the historical record. The platform for victims to speak their truth fulfills even larger objectives. His story, the things he actually did, juxtaposed against the emptiness of the things he did not do, provides a greater learning for what ails America today. In recent years we have seen many brave individuals share their long-suppressed truths. Truth matters. When perpetrators are protected or even exalted by the media, celebrated by the public, and financially rewarded at grotesque levels, it adds further to a sense of powerlessness for those who are directly affected, but also for those who witness it.

Those who are perceived to be more powerful are also assumed to be more moral. It is assumed that those who have made their way into powerful positions are generally deserving of their status. When a public figure betrays the public trust on national television, telling what turn out to be atrocious lies, the subsequent discovery of these falsehoods sends a message through society.[315] It says lying is normative. It says, "Hey, it's the way we've become, everybody's doing it." Mere signals of virtue become more important than facts.

And we should not forget the individuals who are affected when their trust is taken. There are many more than those included in these pages.

*We're supposed to take the view*
*that his crimes are victimless.*
J. Westhoff on *Catch Me If You Can*, 2002[316]

Let's be clear. Victims of non-violent crime carry significant health effects. Not only a litany of physical health problems—especially heart disease, diabetes, depression and stroke—but also psychological disorders magnified by shame and diminished self-worth.[317,318,319,320] This is especially so with betrayal by someone who was trusted. It's a vicious cycle with long-term implications. Powerlessness erodes trust more generally. People see the world in a more negative light.

Loss of trust persists for years. Indeed, there were a number of people who were contacted for this book who, though supportive, were too troubled to share their stories in these pages—still traumatized, intimidated and fearful of the power afforded to the perpetrator by his celebrity.

*When we discover that someone we trusted can be trusted*
*no longer, it forces us to re-examine the universe, to*
*question the whole instinct and concept of trust . . . we are*
*thrust back into some bleak, jutting ledge, in a dark*
*pierced by sheets of fire, swept by sheets of rain, in a world*
*before kinship, or naming, or tenderness exist; we are*
*brought close to formlessness.*
Adrienne Rich, 1977[321]

But it runs even deeper. At larger scales, involving the general public, such betrayal can induce widespread cynicism. It leads to generalized distrust of actual experts. That's a particularly dangerous outcome in our modern world where denial of expertise is increasingly common. We lose our rudder and our compass altogether.

In 2017, the renowned physician-scientist Sir Michael Marmot reminded us that there are two sides of the post-truth coin. On the one side, there is the obvious lie. And on the other, the bulk resources and immense effort required to dismantle the lie.[322] Without truth, and with the wearying, tiresome act of continually having to debunk falsehoods, the whole system crumbles.

*Deception has become the modern way of life. Where once the boundary line between truth and lies was clear and distinct, it is no longer so. In the post-truth era, deceiving others has become a challenge, a game, a habit.*
Ralph Keyes, *The Post-Truth Era: Dishonesty and Deception in Contemporary Life,* 2004[323]

At some point, the fantasy and flim-flam must wear off. Once the veil is lifted, the myth is shattered, and no amount of celebrity spin can restore the illusion once broken. And the once-spellbound media will help turn that tide against a fallen hero—as Evel Knievel had learned.

In the summer of 1977, just as Abagnale shot to fame, fading hero Evel Knievel was in a downward spiral. He had tried a final shot at fame with his own big-name film production, *Viva Knievel!* And decided to star in the picture himself—"bearing out P.T. Barnum's thesis on the gullibility of the American public," wrote one sharp critic.[324] But the film followed a trajectory similar to Knievel's ill-advised shark jump. Resolutely downward. Scorched by film critics, it sealed Knievel's fate.

"It's not autobiographical, merely autoerotic . . . infused with worship of an image," wrote film critic Desmond Ryan. "Not only will it hear no evil and speak no evil about Knievel, it will not even address itself to the moderately interesting question of *who* he is, and *why* he does what he does.[325]

The show was over. The public had finally seen the reality.

*Abagnale's lecture may be the best*
*one-man show you will ever see.*
Tom Hanks

# CHAPTER 24
# Return to Baton Rouge

*The most ominous cultural divide lies between those who*
*chase after manufactured illusions and those who are able*
*to puncture the illusion and confront reality.*
Chris Hedges, 2009 [8]

None of us quite expected what happened next. In February
2020, as the major contributors to this story were reviewing the
completed manuscript for this book, an unanticipated new
chapter started to unfold. With a strange life of its own, the story
took a new twist as Paula Parks discovered our central character
was about to make an appearance in her hometown—just about
fifty-one years to the very day he had been jailed in Baton Rouge,
after stealing from her family.

Frank Abagnale was scheduled to hold a book signing and
give the luncheon keynote address at the Louisiana Association
of Business and Industry (LABI) annual meeting in Baton Rouge
on Tuesday, February 11, 2020. Paula only learned of this just
days before the event and was immediately overcome with a
powerful mix of emotions. She felt renewed outrage that the man
who had stalked her, hurt her parents and deceived their
community would once again be in their midst spinning lies—this
time celebrated and paid a good round sum for doing so.

Frank Abagnale may have been selling the same lies for decades, but this time it was so close to home. Too close. There was also an overwhelming desire to finally confront him. Paula knew she might never have the chance again. A strange and powerful karmic synchronicity seemed to be drawing their paths together again after more than fifty years. It was too much to ignore.

She started playing dozens of scenarios in her mind.

Just imagining the range of dramatic possibilities was therapeutic. A private confrontation? A more public challenge? Or should she just leave this in the hands of the local media? It was an incredible story with a local twist. The local paper would surely be interested and would know far better how to handle the situation. In that moment came a new sense of empowerment in just knowing that she *could* influence his fate, at least on that day—*if* she chose to. There might be some personal closure and satisfaction, but was it the right thing to do? Would it achieve anything?

Paula spent all day deciding what to do.

She was well aware that very few in the media had shown any interest in the veracity of Abagnale's outlandish claims. Most had served only to glorify him. In forty years, barely a handful had done *any* significant investigation or challenged him. But one of them was from her own local paper—the *State-Times*, now *The Advocate*.

Years before, local Baton Rouge journalist Fayette Tompkins *had* challenged Abagnale—especially the outrageous claim he worked for Attorney General Jack Gremillion, the respected member of their Baton Rouge legal community.[71] In 1981, when the con man was promoting his new book *Catch Me If You Can,* Tompkins had alerted his readers to the serious doubts over Abagnale's claims, in a series of stories that ran in the *State-*

*Times*.[71] In particular, Tompkins had taken an interest in Paula's family's story and interviewed both of her parents, Bud and Charlotte Parks. He had reported how the con man moved into their house and accepted their hospitality while he was stealing from their checking account.[35]

Tompkins even revealed that Abagnale had been jailed in Baton Rouge after his arrest for vagrancy, forgery and theft.[114] The report also featured an interview with then-retired AG Jack Gremillion himself, who confirmed that Abagnale had never worked in his offices.

"Far as I'm concerned, he is a fraud," Gremillion told Tompkins, his Louisianan accent audible through the printed word.[71]

Years later, Paula could only imagine Jack Gremillion's outrage if he had lived to see Abagnale telling the world he got the job as an assistant attorney general through Gremillion's own daughter!

"I met a girl whose father was the attorney general in Louisiana and I ended up telling her I had a law degree," Abagnale told the fawning host in a recent 2018 PBS interview.[326]

Paula knew how grateful her parents were to Fayette Tompkins (who later worked with *The Advocate* when the *State-Times* closed its doors). They had really admired the journalist for pursuing the truth when others had not been interested. Tompkins had long since retired, but Paula hoped that there were now others at *The Advocate* who would be interested in bringing the truth back into focus. After fifty years, enough was enough!

After much deliberation, Paula decided on two things.

The first was personal. She *would* attend the event. If she didn't seize the opportunity, she knew she would regret it later. Paula planned to speak to the grifter privately to make it clear how much pain he had caused her family, amplified by the decades of his lying since. She had no desire to cause a ruckus or challenge him in front of his audience. But she would make it clear to him that she knew of his lies. That it was her hope that he would choose to *finally* tell the truth—and own it.

The other thing was to contact *The Advocate*. She would alert them to this unique opportunity—to expose the truth and set the story straight. It was such an important story, and she hoped that they would see that. How could they not? After all, the man continues to claim that he worked in the offices of the attorney general in Baton Rouge for close to a year!

Indeed, the young reporter Paula spoke to at *The Advocate* seemed fascinated and surprised to hear the story. The journalist immediately appeared to understand both the local importance and wider significance—an amazing opportunity. Paula arranged to email them the court records and previous reporting which exposed Abagnale's lies. The journalist sounded excited to investigate further and to attend the event. But first, the reporter said, it would need to be cleared with the bosses at *The Advocate*. The reporter had all weekend to look into it and would call Paula back before the event.

With the larger story now in the hands of *The Advocate,* Paula turned her mind to what she would personally say to Frank. Would she tell him that she still had his letters? The photos? That she had his own parents' letters? That she knew he was in Great Meadow Correctional Facility for almost the entire period he claimed to be posing as a lawyer, doctor and a pilot? She made notes on what she might say. She hoped for meaningful discourse. In the end, it would all depend on how he reacted. It was more nerve-racking than she imagined. She hoped that *The Advocate* reporter would be there to witness it—especially if Abagnale refused to acknowledge her or tried to intimidate her.

But Paula heard nothing more from the journalist. Or anyone else at *The Advocate*.

"Their silence spoke volumes," said Paula. "With each passing hour it looked like they were going to crush the story. They had all the information—his criminal record in Baton Rouge and Fayette Tompkins' previous columns debunking him—and they must have deliberately decided not to act on it. I can only assume they didn't want to rock the boat."

Paula wondered if the journalist would still turn up. But as the event approached it was more and more likely that the bosses had already blocked the story.

"That was pretty disappointing," said Paula. "I figured I should dress all in black because the truth was dead. And no one seemed interested in reviving it."

The message seemed clear. Frank Abagnale was famous. She wasn't. The establishment appeared more interested in protecting the liar, and the group that invited him, from embarrassment than informing the public of the truth. This should have been no surprise. It had been happening for decades. But Paula had just hoped that with the local interest *The Advocate* might stand up for truth, as they had stood behind Fayette Tompkins' gutsy reporting in 1981. And this time, in the digital age, it might create a more lasting ripple effect. But no.

It didn't matter. She would go anyway. Even if she had to face her nemesis alone—she would.

*The traditional role of reporting [begins] with the assumption that those in power have an agenda and are rarely bound to the truth ... it is the job of the journalist to do the hard, tedious reporting to expose these lies.*
Chris Hedges, 2009[8]

\*  \*  \*

Fayette Tompkins had retired from journalism. But he remembered the story well. And he remembered Paula's family. He was still living in Baton Rouge and was also unimpressed to discover that Abagnale was returning to repeat his old lies. It had been astounding to see the trajectory of Abagnale's career in the decades since his journalistic search for truth and listening to victims' voices led him to expose the self-professed Great Imposter as a fake.[71]

He, too, hoped that the story he had started at the *State-Times* might be revived with far more impact than he had been able to achieve almost forty years earlier. Fayette had been one of the very few to elevate the work of fellow journalist Stephen Hall, who had been the first to expose Abagnale's deception in 1978 for the *San Francisco Chronicle*. Under any threat of media scrutiny in the past, Abagnale had quickly retreated and canceled events—as he had after Hall's piece—a sure sign of how flimsy his lies were, caving with even the smallest effort to push against them. The problem was that there had been so little pressure of scrutiny since. And so, it seemed that Abagnale had been free to truly become a great imposter after all.

Fayette Tompkins explained all this when he was contacted by this author in early 2020. He was pleased to learn that Paula Parks would be attending Frank Abagnale's event. He was also considering it himself.

Fayette knew that this *could* be a big story. Really big. More than it had been in his day—because of the film and the vast public profile Abagnale now commanded. As a seasoned newsman, Fayette also knew that if a younger reporter from *The Advocate* was going to write a piece, and he hoped they would, that last thing that they would want was one of the old guard like him getting involved. Out of respect for former colleagues, he did not want to interfere. If Fayette went at all, it would have to be as an observer. A concerned citizen. Very concerned.

\* \* \*

Paula still carried a flicker of hope that someone in the media might take an interest. She took great comfort that she was not really alone. As her new friend, this author, Alan Logan, also understood the depths of the story and was providing moral support from a distance. But we both knew this was Paula's part of the story, and she had to make her quest alone. There couldn't be any diversions or distractions from Paula's purpose.

And so, while Abagnale most likely slept soundly, Paula had a long and sleepless night. She knew she might only have a matter of moments in a book-signing line to make her points. Most of all, she wanted to remember everything and hoped she would not be too overwhelmed to take it all in. Paula still really needed an impartial witness who understood the significance of the moment.

As she got ready the next morning, Paula's thoughts were with her parents. She had decided to ask Abagnale to sign a book for them—to inscribe it with an apology, no matter how insincere it might be. Paula felt that her parents were with her as she nervously made her way to the conference venue—not knowing what lay in store for her.

\* \* \*

Over the weekend, the author had reached out to Fayette Tompkins. Both in appreciation of his work and to let him know that Paula had contacted *The Advocate* and was planning to go to the event. In the meantime, Fayette had been considering how he might help. He knew what they might be up against. Which is to say, the power of willing believers. Even when presented with incontrovertible evidence, people still preferred to believe the con man.

"I still don't understand it," said Fayette. Ironically, the biggest pushback he remembered was when he went onto a university campus.

"I was covering Abagnale's 1981 appearance at Tulane University in New Orleans for an article, and the accumulating evidence was disproving his claims," recalled Fayette. "But the students rallied around him in what seemed like protective hero worship. They made it clear I was not welcome."

The Louisiana Association of Business and Industry would likely be even less sympathetic to any efforts to undermine the reputation of their star attraction.

By Monday evening, hearing there had been no further word from *The Advocate*, Fayette was considering other options. He was retired, but he still had contacts of his own, including someone who had no fear of speaking truth to power.

On Tuesday morning Fayette confirmed he would be there. And that he would be bringing a friend—Tom Aswell from the *Louisiana Voice,* an important outlet created to provide the citizens of Louisiana an inside look at those in power in politics or public life. They would try to intercept Paula before she went into the venue.

\* \* \*

Paula had already arrived at the Crowne Plaza Executive Center on Constitution Avenue. The main event was Abagnale's luncheon keynote lecture, but he would be holding a book signing beforehand from 10:30 a.m. What stuck in her throat the most, was that she had to pay two hundred dollars to get in the door! But it was worth it.

She was still outside collecting her thoughts when she got the call to wait for Fayette Tompkins and Tom Aswell. It was a relief to have moral support on the ground. Paula is known for her confident, fearless attitude to life, but even she admitted that this was hammering her nerves. It annoyed her that she had let a man, who was oblivious to her, have this effect on her. Not for long.

Fayette and Tom assured Paula that they were only there to observe. Not to interfere. It was her show. They would not disclose who they were. It was forty years since Fayette had challenged Abagnale, and he probably would not recognize the journalist. Tom would be carefully watching the interaction for a story on his popular blog on the *Louisiana Voice* website, "Graft, Lies and Politics—A Monument to Corruption." Paula thought that seemed like a fitting home for a story on Abagnale.

It seemed strangely surreal to Paula as they made their way across the crowded lobby to where the book signing was scheduled to begin. The conference area was already thronging with attendees for what was anticipated to be a packed ballroom for the luncheon keynote event.

But the signing area was distinctly quiet in comparison. And the man sitting at the table signing books looked disappointingly small and insignificant. There he was with a big stack of his books, including a new release. Paula begrudgingly purchased a copy of *Catch Me If You Can* and stood in the short line to have it signed. She did not have long to collect her thoughts. It was all happening too quickly. Tom was close behind her to her right— watching but saying nothing. Fayette was not far behind him, making sure they did not appear to be together.

Suddenly she was standing in front of the table. Abagnale was looking up at her.

"Do you know who I am?" she asked. He clearly did not, muttering something she did not understand. He seemed to think she was the wife of some LABI delegate who evidently was a big fan.

She suddenly realized that her name badge had likely confused him.

"Paula Parks," she said clearly.

No acknowledgment. No reaction.

"I was the Delta flight attendant, who was there when you started your scam," said Paula.

Still nothing. He just stared at her.

"You knew my parents—Charlotte and Bud Parks," she added. "I would think you might remember after what you did to them," persisted Paula.

"Do you want me to sign the book?" was all he said.

"You lived with them. You stole from them," she tried again.

Now Paula was convinced she saw his gaze falter. Even if only ever so slightly.

"So, do you want me to sign the book?" he deflected again.

"Yes, I want you to sign the book to my parents," Paula said calmly, although the world seemed to have disappeared and she was lost in time, "and I want you to write that you are sorry for what you did to them."

Frank Abagnale Jr. made no protest. He reached out to take the book that Paula was rotating toward him. In his well-practiced flamboyant script, he started writing "To Charlotte and John," as she had instructed.

"Now, write that you are sorry," she reminded him. If others in the line thought this was odd, no one said a thing.

He dutifully wrote the word "Sorry!" And underscored it twice. Just as he had double-underlined "I beg for it" in his plea for help to Reverend Underwood in exactly the same way, fifty years earlier. There seemed little sincerity in his action now. Just as there had been no sincerity then. His actions were those of a man trying to comply with a strange request from a woman he silently claimed not to know. He was avoiding a scene.

There was still no acknowledgment. He seemed to still be pretending that he did not know her. But he did seem unsettled. Perhaps he was worried about what she might say next. She was tempted to remind him of his letters, and how he wrote "I'll never forget what I did to them for as long as I live" and "I think of that 24 hours a day. I'll be sorry for the rest of my life." But she decided against it.

Instead, she decided to challenge him on something that he could not deny—facts in public record.

"You were arrested here in Baton Rouge," she reminded him. Even if the mind of former convict was a little foggy, he would surely remember he was arrested on Valentine's Day—for stealing from the very same Charlotte and John he had just signed a book to. "Why don't you ever tell people *that* in your talks?" she challenged him.

That's the instant his demeanor changed.

Now he looked "nervous as hell," according to Paula. His composure was momentarily broken. Tom, watching on, saw it too. They all did. Abagnale had started writing the date in the book above his signature as she spoke and clearly faltered. He miswrote. Paused. Started scribbling a correction. Then stopped again as he considered his answer.

"That's because I work for the FBI," was his cockeyed retort. It was not a denial. It was a deflection and a dismissal. They both knew that he was *not* working for the FBI when he was arrested in Baton Rouge. He had only just been released from prison. And it made no sense as an explanation. Did he think that she would be bedazzled by his mentioning the magical three letters FBI? Was that supposed to excuse him from any further questions? She suspected he had used it as a shield for decades. And she was not impressed.

"But really—why don't you tell people that you were arrested here?" asked Paula again, realizing that she had hit a nerve.

*Secrecy and deception allows small men*
*the chance to feel big.*
Professor Gerard DeGroot[327]

Now Abagnale was more obviously avoiding eye contact with her. Tom saw that too. Abagnale's pen was still poised before he added the year to the date—in the wrong place on the page.

"I *still* work for the FBI," was all Frank Abagnale said. This time it sounded more like a threat. And a final dismissal. He was already looking beyond her to the next customer in the line. Making it clear her time was up.

"The windbag who always seems to have plenty to say about everything was strangely silent," Paula said later, recalling her exasperation.

Indeed, Abagnale famously provides off-the-cuff monologues, especially about ethics and "the dire lack of morality in our society today."[183] On a normal day, a simple question will likely be met with a lengthy sermon on how American prisoners have it easy, why Jewish families send their children to Catholic school, and how Johnny Carson dumped the Pointer Sisters during live taping to extend his time with the reformed con man—because "Johnny just loved me."[183, 328,329] But this was far from a normal day in the life of America's grifter.

The next moment Paula found herself walking out of the room, Tom and Fayette following not far behind her. It had all happened so quickly. She felt totally deflated. He looked so small. A Lilliputian character with behavior to match. He was not even big enough to acknowledge her—or take the opportunity to have a sincere conversation. The golden ticket out of the looking glass world and into redemption was right there for him to grab. If his letters to her parents meant anything, if his claims of redemption ever since meant anything—he would have taken the chance.

But the con man had not changed at all. She didn't really know what else she could have expected.

Tom and Fayette both reassured her. And as they were standing outside in the hotel corridor, a man approached them.

"Are you Paula?" he asked.

She nodded and said that she was, curious.

"This is from Frank," he said and handed her another book. The man appeared to be one of the professional booksellers handling the event.

Paula saw that it was Abagnale's new release, *Scam Me If You Can*. As if. She had no interest in it. Mister bookseller said Frank had inscribed it to her. Frank knew fine well who she was. Was he so tone-deaf to think that she would want his silly book? Or was he just trying to annoy her? That was more likely.

The bookseller man just stood there, expectantly. It was weird that he wasn't walking away.

After the silence went on a second too long, he said, "You have to pay for it."

"What!?" Paula was astounded.

"It has been signed to 'Paula,' so you have to pay for it now," said the man who was oblivious to the complex fifty-year history that hung across the moment. Abagnale, she was told, didn't pay for the book. Paula had to just laugh bitterly. The millionaire con man had already left the ballroom floor, leaving yet another unpaid bill. Some things never change. He was a living fossil.

Refusing to be scammed again, Paula politely gave the book back to the confused seller. Unless the bookseller could track down Abagnale or find another woman named Paula who wanted the book, he was going to have to absorb the loss. Whoever paid for it, they might not realize that it could be worth something one day! But she sure as hell was not taking it home. She was already out two hundred dollars for the event ticket, and more for the fantasy-filled *Catch Me If You Can* book.

As they returned to the main reception area, Paula thanked Fayette, who said he would not stay for lunch. She would have happily followed him out the front door but had resigned herself to stay to watch the performance, to see if Abagnale would stick to his well-memorized script. Knowing she was sitting in the audience, would he still have the audacity to persist with his well-scripted bald-faced lies? Was he wondering if she had brought the press? That he might be heckled? He had nothing to fear on that front. At least not for now. She had just given him the perfect opportunity for honesty but, based on what she had seen, Paula seriously doubted he would *ever* consider telling the truth.

*No legacy is so rich as honesty.*
William Shakespeare, *All's Well That Ends Well*[330]

Paula made her way into the banquet hall, already packed with an adoring crowd of the LABI elite. A privileged few "posed for photos with the beaming author who, in his expensive suit and silver hair, came off as some elderly corporate CEO," as Tom Aswell described the scene after the event.[331]

Mr. Abagnale seemed to grow in the light of the attention, like a strange monster feeding off the energy of others, thought Paula. In those moments, Paula was transported over fifty years back to when this very same creepy man, using false pretenses to obtain her flight schedule from her employer, had stalked her from city to city, before moving into her parents' home behind her back. Sleeping in her bedroom. And here he was, a half-century later, feasting on the limelight and pretending he didn't know her. Taking photographs with a fawning lieutenant governor.

If she told the others sitting at her table, none of them would have believed it. A surreal parallel universe, but real—hidden from view by layers of dishonesty and deception.

Clips from Spielberg's *Catch Me If You Can* dazzled the audience as Abagnale stepped onto the stage, reinforcing his stature and reminding all of his incredible pedigree! The man in the spotlight, Abagnale, didn't just use the coin of the realm, he was minted into it—described by organizers as "a decorated FBI agent."[332] That was a new one to Paula. As usual, though, he began reciting the monologue of his well-worn tales—and all the many lies Paula knew she could prove to be untrue.

The speaker's pants were on fire. His wooden nose grew longer. Paula promised herself not to react, not to douse him with cold artesian water, as the camp counselors did in 1974. As she'd tossed and turned the night before, she had been afraid she could not trust herself to resist the impulse to stand in her seat and yell, "You're a liar! Much of this is untrue! You are still conning everyone with tall tales!"

Instead, she watched the admiring and amused faces around her table in the luminous blue light. It took all Paula's self-control not to walk out. And it was worth it.

Though famous for his seamless monologues, the usual cadence of his speech was uncharacteristically broken in several places, as he stumbled slightly in making several necessary detours from the script—around Baton Rouge. Others may not have noticed. But Paula did. He had said the same thing thousands of times—much as it had been recorded recently at his

Talks at Google. Since starting *The Greatest Hoax* project, Paula now knew his pattern well. She could tell he made several obvious omissions and bumbles—obvious to her at least.

Although all his other falsehoods stayed firmly in place, he spent far more time than usual preaching about morals and ethics, and the importance of family.[332]

"He was really laying it on thick," said Paula, "I almost choked on my food at the sheer hypocrisy."

She could not help wondering if he was also sending her a clear message—he'd achieved redemption—there was no need for her to dig up the past.

"Except that his every ongoing lie is evidence that he has *not* changed," said Paula.

"It's a burden I live with every day," Abagnale humbly told his audience,[332] as those around Paula nodded in admiration.

"I don't believe it for a moment. He had every opportunity to acknowledge that burden to me personally and have an honest conversation about faith and family, and maybe Reverend Underwood, who saved his life," she said. "It was there to take on a silver platter. But he didn't."

She kept thinking, "Have you no sense of decency, sir?"

Paula wondered if the only burden he had really ever lived with was the fear of discovery. She would never forget the smell of fear when he boarded her plane in 1969, just days after he was released from Comstock prison. Or how he had driven well under the speed limit all the way to Baton Rouge to avoid detection. She had seen the fear in his eyes.

There had been little trace of that fear today. Now he was encased in a world of wealth and privilege, insulated by fame. Politicians desperate to be photographed with him. Somewhere, somebody must be building a statue of this man. But, as he'd handed the inscribed book back to her earlier, she thought she recognized a brief flicker of that same fear in his eyes.

"It has been so long since anyone challenged him, or threatened to expose his lies, I think that he has forgotten that fear," said Paula. "But maybe he will remember it again now."

\*   \*   \*

Fayette Tompkins was on the lookout for an article in *The Advocate* but saw nothing. The only column that came out that day was a puff piece in a local business outlet, celebrating the LABI event and their star attraction.[332]

Paula had arrived home utterly exhausted and deflated.

"At least you didn't end up in jail," her husband said, relieved to know that she had not been arrested for brawling or causing a public disturbance.

"That is still on my bucket list," she joked, half wishing that she had made more of a scene.

Later that day, she called this author, Alan, to share her account and debrief.

"I don't know why I'm so disappointed in today," she told me. "He just seems so passive and small. I wanted more of a result from my confrontation, I guess."

But we each knew that this was just the beginning. We hoped that Tom would still write a story that would open a small portal to the truth—one that could pave the way for a much bigger story.

\*   \*   \*

Two days later, Tom Aswell published his scathing story in the *Louisiana Voice*. He described the event as "a carnival sideshow" and entitled it with a challenge—*Did LABI pay a five-figure fee to get flim-flammed by self-proclaimed flim-flam artist at its annual luncheon Tuesday?*[331]

He framed the story around the encounter between Abagnale and Paula, explaining her connection with Abagnale's more shady past, which was rather darker than the version he was now peddling. The article also revisited Fayette Tompkins' stories, with links to the original articles, outlining how Abagnale had been arrested in Baton Rouge for stealing from the Parks family and others. He also linked other decades-old articles which clearly debunked many of Abagnale's ongoing claims—including how Abagnale had fled from the college speaking circuit, refusing to sign the truth affidavit after Professor Bill Toney's systematic efforts to disprove his stories.

"Which raises other questions about his claims as he travels around the country collecting generous speaking fees, which have mushroomed in the aftermath of the movie," wrote Tom Aswell.

"He suddenly developed a conscience about speaking to 'young, impressionable minds,'" wrote Aswell, regarding Abagnale's dubious justification for canceling his college speaking engagements—that it would open him to unnecessary controversy. "That seems a somewhat thin excuse, given the fact that Abagnale has professed to leading a life of considerable controversy for virtually all of his adult life."

That conscience no longer seems to be stopping Abagnale from continuing to tell the same stories to audiences of all ages.

"I'm very popular on college campuses," Abagnale was proud to share only recently.[163]

Aswell expressly outlined the efforts that had dismantled Abagnale's absurd claims about working for the Baton Rouge AG's office, including comment from now-retired Assistant Attorney General Ken DeJean.

Paula was pleased to see that Tom concluded the piece with Abagnale's questionable efforts to dismiss and shut her down by dubiously claiming that he doesn't mention Baton Rouge because he "still works for the FBI."

Using "the FBI" as his shield to deny his *real* crimes against her family in Baton Rouge in 1969—ones he was convicted of— was illogical. Even more illogical was using "the FBI" to justify his highly profitable story of *fake* crimes, like pretending to be their assistant state attorney general—a lie that helped make him a millionaire. Many now believe that Abagnale's "work" for the FBI has been minimal but allowed him to spin an evermore mythical web over the years. He was known to do this with other enterprises—claiming he "worked" for businesses like Neiman Marcus after only giving a lecture to staff.[56] Working for the FBI, even if true, did not justify the way he seemed to be using their shield as a bullet proof vest.

Paula could not help recalling her own "work" assisting the FBI when they interviewed her in connection with Abagnale's "wanted" poster in 1978.

*       *       *

*They* [the FBI in 2008] *celebrated their 100th*
*anniversary and did a big coffee table book and talk about*
*me* [as] *the only person they ever did that with . . . The*
*Director of the Bureau at that time wanted* [my] *ability.*
Frank W. Abagnale, Talks at Google (2017),
claiming that he was uniquely released from the
federal prison, recruited to work directly at the
command of then FBI director Clarence M.
Kelley, and that Kelley gave him various cloak-

and-dagger assignments in military bases,
hospitals, and a lab in New Mexico.

❖

In 2008, the FBI Office of Public Affairs did indeed publish an impressive 100th-anniversary coffee table book (*FBI: A Centennial History*. ISBN 978–0160809552). But despite his bold claim of being featured in the comprehensive volume, Frank W. Abagnale's name does not appear anywhere.

\* \* \*

The article lifted Paula's spirits. Not because she expected it to have wide reach—that was not the goal yet—but because there were signs that it resonated with people. Even if *The Advocate* had not taken an interest, others in the community were actually listening—and many were supportive and sympathetic. Maybe times were changing. She hoped so.

"I knew my reunion wasn't going to lead to instantaneous change. It takes time to dismantle a myth embedded so deeply in the social fabric," she said. "You have to work around the edges, that's how change works, gather more people who see the falsehoods, injustice and inequity, and working your way to the core."

Later that day, Paula was on the phone to one of her good friends. She asked if her friend's husband was still a subscriber to *The Voice*. Oh yes.

"Ask him if he has read today's article," said Paula, as her friend relayed the question to her husband.

"Oh, definitely," Paula heard him say, he read it, adding how much he enjoyed reading the very revealing piece—which was as much a commentary on the corruption of selling celebrity in a post-truth inverted reality.

"You realize that was Paula," said her friend to an astounded husband.

"Our Paula!?" she heard him shouting. "I can't believe it! Wow! Amazing!"

So many of Paula's friends were impressed and proud of her. She was not seeking validation, but it was good to hear all the same. She had still not told anyone about the book. If they were surprised now, wait until they heard about *The Greatest Hoax*. But she was not ready for that yet.

\* \* \*

Like many who *actually* knew Abagnale, Paula had stopped telling people about the *real* true story years before—because most could not believe it. Attorney Paul Foreman, who knew Abagnale at the time of his arrest in Friendswood, said the same. Legal colleagues in Texas were dubious when he told them about Abagnale's antics as a camp counselor in 1974. Mark Zinder also stopped mentioning Abagnale. The frustration of being disbelieved was not worth it. Better to just never mention him.

Fayette Tompkins had certainly seen the power of belief. He still remembered how the students at Tulane had seemed to be mesmerized by Abagnale's spell. Borderline worship. Even people who had never met him didn't want the story to be untrue. Fayette had not received any opposition from his editors back in the 1980s—they had no hesitation in supporting his story.

Indeed, at least two other news outlets in Louisiana were appalled by the 1981 Tulane lecture, writing a joint editorial:

"Today's 'heroes' are not easy to find, and if the kind of example set before the student body at Tulane recently is any indication of what our youth has held up to them as role models, we have no one to blame but ourselves. Invited to speak last week at Tulane's McAllister Auditorium was Frank Abagnale, con man deluxe. And for his efforts he is a national celebrity. Surely there are better images of 'success' to set before our youth."[333]

But the belief has only grown. The celebrity has grown exponentially. It was two decades before the movie had made *Catch Me If You Can* folklore and built its main character into a tragic, misunderstood, iconic figure. It is a situation that has become all too familiar. The more famous, the more powerful its protagonist, the less likely that a story will be challenged, even if the evidence to do so is clear.

Award-winning author Rebecca Solnit has warned that too many in the establishment, mainstream media "let people who have been proven to tell lies, tell more lies [which] get reported without questioning."[334]

Addressing graduates at her alma mater, the University of California Berkeley, she urged the next generation of journalists to restore public trust and understand what it truly means to "break" a story—it means smashing up the dominant status quo bias of simply believing people in authority, the rich and powerful. She inspired the fresh graduates to boldly investigate the truth. Break up falsehoods to make news.

"Dominant culture mostly goes about reinforcing the stories that are the pillars propping it up . . . they are too often stories that *should* be broken," she told the journalism graduates. "Examine the stories that underlie the story you're assigned, maybe to make them visible, and sometimes to break us free of them. *Break* the story!"[334]

But perhaps it falls to all of us to be part of this process, building truth from the grassroots, and rebuilding a culture where deliberate deception and falsehood does not thrive unchallenged. Especially when false narratives seem as prominent as ever.

Never before in human history have the stakes been so high. We must protect ourselves against grandiose narcissists and Machiavellian purveyors of falsehoods. These are the people, research shows,[335,336] who are willing to lie, cheat, and steal in order to obtain their objectives—to tell us black is really white, and the moon is just the sun at night.[337] These are the people that satiate their gluttony with short-term interests at the expense of humanity and the health of our planet. Many of them rise through the ranks to take influential podiums in the Western world. These individuals, verbal strongmen with greedy aims masked by spurious claims, are society's largest threat.

Research reveals that liars prefer to embed their lies into a mixed bag of otherwise truthful statements.[338] We need to be educated at an early age on how that works.

At this vulnerable time, with so many grand challenges, the importance of separating fiction from fact has never been higher. Understanding the ways and means by which grandiose narcissists and authoritarians disrupt well-being at community, institutional, national and planetary levels—how they spread lies and hoaxes—is an urgent mission.

*The ability to amplify lies, to repeat them and have*
*surrogates repeat them in endless loops of news cycles, gives*
*lies and mythical narratives the aura of uncontested truth.*
Chris Hedges, 2009 [8]

# CHAPTER 25
## Legacy of Truth

*Real reporting is nothing more than the best obtainable
version of the truth. Getting at the truth is hard work. It
requires making phone calls, knocking on doors, spending
hours with people who know the subject, and most
important of all, giving credence to information that might
be contrary to the reporter's preconceived notion of the story.*
Carl Bernstein. 1990[339]

Stories are powerful. They make us who we are as individuals, as
communities and as societies. They create the narratives that
bring us together, but also have the power to pull us apart. And
so, the stories we choose are important. As is the understanding
that we have the power of choice in creating better stories for a
healthier reality—for each and for all.

Storytelling is a universal human trait. It is a feature of culture,
society, language, behavior and psyches the world over, without
known exceptions. Study of the few remaining traditional hunter-
gatherer groups—societies that reflect our ancestral heritage—
show that storytelling has been an evolutionary asset, promoting
cooperative social behavior, equity, purpose, respect and
egalitarianism. Skilled storytellers held the cultural identity of the

group and were as important, if not more, than the hunters or the gatherers.[340]

Myths, and more specifically, mythical heroes, are also part of the human condition. We grow up on fables, legends and parables. Their purpose is to teach us about life, love, ethics and morality. To pass on knowledge and create awareness. To inspire purpose and encourage good judgment. These stories do not need to be true to be positive. But we *know* what they are. And that they are told with good intention, usually embodying a higher truth for the benefit of the recipients. When we enjoy George Lucas's *Star Wars* films, we know Luke Skywalker isn't real, but we recognize the timeless messages of the modern legend, and the deeper purpose layered within it. We share the fundamental and unifying elements of the mythology.

> *A hero ventures forth from the world of common day into a region of supernatural wonder ... the hero comes back from this mysterious adventure with the power to bestow boons on his fellow man.*
> Joseph Campbell, *The Hero With a Thousand Faces*[341]

This is very different from gross misinformation and deliberate disinformation—stories that are calculated to exploit, control and manipulate. The intention is very different. These are often told with thoughtless, selfish or malicious intent usually for the benefit of the storyteller, rather than the recipients. Such stories do not usually serve a higher truth and may damage individuals and undermine communities. They seek to shroud awareness. They are not told with love but can satisfy selfish motives.

The problem for modern societies is that narrative and

storytelling have become the domain of those with largely ulterior motives—usually power and profit. From large corporations and political factions to individuals seeking fame or fortune. Today, stories are the tools of advertising to create appetites for our consumer reality, whether it is selling entertainment or products or influencing opinions for political agendas. Narrative is used to capture the emotions, beliefs and behaviors of consumers for the large-scale profit of the storytellers.[340] Often at the expense of the health of individuals, communities, the environment and deeper societal values. Stories of deeper purpose and meaning are neglected or forgotten.

But awareness is creeping in. It is a time of reawakening. A time for challenging forces that have dominated others through greed, fear or intimidation. There is a renewed hunger for truth. For justice and righting past wrongs. For retelling stories that have been corrupted by self-interest or financial gain. And growing intolerance for those who control or suppress truth. That includes Hollywood moguls once considered untouchable.

Ignorance is not bliss. It is a lesser state of being. Especially if it has been created through propaganda and deliberate deception to limit us. Awareness restores power—the power of choice. We cannot change what we cannot see.

If we want to change the world, we need to take on the big stories that have corrupted it. These are the ideals that lie beneath the telling of this story, and why we chose to tell it.

The purpose here is truth, awareness and the kind of justice that comes from shedding light on falsehood so that something better may grow. It is not retribution. It is not vengeance. It is for the love of truth, in a world that needs more love.

\* \* \*

Reverend Underwood was a man of stories. He used them every day. Sharing stories of hope, kindness and purpose for the betterment of his congregation and his wider community. Frank was almost twenty-one when he came to the reverend's church in 1969. The story that later became *Catch* did not even exist yet. There had been no fantastical escapes. Or international travel. Frank had spent most of the previous four years in prison for petty crimes. His teenage travels had been from one jail to another. When the reverend eventually learned Frank Abagnale's *real* story, he accepted him anyway.

Within weeks of his release from prison in New York, Abagnale found a home with Bud and Charlotte Parks—his first home, perhaps, since his own home had been broken by divorce. The family welcomed him. Although he tried to hide the truth, his own behavior quickly betrayed him, and his criminal past came to the surface anyway. Had he trusted them with his truth before he took theirs, he would have learned just how kind they were.

His was not the story of a teenage mastermind, it was the story of a troubled adult who had arrived in a community that would have been prepared to help him. Did Abagnale really find so little value within himself that he thought he had to pretend so others would like him? He said as much in his letters. If they can be believed.

"I have always found that I had to be a fake to find someone who cares," he wrote in 1969, as he was pleading for forgiveness and asking for the opportunity for reform.

Reverend Underwood did everything he could to get Abagnale psychiatric help and avoid what could have been a ten-year sentence in one of the harshest prisons in America. But that effort was also abused when Frank violated his probation and absconded. There is nothing heroic or daring about that. Even then, the reverend found forgiveness.

There was no story of reform. More petty crimes followed. Stolen cars. More forged checks. More kind people abused. More arrests and prison terms. Theft at a kids' camp. Deception at an orphanage that his parole officer decided not to report. Accusations of fraud by Aetna. None glamorous at all. And with no resemblance to his later claims.

This was the story of Frank Abagnale that Paula Parks knew.

But suddenly a new story appeared. The story of Frank Abagnale that Mark Zinder knew and believed, like most of the world, at least initially. A colorful hoax. Filled with fantastical capers, dishonesty and the illusion of reform for profit. Not merely alternative facts, but a complete alternate reality. A story that was falsely marketed and sold—as truth—for fame and fortune.

Undoubtedly, in the decades since, Abagnale's years of experience consulting in white-collar crime, document forgeries, cyber-security and the like have forged legitimate expertise. On that score, Abagnale cannot be challenged.

There is also little doubt that Abagnale has earned the title of great con man on his resumé. *Not* based on his tissue-paper thin history of forging some checks and briefly wearing a pilot's uniform—but because he has *lied about his past* and benefited from those lies for so long. The fact that his hoax has convinced so many, for so long, so far around the world, probably does earn him the accolade of "The Greatest Con Man"—although society would do well to ask if that is something to be valued. The hoax has devoured so many in its slithery travels, including prestigious institutions and trusted media outlets, like a coldblooded reptile that swallows a deer, whole.

However, his efforts to steal the ultimate title of The Great Imposter from Ferdinand Demara have failed—because

Demara's fantastic lives and careers were actually true and documented as they occurred.[342] And later, Demara's biographer, Robert Crichton, traveled to the places where his subject had been an imposter, *with* Demara, to verify what he had done—from the people who knew him at each location. If Abagnale's biographer Stan Redding had tried that—which he clearly did not—the game would have been up immediately. Demara retains his Imposter title. Hands down.

But there is no arguing that Abagnale's tenure as a grand hoaxer has lasted far longer than others—forty years and counting. After the death of showman Evel Knievel, there was a revival in interest about the man who once burned so brightly in the early 1970s. Mostly, the revisionist history on Knievel eludes the fact he flickered out almost as quickly as he arrived—no longer welcome. Once the switch was flipped—the truth was contagious. Nostalgia now paves over much of the facts.

> *Five years ago* [Evel] *was sitting on top of the world.*
> *Regardless of how ignorant, crude or absurd his public*
> *statements were, he nearly always was treated like a*
> *genuine American hero. But today, time, the law and the*
> *truth have caught up with Evel Knievel. No longer the*
> *recipient of undeserved respect and celebrity-worship by*
> [the] *misguided,* [Knievel] *now is almost universally*
> *recognized for his true self.*
> Gary Deeb, 1982[343]

Even a fallen hero will still have some believers—some in the chambers of commerce, where Abagnale has also been so popular, still believed in Evel Knievel. In September 1985, Knievel was invited back to Twin Falls, Idaho, the site of his unsuccessful canyon jump a decade earlier. His friends at the local chamber of commerce decided it was time to unveil a stone monument at the site to mark the occasion and offer a marquee event worthy of a hero's welcome.

Only fifty people showed up. But, still shouting from a flatbed truck, Knievel told his ardent fans that "the canyon was a stage, and the world was my audience," although nobody much was listening anymore.[344]

As the truth of Frank W. Abagnale becomes known, will it become contagious? Will romanticized misinformation and revisionist history continue? People who have been conned sometimes hold a strange admiration for those who conned them—but we hope that the value of truth will be held higher. There is so much more at stake.

Abagnale has shown, to great effect, how powerful a story can be in transforming reality. There is no question that he transformed his life to achieve vast fame and wealth. He may even have actually *achieved* his claim of being "The Greatest Con Man" in the end, but at the expense of the very ethics and moral code he was claiming to represent. Recall the FBI motto: Fidelity, Bravery and Integrity. One cannot stand at a podium and lie about the past, while fantastically clinging to the fundamental definition of integrity. From its Latin root, *integer*, integrity means adherence to whole truth. Not the deception of partial truth or overt lies.

A story of reform based on deception is not reform at all. It is the very opposite. It is a further betrayal of the truth. It should have no place among our modern legends, save as a cautionary tale.

The case of Frank W. Abagnale should indeed be remembered for what it teaches about discerning facts from fiction—and the *intent* behind a story. The myth of *Catch* may be a wonderful, engaging and inspired story. People love it. It is entertainment.

But it is a fiction sold as truth. All the while, the real truth is hidden. And that is deception.

*   *   *

Stories do not really ever end while they are still in our minds. They are added to by our every thought. And when a story is broken, we can change it. That is our purpose here. To do as Rebecca Solnit advised the graduates—to break the story.

When this project began, we were strangers. Paula had been trapped in the awareness that the truth lay dormant, despite her efforts to bring it to light. And she had no plans to rejoin the story. Mark was also trapped in a decades-long hibernation. But without their voices and personal experiences, this book would have been another academic exercise by the author. Instead, Paula and Mark agreed to become part of this story again in order to change it—so together we could tell the true story.

We are indebted to the many others who have added their experiences in this journey of discovery. With the author's extensive research, and the many other voices willing to join our quest, together we have told the truth as completely as we can, contextualizing it in the bigger picture of why it matters. For all of us, this speaks to the much bigger issues that challenge our society today.

This is not about "catching" Abagnale because "we could" . . . it is about releasing the truth and releasing all those bound in the lies, and the frustration of those lies—including the man at the center of it all. The truth presented here offers a key to open a lockbox of lies. There is no value in retribution. There is already too much fear and hatred in the world. Shining a light is intended to dispel that, not to humiliate but to heal all those affected.

We are not the first to try. We tread with the benefit of the footsteps of others—like Stephen Hall, Ira Perry, Fayette Tompkins, Linda Stowell and Bill Toney—whose valiant efforts failed to displace the powerful hoax. But for the first time, we have been able to show the impossibility of his claims by providing an accurate timeline that shows exactly where *he really was,* and share the stories of those who lives he touched along the way.

Now it is time to answer one great story with another. Each story that goes before makes the next greater for what must be overcome. Building an even greater shared story toward a greater truth—far more powerful than what was—for what can be learned by all in the process. And the character at the center may yet triumph, by stepping into the truth. That is not our choice to make. But we offer a key to a captive, that we may all be free.

The story of the future is ultimately written by all of us. By the choices we all make as we ask—what kind of stories do we want to shape our world and the world of our children?

# AFTERWORD
## Assuredly Not the Last Word on the Myth

*When I first heard the name Clouseau, he was a little
nothing, just another police officer in a small village far
from Paris. He was the village idiot, I think.*
Chief Inspector Dreyfus, on Jacques Clouseau,
The World's Greatest Detective

The world cheered. Inspector Clouseau had saved the day, the
Pink Panther diamond was restored, and the president was about
to decorate the "The World's Greatest Detective"—yet again!
Defying his own intelligence and in spite of himself, the
bumbling detective continued to stumble into triumph and
perpetuate the myth of his own greatness—all the while believing
the illusion of it.

It was during my work on this book, examining Abagnale's
antics between 1974 and 1976—from Camp Manison to
Blackmon's garage and Westbury Square—that I couldn't help
notice the newspapers at the time featured the film *Return of the
Pink Panther*. Peter Sellers back in the role he was made for. It
allowed my imagination to drift ... to how "The World's
Greatest Con Man" might fare against "The World's Greatest

Detective." An amusing clash of titans in my mind. But it opened another unexpected line of thought as I suddenly began to see *The Greatest Hoax* in rather a different light.

But first . . .

The origin of *The Greatest Hoax* dates to the summer of 2017. While I was researching misinformation, pseudoscience and post-truth, I stumbled across the forgotten story of another con man, "Doctor" Robert Vernon Spears, who adopted many identities as he perpetrated confidence schemes and much more over the course of five decades. My interest in the devious but evidently charming con man became the basis of my last book, *Self-Styled: Chasing Dr. Robert Vernon Spears* (Glass Spider Publishing, 2019).

It was in the course of researching and publishing *Self-Styled* that comparisons with other famous con men became inevitable—most notably Frank *"Catch Me If You Can"* Abagnale. Indeed, even the Kirkus review of *Self-Styled* made this comparison. Extensive research had allowed me to chronicle Robert Spears' life story through mountains of historical newspaper accounts, police records, court documents and medical fraternity journals—all providing a clear trail of his life and crimes as they occurred. This is also the case with other famous imposters, like Ferdinand Demara, whose story was told in Robert Crichton's 1959 book *The Great Impostor* (Random House). Extensive records and contemporaneous documents verify their stories.

Not so with Frank W. Abagnale.

After reading Abagnale's 1980 autobiography, *Catch Me If You Can* (Grosset and Dunlap), I went back to the archives for verification—police, court and journalistic records—but unlike with Spears and Demara, I found almost no evidence to substantiate Abagnale's claims. The facts I did discover allowed me to rotate the Janus face to its correct side—and a wholly different story began to emerge.

Instead, it was the picture of a bumbling, fumbling, small-time grifter—an Inspector Clouseau of con men. A young man who, despite himself, seemed to cruise to later-life titles of greatness. Certainly not because he was a master thief. Quite the opposite—his "career" was peppered with amateur mistakes. He was efficiently inept. Easily caught, time and time again. People saw through him. Daftly, he used his own name wherever he went and on the handful of Pan Am checks he wrote, apparently foiled his own escape by tampering with the laminate on a perfect forgery, and had his bright-yellow getaway car double-branded with the word "Bandit" so police had no problems finding him!

Strangely, he also seemed plagued by bizarre coincidences, which only added to his rapid undoing. Like driving cocksure into a remote northern Californian town to try his hand at opening a bank account, only to discover he had picked the *very* place that was home to the country's leading paperhanger hunter. Like choosing an obscure kids camp to work his cartoonish furloughed Delta pilot ruse, only to learn his co-worker was daughter to an *actual* Delta captain. Like attempts to recruit beautiful young stewardesses from a college campus with creepy "health checks" only to have a male co-ed with airline experience show up looking for a job. Like setting up office in an orphanage, where, as chance would have it, his parole officer used to be the superintendent! A would-be comedy of errors had there not been actual victims.

Too often, he was assisted by well-meaning people before they inevitably realized his dishonesty—and that he was stealing from them. Even when he was convicted, he seemed to get off lightly. Like when he was convicted of ripping off the older couple who had invited him in to live with them in Baton Rouge. Even recently, when asked about it by the couple's daughter, he used his illogical but ever-ubiquitous "because, FBI" excuse.

*That damn Abagnale uses my name all over the place, but I've never even met the guy.*
Robert Russ Franck, Retired Director of the FBI's Houston Division. 1978

None of the actual events resemble the fictionalized account that the world believes today. Not even close. Yet, somehow, despite it all, the biggest name in the history of Hollywood took him on and soon the world was celebrating him as "The World's Greatest Con Man." He fell ass-backwards into an "ambassadorship" with an older person lobby group, even as his older person victims were still awaiting restitution! He became a de facto spokesperson for "the Bureau"—telling listeners how he has taught ethics at their academy, and even the Lieutenant Governor of Louisiana has introduced him as a "decorated agent." What's more, he sauntered onto the big stage at Google Inc.,—global authority on fact-checking—to tell the choked-up "Talks at Google" crowd he was an assistant attorney general etc., that it was the filmmakers, not him, who concocted that nutty airplane toilet escape, that his mother never remarried, that he never laid eyes on or spoke to his dad after he ran away at 16, and that he was "arrested only once" in his life, and on and on . . . and on it goes!

All this in the hypervigilant "fact check" era after the 2016 election, yet more than enough hot air to break whatever misinformation meter Google/YouTube normally uses. Much like Inspector Clouseau, perhaps he too has begun to believe his own myth. Or perhaps he will argue it was all his greatest con?

It is certainly poetic that the cameo role Abagnale played in

Spielberg's film was a French gendarme arresting himself. Not to mention the uncanny physical resemblance with Peter Sellers as Inspector Clouseau.

In the end, of course, Clouseau is always the winner, mostly thanks to the toil of those around him. He rose up through the ranks to become the "greatest detective of all time," despite his massive ego, incompetence, proneness to infatuation, and penchant for unnecessary disguises. His international reputation soared, and before we knew it, all the elite organizations in the world wanted Clouseau's genius. He was introduced as a decorated agent. But select people knew the truth of how and why the not-so-great detective was exalted. Sound familiar?

It brings to mind one of the more hilarious scenes of the *Pink Panther* movie franchise. When the Clouseau is presumed dead in a fiery collision, government leaders force Chief Inspector Dreyfus, his long-suffering superior, to give the eulogy at the funeral. The apoplectic Dreyfus chokes on the falsity of the words he is made to read.

"He was admired and respected [by] all those who were fortunate enough . . . enough . . . enough to know him," Dreyfus says, visibly gagging as the congregation believes he is struggling with grief. "He was, above all else, a modest man."

In our real-world of post-truth, words to celebrate Abagnale are far more effusive. There is no hesitation in repeating hyperbole while simultaneously promoting his modesty.

"He is much too humble and understated for what he has been able to give back to the world in sensitive parenting messages, ethical guidelines, and moralistic stories that inspire," wrote one such Abagnale admirer recently. "He is a redemption realized."[183]

And mostly Abagnale's audiences hoot and cheer and could not agree more. Few know that the "life story" so many admire is largely untrue, and that in believing it they are victims of a far greater hoax. But the reactions among those who do know the truth are not unlike Inspector Dreyfus—nauseated, not so much by his original transgressions, sinister as some of those crimes might have been, but by the perennial bald-faced propagation of false glory.

*   *   *

All this may seem like good fun. That is, until we are reminded that this isn't the comedic genius of the fictional *Pink Panther*. Our Greatest Con Man injected himself into the lives of real people. I realized that the hidden truth needed to be shared. But, to be made meaningful, I knew I would need to bring the research and facts to life with the voices of the real people who had been part of that story.

Indeed, earlier fact-based rebuttal of Abagnale's claims had come to nothing. The impressive efforts of journalists Stephen Hall in the *San Francisco Chronicle* (1978), and Ira Perry in *The Daily Oklahoman* (1978), had clearly dismantled Abagnale's story, and yet had been largely ignored. Newsmen have received Pulitzers for less than Perry's reporting. Their heroic efforts had focused on convincing proof that he *wasn't where he said he was* when he claimed to be working as a doctor, a lawyer and a professor. And that should have been enough. But it wasn't. The fly in their ointment was that they had not really traced his actual movements and were unable to report *where he really was*.

That was my seam. But I only got there by reaching out to hear Paula Parks' story.

In Paula, I discovered a strong, no-nonsense, fearless woman with a quirky sense of humor. Paula was delighted to hear that I was looking into Frank Abagnale's real crimes. "Have I got a story for you," she said only moments into our first conversation. And I got more than I bargained for!

We built trust and friendship as Paula shared her memories. But there was also an unexpected treasure trove—letters written by Frank himself, and both of his parents after he had victimized Paula's parents, stolen from her little brother and deceived many in their church community. Paula said she knew the time had finally come to unbolt them. The collection had been under lock and key for fifty years—waiting for this moment. She was not bitter, but she wanted the truth known. And she wanted people to understand the deep betrayal her family felt—not just for how badly he had treated them, but for the decades of deception that followed.

Remarkably, it was the one person depicted as a villain in *Catch Me If You Can*, the film—Abagnale's mother, who was cruelly portrayed as lower Westchester's sleep-around gold digger—who was the con man's undoing. It is hard not to imagine that she was hurt by how she was characterized in the film. And perhaps it is fitting that, in the long-confined letters held by the Parks family, the real Paulette Abagnale left the vital clue. Her words jumped off the page: "He has spent three years in Great Meadow Correctional Institution in Comstock, New York. Two years the first time, [he] came home and was writing checks a week later, spent another year in Comstock and was writing checks again three days after his release."

In those two fossilized sentences, without knowing, she torpedoed the hoax her son would later invent—revealing why he could not have been gallivanting around the world during his late teen years.

Without this disclosure that he was in Great Meadow, it is doubtful anyone would have discovered the ruse. Recall, in order to avert all interest, Abagnale has long maintained he was "arrested only once" and that, he says, was in France. He didn't deny earlier brushes with the law but claimed in his autobiography that his dad used clout to have his records erased. The New York State Archives show otherwise. They answered my query and confirmed Paulette's words—that is, Abagnale's Great Meadow records, including his parole violation—and working backward to Tuckahoe, it turned out there were plenty of records. When triangulated with information embedded in the Baton Rouge police and court records vis à vis Boston, the hoax imploded. Or from another perspective, grew even more grand.

What began as an intellectual exercise was transformed in new and meaningful dimensions. Fact gathering could cast away depictions of the "victimless crimes" in Spielberg's *Catch Me If You Can*. Public records became a disinfectant light. It was no longer plausible to nod in bovine agreement with the Hollywood enablers that wrapped his myth in swaddling clothes. DiCaprio said, "It would never be a situation where he [Abagnale] would steal from someone personally," and Spielberg concluded that "a lot of [it] was very innocent."[173]

Thirty years after stealing from a series of families and small businesses, Abagnale can be seen in the *Catch Me If You Can* special features DVD repeating his false tales—you already know them well. In every case, the implication is that the BYU students, the attorneys, the medical interns, everyone who ever believed each of his alleged ruses were gullible nitwits by default. Considering the whole thing is a "ruse about a ruse" that logically includes the viewer.

Given how many copies were sold, the basements and attics of Every Town, USA, are undoubtedly littered with that special features DVD. Now knowing the facts as they *actually* are, it is worth dusting one off and watching. They'll tell you about the extensive research on authenticity—of the film *sets*, that is, right down to replicating era-specific doorframes! They won't tell you about research on the veracity of the *story* itself. The ensemble is seen huddled together with the subject of their "true" story. It takes on the air of a cabal. The only thing that seems missing is the ghost of Mr. Hubbard making an appearance, in naval-style dress and skipper hat, of course, with a wink and a nod. It is easy to see why those who had tried to speak truth had been ignored or intimidated by the bravado of illusion.

> *I just think he was a victim of his own innocence.*
> Steven Spielberg on Frank Abagnale.[173]

What shocked me was that such little effort had been made to verify Abagnale's story over so many decades, and that the myth had been propagated through soft media, and then amplified by Hollywood—all while claiming it was inspired by a "true story." As many sources contacted for this book can attest, only in a fantasy world of hallucinogenic oblivion is Abagnale "a victim of his own innocence." At the same time, his exaltation to the exclusion of faceless others is as American as apple pie—the embodiment of the glamorization of grift, the culture of cool, and the sugar admen work with to peddle propaganda. The epitome of post-truth.

Apart from Great Meadow, it was not even that difficult to uncover the truth. It is hard not to imagine that others with far greater reach and resources (read: titans of print and television media, with framed awards and golden trophies on their mantelpieces) had either not looked, or worse, decided to ignore what they found. And certainly not listened to people like Paula Parks, who had tried to make the truth known.

As Paula and Mark mentioned in the Preface, this isn't Abagnale's story. He already pulled the trigger on that—told it and sold it four decades ago. Nor is it a challenge to his contemporary legitimacy as a skilled security expert. He is, as we say in Belfast, no mug. On certain matters it can be accepted that he is a "hard man," an individual acquainted with criminality who is "clued-up," and "well-sussed." Even early on, Hall, Perry, Toney, and Tompkins were largely disinterested in his claim to expertise. Rather, this is about the people who interacted with him, real people with names and faces who were surgically excised from a fantasy. And still are.

It was a privilege to support and unite these important personal narratives and witness accounts with evidence-based public documents. Their stories are illuminated thanks to quality journalism, police records, court documents, penitentiary files, New York State Archives, United States National Archives, Swedish National Archives and the National Archives of France. Although many reporters were merely uncritical stenographers repeating Abagnale's claims, their efforts in doing so have still been an invaluable service to history—because from 1977 to 2002, they captured highly divergent quotations from a single man.

In the course of my research, I also uncovered the forgotten efforts of Bill Toney, an academic criminal justice professor who had been appalled by the proliferation of falsehoods. He was also a private investigator with a background in law enforcement and the military and had a low tolerance for Abagnale's blatant lies and had collected an accordion file full of evidence. Toney's work led to calls for Abagnale to sign a truth affidavit before speaking engagements in 1982—Abagnale's refusal spoke volumes. Toney's work was a compass pointing to Mark Zinder.

Mark had become well known in other circles since, but I soon learned that he had been Abagnale's booking manager at the time Bill Toney challenged the con man's claims. It was also clear from 1982 news articles that Mark had been shocked and confused by the reports, and no longer clear on what was true or untrue. Obscure college magazine records also showed that Mark had parted ways with Abagnale soon after—there must be a deeper story there.

Mark had been close to Abagnale and probably knew more about him than almost anyone in the early days of Abagnale's rise to fame. When I reached out to Mark, he told me I had his attention immediately, and I will never forget what he said next, "I've been waiting for this phone call for over thirty years."

Mark is a deeply caring, honorable and good-hearted person. We bonded quickly. It was immediately clear that he carried emotional scars—the depth of which he had not even realized himself until we began talking about it. He also harbored considerable guilt for his unintended role in promoting the "pretend pretender" throughout North America.

I soon learned that if anyone was a victim of their own innocence, it was Mark Zinder. He didn't just have a ringside seat at the match—he had been promoting the whole act. Like the rest of the world, he had been conned by the hoax, but his story was so up close and personal. He had been under the spell of the illusion and had been rocked by others' discoveries and his own guilt on many levels. Mark could have taken the easy road of leaving the past in the past, but for the fact that it was not the past—and Abagnale continues to deceive the world to great acclaim. Stepping into the light was the only choice.

And then there are all my new friends from Texas and Louisiana, who worked with Abagnale at the summer camp in Friendswood in 1974, before his arrest in Galveston County. I can't thank them enough for their hospitality and their stories during my travels through Texas and Louisiana. It was wonderful to see the bonds between old friends, and their enthusiasm to become part of this story. It was also a joy to see some of them reunited after more than forty years—and have them provide invaluable perspectives for this narrative.

Spielberg's version of Abagnale's magnificent story is centered around the mid-1960s—painted as an idyllic, upper-middle-class Sinatra-infused Shangri-La. A myth within a myth. As professor of history Gerard DeGroot notes, most often the myths of the Sixties are boxed as "a collection of beliefs zealously guarded by those keen to protect something sacred."[123]

By now, you know where Abagnale really was between 1965 and 1969. Mostly, he was Great Meadow inmate #25367. In reality, his truly grand adventure began in mid-to-late 1970s Houston. It is far more fitting. And humorous. The Camp Manison alum were quick to point that out. Houston at that time was a hustler's paradise. Where you have shoals of convention hall characters trying to pull in investment dough in the energy sector, real estate speculation and space city dreams, you have a metro where working an angle is expected. And there were plenty of Bonnies to the Clydes—*Cosmopolitan* magazine separated Texan women by geography and personality, identifying the Houston Hustler, who "outcusses, outdrinks and outschemes a good ol' boy any day."[345]

Certainly not the stuff of Spielberg's Sinatra era. Instead, it was 100,000 watts of hardhat rock on KLOL-FM, thumping into a CB-equipped Plymouth Duster. Shag carpet and reality in kaleidoscope. Steve Miller Band's *Take the Money and Run* was dominating the airways. Hooh, hooh, hooh.

The now-defunct Men's Tie Foundation of Manhattan voted Houston as "America's Best Dressed City" of 1977. They might have been having a laugh because their accompanying photo shows business attired everymen walking Houston's downtown streets looking like goons tailing Jim Rockford. The Camp

Manison crew have had some giggles imagining an alt soundtrack to the actual events. What would be on the 8-track when Abagnale was booting along I-45 with a bus full of camp kids? Or on his way down to McAdams Junior High, his first screen test? In any case, the chemical plant that brewed up a few molecules of truth within a molten mix of a con man's fantasy was located in Houston. Stan Redding, described as one of the biggest liars ever to emerge from the state of Texas (and that's saying something!), Leo *"Duck-and-Cover"* Langlois, the man celebrated as the hidden gem among America's hidden persuaders, and of course, Abagnale, the Bronx bezonian. What a team of skilled alchemists. The hoax, made with brittle metal around the time of the American Bicentennial, has surely outlasted the temporal imaginings of its conjurers. Like an old carny ride missing its rivets, it will be consigned to the ash heap of history.

We all have many questions for Frank William Abagnale. And perhaps some will yet be answered. Professor Toney knew that simply asking Abagnale to provide facts on his life, or the lives he inserted himself into, was a fool's errand. That's why he developed the interrogatories. It seems past time to dust-off the truth affidavit.

Still, it is nothing short of amazing to see Abagnale four decades on, still peddling his homespun "autobiography" at book signings. To watch eager devotees line up for a copy, after forking over cash or credit cards. To watch him inscribe his book, the one colorfully cover-wrapped with the silhouette of a scantily clad long-legged female in high heels. Lurking in the background is a dark uniformed figure with a black leather bag—reminiscent of when the autobiographer himself was arrested in Tuckahoe with a similar bag containing Japanese-made handcuffs. Stamped with the words "True Story" and "The basis of the hit DreamWorks movie—now a Broadway musical," the cover belies the fading fantasy that lays—and lies—within.

And that appetite has not dulled with time. His relatively recent Talks at Google presentation alone has been viewed over seven million times and counting. It might seem like hyperbole to entitle this book *The Greatest Hoax on Earth*. But if you step back, you can see an unprecedented beclowning of the upper reaches of power and/or vital institutions that otherwise act as an important societal glue. Our major media outlets, academia, elite tech companies, intelligentsia, politicians, aristocrats of Hollywood, household-name associations, and of course, "the Bureau." That's a problem, because our system, the entire enterprise, only works if we trust the truth within. Eugene Stewart, senior FBI agent and later Delta's security director, knew that. He surely knew that if he, in either of those roles, fabricated his bio in a media interview or at a podium, it would've meant immediate dismissal.

Even though Stephen Hall debunked Abagnale in 1978, the bankers who promoted Abagnale's talk were not concerned. Upon learning that most of Abagnale's tales were fantasy, one banker told Hall that it was still "funnier than hell." An honest summation. Four decades on, our large-scale amusement is unbridled to the point that everything has become funnier than hell—entertaining liars are in positions of immense societal power.

When any authoritative man at the podium entertains us to apathy about facts and truth, large-scale looting of human values is a downwind consequence. Victims with names are canceled. It might not be illegal, but it's a far more dangerous racket. Especially when the perpetrator is the one professing to drain the bog and protect the vulnerable from swindling.

## ALAN C. LOGAN

*And I would've gotten away with it, too, if it weren't for those meddling kids.*
Said almost every unmasked imposter
on *Scooby-Doo*.

It will be interesting to see if those who were complicit—willing or unwitting—are prepared to grapple with this cautionary tale. Examine their own role, as Mark Zinder has done. Will Paula Parks and Jan Hillman get invited to an exclusive London pub to celebrate truth and light up a King of Denmark cigar?

The looking glass reality of Abagnale has become so bizarre that it brings to mind another 1970s phenomena, the most famous animated show about imposters—Scooby-Doo. Our imposter has been pretending he posed as a supervising pediatrician, assistant attorney general and a PhD professor, and that he circumnavigated the globe cashing seventeen thousand checks. He sure had the gang, which is to say all of us, fooled for a while. Something like forty years. When Scooby-Doo's meddling kids reach in to pull off the mask of the imposter, they reveal the individual's true identity. But that's not what's happened here. Meddling kids Paula and Mark have pulled the mask off the imposter to reveal . . . an imposter. We still don't know who he is.

Would the real Mr. Abagnale please stand up?

Alan C. Logan

# Acknowledgments

Breaking up the hardened concrete surrounding one of the greatest hoaxes in human history—the astrodome of absurdity—required a wrecking ball of facts and evidence; operating the crane would not have been possible without valuable support from individuals and institutions throughout North America. The author is deeply appreciative to many librarians, archivists, historians, police and court officials, and assorted professionals.

In particular, the author would like to acknowledge:

- Dr. Maria Jenmalm, Linköping University, Sweden, who facilitated the introduction to Jan Hillman and Harry Andersson.
- Dr. Anders Persson, Swedish Prison and Probation Service, who kindly assisted me in understanding the appropriate steps to obtain Swedish court records.
- Åsa Broström, Archivist, Swedish National Archives, Stockholm
- Marcus Broberg, Archivist, Swedish National Archives, Lund
- Dr. Jean-Lucien Sanchez, French Department of Penal Administration, Office of Research and Statistics, who kindly assisted me in understanding the appropriate steps to obtain Perpignan records.
- Valérie Marillier, Archivist, French National Archives
- Dr. Valerie Verhasselt, University of Western Australia, for French translation.

- Detective Andrea Pinto, Tuckahoe Police Department, Tuckahoe, NY, for finding a treasure trove of records; a new distinction added to the legendary Chief Henry Norman.
- Beverly Gutting, Records Clerk, United States District Court, Atlanta, GA
- David Price, Records Clerk, United States District Court, Salt Lake City, UT
- Lucia Mena-Sanchez, Operations Specialist, United States District Court, Sacramento, CA
- Nathan G. Jordan, Archives Specialist, National Archives at Atlanta, GA
- Ketina Taylor, Archivist, National Archives at Fort Worth, TX
- Carey Stumm, Archivist, National Archives at New York City, NY
- Andrew Merwin, Archivist, National Archives at Denver, CO
- Tim Anderson, Archives Technician, National Archives at Riverside, CA
- Kalem O'Dwyer, Archives Technician, National Personnel Records Center, St Louis, MO
- Hayden Burton, Deputy Clerk, Criminal Records, East Baton Rouge Parish Clerk of Court
- Kayla Brennan, Research Coordinator, National Association for Campus Activities
- Caitlin Jones, Head of Reference, Massachusetts Archives, Boston, MA
- Suffolk County Superior Court, Clerk of Court, Boston MA

- Boston Municipal Court, Clerk of Court, East Boston, MA
- Lauren Knight, Clerk of Court, East Baton Rouge
- Texas State Library and Archives Commission
- New York State Archives
- Baton Rouge Police Department, Records Division
- Galveston County Sheriff's Office, Records Division
- Friendswood Police Department, Records Division
- Westchester County Police Department, Records Division
- University of Michigan, Dearborn, Campus Archives

Special thanks to award-winning poet, writer and editor extraordinaire, Murray Reiss of Salt Spring Island, British Columbia, Canada. He is an advocate for human rights, a noted environmentalist and lives a life dedicated to promoting planetary health and peace. Murray worked tirelessly to edit the book for style and substance. Like all top-flight editors, he chiseled the manuscript as an advocate for the reader.

For his legal services and his extensive review of the manuscript I am especially grateful to Paul C. Rapp, Esq., a national expert in libel law. I also thank my brother William F. Logan, Esq., for his expert advice and support. Paula Parks, a dyed-in-the-wool LSU fan, may not like that he is a Notre Dame Law grad, but we can all get along.

L. Paul Foreman, Esq. Thank you for sharing your story, opening the door to many of the Camp Manison alum, and for deft editing skills on several chapters.

Curtis Clarke. What can I say, other than to highly recommend the fine Cajun cuisine at Evangeline Cafe in Austin, Texas!

And to my great love, my soul mate Susan L. Prescott—an *actual* pediatrician and *actual* professor . . . just not an attorney general, that I know of! Thank you for all your encouragement, your tremendous input into the manuscript at every step of the way, and for sharing this fantastic journey.

# About the Author

Alan C. Logan is an award-winning author, historian, and social commentator. Born in Belfast, Northern Ireland, he was educated there through the peak of the Troubles. This cultivated a fine-grained appreciation of the impact of conflict, injustice, and inequality on individuals and societies. He obtained his liberal arts degree from the State University of New York, at Purchase. Alan has published extensively on the history of science and medicine, and is the co-author of *Your Brain on Nature* (Harper Collins, 2012) and *The Secret Life of Your Microbiome* (New Society, 2017). More recently he has turned his attention to cults, con men and post-truth. His true-crime non-fiction book *Self-Styled: Chasing Dr. Robert Vernon Spears* (Glass Spider Publishing, 2019) was a Feathered Quill Award Finalist.

# Bibliography

[1] Ramstad E. Teaching how to catch a thief. *Star Tribune (Minneapolis, Minnesota)*. 2015; Wednesday 13 May, Pages D1, D2.

[2] Chisholm AR. Why are artistic lies successful? *The Age (Melbourne, Australia)*. 1961; Saturday, 4 Feb, Page 19.

[3] Ghent WJ. Some popular hoaxes. *The Independent* 1913; 75:615-618.

[4] Michaelis DT. Will the real John Phillips please stand up. *Princeton Alumni Weekly*.Mar 21, 1977 p 11-13.

[5] Anon. Suspense, fun, being added to 'Tell the Truth.' *The Daily Reporter (Dover, Ohio)*. 1967; Friday 13 Oct, Page 20.

[6] Wise J. Deadly mind traps. *Psychology Today*. 2012; Jan.

[7] Abagnale FW. Luncheon lecture at the Bank Administration Institute Conference, California. 1994.

[8] Hedges C. Empire of Illusion: The end of literacy and the triumph of spectacle. *Bold Type Books New York, NY*. 2009.

[9] Andy Warhol. From A to B and Back Again. Harcourt Brace. 1975.

[10] Barbara Goldsmith. The Philosophy of Andy Warhol. *New York Times*. 1975; September 14, Page 238.

[11] Magnus C. 13 sharks no problem, landing lays Evel low. *The Pittsburgh Press, Pittsburgh, Pennsylvania*. 1977; Tuesday 1 Feb, Page 36.

[12] M. Did the public get 'snake-bit'? \ *The Times Herald, Port Huron, Michigan*. 1974; Monday 9 Sep,Page 1.

[13] Jones J. 'I stand by what I did', Knievel says. Acused of beating book author with a baseball bat. *The Los Angeles Times, Los Angeles, California)*. 1977; Thursday 22 Sep, Page 10.

[14] Saltman S, Green M. Evel on Tour. *Dell Publishing New York, NY*. 1977.

[15] D. He's some national hero. *Tinley Park Star-Tribune (Tinley Park, Illinois)*. 1974; Thursday 26 Sep, Page 8.

[16] Anon. Dickinson chamber to hear hoakster. *The Galveston Daily News (Galveston, Texas)*. 1977; Tuesday 25 Jan, Page 1.

[17] Meyer J. Flim-flam man flips coin. *The Port Arthur News (Port Arthur, Texas)*. 1977; Wednesday 18 May, Page 1.

[18] Sidey H. America's mood. *Time Magazine*. 1977; Jan 24, Page 8.

[19] Gallup G. Public shows least confidence in big business. *The Evening Sun (Baltimore, Maryland)*. 1975; Thursday 17 Jul, · Page A2.

[20] Anon. Seminar on crime planned. *The Galveston Daily News (Galveston, Texas)*. 1977; Thursday 10 Feb, Page 3.

[21] Sussman S. A real conartist…everyone believed what he wasn't. *Galveston Daily News, Galveston, Texas*. 1977; Thursday January 27, Page 2.

22 Sussman S. Frank was believable. *Plano Daily Star-Courier (Plano, Texas)* 1977; Friday 11 Feb, Page 8.

23 Sussman S. Con-expert was easy man to believe. *The Port Arthur News (Port Arthur, Texas)*. 1977; Sunday 13 Feb 1977, Page 19.

24 Sussman S. $2.5 million in hot checks passed. *The Brownsville Herald (Brownsville, Texas)*. 1977; Monday 14 Feb, Page 38.

25 Anon. Hoffman and Olivier filming in New York. *The News (Paterson, New Jersey)*. 1975; Wednesday 29 Oct, Page 41.

26 Sowell L. Ex-con recalls flim-flam skill in talks on white-collar crime. *Arizona Republic (Phoenix, Arizona)*. 1981; Monday 15 Jun,Pages 13 and 14.

27 Maclin G. Con man tells his wild story. *San Antonio Express (San Antonio, Texas)*. 1977; Sunday 1 May, Page 102.

28 Evans W. Master thief: Con artist's career told. *Spokane Chronicle (Spokane, Washington)*. 1981; Thursday 5 Nov, Page 33.

29 Redding S. Imposter! *Houston Chronicle Sunday magazine*. 1977; Sunday June 19, Pages 5-9.

30 Domeier D. Forger banks on legitimate gamble. *The Dallas Morning News*. 1978; Friday 15 Sept, Page 15A.

31 Breznican A. Movie brings colorful capers back to haunt Frank Abagnale. *Times Colonist (Victoria, British Columbia, Canada)*. 2002; Saturday 28 Dec, Page 48.

32 Minutes Australia. Real life Catch Me If You Can con artist reveals tricks. Oct 14, 2019 https://www.youtube.com/watch?v=3UmcxQto7UU.

33 Anon. A substitute for the plain word "liar." Napa Journal (Napa, California) 1908; Thursday 20 Feb, Page 4.

34 Baker B. Con artistry came naturally to Abagnale. *The Palm Beach Post (West Palm Beach, Florida)* 2002; Thursday (19 Dec, Page 84).

35 Tompkins F. BR family says renowned imposter took its money. *State Times Advocate* 1981; Monday 27 Apr, Pages 1B and 9B.

36 Editors. Mythomania When lying hurts the liar. *Popular Science*. 1921; April 98:39.

37 Susan Margolis. Fame. *San Francisco Book Company Inc San Francisco*. 1977.

38 De Cordova F. Johnny came lately. *Simon and Schuster New York, NY*. 1988.

39 Caen H. Sunday brunch. *San Francisco Examiner*. 1951; Sunday 8 Jul, Page 25.

40 Anon. Dettner to marry model. *The San Francisco Examiner (San Francisco, California)*.Saturday 29 Dec 1956, Page 3.

41 Steger P. Shirley Wood in town. *San Francisco Chronicle*. 1979; Tuesday 8 May, Page 20.

42 United Press International. Shapely brunette will meet Nikita. *Trenton Evening Times*. 1963; Sunday 11 Aug, Page 1, Television for the Week Section.

43 Tennis C. Johnny Tonight! *Pocket Books New York, NY*. 1980.

44 Adelson S. Johnny Carson Does the Talking, but Coordinator Shirley Wood Puts the Cast on the Couch. *People*. 1982; October 25

(https://people.com/archive/johnny-carson-does-the-talking-but-coordinator-shirley-wood-puts-the-cast-on-the-couch-vol-18-no-17/).

[45] Creamer B. A con man's con man. *The Honolulu Advertiser (Honolulu, Hawaii)*. 1978; Friday 7 Jul, Page 49.

[46] Sachs S. Historian admonishes modern novelists in address to librarians. *The Pittsburgh Press (Pittsburgh, Pennsylvania)*. 1988; Thursday 28 Apr, Page 30.

[47] Hall S. What comic book come-ons really deliver. *San Francisco Chronicle*. 1978; Saturday 23 Sep, Page 4.

[48] Hall S. Johnny is conned. A convict who makes up crimes. *San Francisco Chronicle*. 1978; Friday 6 Oct, Pages 1 and 16.

[49] Abusaid S. Fifty years of healing. https://www.mdjonline.com/news/austell-s-cobb-hospital-celebrates-th-anniversary/article_7937b3ee-66e3-11e8-8c7d-3fe95cedf182.html

[50] Horne J. Patients get hospital preview. *Marietta Journal*. 1968; Sunday 26 May, Page 7C.

[51] Associated Press. Girl in murder case identified. *Star Press (Muncie, Indiana)*. 1935; Saturday 30 Nov, Page 1.

[52] Anon. Con-man's legal scam - with cops as victims. *San Francisco Examiner*. 1978; Friday 6 Oct, Page 9.

[53] Caen H. And so on. *San Francisco Chronicle*. 1978; Wednesday 11 Oct, Page 33.

[54] Anon. How to invest in real estate. . *Berkeley Gazette*. 1978; Saturday 23 Sep, Page 15.

[55] Simon R. Shyster Capitalizes on Years as MD, Lawyer, Pilot. *The Pittsburgh Press (Pittsburgh, Pennsylvania)*. 1978; Monday 23 Oct, Page 17.

[56] Perry I. Inquiry shows 'reformed' conman hasn't quit yet. *The Daily Oklahoman* · 1978; Thursday 14 Dec, Pages 1 and 32-33, and 36.

[57] Schmoyer D. NAU speaker has led life of imposter. *Arizona Daily Sun*. 1982; Wednesday 24 Feb, Page 6.

[58] Niccolò Machiavelli. The Prince. Unabridged edition. *Dover Publications Mineola, NY*. 1992.

[59] Anon. 3 Texans are Winners. *San Antonio Light*. 1977; Sunday 24 Apr, Page 8.

[60] Logan AC. Self-Styled-Chasing Dr. Robert Vernon Spears. *Glass Spider Publishing, USA*. 2019.

[61] Berthiaume E. Con artist goes straight. *Stevens Point Journal (Stevens Point, Wisconsin)*. 1989; Tuesday 7 Feb, Page 2.

[62] Schlosser J. Making it pay: con puts his know-how to use. *Greensboro News and Record*. 1987; Wednesday 25 Feb, Pages B-1 and B-10.

[63] Simon R. No new worlds for him to con. *The Boston Globe*. 1978; Friday 6 Oct, Page 25.

[64] Worldwide News Service. Girls on break: On wings for the summer. *Trenton Evening Times*. 1967; Monday 21 Aug, Page 8.

[65] Wholer M. Stewardess works way up ladder to management post. *Oregeonain (Portland)*. 1971; Friday 24 Dec, Page 22.

[66] Anon. Gold wings take a batch of pretties all over the world. *The Pittsburgh Courier (Pittsburgh, Pennsylvania)*. 1971; Saturday 28 Aug, Page 12.

[67] Vantoch V. *The Jet Sex: Airline stewardesses and the making of an American icon.* University of Pennsylvania Press. Philadelphia, PA; 2013.

[68] Mark Zinder Personal Collection. American Bankers Association, American Institute of Banking Convention, Dallas, Texas. Frank Abagnale speech. 1982.

[69] Herzog D. Business fraud tips con's specialty. *The Daily Sentinel (Grand Junction, Colorado)*. 1979; Wednesday 22 Aug, Page 1.

[70] Texas Property Code, Westlaw Editors 2006 Thomson West Publishing Group, St Paul, MN.Chapter 22.

[71] Tompkins F. Is the great imposter a great imposter? *State Times Advocate.* 1981; Friday 24 Apr, Pages 1B and 7C.

[72] Simon R. Professional con man a nice guy, even before he went straight. *The La Crosse Tribune (La Crosse, Wisconsin)*. 1978; Sunday 15 Oct, Page 6.

[73] Schemmel B. Infant Cobb General is walking early. *Marietta Journal.* 1968; Sunday 1 Dec, Page 1.

[74] Naar I, Heimowitz M. Candid con artist reveals crimes. *The Daily Collegian (University Park, PA)*. 1980; Tuesday 9 Sept, Page 1.

[75] Miller S. Help from a con man. *Baxter Bulletin (Mountain Home, Arkansas)*. 2003; Monday 17 Feb, Page 1.

[76] Mark Zinder Personal Collection. Listen to a Legend. Frank Abagnale. *Cassette Productions Unlimited Inc Irwindale California* 1984.

[77] Powell K. Eugene H. Stewart, 83, FBI agent, security expert. *The Atlanta Journal Constitution.* 2001; Wednesday 14 Feb, Page C6.

[78] Anon. Stewart joins Delta. *The Evening Star.* 1968; Monday19 Feb, Page A22.

[79] Associated Press. State bar honor's news media's work. *Del Rio News Herald.* 1984; Thursday 11 Oct, Page 9A.

[80] George Orwell. *All Propaganda is Lies: 1941-1942. Complete Orwell.* Martin Secker & Warburg Ltd. London, UK; 1999.

[81] Anon. Home of Hughes case witness is ransacked. *Tucson Daily Citizen (Tucson, Arizona)*. 1972; Wednesday 16 Feb, Page 6.

[82] Anon. Tucson woman ties burglary of home to Hughes book case. *Arizona Republic (Phoenix, Arizona)*. 1972; Thursday 17 Feb, Page 11.

[83] Biederman E. CIA aide spying on ex Hughes aide claimed. *Nevada State Journal.* 1975; Wednesday 28 May, Pages 1-2.

[84] Anon. No Hughes documents said stolen. *The San Bernardino County Sun (San Bernardino, California)*. 1972; Thursday 17 Feb, Page 9.

[85] Perry I. Abagnale replaced. 'Con Artist' cancels. *The Daily Oklahoman (Oklahoma City, Oklahoma)*. 1978; Friday 15 Dec, Page 1.

[86] Herzog D. Business fraud tips con's specialty. *The Daily Sentinel (Grand Junction, Colorado)*. 1979; Wednesday 22 Aug, Page 1.

[87] Frank W. Abagnale with Stan Redding. Catch Me if You Can. *Grosset and Dunlap New York, NY First Edition*. 1980.

[88] Anon. Reviewing new books; Catch Me if You Can. *Kenosha News (Kenosha, Wisconsin)*. 1980; Monday 6 Oct, Page 19.

[89] Vondracek S. Man who was somebody else. *The Anniston Star (Anniston, Alabama)*. 1980; Sunday 7 Sep, Page 13C.

[90] Wheeler E. *The Los Angeles Times (Los Angeles, California)*. 1980; Sunday 5 Oct, Book Review Section, Page 14.

[91] Manor R. Bad check artist no better at books. *The Berkley Gazette*. 1980; Sunday 24 Aug, Page 26.

[92] Stowell L. Ex-con recalls flim-flam skill in talks on white-collar crime. *Arizona Republic (Phoenix, Arizona)*. 1981; Monday 15 Jun, Pages 13 and 14.

[93] Anon. FOP seminar features 'retried con artist.' *Lancaster Eagle-Gazette (Lancaster, Ohio)*. 1985; Wednesday 10 Apr, Page 16.

[94] Anon. Your birthday and horoscope for Friday Feb 14. *State Times Advocate Minnesota)*. 1969; Thursday 13 Feb, Page 12-B.

[95] Baton Rouge Police Department. Case File 3857. City of Baton Rouge, Louisiana. 1969.

[96] Beales R. Ex-con artist prospers by sharing tricks of the trade. *Austin American-Statesman (Austin, Texas)*. 1977; Wednesday 20 Jul, Page 15.

[97] Associated Press. Criminal know-how turns into profitable business. *Battle Creek Enquirer (Battle Creek, Michigan)*. 1980; Sunday 21 Dec, Page D-10.

[98] Associated Press. Ex-criminal now prevents crimes. *Longview News-Journal (Longview, Texas)*. 1980; Wednesday 19 Nov, Page 18.

[99] Abagnale, Frank, Jr. DCII - 1111507; Great Meadow. New York State Archives. New York State Department of Correctional Services, Central Depository Inmate Summary Cards. #150931.

[100] Anon. Black picture told BR high schoolers by Angola prisoners. *State-Times Advocate (Baton Rouge, Louisiana)*. 1969; Friday 10 Jan, Page 4.

[101] Murphy JD. Prison reform: Nothing has changed. *Times-Picayune (New Orleans, LA)*. 1976; Sunday 25 Jan, Sec 9, Page 10.

[102] Stagg EW, Lear J. America's worst prison. *Collier's*. 1952; Nov 22, Page 13-16.

[103] Anon. New employee needs are cited in State's corrections system. *State-Times Advocate (Baton Rouge, Louisiana)*. 1969; Monday 10 Nov, Page 3.

[104] Editors. Prison vocational training classes improvements urged by committee. *State-Times Advocate (Baton Rouge, Louisiana)*. 1969; Friday 21 Mar, Page 15.

[105] Adams G. Convict guard evils outlined in petition. *The Morning Advocate (Baton Rouge, Louisiana)*. 1970; Tuesday 15 Dec, Pages 1 and 6.

[106] Parks Familiy Archive. Letters to Reverend Early Underwood and the Parks Family (From Frank Abagnale and members of the Abagnale family). *From Baton Rouge Jailhouse*. 1969; February - March.

[107] Talks at Google. Frank Abagnale: "Catch Me If You Can" Nov 27 https://www.youtube.com/watch?v=vsMydMDi3rI. Published 2017. Accessed January 15, 2019.

[108] Hinckley D. In crime game, pen is mightier than the gun. *The Cincinnati Enquirer (Cincinnati, Ohio)*. 1982; Sunday 28 Feb, Page 64.

[109] Parker DW. Election advertisement. *State Times Advocate*. 1962; Sunday, Aug 26,. pg 2-B.

[110] State of Louisiana vs Frank W. Abagnale. Letter from Dennis R. Whalen to the Court. East Baton Rouge Clerk of Court, Records. 1969; April 11 Ref: 69.103, 69.104.

[111] State of Louisiana vs Frank W. Abagnale. Letter from Chester A. Williams, Jr., M.D., and Russell M. Coco, M.D. to Judge Elmo E. Lear. East Baton Rouge Clerk of Court, Records. 1969; April 26, 1969. Ref: 69.103, 69.104.

[112] State of Louisiana vs Frank W. Abagnale. Summary documents. East Baton Rouge Clerk of Court, Records. 1969; Ref: 69.103, 69.104.

[113] State of Louisiana vs. Frank W. Abagnale. Warrant issued by Judge Donovan Parker. East Baton Rouge Clerk of Court, Records. 1969; Sept 15,. Ref: 69.103, 69.104.

[114] Tompkins F. Imposter was jailed here. *State Times Advocate*. 1981; Tuesday 28 Apr, Page 16-D.

[115] Durkin J. Reformed criminal works for the law. *The Item (Sumter, South Carolina)*. 1982; Wednesday 29 Sep, Page 5.

[116] Durkin J. Impersonator turns to helping people after time in prison. *The Gaffney Ledger (Gaffney, South Carolina)*. 1982; Wednesday 29 Sep, Page 30.

[117] Lawrence K. One-time con man helps others fight crime. *The Daily Item (Sunbury, Pennsylvania)*. 1981; Friday 18 Sep, Page 3.

[118] Harman L. Imposter's life on the run. *The Auburn Plainsman*. 1980; Thursday 17 Jan, Page A10.

[119] Ripp B. Penmanship improved his fortune. *Albuquerque Journal*. 1980; Friday 29 Feb, Pages A1 and A2.

[120] Eaton C. 1980s oil bust left a lasting mark. Houston Chronicle. https://www.chron.com/local/history/economy-business/article/The-1980s-oil-bust-left-lasting-mark-on-Houston-9195222.php. 2016; Aug 21.

[121] Stroud J. Ex-bad check artist cleaning up by telling all. Man talks prevention. *St Louis Dispatch (St Louis, Missouri)*. 1979; Sunday 18 Nov, Page 1E.

[122] Scruggs C. Con man to help crime stoppers. *The Item (Sumter, South Carolina)*. 1983; Friday 28 Jan, Page 2.

[123] DeGroot G. *The Sixties Unplugged*. Harvard University Press. Cambridge, MA; 2008.

[124] Press. 'Great Pretender' is exposed in Maine schoolmaster role. *The Bridgeport Post*. 1957; Friday 15 Feb, Pages 1 and 8.

[125] United Press. Laundry marks identify 'Dr Jones' as imposter. *Tyler Morning Telegraph (Tyler, Texas)*. 1955; Saturday 24 Dec, Page 1.

[126] United Press. 'Master Imposter' is held in Florida as hot check suspect. *Lubbock Morning Avalanche (Lubbock, Texas)*. 1956; Thursday 5 Jan, Page 1.

[127] United Press. Texas prison guard, claimed Peabody degree, identified as 'Great Imposter'—flees job. *Nashville Banner (Nashville, Tennessee)*. 1955; Thursday 22 Dec, Page 12.

[128] Associated Press. Naval surgeon hoax. *The Lethbridge Herald (Lethbridge, Alberta, Canada)*. 1952; Friday 25 Jan, Page 17.

[129] Associated Press. Double desertion charge is made against Demara. *Spokane Chronicle (Spokane, Washington)*. 1946; Saturday 2 Nov, Page 6.

[130] Anon. 'Great Imposter' is posing again. *Courier-Post (Camden, New Jersey)*. 1970; Thursday 8 Jan, Page 4.

[131] United Press. Canada to discharge phony doctor. *The Austin American (Austin, Texas)*. 1951; Wednesday 21 Nov, Page 24.

[132] United Press International. Great imposter is posing again. *Courier-Post (Camden, New Jersey)*. 1970; Thursday 8 Jan, Page 4.

[133] Selix C, Ramstad E. Guy was so good he once got napkin cashed. *Brownsville Herald (Brownsville, Texas)*. 1980; Sunday 29 June, Page 1C.

[134] Ring RH. Cons came quickly—and it's still hard to tell: Frank finessed firm future, in spite if those prison 'nightmares.' *Arizona Daily Star (Tucson, Arizona)*. 1981; Sunday, 5 Apr, Page 23.

[135] Kewson A. After frauds and escapes former conman advocates the straight life. *The Red and Black (University of Georgia, Athens)*. 1980; Wednesday 21 May, Page 3.

[136] Grady P. Former con artist tells how he bilked millions. *The Tribune (Scranton)*. 1983; Friday 21 Apr, Pages 3 and 7.

[137] Ripp B. Penmanship improved his fortune. *Albuquerque Journal*. 1980; Friday 29 Feb, Pages A1 and A2.

[138] Gould L. Real life con artist. His stage was the world. *Green Bay Press-Gazette (Green Bay, Wisconsin)*. 2002; Friday, 27 Dec, Page D-3.

[139] Coursey C. Former con man lays out the law. *Colorado Springs Gazette Telegraph*. 1978; Tuesday 22 Aug, Page 8.

[140] Frank Abagnale and Bud Yorkin Production. Option Agreement for The Frank Abagnale Story. Copyright Office of the United States. 1979; Document Number: V1751P230.

[141] Anon. 'Con artist' will speak. *The Galveston Daily News (Galveston, Texas)*. 1977; Monday 7 Mar, Page 15.

[142] Zorn E. Checks and balances: A con man 'retires.' *Chicago Tribune*. 1980; Thursday 20 Nov, Section 2, Pages 1 and 6.

[143] Anon. Community news. Alpine banks celebrates 20 years. *The Daily Sentinel (Grand Junction, Colorado)*. 1993; Thursday 28 Jan, Pages 29-30.

144 Stevens WK. At last, Sunbelt comics stand up to be counted. *The Dallas Morning News* 1981; Sunday 11 Jan, Page 4F.

145 Plotkin J. Flew a crooked sky. *The Nashville Graphic (Nashville, North Carolina)*. 1982; Thursday 13 May, Page 7.

146 National Archives of France. Perpignan Penitentiary Files. Frank W. Abagnale. 1969; Document #2870W20.

147 Mekeel T. Con man turned business advisor tells visitors bureau of life of crime. *Lancaster New Era (Lancaster, Pennsylvania)*. 1987; Tuesday 17 Nov, Pages 26, 27.

148 Eliason G. A great liar, imposter now among good guys. *Reno Gazette-Journal (Reno, Nevada)*. 1988; Sunday 31 Jan, Pages 1D and 3D.

149 Wilson C. One-time fraud expert cashes in as consultant. *Times Colonist (Victoria, British Columbia, Canada)*. 1996; Saturday 8 Jun, B3.

150 WGBHForum. Catch Me If You Can: Frank Abagnale's Story. *https://www.youtubecom/watch?v=x0fEA0MsiV8*. 2010; November 30.

151 Frank Abagnale Interview. SVT/NRK/Skavlan, [https://www.youtube.com/watch?v=p7OQ91wj5E0] 2014; Sep 8.

152 Mier J. World's greatest con artist speaks at MTSU. *The Daily News Journal Accent (Murfreesboro, Tennessee)*. 1981; Sunday 6 Sep, Page 9 and 11.

153 Moss D. Imposing master thief shows he as all it takes to be one. *Fort Lauderdale News (Fort Lauderdale, Florida)*. 1981; Friday 17 Apr, Page 13.

154 Graham C. Former con artist describes career. *The Times (Shreveport, Louisiana)*. 1986; Friday 18 Apr, Page 14.

155 Hundley W. 'Great imposter' tells tricks of hot check trade. *Longview News-Journal (Longview, Texas)*. 1978; Thursday 11 May, Page 13.

156 University of Arizona Alumni Association. Alumni Reflections, Paul J. Holsen. https://arizonaalumni.com/article/alumni-reflections. Published 2012. Accessed May 12, 2020.

157 Paul J. Holsen II. *Born in a Bottle of Beer: From Jungle Pilot to the CIA*. United States of America, 2014.

158 Anon. Fake recruiter charged by FBI. *Arizona Daily Star*. 1970; Saturday 21 Nov, Page 34.

159 United States vs. Frank Abagnale. National Archives, Denver CO.CR-5-71.

160 United States vs. Frank Abagnale. Northern District of Georgia. National Archives, Atlanta, GA.CR-H-270.

161 Say S. Marietta Journal. 1970; Monday 2 Nov, Page 10.

162 Holsomback B. Man of many faces trying a new one. *Fort Worth Star Telegram*. 1977; Wednesday 9 Nov, Page 20.

163 Conway C. Frankly Abagnale. *Charleston Home and Design*. 2014; Spring 106-117.

164 Anon. 'Catch a thief' seminar at civic center June 20. *Marietta Journal* 1979; Sunday, Jun 10, Page 24.

[165] Baker B. Portrait of the con artist as a young man. *The Los Angeles Times (Los Angeles, California)*. 2002; Friday 6 Dec, Page 1.

[166] Editorials of the Tribune. Get tougher with the Skywaymen. *The Tampa Tribune*. 1972; Sunday 11 June, Page C1.

[167] Buzz Aldrin. Return to Earth. *Random House, New York, New York* 1973.

[168] Anon. Private camp day held on Bay. *The Baytown Sun (Baytown, Texas)*. 1950; Monday 12 Jun, Page 14.

[169] Anon. New Safety and Health Act will make summer camp happy outing. *The Mexia Daily News (Mexia, Texas)*. 1974; Tuesday 28 May, Page 5.

[170] Paternoster L. Ex-con man talks prevention. *El Paso Times (El Paso, Texas)* 1978; Saturday 5 Aug, Page 15.

[171] Holly Wood. $5 investment pays off for Frank Abagnale. *New Braunfels Herald Zeitung, New Braunfels, Texas*. 1979; Thursday 21 June, Page 11.

[172] Hannah J. Check the check, expert advises. *Dayton Daily News (Dayton, Ohio)*. 1991; Wednesday 12 Jun, Page 22.

[173] Special Features - A personal look inside the film. Catch Me If You Can. *Dreamworks Home Entertainment, 100 Universal City Plaza, Universal City, CA*. 2003.

[174] Anon. Houston man arrested for Camp Manison theft. *The News (Friendswood, Texas)*. 1974; Thursday 5 Sep,Page 1.

[175] Frank W. Abagnale with Stan Redding. Catch Me If You Can. *Broadway Books, Movie tie-in Edition, Broadway NY*. 2002.

[176] Kennedy K, Kennedy Z. Friendswood Secrets to Success. *Self-Published Friendswood, TX*. 2014.

[177] Anon. 229 cases filed in Dickinson. *Galveston Daily News*. 1971; Thursday 28 May, Page 8-A.

[178] Precinct #6 Felony Cases—JP William T. Fuhrhop *Galveston Daily News*. 1974; Thursday 28 Nov, Page 11-B.

[179] Kothmann C. Catch and release: Local counselor assisted Abagnale of 'Catch Me If You Can' fame with changing from conman to respected expert. *Uvlade News-Leader*. 2003; Feb 6. Page 4.

[180] Frank Abagnale. Letter of Recommendation: James P. Blackmon. 2002; April 1 (accessed from http://friendsofcriminaljustice.org/press-and-testimonials/ ) July 4, 2020.

[181] Anon. Great imposter to speak at Friendswood annual Chamber banquet *The News (Friendswood, Texas)*. 1977; Monday 12 Dec, Page 1.

[182] Hunt S. Bona Fide. Chalreston Magazine Web site. https://charlestonmag.com/features/bona_fide. Published 2010. Accessed July 5, 2020.

[183] McQueeny WT. *The Rise of Charleston: Conversations with Visionaries, Luminaries & Emissaries of the Holy City*. Charleston, South Carolina: The History Press; 2017.

[184] Malkoff M. Interview with Frank Abagnale. https://carsonpodcast.com/frank-abagnale/. Published 2016. Accessed July 20, 2020.

[185] Daily Court Review, Houston, Texas, United States. 1976; April 14, Page 7.

[186] Mason D. Crime unites Houstonians. *The Dallas Morning News*. 1980; Monday 16 June, Pages 1 and 22A.

[187] Anon. Ex-conman, forger to speak to Chamber. *The Bellaire Texan (Bellaire, TX)*. 1978; Wednesday 15 Feb, Page 10.

[188] Anon. Hoaxter set for Dickinson Banquet. *Galveston Daily News, Galveston, Texas, US*. 1977; January 5, Page 11.

[189] United States Navy. Navy Recruitment Brochure. *US Governmnet Printing Office*.1965 0-778-938.

[190] Abagnale FW. US Social Security Act. Application. Dated 01-19-1937. Employer, Ford Motor Company, 1937.

[191] Advertisement. Printing needs. FW Abagnale at Gramercy Stationary. 284 Madison Ave. *Winged Foot*. 1950; Vol 61, pages 38, 42, 46.

[192] State of New York ToEC. Sale Deed, 12th January. 1948; Liber 4598:pages 363-364.

[193] Anon. Fishing Action Good, Despite Billfish. *Fort Lauderdale News (Fort Lauderdale, Florida)*. 1959; Sunday 15 Mar, Page 59.

[194] National Archives and Records Administration. General Declaration, Inward Transportation to the United States. Chalks Flying Service. N3945C Bahamas to Miami, April 21, 1955.

[195] National Archives and Records Administration. General Declaration, Inward Transportation to the United States. BOAC. BA437 Bahamas to Miami, Mar 22, 1958.

[196] State of New York ToEC. Sale Deed, 7th May. 1956; Liber 5580(pages 146-147).

[197] State of New York ToEC. Sale Deed, 15th June. 1960; Liber 6022:pages 274-275.

[198] United States vs. Frank Abagnale. United States District Court, Northern District of California.CR-14374.

[199] Police Department, Tuckahoe, NY. Abagnale, FW.File #42-0-60.

[200] Associated Press. Go to Army or to jail, youth told. *The Lawton Constitution (Lawton, Oklahoma)*. 1966; Thursday 12 May, Page 21.

[201] Anon. Youth not ready to join army, goes to jail instead. *The Tampa Tribune (Tampa, Florida)*. 1961; Tuesday 21 Nov, Page 17.

[202] National Personel Records Center. Freedom of Information Act (FOIA) request. *National Archives*.2-23354946928.

[203] Hodgins P. Catch me: Life is good after being caught. *Santa Ana Orange County Register, Santa Ana, California, US*. 2013; June 23, Page 87.

[204] Anon. Teen seized in Parkway check case. *Tarrytown Daily News*. 1965; Friday Jul 16, Page 26.

[205] United States vs. Frank Abagnale. United States District Court, Southern District of New York.65-CR-663.

[206] Lee W. City police sergeant will end career after 25 years. *Eureka Humboldt Standard (Eureka, California)*. 1974; Sunday 7 Jul, Page 8.

[207] Anon. Grocery store camera catches check forger. . *Eureka Humboldt Standard (Eureka, California)*. 1965; Saturday 27 Mar, Page 7.

[208] Anon. Check officer warns merchants after fraud here. *Eureka Humboldt Standard (Eureka, California)*. 1963; Saturday 5 Oct, Page 3.

[209] Anon. Credit women to hear officer on bad checks. *Eureka Humboldt Standard (Eureka, California)*. 1963; Tuesday 17 Dec, Page 14.

[210] Anon. AWOL Navy man held here as master forger. *Eureka Humboldt Standard (Eureka, California)* 1963; Saturday 29 Mar, Page 3.

[211] Associated Press. Odessa native is accused in hot check case. *The Odessa American (Odessa, Texas)*. 1963; Friday 29 Mar, Page 15.

[212] Fogg S. Rubber check writers costlier than robbers. *Kingsport News (Kingsport, Tennessee)*. 1965; Saturday 10 Apr, Page 10.

[213] Anon. Federal charge for N.Y. youth. *Eureka Humboldt Standard (Eureka, California)*. 1965; Tuesday 22 Jun, Page 11.

[214] Beckett P. Con men in the atomic age. *Detective Year Book Astro Publishing New York, NY.* 1949.

[215] Anon. Teen seized in Parkway check case. *Bronxville Review Press and Reporter.* 1965; Thursday 22 July, Page 12.

[216] Classified Pages. *The Philadelphia Inquirer (Philadelphia, Pennsylvania).* 1966; Sundayt 16 Oct, Page 137.

[217] Classified Pages. *The Philadelphia Inquirer (Philadelphia, Pennsylvania).* 1966; Sunday 20 Mar, Page 130.

[218] Commonwealth of Massachusetts vs. Frank W. Abagnale. East Boston Court Records. Docket #4923, Docket #4924, Docket #4925 1967.

[219] Commonwealth of Massachusetts vs. Frank W. Abagnale. Suffolk County Massachusetts, Superior Court. Docket #30675, Docket #30676, Docket #30677, Docket #31020. 1967.

[220] Anon. 7-year-old girl found here with 'therapist.' *Ukiah Daily Journal (Ukiah, California).* 1968; Thursday 25 Apr, Page 3.

[221] Anon. Banquet will honor co-op job providers. *El Paso Times.* 1978; Sunday 19 Feb, Page 36.

[222] Zahn L. He turned negatives into positives. *Kenosha News (Kenosha, Wisconsin).* 1982; Wednesday 3 Mar, Page 38.

[223] Clark G. It takes a thief. Ex-king of con artistis delights, terrifies bankers. *The Province (Vancouver, British Columbia, Canada).* 1994; Friday 11 Feb, Page 2.

[224] Chudina J. Master thief now spends time battling white collar crime. *Johnson City Press.* 1982; Saturday 23 Jan, Page 1.

[225] Ashcraft D. Readers' View. *The Baytown Sun.* 1981; Thursday 21 May, Page 8-A.

226 Raison C. Catch me if you can. *The Baytown Sun*. 1981; Thursday 14 May, Page 1B.

227 Whittington D. The great imposter. *Weekly World News*. 1981; April 7, Page 17.

228 Walter J. We hear America speaking; fame too! *The Washington Star* 1978; Tuesday 1 Aug, D1-D2.

229 International Platform Association. A Retrospective, 1902-2001, The 1978 Annual Conference Notes.Page 27.

230 Langston S. Paris High School DECA students attend Sales and Marketing Executives of Dallas workshop. *The Paris News (Paris, Texas)*. 1982; Sunday 10 Oct, Page 7.

231 Dagley J. Con man speaker under fire, now leaving college circuit. *Columbus Daily Enquirer*. 1982; Thursday 21 Oct,Pages A1-A2.

232 Sullivan G. Great Imposters. Scholastic Books. New York, NY. 1982.

233 Lohr L. Promoting talent for campuses. *The Evening Sun (Baltimore, Maryland)*. 1983; Friday 18 Feb, Pages D6 and D9.

234 Silverman D. Dinner speaker is new role for 'Great Imposter.' *San Antonio Light* 1982; Friday 10 Dec, Page 1E.

235 Morgan S. Abagnale Steals CC Meeting Show. *The Shreveport Journal (Shreveport, Louisiana)*. 1983; Wednesday 12 Jan, Page 48.

236 Garrison B. Former Con Artist Fascinates Audience. *Johnson City Press Chronicle*. 1983; Friday 14 Jan, Page 8.

237 Anon. Frank Abagnale, known as the "Great Imposter" has cancelled. *The Michigan Journal Vol 12, Issue 19, Jan 19th Pg 2 University of Michigan, Dearborn, Campus Archives*. 1983.

238 Plank T. The greatest con man ever. *The Independent-Record (Helena, Montana)*. 2018; Friday 31 Aug, Pages A1 and A8.

239 281st Judicial District Court of Harris County Texas. W.T Toney Jr. vs. Frank W. Abagnale, Jr.; Number 83 –07759.

240 Harris County District Court. NM vs. Frank W. Abagnale and Associates.Case Number 85-62400.

241 Harris County District Court. JB vs. Frank W. Abagnale and Associates.Case Number 85-14591.

242 Rogers T. Reformed con artists teaches others how to avoid hustlers. *The Tennessean (Nashville, Tennessee)*. 1985; Sunday 15 Sep, Page 9.

243 Stowell L. Ex-convict uses his experience to help companies catch thieves. *Arizona Republic (Phoenix, Arizona)*. 1981; Tuesday 12 May, Page C1.

244 Paternoster L. Ex-con man talks prevention. *El Paso Times (El Paso, Texas)* 1978; Saturday 5 Aug, Pages 1B and 2B.

245 Dean R. Would you accept a check from this man? *Evening Star (Washington DC)*. 1978; Wednesday 22 Mar, Page 1B.

246 Gillan B. Dan down, pasted by postings. *The Philadelphia Inquirer (Philadelphia, Pennsylvania)*. 2004; Sunday 19 Sep, Pages C1 and C3.

[247] Seiler A. 'Catch Me' made money before the movie. *Journal and Courier (Lafayette, Indiana)*. 2003; Monday 6 Jan, Page 23.

[248] West M. Ex-con tells chamber he regrets crime spree. *The Daily News-Journal (Murfreesboro, Tennessee)*. 1986; Friday 24 Jan, Page 1.

[249] Wynne CC. Ex-con man narrates schemes. *Carlsbad Current-Argus (Carlsbad, New Mexico)*. 1987; Monday 29 Jun, Page 3.

[250] Wilson C. One-time fraud expert cashes in as consultant. *Times Colonist (Victoria, British Columbia, Canada)*. 1996; Saturday 8 Jun, B3.

[251] Butters WS. Ex-con artist prefers family, fatherhood over fraud. *The Signpost (Ogden, Utah)*. 1995; Friday 13 Jan, Page 3.

[252] Heywood J. Crime can pay on your resume. *The Age*. 1999; Wedesday 17 Mar, B1.

[253] Labutta E. The Prisoner as One of Us: Norwegian Wisdom for American Penal Practice. *Emory International Law Review*. 2017; 31:329-359.

[254] Yukhnenko D. et al. A systematic review of criminal recidivism rates worldwide: a 3-year update. *Wellcome Open Res*. 2019 Nov 13.

[255] Fazel S. et al. A Systematic Review of Criminal Recidivism Rates Worldwide: Current Difficulties and Recommendations for Best Practice. *PLoS One*. 2015; 10(6):e0130390.

[256] Kremer J. Man paints a collage of deceit in life. *The Times Herald (Port Huron, Michigan)*. 1982; Thursday 4 Feb, Page 21.

[257] Leonardo Di Caprio on Abagnale. ABC 20/20 with Barbara Walters. 2002; Friday, Nov 22.

[258] Seiler A. Options on 'undoable' film catch up with author. *Public Opinion (Chambersburg, Pennsylvania)*. 2003; Monday 6 Jan, Page 15.

[259] Fine M. Film brings past back for Abagnale. *Fort Collins Coloradoan (Fort Collins, Colorado)*. 2002; Sunday 22 Dec, Page 25.

[260] Hooper B. Caught on film at last. *National Post (Toronto, Ontario, Canada)*. 2002; Tuesday 24 Dec, Page 33.

[261] Anon. Hard to Catch Leonardo. *The Province (Vancouver, British Columbia, Canada), reporting on USA Today article*. 2002; Thursday 19 Dec, Page 82.

[262] Baker B. The truth? Just try to catch it if you can. *The Los Angeles Times (Los Angeles, California)*. 2002; Saturday 28 Dec, Pages E1 and E15.

[263] Maulden B. 'Catch Me If You Can' captures an era's sympathetic soul of a gifted grifter. *Times-Press-Recorder (Arroyo Grande, California)*. 2002; Friday 3 Jan 2003, Page 4.

[264] Seiler A. Contradictions abound in film about con man's life. *Marshfield News-Herald (Marshfield, Wisconsin)*. 2002; Sunday 29 Dec, Page 26.

[265] Dicker R. Spielberg's personal stake in 'Catch Me.' *Hartford Courant*. 2002; Sunday 29 Dec, Page G7.

[266] Smiley Anders. The Big Con. *Advocate (Baton Rouge)*. 2000; August 3, Page 31.

[267] Griffin, J. . Con caper is real thing. *Montreal Gazette*. 2002; Tuesday 24 Dec, Page D1.

[268] Anon. A reel reunion. *The Atlanta Constitution (Atlanta, Georgia)*. 2003; Monday 13 Jan, Page C2.

[269] Anon. Obituary. Shea, Joseph. *The Atlanta Constitution (Atlanta, Georgia)*. 2005; Sunday 7 Aug, Page E7.

[270] Garner J. Spielberg makes young con man's story fun to watch. *The News Journal (Wilmington, Delaware)*. 2002; Wednesday 25 Dec, Page 52.

[271] Abagnale FW. The Film and the Filmmakers. Catch Me If You Can. *Newmarket Press, New York NY*. 2002.

[272] Breznican A. Caught up in capers. *Santa Cruz Sentinel (Santa Cruz, California)*. 2003; Friday 3 Jan, Page 12.

[273] Ebert R. True story of young con artist premiers. *Kenosha News (Kenosha, Wisconsin)*. 2002; Tuesday 24 Dec, Page 31.

[274] Dargis M. Is Spielberg too big for small tales? *The Los Angeles Times (Los Angeles, California)*. 2002; Wednedday 25 Dec, Pages E1 and E22.

[275] Frank Abagnale, the author of 'Catch Me If You Can', interviewed by Sarah Montague on BBC HardTalk https://www.youtube.com/watch?v=A4JDlcpoA4M In: 2011.

[276] Seiler A. Catch Me Movie may be the True Con Job. *Argus-Leader (Sioux Falls, South Dakota)*. 2002; Friday 27 Dec, Pages 1D and 6D.

[277] Correll Griggs C. Unsolved mystery: 20-year-old forgery case haunts former detective now living in Gaffney. *The Gaffney Ledger (Gaffney, South Carolina)*. 2003; Friday 13 Jun, Page 15.

[278] Rowland J. Forgery 'pro' demonstrates how it's done. *The Palm Beach Post (West Palm Beach, Florida)*. 1981; Sunday 24 May, Page 39.

[279] Anon. Two take clue from lecturing con man. *The Daily Sentinel (Grand Junction, Colorado)*. 1981; Saturday 11 Apr, Page 3.

[280] Kipling R. Kipling on Twain. *The Philadelphia Inquirer*. 1890; Monday 18 Aug, Page 8.

[281] Anon. Fort Worth newspapermen share Associated Press contest prizes. *Fort Worth Star-Telegram*. 1957; Sunday 20 Jan, Page B1.

[282] Anon. Headline award winners to be honored Saturday. *Austin American-Statesman (Austin, Texas)*. 1969; Sunday 26 Jan, Pages 1, 6.

[283] Anon. Headliners honor top newsmen of '66. *The Austin American (Austin, Texas)*. 1967; Sunday 5 Feb, Page A20.

[284] Anon. City Wide Youth Revival: Freddy Gage From Hoodlum to Soul Winner. *The Brookshire Times (Brookshire, Texas)*. 1953; Thursday 2 Jul, Page 3.

[285] Freddie Gage with Stan Redding. Pulpit in the Shadows. Prentice Hall, NJ. 1966.

[286] Seiler A. The Story Behind Catch Me If You Can. *The Province (Vancouver, British Columbia, Canada)*. 2002; Thursday 26 Dec, Page 149.

[287] Ivins M. Education plan beamed in from dreamland. *San Antonio Light.* 1990; Monday 1 Oct, Page C5.

[288] Rahtjen BD. The power of a reformed life. *The Kansas City Times (Kansas City, Missouri).* 1966; Friday 28 Oct, Page 32.

[289] Geist EM. Armededdon Insurance. *University of North Carolina Press, Chapel Hill, NC.* 2019.

[290] Loring C. Meanwhile back at Mission Control. *American Cinematographer.* 1969; 50:978-980.

[291] Langolis Communications Inc. vs Frank W. Abagnale, Jr. The District Court of Harris County Texas 127th Judicial District.Number 78–46103.

[292] Garcia D. Imposter build new image. *San Antonio Light.* 1977; Fri 14 Oct, Page 7C.

[293] Austin E. Ex-con warns group of possible frauds. *Hyde Park Herald.* 1980; Wednesday 19 Nov, Page 7.

[294] Maguire T. Ex-con's life story not typical sad tale. *Star-Gazette (Elmira, New York).* 1980; Friday 2 May, Page 13.

[295] Anon. Compendium of best sellers today…and ten years past. *Wisconsin State Journal (Madison, Wisconsin).* 1980; Wednesday 8 Oct, Page 59.

[296] Anon. Best Selling Books. *Green Bay Press-Gazette (Green Bay, Wisconsin).* 1980; Sunday 12 Oct, Page 99.

[297] Claude Solnik. Famous fraudster on LI: An 'autobiography' full of fiction. Long Island Business News Web site. https://libn.com/2014/06/24/famous-fraudster-on-li-an-autobiography-full-of-fiction/. Published 2014. AccessedJune 24.

[298] Postman N. Amusing Ourselves to Death: Public Discourse in the Age of Show Business. Penguin Books.Toronto, Canada. 2005.

[299] Harris N. Humbug. The Art of PT Barnum. *University of Chicago Press Chicago, IL.* 1973.

[300] IMDb. The 65th Annual Tony Awards. https://www.imdb.com/title/tt1961536/. Published 2011. Accessed January 15, 2020.

[301] Tom Williams. Catch Me If You Can – The Musical. *Chicago Critic.* 2012; Date Reviewed: April 3.

[302] Nerone J. Lying with impunity. *Journalism.* 2019; 20:48–51.

[303] Anon. Fame Game. An interview with Susan Margolis. *Playgirl.* 1978; April:Pages 37-38.

[304] Metz R. The Tonight Show. *Playboy Press Chicago, IL.* 1980.

[305] Abril D. Google Introduces New Tools to Help Journalists Fight Fake News. Fortune Web site. https://fortune.com/2019/03/20/google-new-tools-fight-fake-news/. Published 2019. Accessed March 20, 2020.

[306] Hadfield A. 2020 Lying in an age of digital capitalism. *Text Pract.*34:1–8.

[307] Daniel J. Boorstin. The Image: A Guide to Pseudo-Events in America. *Harper, New York NY.* 1961.

[308] Al-Rodhan N. Post-truth politics, the fifth estate and the securitization of fake news, June 7. Global Policy, Web site. https://www.globalpolicyjournal.com/blog/07/06/2017/post-truth-politics-fifth-estate-and-securitization-fake-news. Published 2017. Accessed December 28, 2019.

[309] Hasher L. et al. Frequency and the conference of referential validity. *Journal Verbal Learn Verbal Behav.* 1977; 16:107-112.

[310] Ellis M. Former con man entertains at annual ETMC dinner. *Tyler Morning Telegraph (Tyler, Texas).* 2003; Wednesday 22 Oct, Page 11.

[311] George-Cosh D. This is the real Frank Abagnale. *National Post (Toronto, Ontario, Canada).* 2006; Wednesday 20 Sep, Page 3.

[312] Girard PF. L'Enfance irrégulière. *Psychologie Clinique Presses Universitaires de France ScHumaines.* 1946.

[313] Eck M. Lies and Truth. *MacMillan NY, New York.* 1970.

[314] Wheeler EJ, Crane F. The most misunderstood of all kind of lying. *Current Opinion.* 1920; 69:833.

[315] Orghian D. et al. How your power affects my impression of you. *Personality and Social Psychology Bulletin.* 2019; 45:495–509.

[316] Westhoff J. Good catch. *Northwest Herald.* 2002; Friday 27 Dec, Sidetracks Section, Page 5.

[317] Denkers A, Winkel F. Crime victims' well-being and fear in a prospective and longitudinal study. *Int Rev Victimol.* 1998:141-162.

[318] Staubli S. et al. Happiness and victimization: An empirical study for Switzerland. *Eur J Criminology.* 2014; 11:57–72.

[319] Shapland J, Hall M. What do we know about the effects of crime on victims? *Int Rev Victimol.* 2007; 14:175-217.

[320] Shover N. et al. Long-term consequences of victimization by white-collar crime. *Justice Q.* 1994; 11:75-98.

[321] Rich A. Women and Honor. *Motheroot Publications, Pittsburgh Women Writers.* 1977.

[322] Marmot M. Post-truth and science. *Lancet.* 2017; 389(10068):497-498.

[323] Keyes R. The Post-Truth Era: Dishonesty and Deception in Contemporary Life. *St Martin's Press New York, NY.* 2004.

[324] Grooms R. Viva Knievel, like Evel, a bamboozle. *Cincinnati Enquirer.* 1977; Saturday 16 Jul, Page B4.

[325] Ryan D. Daredevil shoots for film stardom, but he winds up in the pits instead. *The Philadelphia Inquirer (Philadelphia, Pennsylvania).* 1977; Thursday 14 Jul, Page 6C.

[326] Prairie Public Broadcasting Station. Interview with Doug Hamilton. Prairie Pulse. https://www.youtube.com/watch?v=O9NuMRf-8L0&t=5s. 2018.

[327] DeGroot G. The Seventies Unplugged. Macmillan. London, United Kingdom; 2010.

[328] Leonard D. Con's Checkered Past Gets Hollywood Treatment. Fortune. July 10, 2000. https://archive.fortune.com/magazines/fortune/fortune_archive/2000/07/1 0/283748/index.htm.

[329] Wyoming Chronicle with Craig Blumenshine. Wyoming PBS, September 5, 2018 https://www.youtube.com/watch?v=XcOqXxhwJrM&t=73s.

[330] William Shakespeare. All's Well That Ends Well.Act 3 Scene 5.

[331] Tom Aswell. Did LABI pay a five-figure fee to get flim-flammed by self-proclaimed flim-flam artist at its annual luncheon Tuesday? Louisiana Voice Web site. https://louisianavoice.com/2020/02/13/did-labi-pay-a-five-figure-fee-to-get-flim-flammed-by-self-proclaimed-flim-flam-artist-at-its-annual-luncheon-tuesday/. Published 2020. AccessedThursday, February 13.

[332] Julia Arenstam. 'Catch Me If You Can' subject Frank Abagnale comes to Baton Rouge. Greater Baton Rouge Business Report Web site. https://www.businessreport.com/article/catch-me-if-you-can-subject-frank-abagnale-comes-to-baton-rouge. Published 2020. AccessedTuesday, February 11th.

[333] Editorial. *The West Carroll Gazette (Oak Grove, Louisiana)*. 1981; Wednesday, 13 May, Page 15.

[334] Rebecca Solnit. Call them by their real names. Haymarket Books. Chicago, IL. 2018.

[335] O'Reilly CA, Doerr B. Conceit and deceit: Lying, cheating, and stealing among grandiose narcissists. *Pers Indiv Differ.* 2020; 154.

[336] Azizli N, Atkinson BE, Baughman HM, et al. Lies and crimes: Dark Triad, misconduct, and high-stakes deception. *Pers Indiv Differ.* 2016; 89:34-39.

[337] Ronnie James Dio. Heaven and Hell, Black Sabbath (Single and Album Title) Warner Records Inc. 1980.

[338] Verigin BL, Meijer EH, Vrij A. Embedding lies into truthful stories does not affect their quality. *Appl Cogn Psychol.* 2020; 34:516-525.

[339] Bernstein C. And what about the truth? *Time Magazine.* 1990; 135:52.

[340] Prescott SL, Logan AC. Narrative Medicine Meets Planetary Health: Mindsets Matter in the Anthropocene. *Challenges.* 2019; 10:17.

[341] Campbell J. The Hero with a Thousand Faces. *New World Library Novato, CA.* 2008.

[342] Robert Crichton. The Great Imposter: The Amazing Careers of Ferdinand Waldo Demara. *Random House, New York, New York.* 1959.

[343] Deeb G. Evel Knievel is no longer welcome on television. *St Joseph News-Press Gazette.* 1982; Wednesday 10 Feb, Page 7A.

[344] Associated Press. Knievel returns to site of famous jump but only 50 show up for ceremony. *Salt Lake Tribune.* 1985; Tuesday 10 Sep, Page 8A.

[345] Flake C. What it's like to be a Texas lady. *Cosmopolitan.* 1979; December, pp174-78 and 188.

Printed in Great Britain
by Amazon